MEASUREMENT
OF COMMUNICATION
BEHAVIOR

COMMUNICATIONS

George Gerbner and Marsha Siefert, Editors
The Annenberg School of Communications
University of Pennsylvania, Philadelphia

MEASUREMENT OF COMMUNICATION BEHAVIOR

PHILIP EMMERT
University of Wyoming

LARRY L. BARKER
Auburn University

Longman

New York & London

Measurement of Communication Behavior

Longman Inc., 95 Church Street, White Plains, N. Y. 10601

Associated companies:
Longman Group Ltd., London
Longman Cheshire Pty., Melbourne
Longman Paul Pty., Auckland
Copp Clark Pitman, Toronto
Pitman Publishing Inc., New York

Executive editor: Gordon T. R. Anderson
Production editor: Camilla T. K. Palmer
Text design: Jill Wood
Cover design: Susan J. Moore
Text art: J & R Art Services
Production supervisor: Eduardo Castillo

Library of Congress Cataloging-in-Publication Data

Measurement of communication behavior.

(Communications)
1. Communication—Methodology. 2. Communication—Research. I. Emmert, Philip, 1940–   II. Barker, Larry Lee, 1941–   III. Series: Longman communication books.
P91.M377   1988   001.54   87-35292

ISBN 0-582-28674-3

93 92 91 90 89 88 9 8 7 6 5 4 3 2 1

Contents

Preface

Empirical research methodologies in Communication and the Social Sciences have undergone rapid refinement in the past half century. As computer technology, electronic measurement devices and information retrieval systems proliferated, so did the capacity to operationalize and define significant communication related variables. This text attempts to identify and discuss some of the measurement strategies and instruments which are available to scholars at the onset of the 1990s. All of the authors are experts in operationalizing and measuring constructs in their respective areas and have attempted to synthesize their knowledge in individual chapters in the text.

This volume is designed to serve both as a textbook in courses dedicated to Research Methods in Communication and the Social Sciences and as a professional reference source for students and scholars engaged in empirical research. The specific contributions of this book lie not only in the topics represented in the table of contents, but in the emphasis on "teachability" reflected in each chapter. Authors have provided a variety of instructional aids including chapter study questions, suggested readings, and extensive chapter summaries. Every attempt has been made to make the text readable as well as informative.

The editors of and contributors to this text were saddened by the untimely death of Dr. Aubrey Fisher, who originally had offered to contribute a chapter to this volume. Although Aubrey and his contributions in this volume will be missed, we believe that this book will stand as a tribute to his memory and his desire to further enhance the quality of research in Communication and the Social Sciences.

We would like to thank our many students and colleagues who worked hard to help the book to fruition. Thanks also to Longman Inc. for believing in the importance of this project and in making a strong commitment to enhancing research in the Communication related disciplines.

Philip Emmert, Professor
University of Wyoming

Larry L. Barker, Professor
Auburn University

About the Authors

Janis F. Andersen, Ed.D., *West Virginia University, 1978*, is Professor of Speech Communication and Department Chair at San Diego State University.

Dr. Andersen has authored or co-authored scholarly works in *Communication Monographs, Human Communication Research, Communication Education, Western Speech Communication Journal, Communication Quarterly, Communication Reports*, and *Journal of Applied Communication*. She has also authored numerous book chapters and has presented more than 50 conference papers, presentations, and addresses at scholarly conferences. Her publications and presentations have centered around her interests of nonverbal and interpersonal communication, instructional contexts, general intimacy theories, and communication development.

Peter A. Andersen, Ph.D., *Florida State University, 1975*, is Professor of Speech Communication at San Diego State University.

He is the chairperson of the Speech Communication Association's Interpersonal and Small Group Interaction Division, the SCA Legislative Council and the International Communication Association's Executive Committee. Dr. Andersen has authored or co-authored scholarly works in *Human Communication Research, Communication Quarterly, Southern Speech Communication Journal, Western Speech Communication Journal, Journal of Nonverbal Behavior, Sign Language Studies, Australian Scan of Human Communication, Journal of Black Studies, Communication Monographs, Journal of Thought*, and *Progress in Communication Sciences*. He has also served as Associate Editor of *Communication Quarterly* and *Journal of the American Forensic Association* as well as an editorial board member for 6 of the above journals.

William E. Arnold, Ph.D., *Pennsylvania State University, 1966,* is Professor of Communication at Arizona State University. Dr. Arnold has presented over 110 papers at national and international conferences, written over 40 articles and 6 books on various aspects of communication, including *Urban Communication, Crisis Communication,* and *Communication Training and Development.*

He has served as President of the Association for Communication Administration and the International Listening Association.

Deborah A. Barker, Ph.D., *University of Oklahoma, 1984,* is President of Windward Communications, Inc., a communication training and consulting firm located in Auburn, Alabama. Co-author of *Nonverbal Communication* (2nd edition), Dr. Barker also has authored or co-authored numerous book chapters, articles, and research papers concerning topics such as listening, nonverbal and interpersonal communication.

Larry L. Barker, Ph.D., *Ohio University, 1965,* is Professor of Speech Communication at Auburn University. Dr. Barker has authored, co-authored, or edited 29 books and over 65 articles in professional journals covering such topics as listening, research methods, nonverbal communication and intrapersonal communication.

He has served as president of the International Listening Association, as Vice President of the International Communication Association, and was a recipient of the Robert J. Kibler Memorial Award from the Speech Communication Association. Currently he is serving on the National Board of Examiners for the National Teacher Examination, is President of Spectra Communication Associates, a communication training and consulting firm based in New Orleans, and is an active consultant to Fortune 500 corporations and governmental agencies throughout the United States.

Franklin J. Boster, Ph.D., *Michigan State University, 1978,* is Associate Professor of Communication and Coordinator of Graduate Studies. Dr. Boster's research interests center around persuasion and group dynamics. His work has been published in psychology and law journals, as well as in the field of speech communication. He is currently Associate Editor of *Communication Monographs* and *Human Communication Research.*

H. Wayland Cummings, Ph.D., *Michigan State University, 1970,* is Professor of Communication and Director of the Communication Research Laboratory at the University of Oklahoma.

Dr. Cummings developed numerous computer techniques for assessing language behavior, including his work with SLCA-III (Syntactic Language Computer Analysis), that is currently used by more than 30 universities. He is the author, co-author, or editor of 9 books and more than 60 publications and research papers. He has been a consultant to government, business and industry, and voluntary organizations.

William C. Donaghy, Ph.D., *Northwestern University, 1969,* is Professor of Communication at the University of Wyoming. He has authored or co-authored *The Interview: Skills and Applications, An Introduction to Human Communication, Our Silent Language: An Introduction to Nonverbal Communication*, and *Organizational Communication*, as well as several monographs, book chapters and articles.

Dr. Donaghy has presented workshops and consulted on the Time Series Notation System since 1983, and has been invited to serve as a visiting research professor with Professor Frey at the University of Duisburg. He is currently working on a revised edition of the English language version of the Time Series Notation training manual and a computer program for training TSN coders.

Philip Emmert, Ph.D., *Ohio University, 1965,* is Professor of Communication and Adjunct Professor of Statistics at the University of Wyoming. He received the Outstanding Young Teacher Award from the Central States Speech Association, was selected as a Fellow in Academic Administration by the American Council on Education, is currently Chair of the International Listening Association Research Committee, and has served as a Member of the Executive Committee of the Association for Communication Administration.

Dr. Emmert has served as a reviewer or as a member of the editorial boards of *Communication Education, Journal of the International Listening Association, ACA Bulletin, Journal of the Western Speech Communication Association*, and the *North Carolina Journal of Speech*. He is the author, co-author, or editor of 7 books, and over 36 publications and research papers. His interest areas include research methods, persuasion, communication education, and the social effects of communications technology. He also is a partner in Communication Associates and has been a consultant to various governmental, industrial, nonprofit, and professional organizations in measurement, interviewing, interpersonal communication and previolent conflict management.

Victoria J. Lukasko Emmert, M. A., *University of Wyoming, 1976,* Ph.D., University of Iowa, expected, May, 1989, as an Instructor of Communication and director of the interpersonal communication course at the University of Wyoming. She was the recipient of the Top Four Paper Award by the Communication Theory Interest Group of the Central States Speech Association Conference in 1982 and the Top Three Paper Award by the Institute for the Study of Intrapersonal Processes at the International Listening Association Convention in 1986.

She is co-author of *Interpersonal Communication* (3rd edition), and has authored or co-authored papers in the areas of interpersonal listening, conflict, and gender and communicative power. Her present research interests include interactional analysis of self-disclosure and nonverbal listening. She also is a partner in Communication Associates and has consulted with nonprofit, governmental, and industrial organizations in interpersonal communication and previolent conflict management.

Lynda Lee Kaid, Ph.D., *Southern Illinois University, 1974*, is Professor of Communication at the University of Oklahoma. Dr. Kaid serves as editor of

Political Communication Review and has authored, co-authored, and edited numerous books, monographs, articles, and papers on political communication and research methods. Among her books are *Political Campaign Communication, Political Communication Yearbook,* and *New Perspectives* on *Political Advertising.* Her articles have appeared in *Communication Research, Journal of Broadcasting, Journalism Quarterly, Social Science Quarterly, The Handbook of Political Communication,* and *Communication Yearbook.* Her research has focused on political advertising, the coverage and effects of the mass media, and the political system.

She has served in important leadership roles within the International Communication Association and recently received a Fulbright Award to conduct research on the media in European elections.

James C. McCroskey, Ed.D., *Pennsylvania State University, 1966,* is Chair and Professor of Communication Studies and an Adjunct Professor in Educational Psychology at West Virginia University. Dr. McCroskey has been one of the original Fellows of the International Communication Association, President of the Eastern Communication Association, a recipient of the Speech Communication Association's Robert J. Kibler Memorial Award, a member of the SCA Commission of Communication Apprehension and Avoidance, a recipient of the SCA commission on Communication Apprehension and Avoidance Outstanding Scholarly Article Award, a recipient of the SCA Scholarly Paper Award (3 years), selected to present the Senior Scholar Lecture by the Southern Speech Communication Association, a recipient of the Lyman Award for Outstanding Research Article in the *American Journal of Pharmaceutical Education,* a recipient of the Distinguished Research Award of the Association of Teacher Educators (2 years), recognized by ECA as one of the top ten published scholars in communication (1972–82), and recognized by ECA as Scholar of the Year (2 years.)

Dr. McCroskey has published 14 textbooks, 7 instructional texts, 30 book chapters and sections, 131 articles in national and international journals and presented over 200 papers at regional, national, and international conferences. He has been editor of *Human Communication Research* and is the current editor of *Communication Education.*

Gerald R. Miller, Ph.D., *University of Iowa, 1961,* is Professor and Chairperson of the Department of Communication at Michigan State University. Dr. Miller has authored or edited 10 books, and written book chapters, and journal articles in communication, psychology, and law. He was the first editor of *Human Communication Research* and is the past editor of *Communication Monographs.*

He is past president of the International Communication Association and has been the recipient of the Speech Communication Association's Golden Anniversary Prize Fund Award for outstanding scholarship (four times), the SCA Distinguished Service Award, the Robert J. Kibler Memorial Award from the SCA, was designated as a Fellow by the International Communication

Association and the American Psychological Association, and a Joint Resolution of Tribute from the Michigan Legislature for his National Science Foundation-sponsored research dealing with the courtroom uses of videotape.

Virginia P. Richmond, Ph.D., *University of Nebraska-Lincoln, 1977,* is Professor and Coordinator of Graduate Studies in the Department of Communication Studies at West Virginia University. Dr. Richmond has been recognized as one of the Top Ten Publishing Scholars in major communication journals by the Eastern Communication Association, a recipient of the Outstanding Book Award from the Commission of Communication Apprehension and Avoidance of the Speech Communication Association, a recipient of the Top Four Paper Award for the Instructional Practices Group of ECA, a recipient of the Outstanding Scholarly Paper Award From the Commission on Communication Apprehension and Avoidance of SCA, Vice-President of ECA, President of ECA, a recipient of the Distinguished Research Award from the Association of Teacher Educators, a recipient of the 1984 ECA Past President's Award for Outstanding Scholarship to the field, a recipient of an Outstanding Faculty Member Award given by the Golden Key National Honor Society, and a recipient of the Lyman Award of the American Association of Colleges of Pharmacy for Outstanding Article.

Dr. Richmond has published textbooks in the areas of communication apprehension, avoidance and competence, interpersonal communication, and nonverbal communication. She also has authored several instuctional texts and book chapters. She has published extensively in the major journals and presented papers at regional, national, and international conventions. She is the current editor of *Communication Research Reports.*

Samuel C. Riccillo, Ph.D., *University of Denver, 1974,* is Associate Professor and Director of Graduate Studies in the Department of Communication at the University of Wyoming. He is also a member of the Interdisciplinary Neuroscience Program at UW. He is Project Director of the Neonatal Cry Project.

His research focus is directed toward the neurophysiological relationship of language, speech and communication. His research articles on the development of human communication have appeared in *Brain and Language, The Journal of Auditory Research,* and *The Western Journal of Speech Communication.*

Anne Johnston Wadsworth, Ph.D., *University of Oklahoma, 1986,* is Assistant Professor in the Department of Radio, Television and Motion Pictures at the University of North Carolina, Chapel Hill. Her area of research is political communication, and she has several forthcoming book chapters in this area. Dr. Wadsworth is the co-author of *Political Campaign Communication* and was recently invited to participate in a comparative study of the political environment in the United States and in France during the 1988 presidential elections. She has delivered papers based on her scholarly research at major national conferences.

Introduction

The measurement of communication behavior has been a concern of scholars and researchers for centuries. Even the ancient Greek and Roman rhetoricians attempted to establish criteria to determine the effectiveness of orators and public speakers. In the twentieth century emphasis has gradually shifted to more "scientific" approaches to measuring aspects of communication processes. This text attempts to identify and discuss a variety of issues and approaches that are essential to the scientific measurement of communication behavior.

An ancient proverb states "Any path will get you there, if you don't know where you're going." This proverb relates, to some degree, to the issue of communication measurement. If variables are not clearly identified or if constructs are not adequately operationalized, almost any technique for measuring them might be employed. However, as researchers become more precise in their definitions of variables and as they learn more about the nature of the constructs they are investigating, more specific techniques or "paths" must be identified. The contemporary researcher must clearly understand his/her path of research, *and* must be aware of the variety of different paths that are parallel or diverge from that which he/she is following.

The sections and chapters in this book attempt to identify a variety of different paths or techniques that social science researchers may follow and employ. The first section deals with some basic elements of the communication research process. Chapters in the first section present a foundation for conducting social scientific research in a variety of communication related disciplines. A basic introduction to the philosophy of science is presented to help place the measurement of communication behaviors in a philosophical and historical perspective. Chapters that examine issues and approaches to analyzing data and the use of computers in social scientific research enhance the conceptual base for the text. A final chapter in the first section explores issues and problems associated with the evaluation of research in the social sciences. As a whole, this section, reviews issues and terminology that are important in the understanding of approaches discussed in the second section of the text.

Actual procedures and techniques that are related to the measurement of communication are included in the second section of the text that begins with an orientation to measurement processes employed by social scientists. Successive chapters discuss specific instruments and approaches to measurement of communication variables. These include scaling techniques, attitude measurement, semantic differentiation, survey techniques, content analysis, interaction analysis, unobtrusive measurement, psychophysiological measurement, and nonverbal measurement techniques.

Each chapter in the second section includes such components as the identification of step-by-step procedures to follow when using the measurement technique (or measuring instrument), reliability and validity considerations, sample studies using the approach or instrument, and a criticism of the approach or technique from a practical point of view.

The chapters in this text attempt to cover a wide range of issues and approaches to the measurement of communication behavior. However, no text could adequately address all approaches and techniques in a single volume. Students are encouraged to examine the annotated readings at the end of each chapter and to explore the books that are identified. By reading the chapters in this text and consulting the suggested readings, both beginning and advanced researchers should become more proficient at measuring a variety of significant communication behaviors.

MEASUREMENT OF COMMUNICATION BEHAVIOR

PART 1

Basic Elements of Communication Research

The title might better be "Basic Elements of Quantitative Empirical Communication Research." We do not presume to cover all communication research in this part of the book, nor even in the whole book. There are many qualitative approaches, and other non-quantitative research methods that are being used effectively by communication researchers. However, there is a variety of approaches to studying communication that can probably trace their roots back to Franklin Knower's early attempts to quantify communication behavior in the 1940s. These various approaches to communication research represent a significant part of the disciplines of the communication arts and sciences. Certainly, these disciplines have enjoyed much of their extreme growth during the same period, especially from the early 1960s to the present, when these quantitative methods were used so extensively. It is our feeling that the use of these quantitative methods made a significant contribution to the research base of the communication arts and sciences. Further, it is our expectation that quantitative research methods will continue to be of major importance in the research efforts of communication researchers.

It should be apparent that no single volume can cover all communication research methods. Likewise, we would be foolish, indeed, to pretend that this single volume could even cover all quantitative methods alone; however, we do feel it is reasonable to say that in this volume we can address the major issues in quantitative and empirical research in communication for the beginning or not-quite-beginning researcher's consideration. We intend to provide both a starting point for some researchers and a reference point, or an anchor, for others.

In order to accomplish these goals we begin with a consideration of basic empirical/quantitative issues in communication research. The first chapter in Part One, "Philosophy of Science," by Peter A. Andersen, introduces the reader to basic theoretical issues that should serve as a foundation for theory and research in any behavioral science. In fact, the relationship of theory to research relative to quantitative/empirical methods poses vexing questions for communication scholars that Andersen considers in this chapter.

Chapter 2, "Analyzing Data", by Gerald R. Miller and Frank Boster, considers the relationship between the data obtained in a quantitative study and the statistical manipulation of that data for purposes of inference drawing. Miller and Boster's discussion addresses questions researchers are well advised to consider if their objective is valid inference from quantitative data.

Of course, computers have been a basic tool of the quantitative researcher for years, but recent advances suggest new directions for the communication scholar, as suggested by H. Wayland Cummings in Chapter 3, "Using Computers." Cummings addresses practical and theoretical issues in the use of computers in communication research, including discussions of mainframe, mini-, and microcomputers and software.

Finally, in Chapter 4, "Evaluating Research", Larry L. Barker explores the vexing problem of evaluating quantitative studies conducted by other researchers. For any study to be of use to a discipline it must be interpreted and critically evaluated. Barker's comments suggest basic questions that should be addressed by any scholar in the analysis of extant empirical/quantitative studies.

CHAPTER 1

Philosophy of Science

By Peter A. Andersen,
San Diego State University

Scientific approaches to communication attempt to reveal more than can be seen with the naked eye. While "common" sense is often useful it does not help us to develop very deep insights into human communication or any other aspect of the world in which we live. Common sense and language still hold that the sun rises, though most children know that science long ago discovered the world actually turns. Common sense holds that people will value a boring job more if the pay is higher, though dissonance theorists have demonstrated the opposite years ago. Common sense holds that very nervous speakers get better with practice though research showed they actually lose confidence from speaking if their anxiety is too high. Without systematic scientific research it would be difficult to overcome superstition and myth and to replace it with dynamic, objective knowledge.

Science is a process of searching for regularity and order. Few of us believe that events just happen. Instead, events affect other events. The physicist looks for patterns in the behavior of particles; the biologist looks for patterns in the behavior of cells and organs; the social scientist looks for patterns in the behavior of people. Communication scientists are interested in how people think and feel, plan and create, act and react in the communication process. The field of human communication is far more complex than many related sciences since it deals with active agents capable of independent thought and action. Moreover, since human communication is hierarchically governed by the principles of physics, chemistry, biology, psychology and sociology as well as communication, *all* of these disciplines are relevant to its study.

This chapter will examine the role of science in communication research. The scientific criteria of empirical observation, testability, falsifiability, publicness, self-correction, measurability, objectivity, skepticism, and heuristic value will be reviewed. The tools of science including concepts, constructs, definitions, variables, problems, and hypotheses will be examined. Finally, the purpose of communication theory will be discussed.

SCIENCE IN COMMUNICATION RESEARCH

Science is a process of discovering order amid chaos and regularity in randomness. The terms used to describe the process of science vary greatly. Kuhn (1970) regarded science as a puzzle-solving activity. Ravetz (1973) claimed that traditionally science has been viewed as the pursuit of truth, which has provided high morale in the scientific community and has protected science against its external enemies. However, Kibler (1970) argued that the scientific approach involves establishing probabilities and compiling knowledge, not establishing truth.

Most scientists, including social scientists, hope to discover **laws** of human behavior upon which a firm **theory** can be constructed (Ziman, 1968). In a strict sense, laws of human behavior would be universal and would hold true for all people at all times. Few, if any, such deterministic laws have emerged in the study of human communication or social science in general that can be considered universal in scope (Hawes, 1975). More commonly, communication scientists create generalizations which are probabilistic, not deterministic or universal (Miller & Nicholson, 1976). While this limits the strength and scope of these law-like generalizations they are still useful additions to our knowledge of communication behavior. In practice, most social scientists are content to discover any observable regularity in human action whether or not it has the status of a scientific law. Few, if any, practicing communication researchers gauge the success of a project on whether or not a general law of communication has been uncovered (Miller & Berger, 1978).

Communication researchers often actually uncover communication **rules** that are followed by groups and individuals. The emergent rules perspective (see Cushman and Pearce, 1977), recognizes that individuals make decisions according to certain personal or group rules that are not governed by deterministic laws of nature. In effect, when communication researchers discover regularities or patterns in human behavior they typically do not know if they have found a natural law or cultural rule. What they do know is that for these people, in this place, at this time, they have discovered a pattern that is not random or chaotic. According to Miller (1983) patterns of turn-taking, for example, can be explained by either a laws or rules perspective.

It is likely the regularities in human communication are a function of at least five forces. (1) Natural laws of physiology, biology, psychology and even physics provide possibilities and impose limitations on human actions. Certain movements and actions are constrained by neurological and physical laws of behavior, that affect all human beings (P. Andersen, Garrison & J. Andersen, 1979). (2) Cultural rules are imposed on people within social or regional systems at a nonconscious level. We behave in accordance with these rules because everyone in our culture behaves similarly and we fail to be conscious of any alternative (P. Andersen, Lustig and J. Andersen, 1987). (3) Personal **traits** are predispositions, personal patterns, or habitual actions that have developed within an individual. These are often unconscious but even when they reach awareness such patterns are considered part of our personality. People describe themselves or others with thousands of trait terms like affectionate, nervous, shy or talkative (P. Andersen, 1987). (4) **Relational patterns** are predictable actions engaged in by dyads or small groups. They may be conscious or unconscious, pleasant or unpleasant (Cronen, Pearce, and Snavely, 1979), but their regularity is often striking. (5) Conscious choices probably represent a relatively small number of all communication behaviors (P. Andersen, 1986). Nonetheless, humans can and do engage in planned, strategic, tactical and goal-oriented behaviors that produce conscious, intentional patterns of action.

The five types of communication patterns described above are probably not *all* of the patterns that communication researchers seek to discover. However, each of these courses regularly produce nonrandom patterns of social interaction which can be uncovered by systematic scientific research.

CHARACTERISTICS OF SCIENCE

To qualify as truly scientific, research must meet several criteria that have been established by the social scientific community. These interrelated criteria or characteristics distinguish scientific research from "common sense" or speculative "armchair" methods of research. Thus, scientific research must be:

Empirical

All scientific research is grounded in the principle of **empiricism**, the belief that evidence must be based on careful observation. While intuition, visions, revelations, and reflective thought are recognized as other ways of knowing, all scientific knowledge must be empirically based (Selltiz, Wrightsman & Cook, 1976). The human mind is so creative that it can produce imaginary, fanciful, mythical and superstitious explanations for the events we experience. It is only when these creative ideas are empirically tested that their worth or validity can be ascertained.

Empiricists believe that data must be observable by more than one observer. Until a consensus of observations is formed the observation remains unverified. Unlike many qualitative and rhetorical research strategies empiricism is based on public verification by researchers, not on elitist insights or the opinions of so-called "authorities" (Miller, 1983). Finally, Brockriede (1982) has argued that while logical empiricism has been the chief mode of human understanding during this century it is complemented by personal and symbolic modes of inquiry. So while empiricism is a cornerstone of social science it need not stand alone as a way of knowing.

Indeed, the differences between **qualitative** and **quantitative** research modes are overblown. Both modes can and should be based on empirical observation. Quantitative research is more precise but narrower in focus than qualitative research. Qualitative research is less restrictive but also less precise than quantitative research. Both are indirect interpretations of reality. Recently, the intelligent position that the two methods can complement one another has been advocated by significant scholars (Brockriede, 1982; Rogers & Chaffee, 1983).

Testable

Social and communication sciences must actually test their hunches, hypotheses and theories. Field observations or laboratory studies are set up to test whether creative ideas actually hold water. Relationships among events are empirically tested rather than subjected to only armchair speculation (Kerlinger, 1973). While rhetoricians and social philosophers are concerned with whether an idea or hypothesis is tenable or possible, social scientists must show that the idea or hypothesis is testable and probable (Brockriede, 1983; Rudner, 1966). The reason why *tests* are crucial is explained in the next characteristic.

Falsifiable

Researchers test theories and hypotheses in an effort to **falsify** or disprove them (Lustig, 1986). It may seem odd that research would want to disprove the theories that required so much effort to create. If a theory survives such a test it is supported and the scientific community comes to believe the theory has merit. Popper (1959) holds that empirical tests are valuable only if they actually falsify a theory. Under these circumstances a theory can be discarded and replaced by a better one (Dubin, 1969).

Replicable

Results of a scientific study must be repeatable or **replicable** before a hypothesis, theory, rule or law can be supported or confirmed. Often, textbook writers erroneously include a "principle of communication" based on the results of a single study. As a result, many students develop the bad habit of drawing strong conclusions from inconclusive findings (Tucker, Weaver & Berryman-Fink, 1981). Only after the results of a study have been retested several times should people accept these findings. Preferably such replications should take place in different locations, by different researchers using identical or very similar research methods. The results of any single study could be wrong for dozens of reasons. Only through this process can a body of valid scientific findings be built.

Public

In order to replicate another communication scientist's study, it must be part of the public record. Publication outlets such as books or journals and conference papers are an essential ingredient of the scientific process for many reasons. First, such outlets are the only way other scientists can locate, read, and replicate other scientists' studies. Second, knowledge is built cumulatively when scientists add to and extend each other's findings (Ziman, 1968). Only public research can be part of this process. Third, when details of the methods and results are public other scholars can criticize and compare studies. The process of constructive criticism guards against premature conclusions and promotes improvements in future studies. Facts and theories must survive criticism and testing by other scientists before they can be accepted (Ziman, 1968). Finally, science depends on the public for support. Most scientific studies are supported by the public through government agencies and state universities (Ravetz, 1973). Thus, public dissemination and practical application of scientific findings are essential for public appreciation and financial support to continue.

Self-correcting

Related to the public, critical, replicable nature of social science is the fact that it is a self-correcting process. Both social scientific findings and methods continually are being overhauled and improved. Through replication and extension knowledge is updated, errors in previous studies surface, and theory is adjusted and reformulated (Kerlinger, 1973; Tucker, et al., 1981). Social scientists must not get ego-involved in their old findings which are likely to be improved, corrected or even discarded.

Measurable

All social scientific studies rely on one's ability to measure communication concepts. Anxiety, attitudes, gestures, vocal tones, interacts, turns, talk-time, predispositions, traits, situations, rules and every other communication concept has to be measured before it can be studied scientifically. Measurement typically means quantification but any logical distinction or notation is really a form of measurement. When qualitative analysts note the presence or absence of a behavior they are measuring it at a nominal level (see Chapter 5 for a complete discussion). Quantification involves assigning numbers to events, cognitions, attitudes, or behaviors. Tucker et al., (1981) argued that scientific studies could not be conducted or replicated without quantification. Most, if not all, materials, concepts, and behaviors are quantifiable, though some are not particularly amenable to quantification (Kerlinger, 1976; Tucker et al., 1981). Categories, ranks, ratings, and scores, are forms of quantification. Without some form of measurement, communication researchers could never agree on whether a particular attitude, behavior or pattern was even present. Greater precision in measurement leads to more precise description and understanding of communication phenomena.

Objective

Social scientists should attempt to be unbiased and unemotional about the findings obtained in scientific studies. Frequently, results of a study run contrary to a scientist's hypothesis, world view, or political beliefs. Objectivity requires reporting of one's findings with a minimum of personal bias and distortion. According to Kerlinger (1973) and Polanyi (1958) scientific findings and theories lie outside of oneself and one's personal beliefs and attitudes. Objectivity in hypotheses, methods, and findings are cornerstones of social science (Rudner, 1966). According to Kirk and Miller (1986) objectivity refers to taking the intellectual risk of being wrong that is present in every scientific study. Social science requires sufficient objectivity so that the scientist can admit her/his own theory or hypothesis has been disconfirmed.

Skeptical

Scientists do not accept common sense, obvious conclusions, dogma, or widely held beliefs. According to Tucker et al. (1981) "The history of science contains countless examples of the 'obviously true' turning out to be partially, if not totally, false when put to scientific test" (p. 132). Some beginning students fail to understand the skeptical stance necessary for science. They say, "that's obvious" or "that's just common sense" and call such findings "no-shit-hypotheses" (NSH). There really are not any NSH in the scientific community. Quite frequently the obvious is disproven and the unlikely is true in scientific research.

Heuristic

Finally, science is **heuristic** in that it leads to further hypotheses, theories, discoveries and investigations (Kerlinger, 1973). Paradoxically, each scientific discovery raises more questions than it answers. As we learn something about human communication, more questions emerge. In a sense we know more, but also realize much more is to be known. Polanyi (1958) stated, "It is the plunge by which we gain a foothold on another shore of reality. On such plunges the scientist has to stake bit by bit his entire professional life" (p. 123). According to Hawes (1975) an important criterion in evaluating models and theories is whether they are heuristic or lead to insightful questions and hypotheses. If science has no other purpose it should always be directed toward future discoveries and investigations.

THE TOOLS OF SCIENCE

Scientific research in communication typically uses specific tools to do the work of generating knowledge and building theory. The tools of science are more abstract than those of a carpenter or gardener because much of science involves mainly mental or intellectual activity. Nonetheless, understanding how each of these basic tools is used is necessary to doing scientific research and even to reading it.

Concepts

Concepts are sets or classes of objects, persons or events having common characteristics or attributes. Kerlinger (1973) defines concepts as abstractions formed by generalizations from particulars. Examples of concepts in communication include speech, gestures, communication apprehension, style, attitudes and thousands of other terms that enable us, literally, to know what we are talking about. Any concept can be defined by determining its criterial attributes (qualities it must have to be included in the class), excluding attributes (qualities it can't have to be included in the class), and irrelevant attributes (confusing qualities that it may or may not have). Adequate conceptualization will prevent overgeneralization (the result of having too few criterial attributes) and undergeneralization (the result of having too many criterial attributes). The purpose of concepts is to simplify thinking by including a number of objects, qualities or events under one heading (Selltiz, Wrightsman & Cook, 1976).

Concepts are useful when they are properly defined; they are meaningful when they are systematically related to other concepts (Hawes, 1975). Sets of concepts that are logically and observably interrelated form a conceptual scheme, the foundation of scientific theory (Kibler, 1970).

Constructs

Constructs are scientific concepts. Constructs are intentionally created or adopted by scientists for a particular scientific purpose. Constructs are concepts which express relationships among events, objects and other constructs (Kibler, 1970). Some concepts like talk-time, amount of touch, and speech-rate are obvious and easy to measure behaviorally.

Scientists sometimes create or invent hypothetical constructs that can't be easily observed. They are inferred from observation and presumed to exist (Kibler, 1970). Examples of hypothetical constructs in communication include love, attitudes, cognition, consciousness, anxiety, cognitive complexity, fear, and friendship. These constructs "exist" in communication research even if they can never be directly observed because scientists have defined them into existence (Miller & Nicholson, 1976). The value of hypothetical constructs rests on their predictive power and theoretical usefulness (Kibler, 1970). The danger of such constructs is that scientists may come to believe they really exist and dogmatically cling to these constructs long after they have lost any theoretical or empirical usefulness.

Definitions

Definitions clarify and specify the boundaries of concepts, constructs, variables, theories, and other tools of science. Definitions focus our attention on a common understanding and establish a common ground for scientific communicators (Miller & Nicholson, 1976). Kibler (1970) has argued that a priority task facing communication scholars is the definition of key concepts. Today, fuzzy or nonexistent definitions exist in far too many communication articles and books. Quality communication theory and research require careful and precise conceptual and operational definitions.

Conceptual definitions. Conceptual or constitutive definitions verbally clarify the precise meaning of a particular term. These definitions, which define words with words (Kerlinger, 1973) or constructs with constructs (Kibler, 1970), are language-based definitions. Communication apprehension can be defined as anxiety about actual or future interaction. Immediacy is conceptually defined as interpersonal warmth and closeness. Traditional marriage relationships can be conceptually defined as high in sharing and low on autonomy and assertiveness. These conceptual definitions are meaningful verbalizations of the abstract (Miller & Nicholson, 1976).

Operational definitions. The process of **operational definition** requires scientists to specify concretely the way they create and measure a construct (Miller & Nicholson, 1976). Constructs get defined in terms of observed data, specified procedures (Kibler, 1970) and careful measurement (see Chapter 5 for a discussion of measurement).

Kerlinger (1973) provides two types of operational definitions, measured and experimental. A measured operationalization describes how a score will be assigned. For example, communication apprehension can be measured with McCroskey's (1982) Personal Report of Communication Apprehension (PRCA) and immediacy can be operationalized with the Behavioral Indicants of Immediacy Measure (BII; J. Andersen, P. Andersen & Jensen, 1979). A second operationalization can be done experimentally. Here the details of how a researcher will manipulate a variable are specified. For example immediacy could be operationalized experimentally by having a confederate role-play by smiling, increasing eye contact and touching. In either case the details of a researcher's operationalization should be clearly specified for the benefit of the reader and other researchers.

Good operationalizations are required for a construct to be considered valid (see Chapter 5 for a discussion of validity). Operationalizations are not required for theoretical or conceptual development but are absolutely essential for empirical observations and tests of a theory (Dubin, 1969). Miller and Nicholson (1976) argue that operational definitions should tap as much of the richness of a conceptual definition as is possible. Failure to create an operational definition which corresponds to a conceptual definition creates two problems (Miller & Nicholson, 1976). First, since the scientist has not observed what he or she has professed to observe the outcomes of such research are deceptive and misleading. Second, the loose links between conceptual and operational definitions produces error and inefficiency. Operational definitions should be isomorphic with conceptual definitions.

Variables

The step from operational definitions to **variables** is a small one, indeed. Variables are measured constructs. Plenty of similar definitions for variables have been provided by philosophers and researchers. Variables have been defined as: anything that varies in quantity or magnitude (Kibler, 1970), a symbol to which numerals or values are assigned (Kerlinger, 1973), properties of people or things that vary in quality or magnitude (Miller & Nicholson, 1976), or a property of a thing that may be present in degree (Dubin, 1969).

Using the examples from above, the concept communication apprehension which varies from person to person can be operationalized with the Personal Report of Communication Apprehension (PRCA). The original PRCA is a 30-item self-report measure of an individual's fear or anxiety associated with oral communication (McCroskey, 1982). Scores on the PRCA range from 20 to 120 and vary from person to person. Once communication apprehension can be measured it can be called a variable.

Some authors make a distinction between qualitative and quantitative variables (Kibler, 1970) though Kerlinger (1973) disputes whether qualitative variables really exist. Examples of qualitative variables are a person's gender or hair color. Most qualitative variables can be scaled quantitatively. For example, gender can be rated on a masculinity-feminity scale and hair can be scaled on a dark-light continuum. Variables are useful to researchers because they enable quantitative and statistical analyses of the relationships among variables.

Problems

Most communication research studies begin with a particular conceptual or theoretical **problem**. This often takes the form of a question. For example, do high communication apprehensives display less immediacy and intimacy? Kibler (1970) argued that researchers face a period of perplexity or intellectual encounter where the problem is formulated and precisely stated. This is a critical phase of research leading up to a specific hypothesis. On a broader level, Ravetz (1973) maintains the central focus of science is its problem solving nature.

Hypotheses

Many communication studies test specific research hypotheses regarding the relationship among variables. A hypothesis is a conjectural statement specifying the relationship between two or more variables (Kerlinger, 1973; Kibler, 1970). Hawes (1975) stated that a **hypothesis** is a statement proposing a relationship between two or more different aggregates of facts.

An example of a hypothesis derived from the stated problem is: High communication apprehensives will manifest fewer immediacy behaviors than low communication apprehensives. Note that this statement is conjectural until it is tested in the laboratory or field. Note also that it specifies the nature of the relationship between two variables (communication apprehension and immediacy behaviors).

All research hypotheses, including the above example are tested against the null hypothesis. Null hypotheses suggest there is no relationship among variables and assume human behavior is chaotic and manifests no pattern. Null hypotheses are rarely stated but if we were to state the null for the above example, it would read: There is no relationship between communication apprehension and nonverbal immediacy. Researchers, through confirmation of the research hypothesis, attempt to disprove the null. Until the null is rejected and the research hypothesis supported empirically the presumption is that the null is true. The logic of the hypothetical-deductive model is to reject that behavior is random and chaotic by demonstrating the presence of systematic relations among the communication variables we study.

THEORY: THE GOAL OF SCIENCE

In everyday language people use the word theory as a synonym for hunch or pure speculation. People say, "that's only a theory" or "I wanted to learn something practical and all we got was theory." In science the word theory has a very different meaning. For our purposes theory will be defined as a highly organized set of statements about reality (human communication) logically tied together, and empirically testable. The statements are generalizations, laws, rules, or propositions about reality. In the study of communication the reality we seek to explore and understand is human communication. The statements must be logically tied together and interrelated to form a system of knowledge. Finally, theories must be empirically testable. Each statement in the theory can generate one or more tests that take the form of hypotheses in research studies. Preferably, many of the statements comprising a theory already have been tested and empirically supported.

So, in science, theory is certainly not synonymous with idle speculation. It is an organized system of knowledge that is both the result of research and thinking and the catalyst for more research and thinking. A theory of communication should reveal, describe and interpret an underlying system (what Rudner, 1966, calls an underlying calculus) that governs communication. Communication theories deal with actions and behavior, affect and emotions, cognition and understanding, relationships and associations, as well as patterns and structures.

In the hard sciences, dominant theoretical paradigms provide explanations for a wide range of events. The theory of relativity in physics and plate tectonics in geology are examples of dominant theories. No single theoretical paradigm has achieved dominance in the study of human communication. Instead, mid-range theories provide explanations for particular types or contexts of communication. Examples of such mid-range theories are the Berger and Calabrese (1975) uncertainty reduction theory, expectancy violations theory (Burgoon & Jones, 1976), several theories of immediacy or intimacy exchange (Andersen, 1984, 1985; Cappella & Greene, 1982), and McCroskey's (1984) theory of communication apprehension (though the latter might deny he had developed a theory, it is in fact a theory).

Theory is the goal of the scientific study of communication because it provides a perspective from which to view human communication, a system that can explain and predict behavior, and a warehouse where our knowledge can be stored and utilized. Theory performs important functions of explanation, prediction, and control that make a science of communication possible.

Explanation

Many communication scholars agree that the major goal of theory is **explanation** (Hawes, 1975, Miller & Nicholson, 1976; Monge, 1973; Tucker et al., 1981). Monge (1973) suggests

> The primary purpose of a scientific theory is scientific explanation ... To establish a theory of communication is to seek a set of propositions that explain how communication operates, i.e., why various communication events are related (pp. 5–6).

"Why" questions about communication are raised by people every day: "Why was she mad at me?" "Why do I feel good when I'm around him?" Through theory scientists attempt to answer similar questions. However, science attempts to provide answers free from psychological bias and human caprice (Harré, 1983). In science explanations for an event seek to specify the causes or antecedent conditions which led to the event and specify relevant conditions under which these explanations are likely to be valid (Monge, 1973; Harré, 1983).

Explanations enable us to understand communication. Indeed Dubin (1969) employs the term understanding instead of explanation when discussing this function of theory, to refer to knowledge about the interaction of parts in a system. In his theory-construction primer for undergraduates Lustig (1986) suggested the second of the ten steps is to:

> Create an explanation for the event. Theories are creations of individuals who have thought about their world and asked "I wonder what might account for that?" (p. 452).

Rudner (1966) maintained that the logical structure of explanation is identical with the next function of theory, prediction. He argued that the primary difference is in temporal vantage point. Given our vantage point (the present) a theory is able to explain *why* a given set of events occurred. It follows that if we had such an explanation before the event occurred we could have predicted it.

Prediction

The second major function of theory is **prediction** (Miller & Nicholson, 1976; Tucker et al., 1981). Indeed, Redding (1970) has asserted, "Many writers have maintained that the most important—or perhaps even the sole—ultimate goal of all science is *discovering* and *testing theories* which yield hypotheses subject to tests for predictability" (p. 117). So, the proof of the proverbial theoretical pudding, is its ability to predict.

Is human behavior consistent enough to enable theorists to make predictions? Tucker et al. (1981) maintained for example that:

> College student classroom behavior is fairly predictable; the same patterns occur year after year. Even the most casual observer of human behavior can verify that recurring patterns are the rule rather than the exception (p. 132).

Well-developed theories can predict such diverse communication phenomena as: the conditions likely to produce conflict or reconciliation, whether intimacy will be reciprocated or not, the outcome of election campaigns, the effectiveness of an advertisement, and the conditions under which fear about communication is likely to occur. These predictions have three important benefits: (1) Theoretical predictions can be empirically tested to support or refute the theory on which they were based. Thus, theoretic confirmation, modification or rejection rests on the ability to predict. (2) The pragmatic function of accurate prediction means that the future becomes less hazardous, uncertain and dangerous. Humans constantly make predictions about the future and act on them, though these predictions are far less certain than those derived from communication theories. (3) The final benefit is that accurate prediction can lead to control. If we know the conditions under which conflict takes place, debilitating fear of communication occurs, or relationships break up, we can alter the conditions, control the future, and lead better lives.

Control

Control of communication is not believed universally to be a good thing. Critics of the scientific method of studying communication view control as a potential evil, leading to thought control, behavior control, and restrictions on the freedom to communicate. In an excellent essay Rogers (1982) distinguishes between the empirical (scientific) and critical schools of communication. Exponents of the critical school, according to Rogers, view the empirical school as a "repressive science" whose aim is the control of reality. Indeed, Thayer (1983) argued, "to be scientifically successful would therefore not only be to be humanly (and socially) irrelevant, but to deny all human choice and volition—including, presumably the researcher's own" (p. 87). Similarly, Smythe and Dinh (1983) criticized scientific (administrative) research as an attempt to dominate, profit, control individuals' lives, and maintain the status quo.

Doubtlessly, science or any other form of knowledge can be employed in evil ways. Communication is no exception. Propaganda, brainwashing, false advertising and war-mongering are all conducted more efficiently with theoretical knowledge of communication as their basis. However, free speech, negotiations, critical investigations, and counseling all profit from communication theory. The position taken here is that of Tucker et al. (1981). "The ability to control is not inherently good or bad." Rather, the ethical, moral, or evaluative question arises with respect to how we employ the ability to control. How we prevent communication theory from being used unethically is the subject of another essay.

SUMMARY

This chapter provided the student with a basic understanding of the philosophy of science and its application in the creation of communication theory and conduct of communication research. The chapter began with a discussion of how science differs from common sense. Science is described as a process of searching for order and regularity in behavior.

Communication theory and research seeks to discover the laws, rules, traits, patterns, and choices that underlie the communication process. Science provides the framework for such inquiry through its empirical, testable, falsifiable, replicable, public, self-correcting, measurable, objective, skeptical, and heuristic methods.

Like any craft, science uses special tools to accomplish its work. They include concepts, constructs, conceptual and operational definitions, variables, problems, and hypotheses.

The ultimate goal of a science of communication is theory. Communication theory is not a mere set of speculations but a highly organized set of statements about communication, logically tied together and empirically testable. Theories can provide for explanation, prediction, and control of human communication behavior.

STUDY QUESTIONS

1. How does scientific knowledge differ from common sense? What are some similarities?
2. List and describe ten characteristics of science and why these characteristics are essential.
3. List and describe the importance of the seven tools of communication science discussed in this chapter.
4. What is scientific theory? How does it differ from everyday use of the word theory?
5. Why do some critics view the control function of communication with considerable skepticism?
6. Discuss the twin theoretical goals of explanation and prediction. How are they similar? How do they differ?
7. List and describe three benefits of prediction.

ANNOTATED READINGS

Brockriede, W. (1982). Arguing about human understanding. *Communication Monographs, 49*, 137–147.
    An excellent basic reading on philosophy of research and argument. Introduces the both/and paradigm which suggests that alternative perspectives can complement each other rather than compete with each other.
Ferment in the field (1986). *Journal of Communication, 33*, 1–368.
    An excellent scholarly debate about basic issues in philosophy of science, epistemology, alternate theoretical perspectives, and international differences in communication research. Contains 36 articles written by "heavies" in communication research from around the world.
Kerlinger, F. N. (1986). *Foundations of Behavioral Research* (3rd ed.). New York: Holt Rinehart and Winston.
    Considered by many to be the bible of empirical research, this book presents a broad, in-depth overview of science, research methodology, and statistics. Written in clear English and minimizes mathematics, making it readable by the beginning student while still of value to more advanced scholars.
Lustig, M. W. (1986). Theorizing about human communication. *Communication Quarterly, 34*, 451–469.
    A simple, step-by-step primer on theory construction, designed for undergraduates. Fills an important gap as it teaches the steps by which theory can be generated.

Miller, G. R. & Berger, C. R. (1978). On keeping the faith in matters scientific. *Western Journal of Speech Communication, 42,* 44–57.

>   Written by two of the best theorists and quantitative researchers in the field. An eloquent argument for the worth of logical positivism, scientific and empirical research, and a refutation of attacks on social science.

Rogers, E. M. (1982). The empirical and critical schools of communication research. In M. Burgoon (Ed.), *Communication yearbook 5* (pp. 125–144). New Brunswick, NJ: Transaction Books.

>   Provides an excellent overview of the history, geography, differences, and similarities between empirical and critical approaches to the study of human communication.

Rudner, R. S. (1966). *Philosophy of social science.* Englewood Cliffs, NJ: Prentice-Hall.

>   A short information-packed position on the underlying philosophy and logic of social science.

CHAPTER 2

Data Analysis in Communication Research

By Gerald R. Miller,
Michigan State University
Franklin J. Boster,
Michigan State University

The process of social science research can be depicted in numerous ways. Figure 2.1 depicts it in a way that is both generally informative and specifically useful in structuring this chapter. The communal activities of researchers take place in a verbal universe constructed of concepts, propositions, and theories. These concepts, propositions, and theories are communicated to others in the research community, as are attempts at their **empirical verification**—i.e., attempts to arrive at judgments of their probable validity by means of careful, systematic observation. Such attempts ensure that scientific knowledge claims do not remain solely within the province of the community's verbal universe, but rest instead on systematic procedures carried out in the observational universe. To bridge the gap between the two universes some form of **ostensive definition**—i.e., defining by pointing to an example or examples of the concept—is employed, most frequently, operational definitions. After the appropriate observations have been recorded and analyzed, interpretation and discussion of the findings permit researchers to reconstruct the verbal universe and to generate subsequent empirical tests of this reconstruction. The process of verbal construction, bridging, observation, bridging, and verbal reconstruction is ongoing and continuous, with reconstruction ranging from minor tinkering with individual concepts and propositions to major shifts in the guiding theoretical assumptions and positions.

This recurring cycle of scholarly activities conforms closely with classical conceptions of the nature of scientific inquiry (see Chapter 1 for additional discussion of these conceptions). More specifically, the *authority-free* nature of scientific knowledge claims is captured by the requirement for their empirical verification. Recourse to operational definition and careful, systematic obser-

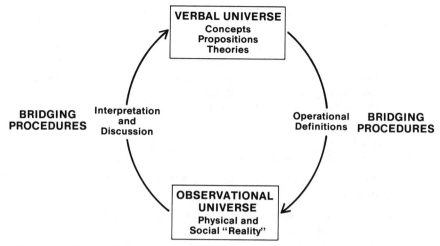

Figure 2.1. The process of scientific research in communication

vation ensure that scientific knowledge claims will be *public* and *reproducible.* Stated differently, such procedures ensure that knowledge claims are communal rather than resting on the authority of a single scholar. Finally, the continuing process of inquiry depicted in Figure 2.1 contributes to the *cumulative* and *self-correcting* characteristics of science.

The observational universe, of course, contributes the data used to verify knowledge claims relating to human behavior. At least two complex sets of problems are associated with these data: The first set concerns the correspondence, or "fit," between the concepts, propositions, and theories of the verbal universe and the data collected in the observational universe; the second set concerns the clarity and informativeness with which data from the observational universe are presented, and hence, their goodness of fit for interpreting and discussing research outcomes. The rest of this chapter is devoted principally to these two broad problem sets.

FITTING THE VERBAL UNIVERSE TO THE OBSERVATIONAL UNIVERSE

Three researchers, two **behaviorists** and a **phenomenologist**, were engaged in a spirited debate concerning candidates for the title of the world's greatest invention:

> "As far as I'm concerned," said the first behaviorist, "the world's greatest invention has to be the radio, for with the radio, we not only can hear everything of note that occurs on Earth, we can also hear voices from

thousands of miles in outer space, such as the Astronauts and Cosmonauts. Yes sir, the radio is definitely the world's greatest invention!"

"Unquestionably the radio is a great invention," responded the second behaviorist. "Nevertheless, my candidate has to be the television, for with the television we can both hear and see what's going on. For example, I can sit here in East Lansing, Michigan, and see and hear Johnny Carson in Los Angeles or New York. Television has it all over radio."

"Well," said the phenomenologist reflectively, "I think both the radio and television are great inventions, but for my money, the world's greatest invention has to be the thermos bottle."

"The thermos bottle?" queried the two behaviorists in unison. "Why in the world would you say that?"

"Look at it this way," responded the phenomenologist," the thermos bottle keeps the hot things hot and the cold things cold."

"Of course, any fool knows that," snapped the two behaviorists impatiently; "so what does that have to do with it being the world's greatest invention?"

"But how does it *know*?" asked the phenomenologist triumphantly.

This whimsical debate illustrates the two broad theoretical allegiances that guide most social science researchers. The behaviorists represent a group of theories often called *motion theories*: Such theories focus primarily on the ways that the environment acts upon individuals to cause them to behave in certain ways. Because of the emphasis on environmental infuence, motion theories are sometimes characterized metaphorically as "pull" theories to capture the notion of the environment "pulling on" the individual. Most stimulus-response learning theories are motion theories, particularly single-stage conceptualizations such as Skinner's (1953, 1957) that eschew recourse to any kinds of intervening processes—i.e., processes occurring inside the person's head. Most social exchange theories (e.g., Thibaut & Kelley, 1959; Homans, 1961) are also conceptually garbed as motion theories, though as we shall note shortly, elements of the alternative perspective inevitably intrude on social exchange processes.

While the humor of our earlier hypothetical debate stems from the logical and psychological incongruity of a thermos bottle actually thinking about and making decisions regarding when to keep liquids hot or cold, it is a widely-shared belief that people do engage in such cognitive, choice-making activities. The second broad theoretical allegiance, *action theories*, rests on the assumption that people act upon the environment by structuring and interpreting it to conform with their needs, choices, and motives, rather than waiting passively for the environment to act upon them. Because of the emphasis on persons acting upon their environments, action theories are sometimes metaphorically described as "push" theories. Probably the most extreme action position is exemplified by rule-following approaches to communication theory (e.g.,

Cushman, 1977; Cushman, Valentinsen & Dietrich, 1982; Cushman & Whiting, 1972; Harré & Secord, 1973; see also Chapter 1), since these positions hold that people create and agree to the rules that guide their communicative behavior. The **coordinated management of meaning** (Cronen, Pearce & Harris, 1982; Pearce & Cronen, 1980) also takes an action-oriented stance, and there is a strong action dimension to most *attribution theories*, which conceive of people as naive social scientists who devote considerable time to constructing reasons for the behaviors of themselves and others (e.g., Jones & Davis, 1965; Jones et al., 1972; Kelley, 1967).

In the day-to-day commerce of research, however, few investigators rely on "pure" motion or action perspectives, turning instead to theories that comprise a blend of the two allegiances. Thus, to return to a theoretical posture mentioned earlier, social exchange theories assume that people's behaviors, including the ways they communicate and the communicative relationships they form with others, are governed by the outcomes—i.e., the rewards divided by the costs—associated with available behavioral alternatives, an assumption that smacks heavily of a motion theory orientation. Nevertheless, the reward/cost metric used to determine outcomes clearly varies from one individual to another, depending upon that individual's needs, choices, and motives. As a consequence, an adequate theory based on social exchange would require elements of both the motion and action positions—i.e., it would posit that particular environmental circumstances predispose persons to respond in predictable ways *but* that the way the environment is structured is partially determined by the emotional and motivational makeups of the involved persons.

In seeking a fit between the theories of the researcher's verbal universe and the data of his or her observational universe, one of the most important steps is developing logically consistent, useful conceptual and operational definitions of individual concepts. Many of the concepts used by communication researchers are **constructs**; i.e., they are labels used to identify real or imagined processes that are not directly observable to the researcher. Indeed, Spence (1944) has argued persuasively that in the behavioral sciences, the activity of theory construction consists largely of introducing and postulating hypothetical constructs that help to bridge the gap between observable variables.

Why are these constructs necessary? Consider the following simple situation: Several persons are asked to express their first thoughts when presented with the verbal stimulus "abortion." In terms of only the objective features of the situation, all of these persons are responding to the same stimulus; consequently, one might anticipate uniformly similar responses. Actually, of course, almost anyone could predict accurately that these people's responses will vary widely. As Table 2.1 suggests, some respondents will present essentially denotative responses indicating that abortion is a medical procedure for terminating pregnancy; others will present connotatively favorable responses having to do with a woman's right to control her own body, and still

TABLE 2.1. EXAMPLES OF INTERVENING CONSTRUCTS LINKAGES

Stimulus	Construct	Responses
"Abortion"	"Attitude"*	1. "A procedure for terminating pregnancy." 2. "A woman's freedom to control her body." 3. "Legalized murder."
Talk for five minutes about your feelings concerning abortion to an audience of 10 peers.	"Communication Apprehension"**	1. "I feel nervous and apprehensive." 2. Increase in heart rate and sweating of palms. 3. High nonfluency and low verbal output.

*"Attitude": "an implicit, drive-producing response considered socially significant in the individual's society." (Doob, 1947, p. 135).
**"Communication Apprehension": an individual's level of fear or anxiety associated with either real or anticipated communication with another person or persons." (McCroskey, 1984, p. 13).

others will present connotatively unfavorable responses indicating that abortion is a crime against the unborn. The researcher seeks to reconcile this wide variance in overt verbal responses by postulating the construct of attitude; the researcher therefore contends that the large differences in response result from varying attitudes about abortion.

Conceptual Definitions

Table 2.1 contains a conceptual definition of "attitude" first presented in a classic article by Doob. Note particularly how some elements of the definition correspond with the previous discussion. To stipulate that attitude is an "implicit response" is another way of saying that attitudes are not directly observable, but rather are *inferred* from other behaviors. That attitudes are arousing or motivating is captured by the phrase "drive-producing response." Finally, the phrase "considered socially significant in the individual's society" differentiates the construct "attitude" from otherwise similar constructs such as "learning." Thus, an attitude is conceived to be a particular kind of learned response; whereas we would not ordinarily say that people have an attitude toward consuming food, but rather that they have learned to feed themselves, we would assert that Moslems and Jews have an attitude about eating pork; Hindus have an attitude about eating beef, and vegetarians have an attitude about eating any kind of meat.

Table 2.1 also contains a second example of a conceptually defined intervening construct, "communication apprehension." This construct represents a particular attitude or predisposition about communicating with others. In this example, the stimulus is not a word but instead the actual activity of talking about abortion to an audience. Once again, the same objective stimulus is capable of eliciting a wide range of responses: Some people will be quite nervous and uncommunicative while others will be generally relaxed and communicative. The researcher assumes that these differing responses to the same objective stimulus result from varying levels of communication apprehension, i.e., varying amounts of fear or anxiety about communicating with other persons.

Obviously, there is no single "right" or "correct" way of defining a construct; in fact, the literature reveals numerous conceptual definitions of the attitude construct. As implied earlier, conceptual definitions are evaluated largely in terms of their scientific utility. Though several criteria determine an overall judgment of utility, the criterion of primary interest here is whether the conceptual definition contains the seeds of clear, useful ways to operationally define the construct so as to bridge the gap between the verbal and observational universes.

Operational Definitions

A term is operationally defined by specifying the operations, or steps, that must be performed to derive its meaning (Miller & Nicholson, 1976). Although this conceptual definition of "operational definition" may sound a bit strange, it can be clarified by pointing to several familiar examples. A cookbook is essentially a series of operational definitions: The meaning of terms such as "beef Wellington" and "German chocolate cake" is contained in the recipes the chef must follow to prepare them. Similarly, a mechanic's manual consists largely of operational definitions; e.g., the term "oil change" is defined by articulating the operations, or steps, that must be taken to change the car's oil.

The "RESPONSES" column of Table 2.1 contains the raw materials for several common types of operational definitions used by researchers. For instance, operational definitions of the construct "attitude" often rely on verbal responses: The researcher specifies a set of operations for obtaining some kind of verbal report from the respondent. The instruction, "Ask each respondent how she or he feels about abortion," is thus an operational definition, though it is crude and lacks much scientific utility because it neither specifies exact procedures for asking the respondents or for recording their responses. The definition could be improved by changing the instruction to, "Give each respondent the statement 'Women should be granted an abortion on demand' and have the respondent check one of five intervals: Strongly Agree, Agree, No Opinion, Disagree, or Strongly Disagree." This change, which corresponds with the Likert scale approach to measuring attitudes mentioned later in this chapter and discussed more fully in Chapter 7, provides all respondents with a uniform stimulus as well as a specific method for coding their responses.

Constructs may be operationally defined in various ways other than verbally. The following are a few alternative ways of operationally defining people's attitudes toward abortion:

1. Solicit contributions from each person for a pro-abortion (anti-abortion) advertisement to appear in the local newspaper. Use the amount of money contributed as an index of the person's attitude toward abortion.
2. Ask each person to volunteer some time circulating pro-abortion (anti-abortion) petitions. Keep a record of the amount of time devoted to this volunteer work and use it as an index of the person's attitude toward abortion.
3. Ask each person to participate in a sit-in supporting the pro-abortion (anti-abortion) movement. Use the person's willingness or unwillingness to participate as an index of her or his attitude toward abortion.

This wide variety of potential operational definitions underscores an important point: *No single operational definition can capture all the complexity and richness of the construct as defined conceptually.* Stated differently, as a researcher seeks to bridge the gap between the verbal and observational universes by operationally defining a construct, some loss of meaning is inevitable. This is one reason why it is important to try to replicate findings of important relationships between communication variables using a variety of operational definitions. When the same findings emerge using various operational definitions, the research community places greater stock in their importance; such consistency of results across varying operational definitions is referred to by some as *convergent validity*.

Table 2.1 also reveals several differing approaches to operationally defining the construct "communication apprehension." The first response illustrates the *verbal self-report* approach; respondents are asked to express their feelings about communicating with others. The second response focuses on *physiological indices* of communication apprehension; the guiding assumption holds that high levels of communication apprehension are signaled by certain bodily states. Finally, the third response stresses *communicative behaviors*; it holds that apprehension results in dysfunctional communication. This third approach can be operationalized either by direct recording of actual behaviors—e.g., the researcher can count such behaviors as nonfluencies or nervous adaptor gestures and time such behaviors as pausing or avoidance of eye contact—or by observer ratings—i.e., raters can observe the communicator and rate a number of the relevant behaviors on some continuum of nervousness or effectiveness. No matter which operational approach is used, it will capture only part of the construct's conceptual meaning. Indeed, examination of the early literature on stage fright using the three differing approaches revealed low correlations among them (Clevenger, 1959), suggesting that the three indices measure different dimensions of the construct.

Conceptual and Operational Definitions:
Motion versus Action Approaches

The earlier distinctions drawn between action and motion theories are closely tied to the question of specifying appropriate conceptual and operational definitions for constructs. This claim can be redeemed by examining how the two approaches relate to an actual research question: the question of the relative persuasive efficacy of using strong fear-arousing message appeals.

One has only to ponder personal experience or humanity's daily activities to ascertain the wide acceptance of the proposition that frightened people are likely to be persuadable people. Children are warned to straighten up their room if they wish to have TV-viewing privileges. Workers are entreated to work harder or lose their jobs. Smokers are reminded they are doomed to premature death from lung cancer unless they kick the habit. Heads of government are told they face military attack if they continue to support terrorist groups. The list of messages resorting to fear-arousing appeals seems almost endless.

Despite the frequent use of such messages, however, grounds exist for arguing that reliance on fear-arousing appeals is persuasively counterproductive. Such appeals may predispose audience members to repress or distort message content, particularly those members who are highly anxious at the outset. The negative consequences emphasized by strong fear-arousing appeals may be so threatening to many recipients that they ignore or "tune out" the actions advocated in the message. In short, messages containing moderate appeals may often be more persuasive than their strong fear counterparts.

If a researcher wished to deal with this problem from a motion theory perspective, a conceptual definition of "fear-arousing message appeals" similar to the one used by Janis and Feshbach (1953) would be appropriate: that is, *appeals that specify the harmful consequences of failure to conform with message recommendations.* This conceptualization places primary emphasis on the message; if an appeal specifies the harmful consequences—e.g., "You should quit smoking (message recommendation) or you will die an agonizing death from lung cancer (harmful consequence)"—it is a strong fear-arousing appeal; if it omits specific mention of such consequences—e.g., "You should quit smoking"—it is not. The two preceding appeals illustrate how to distinguish operationally between strong fear and mild fear messages: The former would contain a number of appeals emphasizing the harmful consequences of failure to conform with message recommendations while the latter would avoid specific references to such consequences.

Conversely, commitment to a more action theory-oriented approach would result in a conceptual definition of "fear-arousing message appeals" that centers on the emotions of audience members: for example, *appeals that elicit high levels of fear or anxiety from message recipients.* Although researchers preparing messages would probably have some hunches about what kinds of appeals to use, this conceptualization is less concerned about the contents of messages than about the ways audiences respond emotionally to the contents. Indeed, the approach can produce vexing, albeit sometimes humorous problems for the investigator. In the late 1960s, one of us was directing a master's thesis dealing with the persuasive effects of strong and mild fear messages. The student involved developed a version of each message and pretested them by asking respondents how fearful they felt when reading the messages. Much to his surprise (and the surprise of his advisor) the persons who read the mild fear message reported higher levels of fear than those who read the strong fear message. When asked how he planned to resolve this sticky problem, the undaunted student responded resourcefully and optimistically, "Oh, that's simple; I'll just change the labels for the messages!" As strange as this solution may sound, its logic is at least somewhat consistent with the action theory approach.

To summarize the difference in the two approaches, the researcher adopting a motion theory perspective is conceptually and operationally freed from the responsibility of asking message recipients how they interpreted and reacted to the message appeals. If the message containing strong fear-arousing appeals were significantly more or less persuasive than the mild fear message *and* if other features of the study were adequately controlled, the difference could be attributed to the manipulated message variable. On the other hand, the researcher operating from an action theory perspective is logically mandated to assess success in manipulating the message variable by obtaining some measure of fear arousal from audience members. Moreover, even if the two messages differ significantly in persuasiveness, this difference cannot be attributed to the fear-arousing message appeals unless the two audiences vary significantly in some post-communication measure of arousal. This fact imposes a problem of retrodictiveness on many action theory conceptualizations; i.e., the researcher cannot *predict* (anticipate a future result) with confidence because it is impossible to determine how recipients will respond to the message until after the fact; rather, the researcher can only *retrodict* (infer from a past result) after identifying the recipients who responded to the message in the required way.

Not only does such retrodictiveness conflict with the goal of a predictive social/behavioral science (see Andersen, Chapter 1), it also provides a tempting loophole for the researcher seeking to provide post hoc, potentially circular "explanations" for failures to confirm research predictions. This is the case particularly when he or she argues from the logic of an action theory conceptualization without performing the needed operations to determine if the conditions for an action theory test of hypothesis have been realized. The point can best be illustrated by an example. Suppose a researcher predicts that a message with appeals eliciting high levels of fear or anxiety ("strong fear-arousing message appeals" as conceived of from an action viewpoint) will be more persuasive than a message lacking such appeals. After exposing audiences to the two messages, the researcher finds no support for this prediction; i.e., the two messages are comparably persuasive. At this point, however, the researcher observes that some audience members exposed to the strong fear message were clearly persuaded by it while others were not. This observation causes the researcher to reason as follows: Those audience members persuaded by the message probably experienced high levels of fear, but those not influenced by the message did not. The researcher then reanalyzes the data using only those audience members for whom the strong fear message had some persuasive impact. This reanalysis supports the original prediction that the strong fear message would be more persuasive.

Notice the circularity in these procedures: The researcher posits a hypothesis, examines the data, throws out the data that do not conform with the hypothesis, and concludes that the hypothesis is supported. The circularity is particularly blatant because the researcher obtained no independent measure of audience arousal; instead, the judgment of arousal was based on responses to the dependent variable itself, namely, whether or not particular respondents were persuaded by the message. If the researcher had obtained a self-report or physiological measure of arousal *apart from* the measure of persuasiveness, the decision to eliminate some recipients from the analysis would be more justifiable, although any after-the-fact decision to throw out data is bound to create logical or statistical problems. Once again, it should be stressed that a motion theory approach centering on the linguistic and semantic characteristics of message appeals enables the investigator to avoid these pitfalls.

Pulling It All Together

This section has examined some of the factors involved in fitting the concepts, propositions, and theories of the communication scientist's verbal universe to the data collection process of the observational universe. For this bridging procedure to occur, clear, useful conceptual definitions of the important constructs must first be stipulated. These individual conceptual definitions themselves typically reflect a primary commitment to either a motion or an action theory perspective, though at the more global propositional and theoretical levels, the two perspectives are frequently blended.

The actual shift from verbal to observational universe is accomplished by means of operational definitions that specify the procedures, or steps, to be taken in order to derive the meaning of the constructs. Any conceptual definition lends itself to various operational definitions, and no single operational definition can capture the entire richness and range of meaning of its corresponding conceptual definition. As a result, findings that remain consistent over a variety of operational definitions are of particular import to the behavioral scientist. Finally, definitions grounded in an action theory perspective pose several logical requirements that are not entailed by definitions founded on a motion theory approach.

FITTING THE OBSERVATIONAL UNIVERSE
TO THE VERBAL UNIVERSE

The primary purpose of scientific observation is to assess accurately the observational universe so that its correspondence with the verbal universe can be evaluated. By so doing, researchers are able to decide on the veracity of hypotheses and theories. Scientific observation may produce two kinds of errors: On one hand, the researcher may reject a theory that accurately depicts the observational universe; on the other, the researcher may fail to reject a theory that does not accurately depict the observational universe. While not totally identical, these errors are closely analogous to the well-known **Type I** and **Type II errors** associated with statistical inference.

An understanding of the researcher's task can perhaps be achieved by likening it to the problem faced by members of a jury. The four possible outcomes of a trial are summarized in Table 2.2. In two instances, the jury's decision corresponds with the actual state of affairs; i.e., the jury finds the defendant "guilty" when in fact he or she is guilty, or the jury finds the defendant "not guilty" when in fact he or she is not. In the remaining two instances, the verdicts fail to correspond with the actual state of affairs. To find an innocent defendant "guilty" closely resembles Type I error, since the jury concludes something systematic has occurred—specifically, the defendant has committed a crime—when in fact it has not. Conversely, a verdict of "not guilty" for a guilty defendant resembles Type II error, since the jury concludes nothing systematic has occurred—specifically, the defendant has not committed a crime—when in fact it has.

Just as the jury can never be absolutely sure of what actually happened, the communication researcher can never be absolutely sure that acceptance or rejection of a theory constitutes the correct decision. Some of the reasons why absolute certainty is impossible will emerge as this section unfolds; suffice it to say for now that some ambiguity is inevitable because the researcher operates with a decision model based on *probability* rather than certainty.

To make an informed judgment of the correspondence between the verbal

TABLE 2.2. SUMMARY OF POSSIBLE DECISION OUTCOMES IN TRIALS AND COMMUNICATION STUDIES

	Defendant "Really Is"	
	Guilty	**Not Guilty**
"Guilty"	Correct Decision	Error (Resembles Type I error in scientific decision-making)
JURY FINDS		
"Not Guilty"	Error (Resembles Type II error in scientific decision-making)	Correct Decision

and observational universes, the researcher must organize all of the obtained observations. Moreover, the researcher must present the observations so that other investigators are able to make independent assessments of this correspondence. These two tasks, organizing and presenting observations, are commonly referred to as *data analysis*.

This section next presents some general data analytic strategies that are employed by researchers. During this presentation, some of the factors that produce premature theoretical rejection and false theoretical acceptance errors are mentioned.

The Visual Organization of Observations: Simple Data Sets

One of the most important and most often neglected data analytic strategies involves displaying research results. The two most frequently used methods of implementing this strategy are table and graph construction. A *table* is a numerical classification of data and a *graph*, or *figure*, is a geometrical classification and display of results. Numerous tabular and graphic methods can be applied to **univariate**, **bivariate**, or **multivariate** data, where univariate data are measurements of one variable, bivariate data are measurements of two variables, and multivariate data are measurements of more than two variables. Regardless of the specific technique employed, however, the purpose of a table or a graph is to clarify empirical results, both for the researcher interpreting the data and for professional audiences reading the presentation of this interpretation.

Several examples of tables are presented below. Table 2.3 summarizes the distribution of scores on a Communication 100 exam. From this display, it can be quickly observed that the majority of students performed quite well, at least

TABLE 2.3. HYPOTHETICAL DISTRIBUTION OF COMMUNICATION 100 EXAMINATION SCORES

Scores (in percentages)	Frequency	Percentage of Students
95–99	2	4
90–94	4	8
85–89	9	18
80–84	13	26
75–79	10	20
70–74	6	12
65–69	3	6
60–64	2	4
55–59	0	0
50–54	0	0
45–49	1	2
Total	50	100

by typical standards; almost two-thirds of the scores fall within the 75 percent to 89 percent range, and fewer than 10 percent of the students scored less than 65 percent.

Were an observer to thumb through test booklets, it is unlikely that the distributional characteristics of these 50 scores could be perceived accurately; 50 scores are simply too much information for most people to process at one time. In tabular form, however, the important distributional information is more easily assimilated. Let us consider some aspects of this table that facilitate information processing.

First, the scores are ordered from the highest marks to the lowest marks, rather than presented randomly. This ordering allows observers to grasp certain quantitative features of the scores with ease. For example, it is quickly apparent that the highest score could have been no greater than 99 percent and the lowest score could have been no less than 45 percent.

Second, the scores are grouped into sets of five numbers; e.g., the category 95–99 includes the scores 95, 96, 97, 98, and 99. Grouping the data results in a loss of information. For instance, the exact scores for the four persons scoring in the 95–99 interval cannot be gleaned from the table; all four could have been 95; the scores could have been spread over the interval, or a host of other possibilities could have pertained. Nevertheless, grouping may permit observers to visualize the shape of a distribution more easily, especially when there is a wide range of scores. Unfortunately, by manipulating the manner in which data are grouped, the skillful but unscrupulous researcher may produce a less-than-accurate depiction of the distribution of scores. Therefore, a set of informal rules for grouping data has evolved (e.g., see Ferguson, 1981, p. 21).

Third, there are columns for reporting both frequency and percentage. The *frequency* column lists the number of persons scoring in each of the intervals, while the *percentage* column lists the percentage of persons scoring in each of the intervals (where percentage = (frequency/total number of respondents) × 100). These figures are particularly useful in clarifying important features of the distribution of scores. For example, there are 13 scores that lie in the 80 percent–84 percent interval and 10 scores that lie in the 75 percent–79 percent interval, a difference of (13 − 10 = 3). Is this difference large or small? Clearly, the answer depends on the total sample size. If there were only 10 respondents, a difference of three between two intervals would be substantial, since three respondents is 30 percent of the entire sample. On the other hand, if there were 300 respondents, a difference of three would be minuscule, since in this case three respondents is merely 1 percent of the sample. In Table 2.3 the percentage column may be used to ascertain the size of a difference of three. Twenty percent of the sample scored in the 75 percent–79 percent range, while 26 percent of the sample scored in the 80 percent–84 percent range, a 6 percent difference. In most situations a difference of this magnitude would not be considered substantial.

Fourth, the table is titled, and this title informs the reader of the meaning of

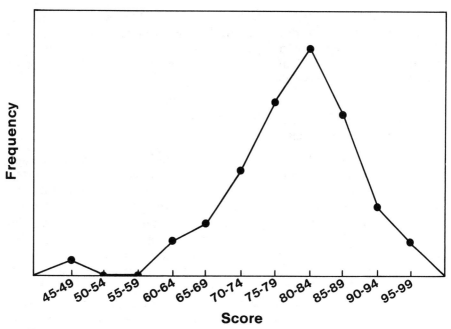

Figure 2.2. Frequency polygon of a hypothetical set of Communication 100 examination scores

the numbers. In this instance, the numbers are Communication 100 examination scores. Clearly, were they something else, such as Graduate Record Examination scores, the meaning imparted to them would differ substantially. It is instructive to consider why.

As you might imagine, the Graduate Record Examination (GRE) is a very difficult test. Given the difficulty of the GRE, scores as high as those presented in Table 2.3 would not be expected. It is this expectation that affects our judgment of these figures. Given the information that these figures were GRE scores, an observer might attribute exceptional intelligence to this group of 50 persons, although a jaded observer might attribute the performance to cheating. These numbers indicate good performance on a Communication 100 examination, although certainly nothing extraordinary. Alternatively, if these scores represented the results of a simple arithmetic examination given to a group of mathematics PhDs, the scores would be judged as dismal. In short, what observers know about the measures from past experience has an impact on their interpretation of data. This fact will assume greater importance when more complex data sets are considered.

These results may also be displayed by graphing them. In Figure 2.2 one type of graph, a *frequency polygon*, is presented. The intervals are arrayed on the *x*-axis, or abscissa, and the frequencies with which these scores occurred are arrayed on the *y*-axis, or ordinate. The shape of the frequency distribution is then plotted across the various intervals. In short, the information in Table 2.3 is presented geometrically in Figure 2.2. The researcher or the consumer of research may gain a quick and accurate understanding of this distribution of scores by examining either the table or the figure.

The Visual Organization of Observations: More Complex Data Sets

Table 2.3 and Figure 2.2 display univariate distribution data, or the distribution of a single variable. To display the characteristics of more complex data sets, more intricate tables and figures must be constructed. For instance, Table 2.4 summarizes a bivariate, or two variable, classification. This table presents the results of a hypothetical experiment in which respondents were exposed to either a high fear-arousing persuasive message, a moderate fear-arousing persuasive message, or a low fear-arousing persuasive message. The numbers under each of these experimental treatments are average (mean) attitude change scores, attitude being measured by a five-point Likert scale.

By examining this table, the relationship between the amount of fear-arousal in a persuasive message and attitude change can be observed. Clearly, as the amount of fear-arousing material in the message increases, attitude change increases. Furthermore, this relationship appears to be *linear*, a linear relationship being one in which the increase in the amount of attitude change is at least roughly proportional to the increase in the amount of fear-arousing material. Specifically, there is an increase in attitude change from the low fear condition to the moderate fear condition ($3.23 - 2.41 = .82$) and the same magnitude of change ($4.05 - 3.23 = .82$) from the moderate fear condition to the high fear condition. Thus, a precise statement of the obtained relationship between the two variables, fear-arousal and attitude change, would be as follows: As the amount of fear-arousing material in a persuasive message increases, there is a proportional increase in audience attitude change.

This same feature of these data is depicted in Figure 2.3. In this figure the **independent variable**, or that variable whose values are uncaused by other variables in the study, is plotted on the *x*-axis, while the **dependent variable**, or that variable whose values are caused by the independent variable, is plotted on

TABLE 2.4. MEAN ATTITUDE CHANGE SCORES AS A FUNCTION OF THE AMOUNT OF FEAR-AROUSING STIMULI IN A PERSUASIVE MESSAGE

	Fear		
	Low	**Moderate**	**High**
Mean Attitude Change	2.41	3.23	4.05

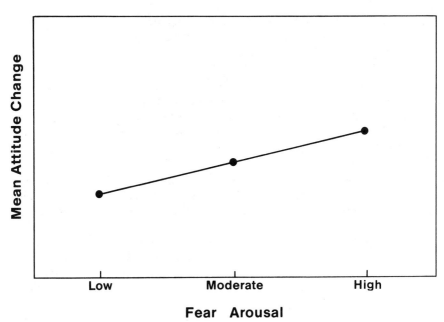

Fear Arousal

Figure 2.3. Relationship between magnitude of fear arousal and audience attitude change

the y-axis. Thus, fear arousal is plotted on the x-axis and mean attitude change is plotted on the y-axis. A line is drawn to connect the mean attitude change values, and since this line is straight, it illustrates that the relationship between fear arousal and attitude change is linear.

Organizing Observations: Statistical Tools

In the main, contemporary behavioral research questions require examining more complex relationships. In fact, multivariate studies frequently include 20 variables or more. Nevertheless, tables and figures can be constructed to characterize the relationships among the variables. With increasing research complexity, however, the relationships among variables become increasingly difficult to extract from tables and figures. Therefore, the behavioral scientist must employ more sophisticated tools to make sense of the data. Generally, these tools are statistical.

In order to arrive at a rudimentary understanding of statistics, some terms must be clarified. A *population* is composed of all units possessing a given attribute or attributes. For example, a researcher might be interested in studying the present population of school teachers in the United States. In this example the person is the unit of analysis, and being a school teacher at the moment is the defining attribute. An investigator might also be interested in studying all humans, past, present, and future. This infinite population is concerned with the person as the unit of analysis, and being a person is the defining attribute.

A *sample* is a subset of a population. Thus, the group of third grade teachers at Marble School in East Lansing, Michigan, is a sample drawn from the population of school teachers in the United States, and 70 members of a Communication 100 class constitute a sample of all humans.

A *parameter* is a characteristic of a population. For instance, the mean income of all United States school teachers at the present time is a parameter. The population is composed of all United States school teachers, and the relevant characteristic is mean income.

Finally, a *statistic* is a characteristic of a sample. Hence, the mean income of the third grade teachers at Marble School is a statistic. The set of third grade teachers at Marble School is the sample, and mean income is again the relevant characteristic.

There are two major problems in the study of statistics. On one hand, characteristics of samples must be described; on the other, sample information is often employed to estimate the value of population parameters. Study of the former problem is termed *descriptive statistics*, and study of the latter problem is referred to as *inferential statistics*. Consider some examples of the two areas of study.

The distribution of Communication 100 scores presented in Table 2.3 can be described, as can any univariate distribution, by four attributes. First, the distribution has some *central tendency*. The central tendency of a distribution refers to how the majority of respondents performed. In this case, most respondents scored in the 70s and 80s. There are statistics, such as the arithmetic *mean* or arithmetic average, the *median* or the middle score in the distribution, and the *mode* or most frequently occurring score in the distribution, that researchers use to describe this feature of a distribution.

Second, the distribution has some *dispersion*, or spread. In Table 2.3, the scores are quite compact. Stated differently, while there are a few outlying scores, most of the scores deviate very little from the distribution's central tendency. Some distributions are quite different; they are composed of scores that are highly dispersed. Researchers employ statistics such as the *range*, or the difference between the high and low scores in the distribution, and the *standard deviation*, or the average deviation of scores from the mean, to describe this feature of distributions.

Third, the scores have some *skewness*. A distribution is skewed to the extent that the scores are asymmetrical. In Table 2.3, high scores are slightly more frequent than low scores; therefore, this distribution would be characterized as negatively skewed. Were the preponderance of scores on the low end of the scale, the distribution would be characterized as positively skewed. Researchers calculate various skewness indices to assess this distributional trait.

Finally, the scores have some *kurtosis*. Kurtosis refers to the extent to which a distribution is peaked or flat. When it is peaked, the distribution is

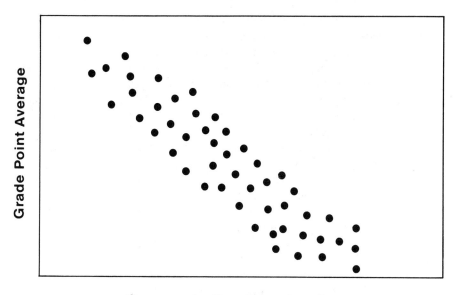

Communication Apprehension

Figure 2.4. Scatterplot of relationship between CA scores and GPA

termed *leptokurtic*; when flat, *platykurtic*, and when exactly the height of the normal, or *Gaussian* distribution, *mesokurtic*. The scores depicted in Table 2.3 are somewhat leptokurtic, although it is difficult to see this distributional characteristic in the absence of a computed kurtosis index.

Descriptive statistics are not limited to characterizing features of univariate frequency distributions. To illustrate a more complex descriptive problem, consider the hypothetical *scatterplot* depicting the relationship between level of communication apprehension (CA) and high school grade point average (GPA) for a sample of first-year college students that is presented in Figure 2.4.

Examination of this figure reveals that, in general, as CA increases, GPA decreases: Those respondents with low CA have relatively high GPAs; those with moderate CA have moderate GPAs, and those with high CA have relatively low GPAs. Moreover, the decrease in GPA is approximately proportional to the increase in CA, so that the relationship between these two variables is linear. The problem for the statistician is to create a numerical index that describes this relationship.

An excellent, and most commonly employed index is the Pearson Product Moment Correlation Coefficient. This measure, which describes the extent of linear association between two variables, ranges from −1.00 to +1.00. A value of −1.00 implies that the two variables have a perfect *inverse relationship*; i.e., as one variable increases the other decreases proportionally and without deviation. A value of +1.00 implies that the two variables have a perfect *direct relationship*; i.e., as one variable increases the other increases proportionally and without deviation. A value of zero implies no linear association between the two variables. As these correlation coefficients move from zero toward -1.00, they imply increasingly strong inverse linear association, and as they move from zero to $+1.00$, they imply increasingly strong direct linear association. Given this brief, nonmathematical treatment of the concept of correlation, the reader should notice that the CA-GPA correlation is negative and substantial, although clearly far less than -1.00.

The concept of *correlation* may be extended both to the multivariate case and the nonlinear case. Coefficients have been developed to estimate the strength of linear association between one or more dependent variables and a set of independent variables (see Harris, 1975). Moreover, there are algorithms that estimate how well various types of nonlinear functions describe bivariate or multivariate relationships (Pedhazur, 1982).

The second major statistical problem, statistical inference, is tightly entwined with the study of probability. Commonly, statistical inference requires that the researcher specify two hypotheses, the *null hypothesis* and the *alternate hypothesis*. The former posits no effect of one or more constructs on another construct or constructs, and the latter posits that the null hypothesis is false. An example should clarify this notion.

Suppose that a researcher performs an experiment in which half the participants attempt to solve problems while working in a group that is highly structured, and the other half attempt to solve problems while working in a group that is very unstructured. Specifically, a total of 25 four-person groups receive the structured group experience, and 25 additional four-person groups receive the unstructured group experience. The outcome of interest is the number of problems solved by the groups.

Upon completion of the experiment, the average number of problems solved in both the structured condition and the unstructured condition is computed. The null hypothesis asserts that structure has no impact on the number of problems solved. Restating this hypothesis more precisely, the average number of problems solved by the structured groups should not differ significantly from the average number of problems solved by the unstructured groups. The alternate hypothesis simply asserts that the null hypothesis is untrue.

The key term in this argument is "significant." When a statistician employs this term it has a very particular meaning; specifically, an effect is statistically significant when the probability is low that one would obtain it given that the null hypothesis is true. Thus, if the mean number of problems solved by the structured groups was 10.75 (standard deviation = 2.00), and the mean number of problems solved by the unstructured groups was 3.12 (standard deviation = 2.00), then assuming the truth of the null hypothesis, it is very unlikely that this mean difference of 7.63 problems would occur. Since such a result is unlikely if the null hypothesis is true, then the null hypothesis is probably not true and the researcher rejects it.

Researchers can make either of two errors. On the one hand, they can reject the null hypothesis when it should not have been rejected. Alternatively, they can fail to reject the null hypothesis when it should have been rejected. As emphasized earlier, these two mistakes are termed Type I error and Type II error respectively. In either case they impair our ability to assess the correspondence between the verbal universe and the observational universe.

While statistical inferences may be drawn concerning a wide variety of statistics and applied to numerous null and alternative hypotheses, it is important to keep in mind that the concepts of *statistical significance* and *practical significance* differ markedly. By practical significance is meant the ability to predict the dependent variable from the independent variable (see Andersen, Chapter 1). Thus, an investigator may obtain a statistically significant result even though knowledge of the independent variable contributes little to his or her ability to predict the dependent variable. Although the factors that contribute to this outcome constitute a number of technical issues beyond the scope of this chapter, some have concluded that the statistical significance test is of little value (for an excellent argument, see Carver, 1978). Though the preceding statement is a little strong for the present authors' taste, the persuasiveness of arguments pointing out the limitations of the statistical significance test should make researchers wary of using it as the *only* criterion for assessing correspondence between the verbal universe and the observational universe. Instead, it must be supplemented by using descriptive statistics to look at the strength of relationship, i.e., how well the dependent variable or variables can be predicted from knowledge of the independent variable or variables.

Pulling It All Together

This section has considered ways of organizing and describing observations that permit relatively unambiguous assessments of the fit of the observational universe to the verbal universe. When undertaking these assessments, researchers may make one of two errors: They may reject a theory that accurately depicts the observational universe or they may fail to reject a theory that does not accurately depict the observational universe.

One way to organize observations bearing on these judgments is in tabular form. Tables permit researchers to summarize the essential characteristics of a large data set so that the implications are more easily grasped by researchers and consumers alike. Tables can be prepared for univariate, bivariate, or multivariate data sets.

Observations may also be presented in graphs and figures, thus allowing results to be displayed visually. As with tables, a large variety of options are available to the researcher, and there are techniques for dealing with data sets of widely varying complexity. At some point, however, the observations become so complex that it is necessary to use other statistical tools for organizing them. The concluding portion of this section describes some of the more basic statistical tools.

SUMMARY

Behavioral science research consists of a process of verbal construction, bridging, observation, bridging, and verbal reconstruction. This chapter deals with two broad sets of problems associated with this process: problems pertaining to the goodness of fit of the verbal universe to the observational universe and problems pertaining to the goodness of fit of the observational universe to the verbal universe. Although the chapter aims for a basic appreciation of fundamental issues, a rudimentary understanding of these two broad problem sets affords a start toward becoming an effective researcher, as well as an intelligent consumer of scientific communication research.

STUDY QUESTIONS

1. Select some of the communication concepts you encounter in your daily communicative activities. Develop a conceptual definition and two or three operational definitions of each of them.

2. Stipulate a "good" operational definition of any concept (good in the sense of its being useful in some way). Stipulate a "bad" definition of the same concept. Explain your reasons for assessing one definition positively and the other negatively.

3. See if you can apply the scientific process depicted in Figure 2.1 to some communicative issue you have come across in your daily activities. It is not necessary to do this formally; rather, you should attempt to work out some informal understanding of how the process can be applied to specific questions.

4. Are you primarily a motion theorist, an action theorist, or a blend of both in the ways you interpret and understand the workings of communication? Explain and justify your self-designation.

5. Suppose that you have performed an experiment in which you have varied the credibility of a speaker. Specifically, the topic of the speech is "The link between smoking and lung cancer," and you introduce the speaker as either a physician (high credibility) or a truck driver (low credibility), so that one-half of your sample hears the speech from the physician and the remainder of the sample hears it from the truck driver. You want to assess how this credibility difference will affect the audiences' attitudes toward smoking. Your thinking is that the high credibility source should produce more conformity to message recommendations than the low credibility source. What is the null hypothesis? What is the alternate hypothesis?

6. You want to survey persons living in the United States to see what television programs they like best. How might you go about it?

7. Imagine that we obtained measures of the number of hours that a child watched television and how aggressive that child was on the playground for a sample of 35 children. We expect to find that the more the child watches television, the more aggressive the child's behavior. Construct a scatterplot that would be consistent with this hypothesis. Now construct one that would be inconsistent.

ANNOTATED READINGS

Anderson, James A. (1987). *Communication research: Issues and methods.* New York: McGraw-Hill.

   A challenging book, but one that contains considerable useful information about the issues discussed in this chapter. Treatment is quite comprehensive and includes a look at both quantitative and qualitative research methods.

Bartz, Albert E. (1981). *Basic statistical concepts* (2nd ed.). Minneapolis: Burgess.

   This volume provides an easily read introduction to the fields of descriptive and inferential statistics. There are formulas and some algebra, but they are minimal.

Bowers, John W., & Courtright, John A. (1984). *Communication research methods.* Glenview, IL: Scott, Foresman.

   Another tough "read" but the outcomes are worth it. Provides examples of the process of definition and of the treatment and analysis of data.

Dubin, Robert (1978). *Theory building* (rev. ed.). New York: Free Press.

   Written by a philosopher of social science, this volume provides a technical, yet reasonably comprehensible treatment of some of the theoretical and definitional issues discussed in the chapter.

Hollander, Myles, & Proschan, Frank (1984). *The statistical exorcist: Dispelling statistics anxiety.* New York: Dekker.

   This book is a series of 26 vignettes concerning decision making, sampling, learning from data, and estimating probabilities. It is easy to read and contains no formulas, only a narrative description of various ways in which statistics are employed.

Kirk, Roger E. (1984). *Elementary statistics* (2nd ed.). Belmont, CA: Brooks/Cole.

   This work provides a more detailed examination of descriptive and inferential statistics. Provides some computer software information and examples.

Rubin, Rebecca B., Rubin, Alan M., & Piele, L. J. (1986). *Communication research: Strategies and sources.* Belmont, CA: Wadsworth.

   A clear, easily read discussion of all aspects of the research process. Chapters 1 and 4, in particular, are relevant to matters examined in this chapter.

CHAPTER 3

Using Computers

By H. Wayland Cummings,
University of Oklahoma

There was a time when a single **computer** filled an entire room and was surrounded by engineers and mathematicians who acted as though they were guards to an inner sanctum. Before computers, it took individuals such as Albert Einstein, in some cases large research teams, to gather data or facts and interpret them in a way that made understanding of our world possible. To say the least, complex problem-solving was dependent on an elite intelligentsia who could occasionally come up with answers that made people feel they heard "God talking."

But the advent of the computer has led to a kind of democratizing of knowledge whereby people now can gain access to a computer, and that computer can store, search, compare, and produce information inaccessible to those in the pre-information age. Some computer enthusiasts have said that time now should be measured as B.C. (Before Computers) and A.C. (Anno Computare, i.e., Year of the Computer). In any event, it is now possible to use a computer to monitor and predict weather patterns around the world, create paintings and sculptures, write music and produce the sounds of a symphony or rock band, or translate English phrases into German and vice versa. It is possible for anyone with normal human intelligence to perform any of these activities, and with the aid of the computer, make inferences about our world that exceed anything that could have been done by the Newtons and Einsteins of a century and more ago. Computer technology makes it possible to address problems that at one time stood in silence, waiting for the right genius to come along.

It is for many sacreligious to even consider that a computer could do what an Einstein, or a St. Augustine, was able to do. And in the strictest sense, this is not what is meant. Indeed, it is intriguing to speculate on what St. Augustine might have said in his fourth century "Confessions of St. Augustine" should he have had an IBM 3083 mainframe computer at his intellectual elbow. We suspect it would have been used for more than word processing. The computer is a technology that provides an extension and amplification of human minds and muscles. What has happened as part of this revolution is that computer engineers have developed high quality solutions to problems we have not yet perceived; that is, we have experienced what it means to be a technology-driven society whereby computers have provided solutions to problems we did not realize we had. The failure of imagination may lie behind much of the resistance to computer use. We find it difficult to manage technologies that have no apparent application, and so we turn our backs on them. We will have more to say about this resistance to computer use later in the chapter. For now it can be said that computers have taken the drudgery out of certain tasks. For example, computers have made it possible to create a measuring instrument using factor analysis that had to be done at one time by hand, in many cases crudely with straight edge, compasses and protractors. It meant that a statistician might take six months to a year to perform a factor analysis of six or eight variables, and then only the simplest kind of procedure could be performed. It meant at one time that some careless error due to inattentiveness or distraction would require recalculation of the entire problem and the loss of four or five months' work.

Another example: Up until the middle 1960s, content analysis as a set of measurement procedures required six months to a year to analyze the messages, often leading to usage of only the simplest of categories. It was not hard to understand why Berelson (1952) noted with some frustration that before one performed content analysis, one had better have a very good reason. Researchers spent more time analyzing data than developing theoretical concepts. The computer has changed all that, and has taken the tedium out of certain parts of the research procedure, releasing time and energy of scholars to focus on other necessary and important activities for knowledge creation and utilization. It may be that the computer is in part responsible for many discovering the impoverishment of their theories. When one seeks to understand an empirical phenomenon, the need to spend months analyzing data allows little time to extend and develop one's theory in testable ways. It is often true that data analysis has become so all-consuming that researchers have become diverted from its meaning and worth. The computer in these instances has provided a technology that makes it possible for reseachers to spend more time on those things which should concern them—the value and meaningfulness of their theories.

This chapter addresses the various uses to which communication researchers can apply the computer, including both the hardware and software requirements. To aid the person who wishes to understand and conduct communication research this essay will: (1) describe in general terms how computers work; (2) focus on what it is that computers process; (3) consider problems for which computers are useful, including some of the kinds of software available for people who study communication; (4) review some of the problems faced by people who exhibit anxiety in learning to use computers; and (5) discuss what it might mean to be a communication researcher in the age of the computer. First, let's take a look at how computers work.

HOW DO COMPUTERS WORK?

Computers are really a type of information processing system which permits a person to input (enter) certain information into an electronically-based system, transform that information in prescribed ways, and then to output that information in some form. We judge the power of a computer on the basis of how much, and how fast, information can be processed. The basic unit of information read by a computer is called a **bit**, which is merely an electronic "switch" which can be said to be "on" or "off." The old-fashioned IBM card (see Figure 3.1) provides an illustration. At any point in the card, which has 80 columns and 10 rows, a hole might be punched. A light may be focused on a column, reading each row in that column. If a light shines through a punched hole, a contact is made, and the switch is on. All other points where the light shines and no punched hole appears, the switch is off. Thus, a bit is a switch which can be on or off, and is the basic unit of information read by computers.

In most cases, however, we as users of computers are not interested in bits, but rather in a **byte**—a slightly higher level of analysis. This is the level at which we can organize bits in a way to stand for a number, a letter, a parenthesis, or an instruction. It is a series of 8 switches, each of which can be on or off, resulting in 256 possible combinations. Thus, a byte is defined as a basic grouping of bits. The "brain power" of a computer is partially measured in terms of the number of bytes it can process at any one time. The early computers processed 2,000 bytes of information, sometimes labeled as 2 **Kilobytes**, or 2K. The "garage

Figure 3.1. An IBM card

hackers" of the late 1960s developed small computers which could process 4K. And in the late 1970s, many microcomputers could handle 16K, 32K, 48K, and even 64K. Today, these capacities are as antique as a Model-T Ford. Micro-computers begin with 128K ranging to 1,000K (1 MegaK) and in some cases much more.

In the early days, computers were often described by the range of their central processing abilities. A large mainframe computer in the 1970s might be able to handle 2, 3, 4, or more million bytes (**MegaK**) of information, while minicomputers were described as being able to process 256K. And personal computers handled at best 64K. Now, what does that mean? It means that a computer could access magnetic cores which could handle the equivalent of 5 million characters (letters, numbers, etc.). Some of those characters could be in what is called **ROM**, or read-only-memory, which means that it is an area of the computer where information is "etched" into memory, and will not disappear even if the machine is turned off (non-volatile memory). Some of those characters are in what is called **RAM**, or random-access-memory, which means that it is in an area of the computer where information is temporarily located into memory, and will disappear should the machine lose power (volatile memory).

But today, many personal computers are larger than mainframe computers of just a few years ago. Many desk-top computers now have 640K bytes of internal memory, while minicomputers have 8 or more MegaK bytes of information, and large mainframe computers have 24, 32, or more MegaK bytes of information. Current engineers claim that soon there will be a desk-top computer capable of handling 4 MegaK bytes of information in its **central processing unit** (CPU), and at a price competitive with many of the higher priced personal computers (perhaps as low as $10,000). The category schema of micro, mini, and mainframe computers are quickly becoming "leaky" and imprecise. The increasing power of the technology requires us to talk about types of computers with blurred boundaries. Indeed, such new terms now appear as "super-minis," "super-computers," and "simultaneous computing capability." Computers no longer have one processor; there may be two or three of them in microcomputers, while large mainframes may have thousands.

It is, then, possible to describe computers by how much information they can process in terms of bytes. But it is also possible to describe a computer on the basis of how fast it can work. For our purposes, however, it is sufficient to be familiar with some specific characteristics of computers. First, computers can move information from one place to another in the form of "words." A **computer word** is comprised of the number of bits that can be moved at a single point in time. A computer which is said to have an 8-bit processor is capable of moving 8 bits in a single time-cycle, and thus computer "words" are comprised of 8 bits. A computer which is said to have a 16-bit processor is capable of moving 16 bits in a single time-cycle, and the computer "words" in this case are comprised of 16 bits. And a computer which is said to have a 32-bit processor is capable of moving 32 bits in a single time-cycle, and as before, the computer "word" is comprised of 32 bits.

The speed of the computer is determined by the number of bits that can be moved from place to place in a single time-cycle and, in addition, the rate or number of time-cycles that may occur in a single second. Computers are often measured in terms of millions of instructions per second, or **MIPS**. The new super-computers are expected to be able to handle 1 billion instructions in a single second, while some microcomputers may handle up to 500,000 instructions per second, or .5 MIPS. The new super-computer "Connection" has 64,000 parallel processors as part of its central processing unit, and is capable of 1,000 MIPS (1 billion instructions per second). The IBM 360 of a few years ago was capable of executing about 10 to 20 MIPS, while the IBM 3081 can execute about 40 or more MIPS. Compare these speeds with an older VAX 11 minicomputer which executes four to six MIPS.

What we know at this point is that computers can be measured by the amount of information they can handle in a central processing unit (CPU), most commonly in the form of kilobytes or K bytes of information. In addition, computers can be measured by the speed with which they process information, and this can be seen in terms of the number of bits that can be processed in a single time-cycle. In addition, the speed of the cycle plays an important part in telling us how many instructions a computer can process per second (MIPS). The super-computers which are but a few short years away will further revolutionize what we can do with computers, and how they may assist us in our work. Now let us take a look at input/output operations of computers.

Input/Output

Computers require that all information to be analyzed—**input**—must be entered in the form of on or off switches (bits). But more generally, we can do this by punching holes in IBM cards for processing by a card reader, or by sitting in front of a keyboard and allowing the mechanics of a typewriter keyboard to transform our information into a form that can be understood by the computer—again, a series of on and off switches. Most large universities are phasing out the use of IBM cards, and instead are using keyboard terminals. There is an increasing use of **optical scanners**, that are capable of reading bar codes or standard type-written manuscripts directly, and then converting them to the appropriate information form for the computer to read. Beyond this, people are also using activated "pencils" (see Figure 3.2) that can be moved across a screen (cathode ray tube, or **CRT**) and then pressing a button on the side of the pencil to enter information. Of course, those interested in games have long been impressed with "joysticks" and "the mouse." The mouse is merely an activated box with a roller on the bottom. As the box is moved across the desk—up and down, right and left—and a button is pushed at a point on the screen where a cursor is following the movement of the box, information is entered and transformed in ways the computer can read.

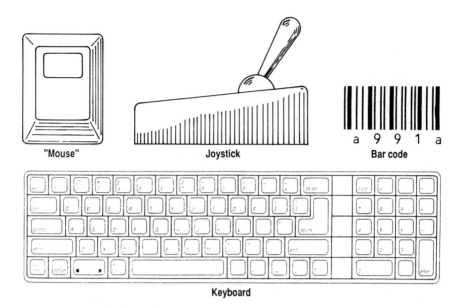

"Mouse"   Joystick   Bar code

Keyboard

Figure 3.2. Some selected input devices

Stated simply, information can be "inputed" into a computer in a variety of ways; we have only mentioned a few that are commonly used. However, information can also be read from electronic sensors that measure heat, heartbeats, or any other kind of data. We also have the ability to transform speech into information the computer can easily recognize. But perhaps most interesting of all is that digital video equipment will permit computers to read films, television productions, even family pictures, and convert those images into information the computer can read.

As for output, computers can produce information in nearly any form desired by the user. We will return to this subject in later sections of this chapter as we pursue some of the uses of the computer for communication researchers.

Auxiliary Memory

Most computers need more than a central processing unit to carry out tasks. When we submit information to a computer, it usually is stored in some appropriate **auxiliary memory** space for use when we get ready (see Figure 3.3). In the early days of computers, information was stored on magnetic tapes. The power of the tape machines was often recorded in the size of reels (7 inches; 9 inches), and the number of bits per inch (bpi) stored on the tape. It was common to have tape machines that handled 800 bpi, but today it is more likely to have 6,250 bpi tape machines. And instead of reel-to-reel tapes, the tape machines now are in the form of cassettes about the size of a beta videotape one purchases at the store.

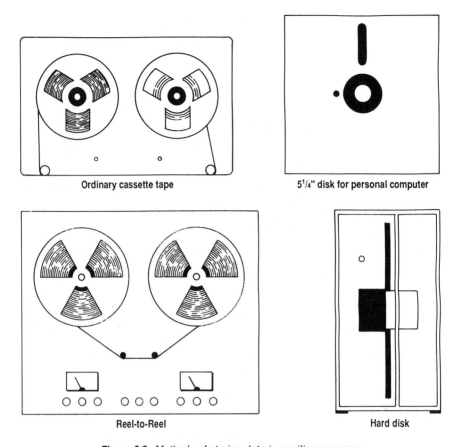

Ordinary cassette tape

5¹/₄" disk for personal computer

Reel-to-Reel

Hard disk

Figure 3.3. Methods of storing data in auxiliary memory

For small microcomputers, it is possible to use standard microcassettes or regular audio cassettes for the storing of information. But the disadvantage of this approach is that the computer must search for information linearly; that is, if you want to run a program entitled "GETIT," and there are 200 programs on the tape, the computer would have to start at the beginning of the tape, and search until it finds a program entitled "GETIT." To say the least, the storage of information in tape memory can be slow and frustrating. Today, tape machines are used primarily to provide "back-up", or "insurance" copies, just in case the working memory medium fails.

An important step forward was made when information was stored on a disk, today the most common method of storing data. The disk has a directory, meaning that it has a table of contents. And thus when a computer wants to get the program "GETIT," it goes to the directory and finds its location. In this way, if "GETIT" is the 196th program on the disk, the computer will skip over the first 195 programs and begin reading "GETIT" immediately. While data is stored linearly on a disk, it is not retrieved linearly; it is retrieved through the use of a directory, or table of contents.

But we now have other methods available to us. Most of the methods are highly elaborated versions of the magnetic disk. The "disk" technology that has revolutionized the music industry is also making large changes in the way computer systems are designed. For example, it is possible to place the entire Encyclopedia Britannica on a single disk (termed CD-ROM) about the size of a long-playing record. The technology has moved so quickly that it is possible to place an entire textbook on a single 3½ inch disk. The average textbook contains about one MegaK of information, and we have a number of personal computers available now that can read 1.4 MegaK of information on a single 3½ inch disk.

Programs

Perhaps there is nothing more frustrating to novices in computing than the intimidation that comes when computer people talk "programming-ese." At the simplest level, a **computer program** is nothing more than a sequence of instructions ordered in a certain way that tell a computer how to read information, how to transform it, and how to **output** that information. We should not look at this kind of process as new, for it is something humans have done ever since cookbooks were invented. For example, Figure 3.4 presents a recipe for white sauce.

What we have done is provide a detailed set of instructions on how to make white sauce. And it is much the same when we write a computer program; it is essentially, though perhaps oversimply, a recipe for creating output from a certain kind of input. Look at the example in Figure 3.4, which is written in BASIC language (more on computer languages later). Please notice that the program represents a set of instructions for the computer. The program is designed to calculate the statistical value of omega squared for an analysis of variance. It is based on the value of F, the number of subjects in the study, and the number of groups.

The numbers in the program in Figure 3.4 are merely an indication of the sequence of steps in the program. It is tradition to number these statements in BASIC in units of 10, permitting an easy change of the program by inserting a new step between 10 and 20, and marking it, say, 11. In any event, the program says first to clear the screen (CLS) of the terminal. Then, six variables are defined at this point as equaling zero. The third step asks the computer to print on the terminal the name of the "recipe," followed by the request that the user enter information—the value of F; the number of groups in the ANOVA; and the total number of subjects in the study. With this information, the equation for calculating the omega squared is presented in steps 70 through 90; the creation of the correlation coefficient based on omega squared is provided in step 100. Then, we ask the program to print out at the terminal the results. Step

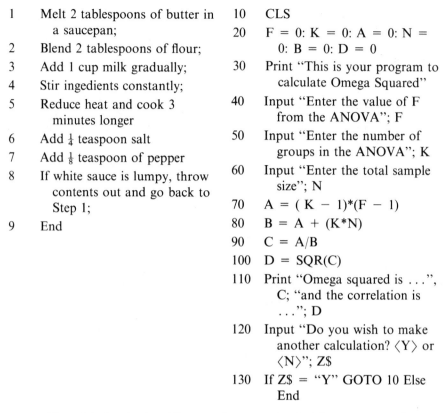

1	Melt 2 tablespoons of butter in a saucepan;
2	Blend 2 tablespoons of flour;
3	Add 1 cup milk gradually;
4	Stir ingedients constantly;
5	Reduce heat and cook 3 minutes longer
6	Add ¼ teaspoon salt
7	Add ⅛ teaspoon of pepper
8	If white sauce is lumpy, throw contents out and go back to Step 1;
9	End

10	CLS
20	F = 0: K = 0: A = 0: N = 0: B = 0: D = 0
30	Print "This is your program to calculate Omega Squared"
40	Input "Enter the value of F from the ANOVA"; F
50	Input "Enter the number of groups in the ANOVA"; K
60	Input "Enter the total sample size"; N
70	A = (K − 1)*(F − 1)
80	B = A + (K*N)
90	C = A/B
100	D = SQR(C)
110	Print "Omega squared is ...", C; "and the correlation is ..."; D
120	Input "Do you wish to make another calculation? ⟨Y⟩ or ⟨N⟩"; Z$
130	If Z$ = "Y" GOTO 10 Else End

Figure 3.4. A recipe for white sauce. A program to calculate omega squared.

120 asks if the user wants to do another calculation, and if so, starts the program sequence again by first clearing the screen and making all variables equal to zero. If the user wants to quit, he/she need only enter N (or any other key except Y) for no, and the program is completed.

Computers basically don't do anything they aren't told to do. What most commonly goes wrong with a "recipe" is that we don't mix the ingredients properly, or we substitute water for milk, or we pour the milk too fast. In other words, we don't follow instructions. However, if the computer "recipe" (program) is written properly we should be able to get good "white sauce" every time. The computer only has the ability (so far) to do what it is told, and to do it exactly the same again, and again, and again—, and again.

There are many kinds of computer languages, some more useful than others, depending upon the task they are designed to perform. These languages are comprised of a syntax with certain rules such that a computer may translate that language into the language of "on" and "off" switches it understands, and carry out the instructions of the programmer. High-level languages are really

TABLE 3.1. SOME REFERENCES FOR LEARNING COMPUTER LANGUAGES

Computer Programming in Basic by Downing Barron's Educational Series, Inc. Woodbury, NY (1984)	Introduction to COBOL by Overbeek & Singletary Addison-Wesley Publishing Co. Reading, MA (1986)
Problem-solving and structured programming in PASCAL 2nd edition by Koffman Addison-Wesley Publishing Reading, MA (1985)	Fundamentals of Fortran 77 3rd edition by Nickerson Little, Brown & Co. Boston, MA (1985)
LISP second edition by Winston & Horn Addison-Wesley Publishing Reading, MA (1984)	Programming in PROLOG by Clocksin and Mellisk Springer-Verlag Berlin (1984)
The C Programming Language by Kernighan and Ritchie Prentice-Hall Englewood Cliffs, NJ (1978)	

descriptive of how abstract those computer languages are relative to the basic machine language of on and off switches that the computer understands. The way to understand a computer language is not different, and really much easier than, learning a modern language. Books are available for the various computer languages, including BASIC, COBOL, PASCAL, FORTRAN, PL/1, and many others. (References for a few of them are provided in Table 3.1).

All computer programming languages must have a "translator." In microcomputers, slow translators are built into the ROM (read-only-memory). The more common method of translating programming languages, particularly in mainframes, is the employment of a compiler. A compiler translates the computer program written in a high-level language into the machine language that the computer understands. What is perhaps most frustrating to computer specialists is that there are so many computer languages that it is difficult for casual users of the computer to stay up to date on the latest versions, let alone the new versions being created continuously. It is important, however, that each researcher become acquainted with at least one programming language in order to meet those specialized needs for which there are no existing programs. There are a couple of terms we need to know, however, that will help us to distinguish the role of programming languages from the rest of the computing system, and that is the distinction between "hardware" and "software."

Hardware versus Software

The term **hardware** is used to refer to the physical properties of a computer system. That may include a terminal to a large mainframe or microcomputer, or it may refer to an optical scanner, a tape or disk machine, the tapes and disks, the printer, or any of a number of other physical elements important to identifying the computer system.

The term **software** refers to the operating systems and computer programs that control the work of the computer as it reads information, performs some function or activity on the information, and then either stores or outputs the information in a form defined by the instructions. A basis now exists for talking about what it is that computers process.

WHAT DO COMPUTERS PROCESS?

It is useful to consider the computer as an information processing system, a point made at the beginning of this chapter. And it is also important to recall that computers have a language or code system by which they process information in the form of "bits," "bytes," and "words." If that were all a computer could do, it would be quite cumbersome for the average user. We have to ask what kinds of information people want the computer to process. There is a terminology regarding the kinds of information processed by computers, that helps to make relevant what the computer can do for users. It is reasonable to consider computers as processors of text, or words; of numbers, or mathematical/logical symbols; and of graphics. First, let us look at the computer as a processor of words and text.

Computers as Processors of Words and Text

The most common use today of microcomputers is that of processing words and text. We use the computer to enter correspondence, memos, research papers, manuscripts for publication, including articles, chapters in books, or entire books. The value of this is that it makes it possible to reduce the drudgery of the mechanical and/or electric typewriter where we have problems with margins, corrections, and additions. One of the early attempts to increase the speed of mechanical typing was the improvement of carriage returns; that is, instead of a handle to push in order to return the carriage to the beginning of the line, it became possible with electric typewriters to press a button on a keyboard, and the carriage would return to the proper place where the next line would begin. But the use of computers as word processors permits this to be done automatically so that one can enter letters of text without ever moving the fingers off the keyboard to return a carriage.

If there are spelling problems, there are dictionaries that permit text to be automatically corrected for spelling. Should there be stylistic problems, there are computer programs that will search the text for the frequency of occurrence of certain kinds of verb forms, or will count the number of times the writer used the phrase, "Of course, ..." Indeed, word processors now give us

	Hardware	Software
Minimal Needs	1. Microcomputer, 128K 2. Tapedrive or "floppy" disk drive 3. Printer	1. Word processing computer program
Ideal	1. Microcomputer 640K 2. 20–60 MegaK Hard Disk Drive 3. Letter quality printer 4. 300/1200/2400 Baud Modem with VT100 emulator capability 5. Optical Scanner	1. Word processing computer program 2. Spelling dictionary 75,000 + words with ability to add to dictionary 3. File Management program 4. Communications Program 5. Daily calendar/project manager program

Figure 3.5. Hardware and software requirements for processing words and texts

solutions to problems in our writing styles that often were visible only to the reader, not the writer. We have provided in Figure 3.5 an array of what we would recommend as the minimal and ideal hardware and software requirements for the processing of words and text on a personal computer.

Computers as Processors of Numbers

The most common use of large mainframe computers is for numeric analysis. If a communication scholar in the late 1960s or early 1970s said he/she needed a computer, it was taken for granted that the individual was interested in some type of statistical or numeric analysis. One of the benefits of the microcomputer revolution is that the average person who studies communication now finds important uses for computers beyond number-crunching.

A significant change is occurring in the use of computers as number processors. The microcomputer has contributed two things: (1) the ability to do simple data analyses such as analysis of variance, chi-square tests, correlation analyses, and with some limitations, factor analysis; and (2) the spread sheet. The spread sheet is basically a matrix of columns and rows, with the ability to write mathematical formulas for the calculation of any value in the matrix. The spread sheet is a kind of computerized "scratch-pad," useful for budget analysis or any of a number of other kinds of numeric analyses that can be understood within a matrix design. Many people in the computer field consider the spread sheet to be the most significant new computer program developed in many years. It has become so important that many software companies have developed spread sheet programs for large mainframe computers. It remains to be determined what role spread sheets might have in communication study,

	Hardware	Software
Minimal Needs	1. Microcomputer, 128K 2. Tape drive or "floppy" disk drive 3. Printer	1. Statistical package for personal computer 2. Spreadsheet for personal computer
Ideal	1. Microcomputer 640K 2. 40–60 MegaK hard Disk drive 3. Letter quality Printer 4. 300/1200/2400 Baud Modem with VT100 emulator capability 5. Optical Scanner 6. Math co-processor	1. Statistical package for personal computer and main frame 2. Spreadsheet for personal computer and mainframe

Figure 3.6. Hardware and software requirements for processing numbers

although it is believed it will do much once scholars become aware of its capabilities. We have provided again in Figure 3.6 what we consider to be the minimal and ideal configuration of hardware and software to process numbers.

Computers as Processors of Graphics

Digital Vision Inc., of Needham, Massachusetts, has developed what it calls "computereyes," a video system which allows films and video tapes to be entered and stored in a computer. It matters not whether the information is from a video camera, a tape recorder, or a video disk. "Computereyes" is available now for the IBM PC, and represents the latest technology in the processing of graphic information by a computer. This is not new for computers, for it has been done for some time with signals gathered from cameras in space. However, "computereyes" represents the first system to our knowledge available for use with a microcomputer. Figure 3.7 provides what we consider to be the minimal and ideal configuration of hardware and software to process graphics.

The most common use of graphics programs is in tandem with numeric analyses, whereby information is formed for presentation as pie charts, histograms, or bargraphs. Many are quite sophisticated, permitting two, three, or more dimensional charts. These charts can then be printed on a standard or color printer, and inserted into manuscripts. Graphics are of special interest to people in business, and are contained in what is commonly called "business packages" of software.

Computers are excellent processors of information. Whether the symbols we wish to process are text, numbers, or graphics, it is necessary for the computer to translate those symbols into the language of bits in order for it to be

	Hardware	Software
Minimal Needs	1. Microcomputer, 128K 2. Tape drive or "floppy" disk drive 3. Printer	1. Graphics Package for pesonal computer
Ideal	1. Microcomputer 1 MegaK 2. 60 MegaK hard disk drive 3. Graphics printer 4. 300/1200/2400/4800 Baud Modem with VT100 emulator capability 5. Graphics co-processor	1. Graphics Package for personal computer 2. Graphics package for large mainframe computer

Figure 3.7. Hardware and software requirements for processing graphics

understood and managed. The computer represents an excellent amplification and extension of the human mind and muscle for the conduct of research. It is time now to turn to some of the kinds of problems communication researchers face that can be resolved by the computer technologies described here.

WHAT PROBLEMS CAN BE ADDRESSED BY COMPUTERS?

It is a modern-day cliché in the age of computers to say that the adoption of this new electronic gadget begins, first, with an understanding of what our job is about. A good computer consultant to any industry begins with an analysis of people's jobs. One does not move computers into a business, and then figure out what they can do for us later. We must begin with a careful analysis of the work that is required, and then and only then can we determine what the computer can and cannot do for us.

And so it is with communication scholars. The work of academicians begins with the need for accurate and relevant information. The university library has lured researchers from near and remote areas in order to locate important information for conducting scholarly work. Thus, one of the primary problem areas computers can address is that of obtaining information.

A second concern of those who perform scholarly work is to analyze and interpret information, whether that information can be found in libraries or whether it is generated by observation of communicative acts. Thus, a second problem area that can be addressed by computers is the analysis and interpretation of information.

And finally, there is the problem of presenting to others the information we have obtained, analyzed, and interpreted. We do this by surrounding ourselves with students who come to the university to study. We also take the results of our work to those in government, business, industry, and voluntary organizations. The fact that scholars have a responsibility for disseminating information to others is a part of all that we mean by scholarly work. The computer is able to address this concern as well. Let us look more carefully at what role the computer plays in each of these activities.

Computers and the Obtaining of Information

Any scholar or professional must be a careful consumer of information. Until recently, most of us have spent much of our time in the library, searching for the latest materials on a topic for research or for instruction. We have searched through the latest catalogues of new books circulated by publishers; we have marched through the library "stacks" to see if a new book of interest was acquired; we have "thumbed through" the subject, title, or author card indexes of a library. This kind of "manual searching," often consuming hours of precious time, is now unnecessary. The scenario at many universities now might look like this: We go to the library and begin our search on the university's computer data base containing all the books currently held in the collection. In some cases, we can perform that search from a personal computer at home, in the dormitories, or in selected stations around the university. We can search by author, title, or subject, or by any descriptor or key word we might like. The computer tells us the location of relevant books, whether the works are checked out. Assuming the books are available, we then need only proceed to check the reading materials out of the library, and go on our way.

But university libraries will not have all the works we might like to have. Thus, we can turn to key word indexes to all the books in print, or to special data bases containing articles published in several thousand journals. Before computers were available we went to Psychology Index, Sociological Abstracts, or the Social Science Citation Index. All of these are now accessible on a computer. For a fee, one can get a microfiche copy of any article contained in these indexes, or a reference to a microfilm file at that university.

Many researchers, however, do not have such a "modern" university library. What then? Knowledge Index of Dialog Information Services Inc., in Palo Alto, California, now permits a person with a personal computer to search numerous data bases such as these from their own home (see Table 3.2 for a partial list of available information utilities and their addresses). It requires only a modem and the appropriate communication software, and the password, account number and local telephone number to access the data base. Knowledge Index permits a search of all journals appearing in the Psychological Index, including *Communication Monographs*, *Quarterly Journal of Speech*, *Human Communication Research*, and *Public Opinion Quarterly* (*Communication Education* is currently not available in this data base, nor are any of the regional journals in speech communication).   Of course, there are 1,300 other

TABLE 3.2. SOME DATABASES FOR USE BY COMMUNICATION RESEARCHERS

Knowledge-Index	Datatimes
Dialog Information Services Inc	818 NW 63rd St.
3460 Hillview Ave	Oklahoma City, OK 73116
Palo Alto, CA 94304	
BRS Information Technologies	Info Master (Western Union)
1200 Route 7	Department 503
Latham, NY 12110	9229 LBJ Freeway Suite 234
	Dallas, TX 75243
Compuserve	Comserve
P.O. Box 20212	Department of Language, Literature, and
Columbus, OH 43220	Communication
	Sage Laboratories
	Rensselaer Polytechnic Institute
	Troy, N.Y. 12180

journals available manually through the library's Psychological Index and Psychological Abstracts, but these same indexes can be accessed electronically via Knowledge Index. In addition, Knowledge Index makes available Sociological Abstracts (which includes abstracts of *Journalism Quarterly*), Books in Print, Peterson's College Data Base, Legal Resource Index, Mathematical Sources, Magill's Survey of Cinema, the National Newspaper Index, and the Academic American Encyclopedia. In addition, Dialog is available through numerous other sources beside Knowledge Index, including Compuserve's IQUEST. Access to these data bases is as convenient from one's home as it is from a library, making it quite unimportant whether a scholar or professional is affiliated with a university having an outstanding library. It may be this represents an open door to the democratizing of famous university libraries, conveying such resources to anyone, anywhere so long as they have a computer, a modem, and a telephone.

Another data base that is quite new, and is available through the mainframe computer systems of many universities around the country, is one called "Comserve." Developed by Timothy Stephen and Teresa Harrison at Rensselaer Polytechnic Institute in Troy, New York, the data base makes it possible to access a growing collection of communication information, including bibliographies, research instruments, announcements of professional meetings, grant opportunities, syllabi, class exercises, job announcements, and even an electronic phone book much like the directory published by the Speech Communication Association. Many universities provide the appropriate software to permit a scholar or professional to query the data base from a home computer, where that university's mainframe computer is connected to the data base via Bitnet. Comserve is the first of what will become many data bases tailored for use by communication scholars, teachers, and professonals. There really is little reason for a scholar or professional not to have a complete review of the literature on a topic with such resources available on such a wide basis. While costs for searching a data base require careful advance planning, it will soon be possible to conduct literature reviews economically and efficiently.

Many scholars maintain unique data bases within their own file cabinets. These may be lectures or papers gathered at professional meetings. They may be working notes for a future article or book, a magazine story clipped to use as an illustration in a speech, or articles on various subjects. These unique data bases become the grounds for our special contributions as both scholars and teachers. However, they are incredibly difficult to maintain, and wasteful of space. In previous years, for example, articles needed to be filed three times—under author, title, and subject—so that we could find the article without too much trouble. Now we have software that permits us to manage our personal files in a simpler way.

Numerous software firms provide the computer programs necessary to permit us to tailor our own file management systems. C. Wayne Ratliff developed a file management system, known today as dBase II, first used on the Viking spacecraft which was sent to Mars in 1976. It later was obtained by Ashton-Tate, which now markets the system for those who have IBM-compatible personal computers. More recently, dBase III is available as an update of the earlier version. The file management system is open in the sense that it permits a person to create a personalized file system. There are many other comparable systems, similarly open, and useful for different personal computers such as MacIntosh, Tandy, and others. In this way, one can take a simple file of 1,000 items and search that file using a wide array of techniques. For example, we can search by author, title, publisher, date of publication, subject (communication, psychology, physics, computers), communication setting (dyads, groups, organizations, social, intercultural, mass, oral interpretation), communication topics such as rhetoric, conflict management, information processing, or problem-solving, and even a notation of who borrowed the folder. Finding a file folder, or a lecture, or a book from one's personal library has led to the frustration of so many, taking minutes, hours, even days to locate. A system such as described here makes it possible to find these items in seconds. The time required to create and maintain a personal file management system is more than compensated by the time required to locate a file, and the sense of reduced frustration when important papers are at one's finger tips rather than lost.

It is fairly obvious that a scholar or professional can use these same "open" file management systems to keep records of test questions, student grades, appointments, or the status of research projects. Many in academe have a reputation as poor record keepers. It is quite clear that not only can the computer, and particularly the personal computer, help us deal with this problem, it can do so simply, efficiently, and with minimum of frustration. The use of computers to obtain and store information for retrieval is expansive and

TABLE 3.3. SOME COMPUTER PROGRAMS FOR USE BY COMMUNICATION RESEARCHERS

TeleVision	Statistics with Finesse	SL-Micro
(Comm Software for Graphics)	(Statistics Package)	(Statistics Package)
LCS/Telegraphics	James Boulding	Questionnaire Service Co
261 Vasser St.	PO Box 339	PO Box 778
Cambridge, MA 02139	Fayetteville, AR 72702	East Lansing, MI 48823
SPSS Inc.	Applied Innovations, Inc.	Statsoft
(Statistics Package)	(Test-scoring programs)	(Statistics Programs and
444 N. Michigan Ave	South Kingstown Office	questionnaire designs)
Chicago, Il 60611	Park	2832 East 10th St.
	Wakefield, RI 02879	Suite 4
dBase III		Tulsa, OK 74104
(Database management)	Harvard Presentation	
Available most computer	Graphics	Pertmaster
stores in local areas	(Graphics Package)	(Project Management)
	Software publishing Corp.	Abtex Software Ltd
	PO Box 7210	2750 El Camino Real
	Mt. View, CA 94039-7210	Mt. View, CA 94040

of high value to us as scholars and professionals. Computers also can be used to help us understand that information, a concern to which we now turn.

Computers and the Analysis and Interpretation of Information

Statistical analysis is perhaps the best known method of analyzing numerical information (see Table 3.3 for some computer programs useful in analyzing information on large mainframes and personal computers). Prior to 1970, universities commonly provided their own statistical packages, along with documentation booklets in their use. It was about 1970 that SPSS (the Statistical Package for the Social Sciences) became available, and was used at approximately 60 installations. The latest version, now labeled SPSS^X, is available at almost any university installation in the country, and also in numerous private and governmental data processing departments. SPSS, along with other widely used packages in medical centers such as the BioMed Package (BMD/P), provided the primary method for analyzing numerical data on a computer. Another package, although first developed in 1966, has become in recent years perhaps the most popular of the statistical packages, SAS, or Statistical Analysis System.

All the statistical analysis systems described in Table 3.3 have today become more than a means of performing statistical tests. They now include graphics packages which permit the construction of color images representing three or more dimensional histograms, or pie charts, or even a tailor-made poster for photographics or use as an overhead. In some esoteric installations, production of slides is tied to a computer system, making quick production of either 35mm slides or overheads possible in high speed. SAS/ETS now includes additional programs for business analysis, forecasting and financial reporting, including a spreadsheet, first written for the personal computer.

A special feature of SPSS^X is a software system which permits researchers to analyze data gathered by the United States Census Bureau, including procedures for deriving demographic statistics for local areas such as school districts, and the production of formatted tables and graphs to display the results. Such a feature makes it of tremendous value to those who conduct field studies, particularly in political and mass communication.

It is quite clear that statistical packages for use on large mainframe computers permit the analysis of large amounts of data. A list of the various statistical procedures is not of use here; anyone who would use them should learn about them coterminously or while taking courses in research methods. What is perhaps most important to note here, however, is that when one is dealing with many variables at a time requiring high amounts of core memory, these packages are still the system of choice.

Some computer specialists are reporting a decrease in the use of these large mainframe statistical packages among social scientists because statistical packages of excellent quality are now available for personal computers. Stacks (1986) reviewed three statistical packages for personal computers, two for computers manufactured by Apple ("Statistics with Finesse" and "SL-Micro"), and one for the IBM personal computer and its compatibles (SPSS/PC$_+$). The latter statistical package is produced by the same organization (McGraw-Hill) that owns the SPSS and SPSS^X.

Many believe today that unless one is conducting research involving the simultaneous analysis of scores if not a hundred or more variables, the statistical analysis of data will be done on personal computers. Simple procedures such as chi square, analysis of variance, t-tests, simple correlations, multiple correlation, and a few others are easily performed by personal computers. It is important to note that the number of subjects in a statistical study is of much less concern than the number of variables when determining whether to use a mainframe or personal computer for analysis. In some cases, statistical packages for use on personal computers are capable of performing factor analysis, cluster analysis, multiple discriminant analysis, and some other techniques commonly used in communication studies.

Beyond statistical analysis, there are other methods available to us. For example, spreadsheets—a method of arraying data in columns and rows— permit us to use the computer screen as a "scratch pad." (Table 3.3 also contains some well-known spreadsheets for both personal computers and large mainframe computers.) For example, we can enter data into columns E and F, say values representing a person's score on the first two examinations in a course. In column G we could create an equation that represents a weighting

$$G = [(.40)^*(E)] + (.60)^*(F)]$$

Columns

	Name	E	F	G	H	I	J	K	L
	Adams	10	20	12					
R	Bostwick	6	18	13.2					
O	Jones	4	11	14.8					
W	Moore	12	6	8.4					
S	Noble	24	10	15.6					
	Peterson	10	24	18.4					
	Smith	20	10	14					
	Zyblonski	20	4	11.2					

Figure 3.8. Spreadsheets

of the scores in columns E and F, such as G = (.40 times E) + (.60 times F). Thus, a person's score on the first test (Column E) is 40 percent of the grade, and on the second test (Column F) is 60 percent of the grade. Column G would represent the person's grade, which combines the relative values of the first two tests (see Figure 3.8).

Perhaps even more useful for students might be the ability to use spreadsheets to play "what if" type simulations, where the student might be able to find out what would be required to get an A for the course by simulating required values in each of the tests and/or papers contributing to the course grade. Of course there are many other important uses for a spreadsheet, limited only by one's imagination. It requires only that one work within a matrix of columns and rows. Equations can be as simple as addition, subtraction, multiplication, and division, or as complex as exponential and geometric functions. The spreadsheet is perhaps one of the most important evolutions in data analysis in the last few years, an innovation which began as a software option for personal computers and now is available for large mainframe computers all over the country. (As noted earlier, SAS now has a spreadsheet available as part of its statistical package.)

Finally, there are a number of computer programs written by such national testing agencies as the Educational Testing Service, which permit the scoring and interpretation of tests taken by students and submitted to a central place via telephone line computer link-ups. For example, the Minnesota Multiphasic Personality Inventory can now be scored via telephone hookup of a computer, with a fairly quick turnaround of scoring and interpretation. At the present time, no such capability exists for scales developed in communication, but as the computer technology develops and becomes more common among people in the field, we project this will occur in communication in the near future. We see a research value in establishing such centralized scoring procedures because it makes possible the establishment of norms, and provides a basis for assessing the generalizability of our constructs.

We have described the use of computers as a useful method of obtaining information, and we have outlined some common methods for interpreting data. Let us now look at some methods for presenting information to others.

Computers and the Presentation of Information

The most common output of information by scholars is in the form of manuscripts: books, chapters in books, articles, and research papers. As teachers, we commonly prepare handouts for students, send correspondence to colleagues, and even exchange data with those who share our interest in certain projects. The computer makes these activities efficient and accurate.

Word processing is perhaps the most important use of computers in the preparation of information for presentation to others (see Table 3.3 for some well-known word processing programs). There are literally scores of word processing software programs, all of which are about equal in their capabilities. There are certain features that might make one package, say "Word Star," more attractive than another, such as Apple Writer. Their features include all that could have been done by typewriters, including underlining, paragraph markings, page numbering, subscripting, superscripting, boldface, and a "spelling checker" to locate certain kinds of spelling errors (spelling checkers won't help the writer who uses "their" instead of "there," and thus do not insure perfect manuscripts). Word processing programs may differ in the ease of their use, or in the safety features designed to protect against loss of a manuscript. Software is now so sophisticated that we can include graphics in the manuscript, add footnotes at the bottom of pages, and provide page headings for identification. There is currently available a word processing program that conforms to the APA Style, 3rd edition (American Psychological Association). The value of computers as word processing systems is great; we can produce manuscripts, letters, and memos with complete case. The letter quality is comparable to that produced by regular typewriters, and the ability to include color graphics in the manuscripts goes beyond our imagination of a few short years ago.

Perhaps more important, however, is the ability to move manuscripts from one place to another via networking. Cummings (1985) described the role of networks for an academic discipline such as speech communication in terms of local, regional, and national systems for exchanging information. Networks are particularly helpful when people exchange data and technical information, making possible the careful and timely review by others of our work. Currently, many academic disciplines gather manuscripts for journals via personal computers connected to networks. This facilitates the editing process and shortens the time from submission to publication for both journals and books.

And further, of course, we can use computers to present information to students in classroom settings. *Communication Education*, a national journal of the Speech Communication Association, regularly reports software available for use in the classroom, including simulations of group problems, communication skill assessment methods, and others. Some scholars, however, will not participate in the computer technology; for a look at some of the reasons let us turn to the issue of computer apprehension.

WHY ARE SOME APPREHENSIVE TOWARD COMPUTERS?

Many have commented that the rapidity of any social change makes it difficult for people to adjust, and often generates high apprehensiveness. Toffler (1970) became perhaps the most important observer of this phenomenon in recent times when he described the problem of future shock. It becomes even more of a difficulty when we recognize that we have very little to say about change; the computer revolution is taking place despite the best efforts of some to pretend otherwise.

Any normal person will suffer from fear of new technologies. Sometimes we are afraid of the costs in jobs. Some are afraid of social consequences. And some are afraid of the need for retraining or change in the way we do work. All of these fears are common and quite normal among those who resist computers. We can be more specific, however, for there has been considerable research conducted over the last five years and a portrait has been drawn of the person must likely to suffer from computer apprehension. He or she is probably: (1) over 30 years of age; (2) lacking in computer experience and knowledge; (3) interested primarily in the humanities rather than in the sciences and engineering; (4) suffering from math anxiety; and (5) female.

The last characteristic requires some explanation. It is quite doubtful that there is anything inherent in one's sex that makes women more computer apprehensive than men, but there is strong evidence that women do more frequently exhibit computer apprehensiveness (Raub, 1982; Webb, 1984; Herkimer, 1985). Most critics of such findings would conclude that this indicates (and we agree) a cultural value system which has not encouraged women to work with technology. Evidence does exist that women are more anxious than men with mathematics because of this culturally-based orientation.

Some argue that with the use of computers, work becomes more abstract, and as decisions are taken over by machines, conceptual skills replace direct experience. We should see from our earlier discussion on programming that computers substitute rules for personal judgment, and this often runs counter to the way many of us prefer to conduct scholarly work. Another argument is offered by Williamson (1983) who believes that most "computerphobes" fear revealing that they don't know anything about computers, or they feel a dumb machine might replace them. Still others feel a sense of loss of control over their lives when faced with learning how to use the computer. All these fears are irrational.

A great deal of research effort has addressed the problem of how to reduce computer apprehension. Most of that research agrees that in-service training is an effective tool in this effort. Price (1986) reports workshops are effective for reducing computer apprehension among teachers; Herkimer (1985) found similar results for college students; as did Howard (1984) for managers in business.

Before one pays a large amount of money to attend a workshop, it is important to know that not all workshops or in-service training programs are successful. A brief training session (Howard, 1984) is generally not successful. And there is little evidence that "relaxation" therapy—a form of which is used to reduce communication apprehension—is effective to reduce computer apprehension (Bloom, 1986). All seem to agree that computer anxiety will decrease as people use the computer, but it takes much longer than might be desirable. Howard argues that experience that avoids the stresses of writing computer programs should be provided over an extended period of time. Widmer and Parker (1984) describe the proper use of in-service training as follows: (1) In-service training should address only the major ideas, not attempt to cover the intricate details of computers; (2) there should be a "hands-on" experience in which people start, stop, and change programs, thus providing a sense of control over the computer instead of mere reaction; (3) emphasize at first only those computer programs (written by others) that are simple to use ("user friendly"); and (4) trainers should take the time to listen to the reasons people give for not using computers to provide insights for developing computer in-service training programs with minimal apprehension.

It is quite clear that many do not participate in the computer revolution out of fear, but this need not be so if we recognize what it can do for our future as scholars. It is often exciting to dream of what will be. It frees our imaginations to explore possible applications of computer technology to the work of communication researchers, teachers, and other professionals. And it just might contribute to a more friendly relationship with the computer for those who are computer apprehensive.

WHAT ABOUT THE FUTURE?

The average person has an inaccurate image of the scholar. The lay person often looks at a university professor's teaching load, and remarks how nice it must be to only have to work 9 or 12 hours per week. As a minister's son, this writer remembers people thinking that "preachers" only worked one hour per week. It, of course, is much more than this. The standard method for the assessment of scholarly work is the contribution made to research, teaching, and service. There is very little research analyzing the work of scholars as we have done with managers in government and industry. The best we know of is anecdotal; it is based on the shared experiences of people in those times when scholars seek to encourage bright young students to enter the profession, and make a life-long commitment to the enterprise.

There are a number of things we would tell those who join the scholarly community. We would argue that they must have good communication skills, including both the ability to write and speak. Peter Cawes (1965) provided an excellent description of what it means to be part of the community of scholars. He explains that the focus of the scholarly community is to do:

> ... two sorts of things: on the one hand, it constructs theories about man and the universe, and offers them as grounds for belief and action; on the other, it examines critically everything that may be offered as a ground for belief or action, including its own theories, with a view to the elimination of inconsistency and error. (p. 5).

Similarly, the work of scholars clearly requires resources which help the scientist to uncover and create meaningful statements about what is going on, and to disseminate that information to others (students, peers, constitutents) as grounds for belief and action. Scholars are information handlers, people who poke around in strange places for "gems" of insight that are inherently interesting, but also are socially useful to others.

Computers are a technological achievement that represent an extension of the human mind and muscle in the pursuit of information. They assist us in locating information in libraries through established data bases; they help us to create personal files of information that assist and extend our ability to gather information. Those same computers also represent a capability for organizing and interpreting information in new and different ways. We can describe what is; we can simulate what might be; we can focus the information in ways that make problem-solving possible. And finally, we can use computers to present information to others. Computers permit us to create messages through word processing procedures, graphics packages, and a host of ways to package and produce information for others.

The view of scholars as those who live the cellular life of monastics is outdated. The new information age requires scholars to be excellent managers of information. Scholars write, but they do not do so in isolation; they rely on the writings and stimulation of others. Scholars speak, but they do not do so only in the classroom; they take their theories and offer them to government or private agencies designed to make life better.

And scholars of the future will use computers. They will do so to search the library of the British Museum, or the library of measurement procedures in some hypothetical "Communication Testing Service." They will be able to send messages, requests for help, and/or answers to questions of inquiring minds anywhere in the world. A famous professor in interpersonal communication is as far as a personal query displayed on a CRT in one's home office. The computer truly represents an extension of mind and muscle; an important lengthening of our ability to conduct and disseminate scholarly work.

SUMMARY

This chapter was concerned with the use of computers as a technology that provides an extension and amplification of human minds and muscles. In order to conduct communication research in an effective way through the use of computers, we described in general terms how computers work; what it is that they process. We considered some of the problems for which computers are useful, including a discussion of the kinds of software that are available for people who study communication; the role of computer apprehension as a condition of many who resist the use of computers; and we completed the chapter by focusing on what it might mean to be a communication researcher in the age of the computer.

How do computers work? We described computers as an information processing system that permits a person to enter information into an electronically-based system, transform that information in some very special ways, and then to produce that processed information according to desired objectives. We found that information is processed in the form of on and off switches (bits), combined into a basic grouping we call bytes. Computers are often measured by the number (thousands or millions—even billions) of bytes that can be processed by the computer's central brain (CPU). The speed of a computer we found was determined in two ways: (1) the number of bits that can be moved from one place to another during a single moment of time (time cycle); and (2) the number of instructions (usually in millions per second, i.e., MIPS) that can be processed in a single second.

There is more to a computer than its central processing unit; that is, the system also contains auxiliary memory storage. Such storage is contained on magnetic tape, the same tape we use for playing music on our stereos; disks, or "platters," including some very recent technology called compact disk—read only memory (CD-ROM).

Computer programs were described as much like a recipe used by cooks. Computer programs are written in special language that provides detailed instructions for the computer system as it reads information, and transforms that information into specified outputs. Essentially, computer programs are primarily responsible for the way a computer transforms inputs into outputs. The programming languages we use are varied, but they typically permit us to tell the computer what to do, with a translator (often built into the computer, but many times with a compiler) made available to allow the computer to understand what we told it to do. When we refer to physical properties of a computer system, we call it hardware; when we refer to operating systems and computer programs, we label these software.

Computers help us in many ways by what they process. This chapter described how they help us to process words and text, including letters, memos, and manuscripts. We found that computers also permit the processing of numbers, including statistical procedures and other mathematical and arithmetic activities. And, we found that computers also permit us to process graphics, including video images obtained with cameras.

There are a number of special problems faced by scholars for which the computer is an ideal technology for the extension and amplification of the human mind. For example, we can search for writings in libraries around the world. We can analyze and interpret information. And we can use the computer to present our information to others. Among the many sources for bibliographic information are Knowledge Index, which contains such data resources as the works listed in psychological and sociological indexes. Others include databases from Compuserve and Comserve, the latter being a library designed by and for students of communication.

A number of statistical packages also were described, including SPSS^X, SAS, and BMD/P, primarily for use with large mainframes as host storage and analysis devices. Recently, however, personal computers have become useful for these activities, including "Statistics With Finesse," "SL-Micro," and SPSS/PC+. The personal computer technology also brought to us the spreadsheet, which is a matrix of columns and rows, and which permits us to use the computer screen as a mathematical "scratchpad." Manufacturers of large mainframe software packages were sufficiently impressed to transport this software technology from the personal computer for use on larger mainframe systems. It is now available with SAS software packages. Finally, national testing agencies have developed software for the use of researchers; namely, there are software packages available to score and interpret measuring devices.

The presentation of information to others was found to be a significant problem faced by scholars. Computers and the attendant network technologies now available allow us to send manuscripts from any point in the world to any other point we desire. It is truly a mark of the "global village." We also can use computer technology in educational settings for student assessment and learning. And we can use the computer as a desk-top publisher if we desire.

We recognize that many resist the use of computers, and much of this is associated with computer apprehension. We noted a number of characteristics of people who tend to be computer anxious, adding that the best method of reducing computer phobia is to provide a careful in-service training program—one that is long term.

Finally, we addressed the future and what it will require of all scholars, but particularly those in communication who are charged with the responsibility to exhibit and train others in good communication habits. The day of scholarship in isolation is over if ever there were any doubt. The computer makes it possible to carry out that most important of our social obligations as scholars: the offering of our theories to others as grounds for belief and action.

STUDY QUESTIONS

1. How do we determine the "intelligence" of computers; that is, if we say some computers are "smarter" than others, on what basis would we make that statement?
2. What does it mean to say that programming of computers is similar to the writing of cooking recipes?
3. What is meant by "hardware" versus "software?"
4. What are the kinds of data that computers process?
5. Scholars are often characterized as problem solvers. What kinds of problems are computers helpful in solving?
6. What is the future of computing for the modern-day communication scholar? Is it possible that "computerphobia" may inhibit the use of computers by these scholars?

ANNOTATED READINGS

Dizard, Wilson P. (1982). *The coming information age.* New York: Longman.
   The late Ithiel de Sola Pool prepared the introduction to this work, describing it as a book that makes possible for the non-technologist to understand the new technologies of computers, semi-conductors, satellites, and light guides. Dizard's work begins with a description of the information age as a new revolution. He is concerned with the stake Americans have in the future of computers, and the need for some kind of public policy regarding the technological venture that is upon us. The book represents a humanistic focus on a technological revolution.
Dordick, Herbert S., Bradley, Helen G., & Nanus, Burt (1981). *The emerging network marketplace.* Norwood, NJ: Ablex.
   This book details the real and potential impact of the computer as an instigator of the new information society. It is futuristic, its primary contribution being the description of the components of computer networks; the emerging trends in networking as a framework for information utilities and its implications for needed public policy; and a survey of the network information services market, including business, government, consumer affairs, and legal, financial, and educational services. The book's text (259 pages) concludes with some key issues such as the problem of privacy, and the new birthbright of information equality. Two excellent appendices contain a description of the use of delphi processes in several settings, and the problem of diffusion of computer innovations.
Heise, David R. (Ed.). (1981). Microcomputers in social research (Special issue). *Sociological Methods & Research, 9* (4).
   This special issue contains a series of articles, including Craig Calhoun's "The microcomputer revolution? Technical possibilities and social choices;" an article by T. W. Collins entitled "Social science research and the microcomputer;"

"Microcomputer data base management of bibliographic information" by Sandra S. Hutton and S. Ray Hutton; "Microcomputers in anthropological research" by Rodney Kirk; "Microcomputers in applied settings: the example of urban planning" by John R. Ottensmann; "The microcomputer in social-psychological research" by Beverly Marshall-Goodell, I. Gormezano, John Scandrett, and John T. Cacioppo; and "Computer simulation of social systems" by Pat-Anthony Federico and Paul W. Figliozze. This book is useful to scholars in a wide variety of research settings to which the microcomputer is uniquely applicable.

Madron, Thomas W., Tate, C. Neale, & Brookshire, Robert G. (1985). *Using microcomputers in research.* (University Paper No. 52). Beverly Hills, CA: Sage.

This 82-page monograph describes the role of microcomputers in the research process. It contains six short chapters, the first describing the several properties of computing systems. Following a short chapter on how to write the research proposal for the obtaining of funding, the authors present chapters on how to use the computer to create and manage grant budgets; the use of computers in data gathering; the process of analyzing and manipulating data; and finally, the use of the computer in the writing of the research report. This publication will assist those who have, or hope to obtain research grants, and who wish to use in the most optimal way the microcomputer technology.

CHAPTER 4

Evaluating Research

By Larry L. Barker,
Auburn University

It has been estimated that scholars have written more documents and reported more research in the last century than their predecessors did in the previous 2500 years. It is also predicted that man's information pool will double again in less than 50 years. This information explosion has created both benefits and problems for the researcher. Benefits are derived from the broadening base of information from which to draw in examining human communication behavior. Problems exist in trying to keep up with the expanding knowledge and data base, and in locating research that has been conducted previously related to a given topic.

Compounding the problem of the rapid expansion of knowledge in this century is the constant demand for academicians to "publish or perish." This fact of academic life has been emphasized even more in the past decade because of economic fluctuations and reduced funding for many academic research programs. Like their colleagues in previous decades, current scholars are encouraged, if not required, to conduct research and publish their results on a frequent and regular basis. Because tenure, rank, and promotions of college professors are based, in large part, on the quantity of scholarly articles and papers a scholar produces, the number of articles and convention papers submitted each year increases. The editors of scholarly journals and the chairs of professional association convention programs must evaluate large numbers of manuscripts and make decisions concerning their quality.

The specific criteria these professionals use in deciding to accept or reject a manuscript fluctuate greatly. However, there are several general criteria for evaluating research that are applied in the majority of cases. This chapter attempts to elaborate on those criteria and help future scholars learn to critically evaluate their own research as well as the research of others. The general topics addressed include evaluating the theoretical base of research, operationalizations and definitions, measurement, design and statistics, data collection, coding and analysis, general research problems, and reporting and publishing results. Consequently, this chapter is written from the point of view of the research critic.

EVALUATING THE THEORETICAL BASE OF RESEARCH

A solid foundation is essential in building relationships, houses, businesses, and governments. It is also essential in establishing a quality or "grounded" research project. The term **grounded theory** is often used to identify those theories which have a solid foundation of previous research and validation preceding their presentation and publication. However, "grounded" theories in the social sciences discipline are rather limited in number. In most cases the social science scholar must assume the responsibility for discovering and reporting related or parallel studies concerning a given research topic. The success of the scholar in identifying, locating, abstracting, and synthesizing previous research is the first criterion of concern to the research critic. For a more complete discussion of the theory building and validation process see Holt (1981) or Kaplan (1964).

Closely related to the presence of a solid theoretical base is the perceived significance of the proposed research topic or problem. Tucker et al. (1981) suggest that the problem or topic must stand the test of such questions as "So what?" and "Who Cares?" Although it is desirable for problems to be perceived as significant by most members of a discipline, there are some researchers who believe that any topic which is scientifically explored has merit as "basic" research. The issue here is not necessarily whether or not there is a place in a given discipline for pure or "basic" research, but the presence of an adequate **rationale** provided by a researcher for initiating a given research project. In other words, a research critic should examine the quality of given reasons for a project when evaluating the overall quality of a research project.

A final consideration in examining the theoretical base for a research project is the logical connection among with research, the rationale for the project, and the specific problem or hypothesis under investigation. Researchers who have not adequately reviewed previous research or who have not "synthesized" it sufficiently may be tempted to make "cognitive leaps" in an attempt to establish their hypotheses or research problems. For example, a given researcher may have found a substantial body of previous literature on "listening comprehension" in preparing to begin a study. However, her topic may actually be focused on "interpersonal listening." The temptation to try to "force" the literature that she has available to relate to her chosen topic might be great. If she yields to the temptation, her problem area would not relate, at least directly, to the bulk of the literature she has examined. This problem of not establishing logical connections between previous literature and the present problem should be examined carefully by concerned research critics.

One difficulty in establishing logical relationships between previous research and a given problem stems from researchers' use of different definitions and operationalizations for the same concept or variable. The following section discusses the need for accurate and complete definitions and operationalizations.

Operationalizations and Definitions in Scientific Research

If we were to ask a college student, an electrical engineer, a television anchor person, and a housewife to define "communication," we would probably get four vastly different responses. Similarly, researchers in different fields often use such terms as communication in different ways, without realizing or specifying their particular definition in their research reports. Such differences often result in confusion among readers, incorrect inferences and generalizations from the results to other variables or situations, and the appearance of contradictory results among studies when, in fact, the different definitions of variables were the "culprits."

Researchers must ensure that definitions used in a given study are accurate, adequate, and understandable by readers of their research reports. Attention to definitions is especially important with regard to (1) specific words or terms in the hypothesis or research question, (2) measurement techniques and devices related to the dependent variable(s), (3) concepts and constructs related to the independent variable(s), (4) characteristics of the sample or population under investigation and (5) variables that may confound or contaminate the research.

In many instances the researcher may need to "operationalize" variables in a unique way. The term "operationalize" means to provide a concrete description or example of a given term, variable or construct. Operationalizations actually become specific definitions of variables and constructs in a given research project. For example, the construct "communication apprehension" may be operationalized as "a score on a set of 24 multidimensional scales related to three primary dimensions of the fear to communicate." However, other operationalizations might also be used to define the same variable. Another researcher might operationalize "communication apprehension" as "the average rating given by a panel of five judges concerning a speaker's manifestations of stage fright." Neither of these two operationalizations of "communication apprehension" is necessarily better or more accurate than the other. The point is that both attempt to define the same term through different means.

When evaluating a researcher's definition or operationalization of a variable, concept or construct, the critic should ask:

1. Is the definition or operationalization *adequate*? That is, does it provide a complete description of all important dimensions of the variable?
2. Is the definition or operationalization *accurate*? Is it a valid and universally agreed on way of viewing a variable?
3. Is the definition or operationalization *clear*? Are the terms or measurement devices described and defined familiar to the majority of report readers and future researchers?

A primary area in the research process where operationalizations become critical is in the measurement of variables. The following section discusses issues in the area of research measurement.

Measurement in Scientific Research

In the previous section the problem of adequate, accurate, and clear operationalization of variables was discussed. Operationalization and measurement of communication variables and constructs is an extremely difficult and time consuming process. Like scholars in most social sciences, researchers investigating communication behaviors and attitudes are confronted with the problem of rather "loose" constructs and variables. This means that such constructs as "attitudes," "communication apprehension," and "communication competence," may be defined, operationalized, and measured in a variety of different ways. There is not necesssarily a "right" or "best" way to measure such constructs. The critic must evaluate the researcher's measuring instruments, techniques, and approaches. One of the primary considerations is the **measurability index** of the variable or construct under observation.

"Measurability index" refers to the degree to which a given variable or construct can actually be measured precisely. Some variables such as height, weight, time, and length can be measured very easily and accurately. These variables would have a rather high measurability index. Other variables dealing with personality, attitudes, opinions, beliefs and cognitive behaviors are less easily and accurately measured. These variables would have a lower measurability index. The critic must evaluate the measurability index of a given variable or construct, and then examine the way in which the researcher attempted to measure it. Some specific measurement concerns include reliability, internal validity, and problems in measuring variables with low measurability indices.

Reliability. A measurement is viewed as reliable if similar results are obtained each time a measurement is made. **Reliability**, then is almost synonymous with "consistency." The research critic should look for evidence in a research report that measurements were checked for consistency or reliability. Correlation coefficients are often reported to indicate reliability indices. If reliability coefficients are reported, the critic should be sure that they are of sufficient magnitude to demonstrate consistency in measurement. Usually reliability (or correlation) coefficients of .60 or above are expected to indicate that a particular measurement is reliable. In some instances indices of a much higher magnitude (e.g., .90) might be required to demonstrate reliability when variables have a higher measurability index.

Internal Validity. The concept of **validity** is mentioned numerous times in other sections of this book. In this instance concern is focused on the **internal validity** of a measuring instrument. Scales attempting to measure "cognitive consistency" might provide very reliable results when given to different groups, but this does not necessarily mean that the scales are measuring what they purport to measure. The research critic should look for evidence of internal validity in any measuring instrument used in an investigation. Several different types of internal validity have been identified and can be examined when evaluating scientific research (Dick and Hagarty, 1971):

1. *Content Validity.* **Content validity** exists if subjects in an experiment are expected to actually "do" the thing that is being tested or measured. For example, content validity would be demonstrated when items on a test directly relate to the concept being measured (e.g., an item such as "I listen easily to most speakers" would have content validity in a test measuring "self-reported listening skills").

2. *Concurrent Validity.* This index involves correlating or comparing one index of a variable (e.g., listening behavior) with a similar but different index (e.g., reading behavior). In instances where several standardized or previously validated tests are available for comparison, the researcher can correlate results of such measures with those in his or her study. The assumption with **concurrent validity** is that two measures of similar traits or variables should produce similar results. If the measures tend to correlate highly with each other they are said to have "high" concurrent validity. If they do not tend to correlate highly, but are attempting to measure similar variables, they are deemed to have "low" concurrent validity.

3. *Construct Validity.* This form of validity usually is assessed through some complex statistical technique such as factor analysis. The principle of **construct validity** is that subparts of the measuring instrument should correlate highly with each other, but have rather low correlation with other subparts reflecting different dimensions of the variable. Through systematic and extensive statis-

tical manipulations, researchers can establish indices of construct validity which can support their claim for overall validity of the measuring instrument (Neale and Liebert, 1980).

The research critic must carefully examine a specific study's validity in an attempt to determine if the measurement of variables has provided an accurate assessment on which to base meaningful results.

Other Measurement Concerns. Several other measurement concerns in addition to reliability and validity have been identified by Blalock and Blalock (1982). These include reactive measurement, interpolated measurement, statistical regression and time of measurement.

Reactive measurement implies that the process of measuring a behavior may in itself create certain reactions in the subjects. These reactions may negatively affect or "bias" the measurement. The research critic must determine if the potential for reactive measurement exists in a given study.

Interpolated measurement concerns the effects of using a particular instrument or measurement device in a situation in which such measurements are not usually used. An example might be to record a speaker's heart rate through a physiograph while he or she is speaking. The instrumentation or devices attached to the speaker could have an effect on the behavior being measured (in this case, heart rate might increase because of the measuring process).

Statistical regression in the measurement process refers to the case when subjects are measured initially to place them in groups and the initial measurement affects later measurements in the actual experiment. The process of taking an initial test might affect (either positively or negatively) scores on a second test during the actual experiment. This process creates an extraneous or contaminating variable in some instances which can not be adequately isolated or accounted for in interpreting final results.

The *time at which a measurement is made* can greatly affect the results of the measurement. For example, if a class of first graders were tested in spelling just after their class had prepared for the county "spelling bee," their scores might have been higher than if the test had been administered before the preparation for the event. Time of day, events surrounding the measurement process, and even season of the year can have "contaminating" effects on some measurement processes.

In examining the measurement process, the critic must not only examine the adequacy, accuracy and clarity of the measurement instrument(s), but he or she must evaluate reliability, validity and other measurement concerns that can affect the study. Measurement provides the foundation for statistical tests and allows for the experimenter to create a "design" that will be most effective in a particular investigation.

Design and Statistics in Communication Research

Abraham Kaplan, in his now classic work titled *The Conduct of Inquiry* (1964), related a story about a small boy who had been given a hammer as a birthday present. The boy loved the hammer and used it daily—on the furniture, the walls, the appliances, even on his father. Of course, the father took the hammer away, but gave the boy a screwdriver as a replacement. The boy immediately proceeded to use the screwdriver on everything in sight—once again, the furniture, the walls, etc. The analogy that Kaplan drew was to statisticians (or would-be statisticians) who knew and felt comfortable using a given statistic. Like the small boy, they believed that their "favorite" statistic should be used in all cases, whether appropriate or not. Therefore some statisticians favor "t" tests, others multivariate analysis techniques, others chi-squares, and so on. Hopefully, we can learn from this analogy and realize that some instances demand a hammer (or "t" test), where others demand a screwdriver (maybe a chi-square). The research critic must know when certain statistics are most appropriate and when convenience or limited knowledge may have tempted a researcher to use a statistic that was not best suited for the study. In this section several considerations concerning the evaluation of statistical and design techniques will be identified and discussed.

Level of Data. A primary consideration when evaluating the statistics employed in an investigation concerns their appropriateness in light of the **level of data** available. In the following chapter definitions of and distinctions among nominal, ordinal, interval and ratio data are presented. A major reason for identifying the level of data available from a given research project is to pick the most useful and "powerful" statistical test or index available. As a rule of thumb, the higher orders of data (i.e., **interval** and **ratio**) allow for the most sophisticated statistical analyses. Lower levels of data (i.e., **nominal** and **ordinal**) use lower level statistical tests. Several statistical texts that might be useful to examine in preparation for evaluating statistical techniques are identified in the "Annotated Readings" section at the end of this chapter. The important consideration in evaluating statistics from a level of data perspective is whether or not the level of data available is appropriate for the statistical test employed.

Randomization and Controls. The primary concern in any experimental or statistical design is to eliminate sources of bias, contamination or error. Researchers have identified two primary means for reducing error—ramdomization and control. **Randomization** is a technique whereby subjects are either chosen from a table of random numbers (see Chapter 9) or are selected based on some probability model. Random selection of subjects, random assignment of subjects to groups, and random assignment of groups to "treatment conditions" are all indices of attempts on the part of the researcher to avoid bias. **Control** is also used to avoid error either separately or in combination with randomization techniques. The use of "control groups," or groups that receive no treatment condition, is the most common attempt at controlling bias. In most studies using control groups, the scores from the control group are compared with those of the experimental group to determine if the treatment condition had a "significant" effect. Other controls in studies include defining the population narrowly to avoid nonrepresentative members, and setting strict time, environmental, lighting, and instructional standards for groups involved in an experiment. Such controls as these help avoid "confounding" within a given experiment.

The presence of adequate controls and randomization is an important consideration in evaluating the statistical and design dimensions of a research project.

Meeting Statistical Assumptions. Most statistical tests can be used accurately only when certain basic assumptions underlying them are met. "F" tests, "t" tests, chi-squares, and multiple regression statistical models all have unique assumptions that must either be tested or accepted by the researcher. Sample size relates to several assumptions underlying many statistical tests. In most parametric tests, for example, there is an assumption that the sample size per treatment group be sufficiently large to approximate characteristics of a "normal" population. (The number 30 is often given as a rule of thumb in identifying minimum sample size per group when employing parametric statistics). A critic of quantitiative research must not only be aware of various statistical options, but must also know the assumptions for each and how they can be tested or "satisfied." The statistical texts identified in the "Annotated Readings" section at the end of the chapter provide explanations of both statistical tests and their assumptions.

Level of Confidence. The **level of confidence** is an exact probability that suggests that results of a given experimental test were "real," and not caused by chance. "Alpha" is the name of the specified probability that allows the researcher to identify how much "confidence" he is willing to have in his results. An alpha level of .05, for example, suggests that the researcher is willing to risk that his results could be achieved by chance in 5 percent of the cases. Similarly, an alpha level of .001 would suggest that the researcher would only risk chance results one time in one thousand. Thus the per cent of risk specified in the alpha level, subtracted from 100 percent would provide a percentage of confidence in a researcher's results. In the above example, an alpha level of .05 would provide a 95 percent degree of confidence in the validity of the statistical results.

However, the alpha level only assesses the probability of chance results when the null hypothesis has been *rejected*. This means, of course, that differences between groups examined were significant as measured by statistical tests. In situations where the null hypothesis is *retained*, predicting confidence is still possible, but is not quite as precise. A value called "beta" is calculated, which relates (inversely) to the "power" of a given statistical test to detect real significant differences. Research critics should be familiar with both alpha and beta levels as well as the concept of power, when evaluating the appropriateness of a given statistical interpretation.

When actual errors exist (or when the chance event occurs that the statistical tests produce invalid results) two types of errors are possible. **Type I** errors are those that occur when the null hypothesis was rejected when it, were the truth to be known, should have been retained. In other words. Type I errors occur when a statistical test indicates that findings are significant—but the effects identified were a function of chance, not the experimental treatment. **Type II** errors are those that occur when the null hypothesis was retained when it, were the truth to be known, should have been rejected. In this case, the experimenter finds no statistically significant difference, but the results actually were different.

There is no way to actually know when these types of errors occur, but they can be statistically estimated. The research critic should be sensitive to these two possible types of errors and examine their potential carefully when evaluating the statistical interpretations in a given study.

The research critic must understand principles of statistics and design as well as the subconcerns of level of data, randomization and control, assumptions, and possible sources of error. These demand training and experience in statistical methods and experimental design. Once the statistical dimensions have been evaluated the critic must examine methods of data collection, coding, and analysis.

Data Collection, Coding and Analysis

Evaluation of methods of data collection, coding and analysis are often difficult if the report of the research is in brief or abstracted form. Most journal articles are shortened in the methodology sections because of limited print space in a journal. This makes it necessary for the critic to make inferences, in some cases, concerning the appropriateness and quality of data collection and coding techniques. Some important concerns in this area of evaluation include evidence of training of the research team, training of "confederates" when used, coding methods, external validity, and the concept of "meaningfulness."

Training of the research team. Evidence of precision and standardization of techniques among the research team is an important index of the quality of a research project. The researcher must demonstrate that instructions have been standardized if multiple research assistants are used. He or she must also demonstrate that concern has been taken to standardize or randomize such variables as sex, race, age, and/or physical appearance of research assistants. As will be noted in the next section, the "experimenter effect" can produce confounding if not controlled adequately. Evidence of pretesting and pilot testing of the experimental conditions by the research team provides further indices of quality in the research process.

Training of Confederates. A **confederate** in an experiment is a person who acts, talks or appears in a given way as a part of the experimental condition. For example, in a study involving group conflict a confederate might be placed in the group to produce different types of conflict. The use of confederates is common, and can be very useful. However, their training must be precise and extensive. Evidence of practice sessions with confederates, pretests, and pilot tests should be included to demonstrate quality in the research process.

Data Coding Techniques. "Raw data" is that which is recorded either by subjects, observers or evaluators. However, the raw data usually must be "coded" into a form that can be analyzed statistically either by hand or by computer. Most modern research programs involve the computer as a research tool. Raw data are usually coded into a form that can be entered into a computer for analysis. The procedures used by a researcher to transfer the raw data into a useful form for analysis are both important and a source of potential error. In evaluating a research project, evidence that coding was "verified" (checked for validity and reliability), that the number of times data were converted or coded within a study was kept to minimum, and that coders were adequately trained is important. "Data cleaning" is a term often used in the area of computer coding and analysis. It represents techniques to ensure that coding is complete and accurate. Evidence of data cleaning is usually an index of quality in a research project.

The use of "sense mark" or computer readable forms in research decreases many coding errors. However, the use of sense mark sheets by untrained subjects can result in subject coding errors. Whatever coding system the researcher uses, it should be as simple as possible, be checked for validity and reliability, and involve the fewest possible transfers of data.

External Validity. Just as important as internal validity is the concept of **external validity** in a research project. External validity here refers to the degree to which the behaviors or attitudes tested in a given study relate to those in the "real world." External validity in the data collection process relates to making the "laboratory" environment in which data are collected as "realistic" as possible. Attention to variables which increase the ability of the researcher to generalize his or her results to real life situations is an important index of quality. The critic can ask such questions as:

1. Is the language used in the experimental treatment condition similar to that used in real life situations?
2. Are the tasks to be performed in the experimental treatment condition those subjects might be asked to perform in real life?

3. Are environmental variables such as room size, decoration and location realistic in light of real world experiences?
4. Are observers or evaluators disguised or hidden from view of subjects so they do not appear artificial or obtrusive?

These and a number of related questions concerning the potential external validity or generalizability of a research project must be thoroughly investigated by the research critic.

Meaningfulness vs. Significance. Two words that are often used rather loosely by beginning researchers are "significant" and "meaningful." In the context of experimental research, the words have very precise but different meanings. The word "significant" should be used in experimental research reports to indicate that statistical significance was obtained in examining the research or null hypotheses. **Significance** really means that the results were determined to be different than would have been predicted from "chance" alone. Because of problems of Type I and Type II errors discussed above, and because of other errors and biases that may be present in a given experiment, the fact that a test was reported to be statistically significant does not necessarily mean that the results are "meaningful."

With very large sample sizes some results can be found to produce significant statistical differences, but the results are relatively meaningless. It is up to the researcher, based on his knowledge of all variables in a research project, to interpret the results in light of not only their significance, but their value or meaningfulness. It should be noted that the words "insignificant" and "nonsignificant" are also often confused or used incorrectly in the reporting of statistical results. The word nonsignificant should be used when reporting that a statistical test did not reach the level necessary to achieve statistical significance. Insignificant, on the other hand, is a rather informal term. It implies that a variable or a result was of relatively small or no importance in the study.

Research critics should make their own decisions concerning the meaningfulness of a given result, in light of the statistical significance obtained. They should also be aware of a variety of other general problems that can affect the quality of a given research project.

General Research Problems

In addition to the specific research concerns and considerations discussed in previous sections, several general research problems must also be evaluated by the research critic. This section poses several questions that should be asked when evaluating the quality of a specific article or manuscript.

Is the Manuscript Written Objectively? Kerlinger (1979) suggests that the "criterion of objectivity enables scientists to get outside of themselves." The idea is to reduce bias by removing their attitudes and desires from the procedures and descriptions of results in a given study. Kerlinger points out, however, that it is nearly impossible for a researcher to be totally objective. Researchers, like most of us, are governed by personal values and motives. However, there are several ways that researchers can attempt to make their research reports more objective. They can relate results to previous studies and theoretical positions; they can demonstrate attempts to avoid bias in sample selection, group assignments and treatment assignments; they can use language that is specific and free from emotional or biased connotations; and they can qualify their results and identify possible sources of bias for the readers of the manuscript.

Is the Manuscript Free from Bias and Error? Given that objectivity is a primary goal of a research report, it follows that demonstrated attempts to reduce bias or error would be equally important in a research project. Some potential sources of bias or error that should be evaluated include:

1. *The experimenter effect.* Blalock and Blalock (1982) suggest that such variables as sex, personality, character, specific behaviors, race, dialect, word choice, and demonstrated attitudes of the experimenter or research assistant can significantly affect results of experimental treatment conditions. This implies that the **experimenter effect** may bias or "contaminate" scores or measurements in some instances. Attempts to randomize or control such effects by the experimenter are needed to avoid negative bias produced by the experimenter effect.

2. *Sample selection.* The need for representative sample selection is emphasized throughout this text. However, the means by which an experimenter obtains his or her subjects can have a significant effect on the outcome of the study. For example, if the subjects are enrolled in a class taught by the experimenter there is some potential bias due to the fact that the subjects (a) already know the experimenter; (b) are more highly motivated than most subjects to perform well; (c) may fear that their course grade is related to their performance in the experiment; and, (d) may distort their responses in an attempt to give the experimenter the results the subjects believe are desired. Similar biases from sample selection occur with "captive" subjects (e.g., those who are required to participate by their boss, a military officer, or a teacher). If the subjects are not selected randomly or in a truly unbiased manner, the results of the research may contain some degree of error.

3. *Practice effect.* The **practice effect** occurs when either a pretest or an initial testing in an experiment serves as practice for future tests. Such practice often tends to artificially improve scores, even without a group receiving a treatment condition. The research critic should see if care was taken to avoid or test for the practice effect in the research. Many research designs can help control for the presence of the practice effect. By having a series of control groups take pretests or initial tests at the same time, and then take follow-up tests at the same time they are administered to treatment groups (but the control groups, of course, do not receive the treatment), the practice effect can be assessed. This is done by comparing pre- and post-scores of the control groups to determine if practice alone has created significant differences. These can be compared to those of the experimental groups to determine if similar differences occurred. When possible, the experimenter should attempt to avoid the potential of a practice effect or use an experimental design that helps control for its presence.

Were Ethical Principles and Practices Upheld in the Research Report? Most universities and government agencies have committees and policies governing "human use of human subjects." Some evidence of compliance with such policies should be identified in a research report when appropriate. For example, it is no longer considered ethical to initiate treatment conditions that might cause emotional trauma to subjects, even if no physical harm is caused. Research with animals, although rather rare in the communication discipline, is also strictly governed by ethical codes (policed in many areas by the Society for the Prevention of Cruelty to Animals). The researcher must be aware of ethical and legal concerns and report ways he or she addressed them in the research report.

Other ethical issues of concern when evaluating a manuscript include the use of "cover stories," by researchers (i.e., telling a lie to enhance the effect of a treatment condition), assuring subjects of anonymity or confidentiality (and keeping it), and "debriefing" subjects when the experiment is concluded (telling subjects what really was happening in the experiment, especially if a "cover story" was used). The violation of ethical practices or their suspected violation on the part of the experimenter is a cause for serious concern by the research critic.

What is the Motivation or Source of Funding for the Research? Although television and the motion picture industry like to stereotype the typical researcher as living in an ivory tower, removed from the pressures of the real world, this is not usually the case. Most research has to be sponsored or partially supported from some outside source. Researchers usually cannot afford to conduct research on their own. The problem with outside support is often "expectations" or pressures to produce significant results. If a university grant is given to support a professor's research, for example, there is substantial pressure for the results to be publishable. Similarly, if a major corporation funds some research, there is some implied pressure that the results be useful to the company. Such pressures may be subtle, or even nonexistent in some cases, but the research critic must evaluate these variables in determining whether pressures may have created "shortcuts," or misinterpretations of some results.

Once these questions have been addressed and answered to the satisfaction of the research critic, a final evaluation must be directed toward the thesis, dissertation, term paper, journal, book, or convention report in which the research appears.

Reporting and Publishing Results

There is some implied credibility connected with the specific medium or outlet where a given research report appears. Obviously, one would give higher credibility to a manuscript published in a "prestige" academic journal than to a term paper in an undergraduate class. Yet, such credibility may not relate in any way to the actual quality or importance of the research. In most cases, however, it is safe to assume that research reports which have been carefully refereed (that is, evaluated objectively by anonymous expert reviewers) reflect higher concern for quality than those unpublished or in nonrefereed journals.

The research critic must begin by evaluating the quality of a given journal or process for selecting convention participants (if the paper is to be presented at a professional convention). Some issues to examine include: how long the journal has been published (in most cases, journals improve in quality and sophistication over time); the qualifications of the editor and associate editors (or reviewers); the percentage of manuscripts rejected by the journal (this information can usually be obtained by writing to the association that published the journal). If the paper is being submitted for a convention program, is it being reviewed "blindly" and by qualified reviewers? Is the journal or convention national or regional? National conventions and journals usually demand higher quality and have higher rejection rates.

If the research report is unpublished (e.g., thesis, dissertation, term paper, or corporate research report) it is often more difficult to assess quality controls. The credibility of such reports usually is affected by (1) the corporation or academic institution from which the research report originated, (2) qualifications or reputation of experimenters, project supervisors or major professors (in the case of theses and dissertations), (3) knowledge of previous reports originating from the same institution or corporation, and (4) evaluation of funding sources or granting agencies that have contributed to the support of the research.

Although evaluation of the medium or outlet for a given research project is not necessarily related to the quality of the research, it is an important consideration and should be examined carefully by the research critic.

A final point needs to be emphasized: probably no piece of social science research that has been published or presented is free from all biases, problems, errors or omissions. What research critics must look for is "relative" quality— not "absolute" quality. Because social science involves human beings, the "humanness" of both subjects and experimenters will usually create some problems. An evaluation of any research must accept that perfection is desired, but not expected. Assessments of quality must be based on a "reality" in which the average experimenter must live.

It is rather easy, actually, to criticize the research of others. It would be useful for most critics to determine if they "could have conducted a piece of research better" when making critical comments about the research of another. Such self-analysis of potential quality can help the critic make more realistic and practical evaluation efforts.

SUMMARY

This chapter has provided several guidelines and criteria that can be used by critics of scientific research. First, the criteria for evaluating the theoretical base of research were discussed. These included such issues as relative value of basic vs. applied research, presence of an adequate literature review and synthesis, and the presence of a logical empirical rationale.

Next, criteria to evaluate operationalizations and definitions were presented. These included such issues as accuracy, adequacy and clarity of definitions and operationalizations. Measurement of scientific research was then discussed, including such issues as reliability, internal validity, and a variety of measurement concerns such as reactive measurement, interpolated measurement, statistical regression and time of measurement.

Several issues concerning design and statistical procedures were identified, including level of data, randomization and controls, meeting statistical assumptions, level of confidence, and types of statistical errors possible in scientific research. Data collection, coding, and analysis were discussed in terms of the training of the research team, training of confederates, data coding techniques, external validity, and the distinction between meaningfulness and significance.

An entire section was devoted to general research problems such as the degree of objectivity in a scientific study, degree of bias and error in a research project, ethical principles and practices required in quality scientific research, and motivation and funding sources for scientific research. The final section of the chapter addressed some issues concerning the credibility of report forms, journals, and outlets. The chapter concluded with a suggestion that research critics temper their criticism in light of the "real world" problems and pressures facing researchers.

STUDY QUESTIONS

1. Identify the primary considerations a research critic should examine when evaluating a researcher's theoretical base for a given scientific study.
2. Identify and discuss the major criteria which definitions and operationalizations should meet in a scientific study.
3. Define and distinguish among reliability, internal validity, and external validity.
4. Define and distinguish among three types of internal validity.

5. Define and discuss reactive measurement, interpolated measurement, statistical regression, and time of measurement.
6. Discuss the role of randomization and controls in statistical and experimental design.
7. Describe the importance of a researcher's level of confidence in interpreting the results of an investigation.
8. Discuss the importance of training of the research team, training of confederates, and data coding techniques in evaluating scientific research.
9. Distinguish between the terms "meaningfulness" and "significance" as used in reporting research results.
10. Discuss the issues of objectivity, bias and error, ethical principles, and funding or support sources as they relate to the quality of scientific research.
11. Discuss criteria necessary to evaluate quality of journals or convention programs.

ANNOTATED READINGS

Blalock, Hubert M. and Blalock, Ann B. (1968). *Methodology in social research.* New York: McGraw-Hill.

This is a landmark text in the area of scientific research methodology. The orientation is toward critical analysis of research problems and techniques. Topics of special interest to research critics include: validity, error, experimenter characteristics, volunteers, situation realism and measurement variations.

Cochran, William G. (1980). *Statistical methods (7th ed.).* Ames, Iowa: Iowa State University Press.

One of the classic statistical tests, written by a pioneer in the statistics field. This text can serve as a useful reference for researchers and research critics alike. Most parametric and nonparametric statistics are identified, defined and illustrated. Sample problems and solutions are included, along with discussions of statistical assumptions, models and applications.

Cooper, Ron A. (1983). *Data, models and statistical analysis.* Totowa, NJ: Barnes and Noble.

A readable introductory statistics text. It includes useful information for the research critic interested in evaluating statistical assumptions and techniques. Topics of particular interest include: Type I vs. Type II errors, parametric vs. nonparametric statistics, statistical assumptions and tests for assumptions, level of significance and level of confidence, and design considerations.

Kerlinger, Fred N. (1979). *Behavioral research: A conceptual approach.* New York: Holt, Rinehart and Winston.

Kerlinger provides a comprehensive treatment of the scientific research method. The text is written from the researcher's point of view, but can be valuable to the research critic as well. Topics of particular interest to research critics include: objectivity and scientific research, variables, values and science, basic and applied research, the influence of research on practice and payoff.

PART 2

Communication Measurement Procedures

Essential to the conduct of empirical studies of communication processes is the reliable and valid measurement of communication and communication-related behaviors. Often, the measurement of some of these behaviors appears to be simple and straightforward; however, most measurement procedures require considerable care and thought if they are to meet social science criteria for reliability and validity.

Chapter 5, "Philosophy of Measurement," by Philip Emmert addresses the issues of reliability and validity from a philosophical-logical perspective. This chapter lays the groundwork for the succeeding chapters in Part Two of the book.

Chapters 6 through 14 each cover a separate measurement process or processes. Each chapter includes a discussion of the history and development of the procedure discussed in the chapter, a discussion of reliability and validity issues concerned with the measurement process, an analysis of research that has included the measurement process, and a discussion of the advantages and disadvantages of the procedure. The topics covered in Chapters 6 through 14 are:

Chapter 6, "Scaling Techniques," by William E. Arnold, includes a discussion of measurement procedures applicable to a wide range of phenomena, ranging from rating scales in a speech contest to employee evaluation forms in industry.

Chapter 7, "Attitude Measurement," by Philip Emmert, addresses the issue of measurement of one of the most frequently used constructs in the social and behavioral sciences. Several different procedures are discussed that have been developed in psychology and communication.

Chapter 8, "Bipolar Scales," by James C. McCroskey and Virginia P. Richmond, is concerned with one of the most frequently used measurement processes in the social and behavioral sciences, the method of the semantic differential. Originally developed to measure meaning, the procedures have been applied in many creative ways likely not anticipated by the developers of the method.

Chapter 9, "Survey Research," by Larry L. Barker and Deborah A. Barker, focuses on a method that goes beyond measurement into sampling, as well as other very practical issues.

Chapter 10, "Content Analysis," by Lynda L. Kaid and Anne J. Wadsworth, is concerned with a measurement technique with a history that stretches back to antiquity. In this chapter, the roots of the technique, along with its contemporary applications, are discussed.

Chapter 11, "Interaction Analysis," by Victoria J. Lukasko Emmert, examines methods of measuring relational characteristics in interpersonal relationships. This measurement approach is closely linked to content analysis, and the reader is encouraged to read Chapters 10 and 11 together.

Chapter 12, "Unobtrusive Measurement," by Janis W. Andersen, addresses the problem of the effect of measurement on the persons being observed. Nonreactive measurement techniques hold great promise for researchers concerned with communication behaviors.

Chapter 13, "Physiological Measurement," by Samuel C. Riccillo, examines the use of measures of physical phenomena as indicators of hypothetical constructs of interest. Although there are problems with these, as other measures, this approach offers potential for researchers who wish to use measures possibly less under the conscious control of subjects.

Chapter 14, "Nonverbal Measurement," by William C. Donaghy, focuses on methods of measuring nonverbal communication behaviors. Of special interest in this chapter is the presentation of the Time Series Notation System developed in Europe.

It is our belief that greater familiarity with more measurement procedures will reduce dependence on any one or two measurement techniques. All too often, we have had the feeling that the "law of the hammer" has been in operation in the social and behavioral sciences. If we only know how to use one tool we tend to use it for everything—whether or not it is appropriate to do so. On the other hand, knowledge of many tools permits us to choose the one most suitable for each different research objective. It is our conviction that Part Two of this book should help scholars have a broader approach to research/measurement.

CHAPTER 5

Philosophy of Measurement

By Philip Emmert,
University of Wyoming

A major portion of this book is devoted to **measurement** because the weakest link in empirical research is often that of the measurement techniques employed by the investigators. How much can you trust the generalizations made from empirical research if you don't believe that the investigators actually observed, or measured, what they thought they observed or measured? This is a critical aspect of any empirical study that cannot be overemphasized.

Any behavioral science must begin with the simple act of description. Prior to experimenting it is necessary for scientists to describe the phenomenon they are going to study and about which they intend to theorize. If we cannot reach agreement about what phenomenon we are studying (to ensure that we observe the same phenomenon, use the same labels for it, and measure it in similar ways) then it is very difficult for us to explain and predict the way that phenomenon functions. Measurement is the basis for achieving agreement among researchers about the phemonena they study.

You probably take measurement for granted. You have used rulers to measure length, measuring cups to prepare food from recipes, stepped on scales to measure your weight, and possibly even taken personality and intelligence tests. In addition, most of us take driver's tests, entrance exams, opinion tests and the like. Growing up in the twentieth century in any Western nation has meant growing up with measurement. We read in the newspapers the results of puplic opinion polls that tell us which presidential candidates are preferred by voters. We read figures that suggest the number of people who are unemployed. We also read about which television programs are being watched by the most people. All of these measurements are part of our lives, so much so that we assume their accuracy and believe them. It rarely occurs to us to consider the process underlying measurement.

HOW DID "SCIENTIFIC MEASUREMENT" BEGIN?

It is one thing to discuss the measurement of length or of ingredients for a cake on the one hand, and another thing entirely to discuss the measurement of "intelligence" or "attitude." When did we first begin to measure phenomena for the purpose of developing social scientific theories, laws and principles that could be empirically studied? Although this book is not in any sense a history of measurement, it might interest you to know that the roots of social scientific measurement go back several centuries.

Measurement by Government

As long ago as the seventeenth century social topics were subjected to quantitative analysis. In the early 1600s as more people began to interact with each other in business, as populations began to grow, and as governments grew more complex it became necessary to describe the population within a country for many reasons. Insurance systems at the time required data regarding birthrates, deathrates, mortality, etc. Likewise, it was important to keep track of the size of a population in order to determine tax rates. Thus, one of the forerunners of measurement in the behavioral sciences could be considered the early attempts of businesspeople and governments to gather information about such phenomena as population size, age, sex, and deathrates.

Today we take data-gathering of this nature for granted. Every ten years in the United States we conduct a census. As we are writing this book the United States is preparing for its 1990 census. We take this for granted as it has been a recurring practice in our country since the nineteenth century. But there was a time when people did not know how many human beings there were in the world, how many males and females there were, or how many people were dying, and when, at what age, and where. Thus, the area of "political arithmetic" was developed in England and spread throughout Europe.

These methods were not always direct. Frequently, as is the case today, people did not wish to answer the questions of a census taker and it was necessary to get some information indirectly. For instance, one breakthrough in determining mortality rates was accomplished simply by checking registration figures on births and deaths. This may seem absurdly simple to us today, but it represented a significant step forward in measurement. Thus, the early beginnings of measurement in the social and behavioral sciences, as well as the natural sciences, might be traced back to the seventeenth century (Lazarsfeld, 1961).

Psychophysics

Following the crude and early beginnings of political arithmetic, an area of measurement sometimes referred to as "psychophysics" developed in the eighteenth century. This approach paralleled the increasingly empirical approach of science in the seventeenth and eighteenth centuries. Science reached a point at which it was no longer adequate for a scientist simply to observe and subjectively record observations, but rather it became necessary to describe with greater precision.

In the eighteenth century one of the early examples of this kind of measurement was that of Pierre Bouguer, who in 1760 devised a means of describing brightness of light in terms of "just noticeable differences" (Boring, 1961). Using crude methods, he moved candles from one distance to another and described the shadow on a screen as being noticeably different or not noticeably different. In doing so he developed a ratio of just noticeable differences which enabled him to quantify illumination. From this point on, others followed, especially in the area of measurement of sensation, developing ways of measuring how we receive physical information. From all of this were developed measurements of sensory thresholds, sensory equivalences and sensory distances (which was another step forward in the measurement of nonphysical stimuli).

Studies of Reaction Time

In the nineteenth century astronomers began to notice that their observations were not always the same. F. W. Bessel, an astronomer at Kunigsberg studied the differences between his and another astronomer's observations. He was aware of other similar cases and began studies of reaction times. Others at the same time continued discussions of reaction time so that many different reactions were being measured, such as reflexes, muscular reactions, cognitive reactions, and judgment reactions. All of this was, of course, a large step toward the measurement of mental phenomena as we do it today.

Studies of Learning

At the same time measurement was progressing regarding reaction time, a German scientist, Herman Ebbinghaus, developed a method of measuring forgetting. In fact, his classic "forgetting curve" is still referred to today by behavioral scientists. Ebbinghaus measured forgetting simply by counting the number of repetitions that were necessary to relearn certain kinds of material. Although he did not follow up his own research, in the late 1800s others did so and carried it forth into the twentieth century so that today many mental measurements can be traced back to the influence of Ebbinghaus (Boring, 1961).

Studies of Individual Differences

Finally, in the late nineteenth century and in the early twentieth century people began to notice that all individuals were not the same. In fact, Adolphe Quetelet and Francis Galton suggested the existence of what has been termed a "normal curve." Many phenomena were distributed within a population so that the large bulk of the population was in the middle and people were spread out on both extremes.

You have, no doubt, observed something similar to this relative to the height of people. There is an average height around which most people tend to cluster. Most American males tend to be around 5′ 9″ or 5′ 10″. Most American females tend to be around 5′ 3″ or 5′ 4″; thus, you can find in any crowd the large bulk of people clustering around these heights with fewer people who are taller than that and fewer people who are shorter than that.

One of the people most responsible for advances in the measurement of individual differences among people was Francis Galton. In the late nineteenth century he published works that investigated different variables and attempted to go even further, to suggest relationships between characteristics of fathers and sons. It is actually from his work that many of the current tests of intelligence and personality have evolved (Boring, 1961).

You can see from this brief discussion of the background of measurement that the measurement procedures we have today and will be considering throughout the rest of this book did not spring, all of a sudden, from nowhere in the mid-twentieth century. Indeed, we owe much to the scholars of the past as we are part of a tradition begun at least 300 years ago. It would be possible to suggest that this tradition began thousands of years ago with the first intelligent human being who attempted to describe precisely a phenomenon he or she had witnessed. To be sure, our quantitative measurements today are more sophisticated than the verbal descriptions of the past, and yet, as we consider the problems with some measurement techniques in the following chapters you may question whether we have advanced much after all.

THE FUNCTIONS OF MEASUREMENT

Having considered some of the background of measurement in the behavioral sciences it is useful at this point to consider the functions of measurement. Why do we find it important to quantify our observations? Why must we measure attitudes? Why must we measure intelligence? Of what value is it to read books on measurement and take courses to learn the logic and philosophy underlying measurement techniques? These are questions many behavioral scientists ask themselves because sometimes it seems such a complicated process that it would be easier left unlearned. Actually, the fundamental processes that are the basis of most measurement procedures are not terribly difficult to learn. As more researchers become more familiar with various measurement procedures and the logic underlying them behavioral research will be much improved.

Abraham Kaplan (1964) suggests that quantitative measurement techniques serve three functions. First, he suggests that measurement "... is a device for standardization, by which we are assured of equivalences among objects of diverse origin." This is a significant advantage. This function served by measurement permits us to standardize different objects from different origins in a way that is not possible without measurement. To use a very simple example from everyday life, when we go into a shoe store to buy a new pair of shoes it is most convenient that a clerk can measure our feet and tell us that we wear a "10-D shoe." After making that statement the clerk can bring out all of the "10-D's" in the store and they are all likely to fit. Although these shoes have come from various manufacturers throughout the country and the world, a standardized measurement procedure assures that the shoes sitting in front of us (with some exceptions) are rather consistent as to size.

This is also the case with some mental tests. Although intelligence testing for employment has been abused in the business world, if we are employers who need to hire people of a certain intelligence level for a job we must be able to determine intelligence levels of the applicants for the job. It would be handy to have a test that permits us to standardize people in such a way that we can hire someone for the job and be somewhat assured that he or she is intelligent and thus, appropriate for the position.

This is why Kaplan suggests that one of the functions served by quantitative measurement is that it does allow us to standardize. This standardization through measurement is what makes it possible for us to compare outcomes of various studies in the behavioral sciences. It is what permits one researcher to understand what another researcher has been studying. If our measurement procedures were not standardized, comparisons from one study to the next would be almost useless.

Kaplan's second function of measurement is that measurement makes "... possible more subtle discriminations and correspondingly more precise discrimination." Without the intelligence tests we use today we might be faced, in hiring people to be computer programmers, with simple descriptions such as, "this person is smart" or "this person is stupid." Those two statements would not be very useful in determining who might be most qualified to become a computer programmer. What we probably need is to be able to say more precisely that a person is in the 10th or 20th percentile of the population in mathematical ability so that we can predict that he or she might be a good computer programmer.

The kinds of intelligence testing we do today permit us to make some relatively fine discriminations as to verbal ability, mathematical ability, and even reasoning ability. We are not suggesting at this point that we actually measure the person's ability, but rather that we are able to measure the way the person performs in each of these areas and thus, can predict the way they are likely to perform in the future.

If we return to the analogy of shoe size, we can see that many measurements are possible. First, there are the two categories of male and female shoe sizes. There are also children's shoe sizes, which are different from adult shoe sizes. Of course, within each of the categories you can have numbers such as 6, 6 1/2, 7, 7 1/2; then one can go to triple A, AA, B, C, D, widths so that a clerk in a shoe store can make rather fine discriminations as to size and fit with shoes. Thus, a function of measurement is to make possible very fine distinctions and precise descriptions. We would not suggest that we can make discriminations that are this precise with measurements in the behavioral sciences. However, as we refine procedures we will improve our ability to make fine discriminations about a variety of variables of human behavior.

Finally, Kaplan suggests that the third function of measurement is to make "... it possible to apply to inquiry available mathematical techniques, whether for purposes of verification, prediction, or explanation." This is probably one of the most important functions served by measurement. We have at our disposal today various statistical techniques, many of which you already may have studied in a basic course in statistics. These techniques permit us, with proper cautions, to infer the existence or absence of significant differences, as well as the presence or absence of relationships among different variables. This, then, enables us to make predictions about how people will perform in school or about their behavior in a voting booth.

Without quantitative measurement we would not be able to make statistical comparisons. We would lose the precision afforded by statistics. The Gallup and Harris polls regarding public opinions on various issues, as well as on presidential candidates every four years, are made possible through the use of descriptive and inferential statistical techniques in existence today. Without the numbers produced by quantitative measurement techniques we also could not make predictions regarding the performance of students in college—at least not with the degree of precision we can today. Not only can we predict how a student will perform in college, but it is also possible to specify the percentage of error in our prediction. In the behavioral sciences today it would be impossible to carry out the experimental studies we perform regularly were it not possible to quantify the phenomena under study. Thus, measurement serves an extremely valuable function: it permits us to make use of the available mathematical and statistical techniques of today.

There is one final function served by quantitative measurement, although Kaplan does not mention it. It is not a "respectable" function. Quantification serves the function of making our science look more "scientific." The numbers look more certain and thus, the public and even our colleagues are more likely to listen to us. In short, quantification is persuasive. As we conduct our experiments our ability to quote numbers makes our conclusions more acceptable to many people. We might mention that this function is a two-edged sword, however. Just as the average person is more likely to believe our results because they are quantified, so we are more likely to place great trust in our numbers. This not necessarily bad, but it does carry with it a significant risk. Too often we believe the results of a study because it is quantified when, as we shall see later in this and subsequent chapters, being quantitative does not necessarily make it right. Thus, this "unrespectable" function of quantitative measurement can both serve us and sometimes mislead us.

WHAT DO WE MEASURE IN THE BEHAVIORAL SCIENCES?

This may be your first contact with the area of measurement, so you may well be asking the question, "It is all well and good to talk about the importance of measurement, but what exactly do we measure in the behavioral sciences? It would be easy to give you a "flip" answer and suggest that we measure everything that can be seen, but in fact, some areas are of greater concern to us than others. There are many variables such as language intensity, attitude, credibility, and the like that have been manipulated as independent variables and have been examined as dependent variables.

One of the interesting distinctions we can make regarding the variables that have been measured is the distinction between those variables we can observe and those we cannot observe. A reasonable question that might occur to you is, "How can we measure something we cannot observe?" This question will seem even more reasonable and important as we continue in this chapter. Also, throughout the rest of the book we will be making an important point: there are variables that are discussed as **hypothetical constructs** in the behavioral sciences, that many behavioral scientists believe they have studied directly, when in fact they have not. In order to make this more clear, we will now consider those variables we can study through direct observation.

Measurement of Observed Phenomena

There are many observable phenomena that we can measure directly. In journalism a frequently cited variable is the length of news stories devoted to a particular topic. When journalists discuss the number of column inches devoted to a particular story or particular subject matter they are measuring a directly observable phenomenon. In so doing they are perfect examples of behavioral scientists studying human behaviors. When a communication scholar or a psychologist measures the distance between people during conversations this is another good example of measurement of observed human behavior.

Likewise, things such as pulse, pupil dilation, loudness and softness of voice, the number of words uttered in a sentence, hair styles, and the number of times a person stutters while speaking are examples of observable communication phenomena. In each of these examples the focus is on an actual human behavior that can be directly observed. Were we "purists" we would suggest that behavioral scientists have no business studying anything other than these directly observable human behaviors. Certainly this would be consistent with some behavioral scientists' perspectives. However, it should be obvious that restricting ourselves to directly observable human behaviors would prevent us from considering many concepts and ideas that are important in disciplines such as communication, education, political science, psychology, and sociology. Having considered examples of those phenomena that can be directly observed, you might ask "Well, what about concepts such as attitude and intelligence?" In order to answer that question we now need to consider unobservable phenomena.

Measurement of Unobservable Phenomena

Of major concern to most scholars in the behavioral sciences is the hypothetical construct. As defined and discussed in Chapter 1 and 2, the hypothetical construct is useful in that it enables us to discuss unseen or hidden phenomena that are theoretically useful. In developing theories of human behavior one of the most useful concepts available to behavioral scientists has been that of "attitude." Other useful concepts have included "intelligence," "meaning," "personality," and "listening." None of these is an observable phenomenon. It is important to grasp the central point that we cannot directly observe a hypothetical construct. Because we cannot directly observe it we cannot directly measure it.

Some people question the notion that we cannot see an attitude. It may even seem to you that you can see a person's attitude about something. On further reflection, however, it becomes obvious that what we actually see are behaviors from which we *infer* the existence of an attitude inside someone's head. When you talk about a friend having a "good attitude" or a "bad attitude" you haven't actually seen an attitude, have you? Rather, what you actually see is a set of behaviors that could include anything from positive or negative statements to nonverbal avoidance behavior or direct eye contact, or the like. From any of the behaviors you might begin to infer either a positive or negative "attitude" on the part of your friend. We hope you can see that something such as "attitude" is locked away inside our heads.

Whatever meaning you have for the word "school" is something only you know (and there are some who question whether we even know ourselves). Other people may infer your meaning from things you say and do or things you don't say or do. Notice that they are forced to infer your "meaning." (The problems involved in the measurement of "attitudes" are discussed in greater detail in Chapter 7 and the measurement of "meaning" is discussed in Chapter 8.) The same thing can be said of "intelligence," which we cannot directly measure but must infer. People who engage in what we call "intelligent behavior" or who respond in what we consider to be intelligent ways to certain kinds of questions we call "intelligent." People who don't engage in "intelligent behaviors" or who cannot respond to questions in ways we consider "intelligent" we call "unintelligent."

This may suggest to you that things such as attitude tests or intelligence tests do not really measure "attitude" or "intelligence." If that is so then you have the right idea. The question then becomes, "What is the basis for our inference of a hypothetical construct based on our observations of actual behaviors?"

To better understand how we make this inference let's take an example of a person who is white about whom we wish to determine the existence or nonexistence of negative attitudes toward black people. If we are following this person in question, (whom we will call Ralph) down the street in our home town we can observe, as Ralph walks down the sidewalk, that he crosses the street and continues in the same direction but now on the other side of the street. At the same time, we observe a black person with whom Ralph would have crossed paths if he had not crossed the street. Some people might suggest that we could infer from his action that Ralph doesn't like black people.

Upon further reflection, however, it must be apparent that there might have been several other reasons why Ralph walked across the street. For instance, he may have seen something in a store window that he wanted to look at, or he may have wanted to get out of the shade and into the sun. Thus, we still don't know whether or not Ralph has an antiblack attitude. If we continue to follow Ralph, however, and observe him walking into a diner and standing while placing an order, rather than sitting in an empty chair that happens to be next to a black person we might begin to suspect that Ralph has a negative attitude toward blacks.

We might suspect this because we have had a chance to observe two different behaviors in two different contexts in which the only consistency in the behaviors was avoidance of a black person. Even so, we might still not infer the existence of a negative attitude toward blacks unless we continued to follow Ralph throughout his day and later heard him make statements in which he indicated his opposition to having a black person move into his neighborhood or his reluctance to work with black people at his job. As we begin to hear statements of this sort and can observe these kinds of behaviors we become more thoroughly convinced that Ralph, indeed, does have negative attitudes toward blacks. The important point in this illustration is that what permits us to infer the existence of Ralph's negative attitude toward blacks is that we can observe a consistency in his behavior regarding an attitude object (black people) in different contexts.

The more examples we could obtain of his behavior in response to black people in different situations, the more confident we would be about our inference of his attitudes. Notice that we are inferring attitudes, and that we are basing our inference on consistencies we can observe in his behavior regarding the attitude object in different settings. This principle is one that is true for inferring intelligence as well. If we were trying to infer Ralph's intelligence we would have to see his responses to different problems, demanding different levels and types of intelligence in different situations. Once we began to observe a consistency in his behavior that we could label either "consistently intelligent behavior" or "consistently unintelligent behavior" we could infer the existence of high or low intelligence, depending on what we have observed.

You should keep this principle in mind while reading Part 2 of this book. Whenever researchers claim to have measured hypothetical constructs (those phenomena which are not directly observable) they are involved in a process of *inference*. This inference usually is based on observed consistencies in behavior.

It is also important to consider that consistencies in the observations from which we infer the existence of a hypothetical construct are based on some kind of theory. Every measurement procedure assumes some kind of theory about human behavior. In the example of Ralph and his attitude toward black people the researcher, at the very least, theoretically assumes that people behave negatively toward things about which they have a negative attitude and that they behave positively toward objects about which they have a positive attitude. In addition, there is a theoretical assumption that people make positive statements about attitude objects toward which they feel positively and negative statements about attitude objects toward which they have negative attitudes. Although all behavioral scientists do not necessarily agree with these assumptions, the assumptions are nevertheless inherent in the example.

As will become apparent as we discuss various kinds of measurement procedures, different kinds of theories underlie the various kinds of measurement techniques. One of the most obvious assumptions inherent in many measurement procedures is the notion that people arrange perceptions and cognitions on a kind of mental continuum. Any procedure that asks a respondent to rate or rank some phenomenon makes this assumption. If we ask a person to evaluate a message source (as will be discussed in Chapter 8) or to rank employees in a company as to their productivity, we are making this assumption.

Another assumption is the premise that phenomena in the world *can* be ranked or rated. As will be apparent in the discussion of nonverbal measurement in Chapter 14 and in the discussions of content analysis and interaction analysis in Chapters 10 and 11, there is an assumption that it is legitimate to order verbal and nonverbal stimuli. Of course, this assumption is necessary if we are to benefit from the third function of measurement suggested by Kaplan, for it enables researchers to convert qualitative observations to quantitative data. Both of these assumptions serve as the basis for all measurement procedures, however, and, depending on the phenomenon we are attempting to describe with our measurements, we should consider their validity at all times.

Since our data collection procedures are theoretically based, their results will reflect the theories underlying them. This means that, to a certain extent, every time we measure a human behavior we are, in effect, collecting biased data in that it is biased by the theoretical assumptions underlying our measurement procedures. This does not mean we should not attempt to measure the phenomena that interest us. It does mean we should not blithely assume that because a measurement procedure produces numbers that the numbers are "unbiased," or "objective." We should critically examine the theoretical assumptions that drive the measurement procedures and determine for ourselves the validity of the assumptions for the measurement procedure in question. We also should begin to demand that researchers state the theoretical underpinnings of their measurement procedures—even though most do not.

All measurement procedures in the behavioral sciences are either attempts to measure human behavior or other phenomena that are directly observable and thus, can be measured directly, or to "measure" hypothetical constructs that are not directly observable, cannot be measured directly, and therefore must be inferred. Whenever we "measure" hypothetical constructs we infer their existence on the basis of some sort of consistently observed behaviors, through the filter of some set of theoretical assumptions. These behavior patterns, along with our theoretical assumptions, permit us to infer the existence of a hypothetical construct in the heads of subjects under study. This distinction is of considerable importance as we consider what can and cannot be accomplished with each measurement technique discussed throughout this section.

Levels of Measurement

Because we have been exposed to measurement every day we tend to take measurement procedures for granted. However, it is useful to keep in mind that measurement is a very complex process and deserving of special attention if we are to be effective as empirical researchers.

Measurement is remarkably like description. You have, no doubt, described many things in your life. For instance, you may have said once to someone, "Yesterday was cold." In making that kind of descriptive statement you have actually used a symbol, the word "cold," which you attached to the phenomenon of the day's temperature. You classified the temperature for the day as "cold" and in so doing performed the most basic kind of measurement. The problem is that there is no standardized procedure for attaching terms like "cold" or "hot" to phenomena like the day's temperature. What is "hot" or "cold" to one person may not be the same for another. This is the function measurement serves in science: It enables us to specify and agree on *standardized procedures* of observation/description. Notice the emphasis on procedures. It is not nearly so important to learn about specific measurement instruments as it is to understand the procedures underlying the creation of those instruments.

Measurement has been defined as "... the assignment of numbers to objects (or events or situations) in accord with some rule" (Kaplan, 1964). This definition of measurement suggests that whenever we attempt to describe a phenomenon quantitatively, be it a person, place, event, or thing we must consistently follow a rule, or set of rules, which prescribes the method for the assignment of descriptive numbers. For instance, if you were to use a ruler to measure the dimensions of the pages in this book, you would be describing the pages in the book according to a set of rules which we have all learned regarding the use of rulers. You are probably so familiar with these rules that you use them without thinking about them consciously. You might even have trouble remembering what it was like to have learned them. You did, however, and this set of rules is what enables you to describe the pages quantitatively—by using numbers as descriptive symbols.

Notice that it does not really matter what kind of a ruler you use in this example. You could use a ruler that measures in inches or you could use a metric ruler that measures in centimeters. The specific measurement instrument is almost unimportant if you are consistent in following the rules for that kind of measurement. The rules for each of these instruments are fairly similar. That is, you go through basically the same operations, whether measuring in inches or centimeters. The measurement procedures are what is of paramount importance. As our discussion in this chapter continues, and as you read Chapters 6 through 14 please keep this in mind. *The procedures are what determine the legitimacy of our measures.*

In the behavioral sciences we have procedures, or sets of rules, for the assignment of numerical values to phenomena that interest us. Typically, behavioral scientists employ measures of many communication variables such as attitudes, meaning, language intensity, credibility, and galvanic skin responses. We will touch on these and other measures throughout this section. Rules of measurement result in procedures that produce at least four different types of data. It is important to consider these levels of measurement in order to better understand the kinds of data produced by different measurement procedures, as well as the implications for us as we analyze that data.

Since there are different kinds of phenomena researchers wish to measure it should come as no surprise that some scholars (Kachigan, 1986) feel that the numbers we use to represent them are different also in reflecting the differences in the "real world objects." After all, numbers are merely symbols and symbols have arbitrary meaning so we must be careful about how we assign numbers to phenomena. Stevens (1946, 1951) suggested the existence of four levels of measurement. They are the "nominal," "ordinal," "interval," and "ratio" levels, or scales, of measurement.

Nominal Scales. Whenever the numbers produced by measurement procedures represent objects or events that differ in *kind*, the numbers have no meaning other than that of a label. For instance, different kinds of fruit, such as apples, oranges, and raspberries differ in kind, not degree. Therefore, if we number oranges as "1", apples as "2", and raspberries as "3", the numbers only serve the function of labeling, or naming the fruit. There are many variables in the social sciences that can only differ in kind. Characteristics such as political party affiliation, church membership, gender, and occupation, can only be differentiated in kind. For instance, there is not a measurable distance between male and female.

By using numbers as labels, or classifications, there are no assumptions made about the distance from one number to the next, eg., from "1" to "2". There is no basis for arranging the objects numbered in any order, in spite of our "common sense" knowledge that "1" comes before "2" and "2" comes before "3". When numbers are used to classify they contain no more information than the letters "X", "Y", and "Z". In essence, although we may be using numbers, the distinctions among the objects they are applied to are qualitative, not quantitative. We have only categorized phenomena, not quantified it, with **nominal scales.**

Because the data produced by nominal measurement procedures are not quantitative, or metric, in nature, parametric statistical tests, such as F-tests and t-tests are not appropriate. There are some nonparametric tests that can be used but they are beyond the scope of this book.

Ordinal Scales. Whenever the objects to be quantified can be ordered, it is possible to represent them on an **ordinal scale**. When objects appear ordered they are said to possess the property of transitivity. An ordinal scale can be thought of as a ranking, since each item on the scale is either above or below the items on either side of it. Speakers in a public speaking contest are frequently ranked from first on down to nth place. This is a good example of ordinal scaling. It is important, however, to note that there are no assumptions made as to the distance from one point on an ordinal scale to the next. First place is not necessarily the same distance from second place as second place is from third place.

Although the values on an ordinal scale are ranked hierarchically, the distance between rankings is unknown. Because of this we are limited as to our interpretation of quantitative differences between ordinal values. Some authorities consider ordinal scales, like nominal scales, to be qualitative since they are also nonmetric scales, lacking information about distance between values (Kachigan, 1986). This would mean that, strictly speaking, one should not use parametric statistics to analyze ordinal data but rather should restrict oneself to nonparametric tests, as with nominal data.

Interval Scales. Scales that have both rank order information as well as equal distances between ranks are **interval scales**. The example most often cited of an interval scale is that of a thermometer. Be it Fahrenheit or Centigrade, we know that the difference between 32 and 33 degrees is the same as the difference between 20 and 21 degrees. Every difference of one degree is the same difference in heat.

Kachigan (1986) points out, however, that 80 degrees F is not twice as hot as 40 degrees F. If these temperatures are converted to their Centigrade equivalents of 26.7 and 4.4 degrees C, the higher temperature appears to be six times as large. How can this be? The answer lies in a major deficiency of interval scales: they lack an absolute zero point. Zero degrees on either a Fahrenheit or a Centigrade scale is an arbitrary point and has no correspondence in the "real world." There is no such thing as "no degrees." Most scholars will accept the analysis of interval data by parametric statistics tests, even though the scales lack the absolute zero point. A major concern, however, is whether the tests performed in the behavioral sciences can even be considered interval.

Attitude tests, intelligence tests, credibility scales, and many other paper-and-pencil tests are usually assumed to produce interval data in the social sciences. There is reason to question, however, whether the difference between IQ scores of 90 and 100 is the same as the difference between 140 and 150. The same is true on a seven-point attitude scale in that the difference between 1 and 2 is likely not the same as the difference between 4 and 5—because of perceptual differences of respondents in the middle as compared with the ends of the scale. Kachigan (1986, 17) suggests that "It is more realistic when trying to scale human dimensions to recognize that our scales are *approximately* of equal intervals—somewhere between an ordinal scale and a true interval scale—and we might distinguish them as *quasi*-interval scales." This may mean that when we use parametric statistics tests on interval data (relative to constructs in human behavior) we would be well advised to interpret our results conservatively.

Ratio Scales. Combining the properties of rank order, equal intervals, and a genuine zero point, **ratio scales** have more information than the other three scales and thus, are considered metric scales. Many nonverbal communication behaviors are easily measured using a ratio scale. For instance, a measure of distance would be a ratio measure, as in studies of the effects of distance on interactions. Scales of inches and centimeters are good examples of ratio scales as they are ordered, have equal intervals, and have an absolute zero. It is, of course, possible to use either inches or centimeters, whichever is convenient, so long as we identify which unit we are using. The numbers by themselves, without the units "inches" or "centimeters" attached, would be meaningless. Other examples of ratio scales include a simple frequency count and percentages, which are used in content analysis, interaction analysis, and some nonverbal measures.

Because ratio scales contain so much quantitative information it is appropriate to analyze data of this type using parametric statistics tests. All mathematical operations are valid to perform on ratio scale data. Although interval scales contain less data, and although many constructs in the behavioral sciences may not permit "true" interval measurement, most behavioral scientists accept the use of parametric statistics in the analysis of interval, or quasi-interval data. As was mentioned earlier, nonparametric statistics should be used to analyze nominal and ordinal data.

The level of measurement in a study is a critical factor in the validity of any research. In evaluating research you should determine whether or not the statistical analysis is consistent with the level of measurement in the study. Likewise, in planning your own research always select your method of analysis with this in mind. As you read Chapters 6 through 14, evaluate each measurement procedure relative to the level of data produced.

RELIABILITY AND VALIDITY

Because we must observe consistency in measurement procedures before we can infer the existence of a hypothetical construct it is necessary to have a measure of consistency. How useful would a measure be if you could not expect to get the same results with it each time you used it—even when measuring the same phenomenon? This would be very frustrating, and would also make it difficult to interpret others' research since you wouldn't know how much of their results were related to what was being studied and how much was the result of fluctuations in measurement unrelated to what was being studied. How consistent the results from a measurement instrument/ procedure are from item to item (from observation to observation), and from one administration to the next, and how consistent they are with the phenomenon we are attempting to measure relate to the concepts of reliability and validity.

Reliability refers to the extent to which the results obtained by a measurement procedure are consistent from one administration to the next and/or internally. If we give a test of communication apprehension to a group of subjects in January and then again in March, will we get the same results? The more nearly the results are the same both times the more reliable the instrument is considered to be, assuming nothing has happened to the subjects that would affect the phenomenon being assessed, communication apprehension. Likewise, we would expect that all of the items in the test should be consistent with each other in the results they produce for us to consider it a reliable measure of communication apprehension.

The **validity** of a measurement procedure, on the other hand, concerns the extent to which it is actually a measure of the phenomenon we say we are measuring. Thus, if we administer a communication apprehension test to a group of incoming freshmen at a university and label some students as "above average" in communication apprehension, others as "average," and a third group as "below average," are their "real communication apprehension" levels as we have labeled them? The extent to which we can answer "yes" to this question is what validity is all about. The more consistent our measurements are with the phenomenon we say is being measured, the more valid the measurement procedure or instrument is said to be. What follows is a consideration of different ways of thinking about reliability and validity and ways of estimating numerical indices of these concepts.

Reliability

The extent to which there is little random measurement error is our basic concern with reliability. The less the form of the test or the testing procedures cause measurement error the more reliable is our test. The fewer extraneous factors, such as the time of day, the nonverbal behavior of the person administering the test, or the temperature of the room, which affect the measurement techniques we are employing, the more reliable the instrument is. In other words, the more the responses of the people we are testing are indicative of the phenomenon of interest and no other unrelated occurrences, the more reliable our instrument is likely to be.

Another way of considering reliability is to think in terms of the repeatability of our measurement. The more we can repeat our measurement procedure and get the same results, the more reliable the instrument is. This is simply another way of saying that the results we are getting should be the result of the instrument and not of irrelevant influences. There are actually two kinds of evidence of repeatability or consistency that we can develop in order to argue for the reliability of a procedure. First, there is the repeatability that exists from one administration of a test to the next. Thus, if we gave the same test three times we would hope to get similar results when giving it to similar people each time.

Second, as we give a test to a group of people once, we would hope that the responses to all of the items would be consistent. That is, if we attempt to measure interpersonal attraction we would hope that if a subject indicated positive attraction toward another person in question one he or she would also respond in a similar manner to subsequent items on our test. If the responses were wildly different from item to item there would be no consistency within the test and thus, no evidence of internal repeatability. If this were the case then there would be an argument for low reliability.

One of the ways that we can quantitatively define reliability is through the use of the correlation statistic. Correlational statistics permit us to quantitatively state the degree of consistency between two sets of numbers, as was discussed in Chapter 2. A high positive correlation, indicative of a direct relationship between two administrations of a test, is evidence of high reliability, or repeatability.

A low correlation, approaching 0.0, is an indication of a lack of repeatability between administrations of a test. Thus, if we administer a test at one point in time and respondents get high scores, the next time we administer it they may get either low or high scores. This is evidence of poor reliability and what we are looking for in tests is high positive reliability.

There are different ways of computing correlations between groups of scores which need not concern you now. Rather, you should conceptually grasp the notion that the higher the correlation between zero and plus one, the stronger the argument that can be developed in support of the reliability of a measurement procedure. The lower the correlation, the weaker the argument supporting the reliability of the procedure. Thus, a reliability coefficient (this is the terminology used for the correlation coefficient when discussing reliability) of .20 would be strong evidence to most researchers that the reliability of a test is too low to be acceptable. Although in theory it would be possible to have a reliability coefficient that is negative it seems highly unlikely that this would ever happen. If it did, the measure would be trash. Likewise, a reliability of .92, would be acceptable evidence of high reliability for most scholars.

Some people wonder what an acceptable reliability coefficient is for a test. The preceding discussion has been phrased to indicate that there is no way to "measure reliability," nor to "prove absolutely" that a procedure is reliable. We can only develop arguments to persuade our colleagues concerning the reliability of our measurements. These arguments are fairly standardized and are, indeed, based on statistical evidence, especially the reliability coefficients that can be computed for measurement procedures. Although there is no hard and fast rule, tests with reliability coefficients of .80 and higher will probably be accepted by most behavioral scientists as reliable. Anything lower than .80 will probably be suspect. There are probably some scholars who would suggest that even .80 is questionable reliability for a test. Their argument has merit, as a test can be no more valid than it is reliable (Werts, Linn & Joreskog, 1974).

At this point, it is important to recognize that there are four primary ways of statistically arguing for the reliability of a test. A conceptual understanding of the methods available for computing these reliability coefficients is important for understanding measurement. They are: test-retest reliability, parallel test reliability, split-half reliability, and internal consistency reliability. In each of these approaches to estimating reliability coefficients, the objective is to determine consistency within the test or between separate administrations of the test. Keep in mind that some researchers consider these methods statistical "measures of measurement reliability," but they are actually statistical tools for developing arguments for accepting measures as reliable. This is so because *reliability itself is a hypothetical construct that must be inferred from observed phenomena.*

Test-retest Reliability. One of the earliest procedures for estimating the reliability of a testing procedure was that of administering the test at two different points in time and computing the correlation coefficient (reliability coefficient) between the two administrations of the test. The discussion to this point has taken this view of reliability because it is an easily understood starting point.

There are, however, problems with this approach to estimating reliability, in that factors other than reliability of the test can cause different results in two different administrations of the test. This can result in low correlations, misleading us into thinking that the test was unreliable. For example, if we administer an attitude questionnaire regarding political candidates it is entirely possible that in the time period between the two administrations of our attitude test a speech could be given or an event could occur that would genuinely change attitudes. If this happened the correlation between test scores would probably be very low and thus, there would be an underestimate of its reliability.

Likewise, if the time interval between the two administrations of a test is too short, it is entirely possible that subjects could remember their prior responses and, consciously or unconsciously, attempt to duplicate them. This would artificially increase the consistency between their scores on the two separate administrations of the test and lead us to believe that the instrument is more reliable than it actually is. When reading **test-retest** reliability coefficients in any study researchers should keep in mind that the reliability coefficient could be either artificially inflated or underestimated. This possibility should be taken into account in determining the time interval between administrations of tests when attempting to estimate reliability.

Parallel Test Reliability. It is possible to avoid the problem of subjects remembering their responses from the first administration of a test by creating parallel or alternate forms of the same test. You have probably experienced something like this in large classes in school. Professors sometimes will administer two forms of the same test, although their intent usually is to prevent cheating, an extraneous factor that would decrease both the reliability and validity of test scores.

It is possible to do something very similar with attitude tests, intelligence tests and other paper-and-pencil tests. It is common with standardized personality and intelligence tests to have more than one form of a test. Thus, a "form A" of a test can be administered to a group of subjects and then, soon afterward, a "form B." The correlation between "form A" and "form B" would be an estimate of the reliability of the test. The obvious problem in computing such **parallel test reliability** is that the forms of the test may not be exactly equivalent. If this is the case people may score differently on the two different forms *without this being the result of low test reliability.*

A low reliability estimate using this approach may result simply from either different content in the items on the two forms of the test or the time interval between the two administrations of the test, as in the case of the test-retest procedure. This approach to reliability results in a correlation coefficient that is indicative of both stability/consistency of the test over time, as well as the equivalence of two forms of the test (Helmstadter, 1964).

Split-half Reliability. Although the parallel, or alternate forms, approach to reliability does correct for the problem of subjects remembering their responses on earlier administrations of the test we are, of course, left with the time interval problem. Another approach to estimating reliability is to develop alternate forms *within* the same test. The **split-half reliability** approach attempts this.

For example, a twenty-item test can be constructed in which all of the odd items are correlated with all of the even items. Another approach would be to divide the test into the first ten items and the second ten items, treating each half as a separate form. The test, although consisting of twenty items becomes essentially two ten-item alternate forms combined into one test. Thus, it is possible to administer the two alternate or parallel forms simultaneously as one test, separating the items into the two halves after administration. This eliminates the problem of time elapsing between administrations and achieves the practical benefit of only having to administer the test once in order to derive a correlation coefficient.

We are, of course, left with a problem similar to that of the parallel or alternate forms approach: That is, how can we be sure that the odd items in a test are necessarily equivalent to the even items? The same problem would exist in the comparison of the first ten items with the second ten items. There can always be content differences which could artificially cause an underestimate of reliability. In addition, there is a problem related to the length of the test. The reliability of a test increases as the length of the test increases—up to a point (Allen and Yen, 1979). Thus, although the measurement instrument of concern may be a twenty-item test we are, in effect, computing reliabilities for two ten-item tests, even though we may ultimately want to administer the twenty-item test.

This suggests the need for a correction so that the ultimate reliability coefficient we derive, (although it is computed between two split-half forms, namely the odd-item form and the even-item form) is an estimate of the reliability of the twenty-item test. In order to correct for this the Spearman-Brown prophecy formula was developed and subsequently modified for purposes of computing the split-half reliability coefficient (Brown, 1910; Guttman, 1945; and Spearman, 1910). This is easily computed today by many mainframe, mini- and microcomputer statistics programs.

Method of Internal Consistency. In order to solve the problems related to the two halves of a test not being similar, another approach to computing a reliability coefficient was developed by Chronbach (1951). This commonly used method of computing a reliability coefficient can be thought of as an estimate of the reliability coefficient of a test with a hypothetical version of itself (Nunnally, 1978). Apparently, Chronbach's Alpha is a conservative estimate of the reliability of a test—that is, the lowest possible estimate. The primary difficulty with this measure is that it is very complicated computationally. However, since this reliability estimate is a part of statistics software available for most computer systems it is relatively simple to obtain regarding any measure we use.

As must be obvious, while it is desirable for us to have quantitative estimates of the consistency achievable with any given measurement procedure, there are problems with the first three approaches to estimating reliability coefficients. Today, the most widely used approach is the **method of internal consistency**, specifically using Chronbach's Alpha formula. Logically, basing our estimate of consistency on the intercorrelations of items on a test, as does Chronbach's Alpha, makes sense. In addition, its ready availability as part of computer software makes it easily usable for researchers.

As is frequently stated throughout this book, quantification does not produce absolute truth. Rather, quantification enables us to specify more precisely some things that we ordinarily discuss in very subjective terms. But even with the greater precision it is still not absolute. Whenever we discuss reliability we are developing arguments for acceptance of our measurement procedures. We should always keep this in mind as we read studies by other scholars, as well as when we are in the process of conducting our own research.

It is also important to note that some measurement procedures will not permit the use of Chronbach's Alpha because the procedures do not involve the use of items on a test that can be intercorrelated. Content analysis, interaction analysis, and nonverbal measures, for instance, all require the estimate of reliability of judges, or raters, as discussed in Chapters 10, 11, and 14. In addition, the special problems regarding reliability in unobtrusive measurement and physiological measures will be discussed in Chapters 12 and 13. However, the essential concerns regarding the reliability of a measure in all procedures are outgrowths of the logic presented here. In fact, actual behavioral observations can be made to fit the same general patterns as items on tests such as we have been discussing (Meister, 1985). If the problems concerned with arguing for the reliability of measurement procedures are great, the problems associated with developing an argument supportive of the validity of a measure in the social and behavioral sciences are even greater.

Validity

At the most basic level the concept of validity revolves around the question of whether or not a measurement procedure measures what the experimenter claims it measures. Thus, if we claim to be measuring size using a metric ruler, the length measured in centimeters would be a measure of size. This ruler would not always be an adequate measure of size, however. If we were measuring the size of a person's foot and we expressed it in centimeters this could be a valid measure of size. However, if we wished to measure the size of a person's body, a measure of length in centimeters might be inadequate because it does not take into account weight as a part of size. Thus, when asking whether or not an instrument is valid we should always ask a second question, and that is, "for what purpose?" Validity is a question of both the purpose to which we intend to put the data obtained, as well as the question of whether or not the instrument actually measures the variable we claim it measures.

A second question concerning validity arises quite often in the social and behavioral sciences, although the question is not often faced directly. As indicated earlier in this chapter, many of the variables studied in the social and behavioral sciences cannot be directly observed and are, therefore, inferred from behaviors that *are* directly observable. These inferred phenomena were called "hypothetical constructs" by Kibler (1970) and are referred to as "constructs" by Miller and Boster in Chapter 2. We have referred to variables such as "attitude" and "intelligence" as examples of these. Establishing the validity of an attitude questionnaire or of an intelligence test is a process that involves considerable inferential leaps. If we were to be totally honest we would have to admit that it is never actually possible to "prove absolutely" the validity of any measurement procedure that is intended to "measure" a hypothetical construct.

Linking Theory and Measurement. Because we cannot see the variable we are measuring in the first place, it is next to impossible to answer the question of whether or not our measurement procedure actually measures that variable. This is an important problem to keep in mind, both during this discussion of validity, as well as throughout this section. At best, our statements concerning the validity of measurement procedures of hypothetical constructs are inferences, as *validity, like reliability, is also a hypothetical construct.*

We never *really* know whether or not we have measured a hypothetical construct. Unfortunately, many researchers forget that it is not really possible to directly measure hypothetical constructs and begin to treat the words that stand for the constructs as if they were "real." The practice of treating a construct as if it were real is called "reification." Constructs such as "attraction," "credibility," "needs," and "communication apprehension" are additional examples of hypothetical constructs. These are "imaginary phenomena" that none of us can see or measure. We can only observe actual behaviors and infer their existence. It is important to remember always that we can only measure behaviors, or observables. Even paper-and-pencil tests measure "paper-and-pencil marking behaviors" (Cronkhite, 1969).

Blalock and Blalock (1968) suggested the importance of the use of **auxiliary measurement theories** regarding our measurement procedures. An auxiliary measurement theory is a statement of the logical linkage between the measurement operations and the hypothetical construct of interest (Blalock, 1982). This is more complicated than it sounds because we usually do not have anything resembling a direct connection between our constructs and the observables we measure that are supposed to reflect the constructs.

It must be obvious, for example, that what we measure when we use an "attitude questionnaire" is more (and maybe less) than just "attitude," as usually defined in persuasion literature. As can be seen in Figure 5.1, a person's "attitude" toward Arabs involves much more than it might seem at first glance. The person's religious beliefs, connection to the oil industry, friendships, political affiliations—all of these things, and more, will have an effect on how he or she will respond to items on an attitude questionnaire about "attitudes

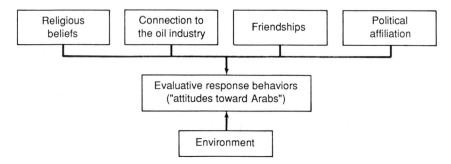

Figure 5.1. Multiple Causes of Evaluative Response Behaviors (Attitudes)

toward Arabs." In addition to those factors within the person, there may also be other factors present in the environment in which the person fills out the questionnaire that affect the way he or she responds.

Each response to each item on the attitude questionnaire is a behavior that has multiple causes. This means that the total score produced by an attitude questionnaire is a gross oversimplification of a multivariate phenomenon in which many behaviors, each the result of many causes, are represented by a single number. It is no wonder that some scholars do not consider attitude questionnaires to be valid. However, it is important to note that the problem we have with attitude measurement is a problem common to most other measures of human behavior. Every behavior has multiple causes, and thus, any single measure of that behavior is a simplification of the hypothetical construct of which the behavior is supposed to be an indicator.

Given the complexity of the connection between the behaviors researchers can actually measure and the hypothetical constructs that they are trying to infer, the importance of specifying the theoretical/logical linkage between measurement procedures and hypothetical constructs should be evident. A traditional approach to establishing this linkage has been the "operational definition." As discussed in Chapter 2, constructs can be defined by the operations, or steps, that must be followed to measure them. When we define a construct this way we are employing an operational definition.

It should be apparent from our previous discussion, however, that the operations performed in any measurement procedure do not really define the construct itself. At best they define another, lower level construct, one based on the measurement operations, whereas the original hypothetical construct of interest usually exists at a much higher level of abstraction. For instance, the semantic differential scaling procedures for measuring credibility (discussed in Chapter 8) do not operationally define credibility, as is so often written, but rather define a lower level construct, such as "evaluative responses to message sources," or "ERMS" (Emmert, 1986). This lower level construct, an **operational parallel**, suggests a construct more directly generated by the measurement operations.

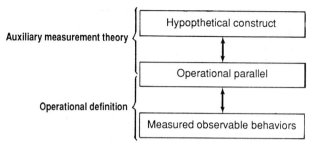

Figure 5.2. Relationship of Actually Measured Behaviors to Hypothetical Constructs

By using an operational parallel, or a lower level construct, to represent our measurement procedures we gain the advantage of being more directly connected to the behaviors actually measured. There is less "abstraction distance" between a measurement and its "operational parallel" than between it and its hypothetical construct. In the credibility example cited above, we actually are measuring behaviors in which respondents evaluatively respond to a message source. We are also reminded that we have not actually measured the construct of credibility, but rather have measured a construct parallel to it, which, in turn, must be logically linked to the more abstract hypothetical construct of "credibility" (see Figure 5.2).

Using a model of source credibility as the auxiliary measurement theory, it is possible to specify, with a greater degree of precision, the variables that are linked to evaluative responses to message sources (ERMS) as shown in Figure 5.3. By so doing, we are able to state more clearly exactly what we have measured and how that relates to the construct with which we are concerned. The model suggests that we have measured ERMS and that they are the product of the interaction of source perception, message perception, mediating cognitive variables and attitudes. Although this is not really a very detailed auxiliary measurement theory, it does suggest a direction we should take whenever we attempt to infer hypothetical constructs from measurements.

Four Arguments for Validity. Although it is difficult to develop arguments for the validity of a measurement procedure, researchers have traditionally used four "standard arguments." These serve to standardize the process for demonstrating validity in a way most researchers will accept. While they usually have been referred to as four *types* of validity, by now you should be aware that they are simply different ways to argue for acceptance of a procedure as valid. These are the approaches to validity most often discussed in the social and behavioral sciences: face validity, content validity, criterion-related validity and construct validity (Babbie, 1986; Zeller and Carmines, 1980; Carmines and Zeller, 1979).

Face validity. If a measurement instrument looks as though it measures what we claim it measures it is said to have **face validity**. This may not seem very

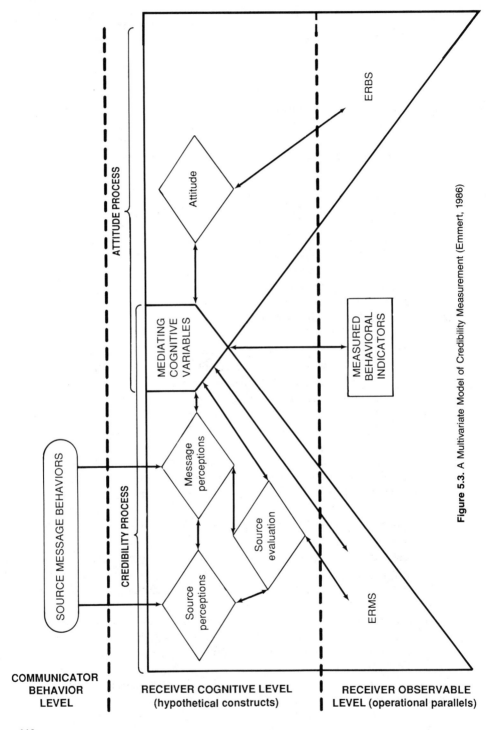

Figure 5.3. A Multivariate Model of Credibility Measurement (Emmert, 1986)

110

scientific, but as will become apparent, given the problems of some hypothetical constructs, face validity is sometimes the best type of validity argument we can develop. Keep in mind that in establishing the validity of our measurement procedures of hypothetical constructs we cannot "prove" validity, therefore, we must develop a persuasive argument for the acceptance of our procedures by other scholars. The face validity of a measurement procedure may be of greater importance than we would ordinarily think.

Our procedures should, at least, *look* as though they tap into the variable we claim is measured. The procedures we use should, at the very least, appear to be consistent with the construct of interest. Again, as mentioned earlier, consistency in our observations is important. Thus if we administer a test of attitudes toward minority groups, the items on the test should at least appear consistent with notions concerning racial prejudice.

Researchers are not, however, concerned with whether a measurement procedure looks valid to just anyone. The determination of face validity should be from the point of view of people who have expertise or experience regarding our construct. In order to determine this kind of consistency it is common to have a panel of experts evaluate the procedures used as to their face validity. Then it is possible to compute the interrater reliability of their judgments, which is an estimate of the extent to which their evaluations correlate. If we, as researchers, can demonstrate that our experts are consistent in their perceptions of the validity of our procedure, we have an argument for its validity. This, of course, is the weakest argument for the validity of an instrument, but sometimes it is the only one we can develop. As you read many empirical studies, you will probably notice that face validity is a frequent argument implicitly assumed by researchers as they write up their research.

Content Validity. Very closely related to the face validity argument is the **content validity** argument. With content validity the question is: Has the total universe of items relative to the construct being measured been adequately sampled? If we have X number of attitude statements potentially available to measure racial prejudices, have we adequately sampled from all of those attitude statements so that the ones included on our questionnaire are a representative sample of the total?

A very good example of an argument for the content validity of a test is that used in education. When giving exams teachers sometimes have students tell them they have given a good test because the items on the test "covered all of the material covered in class." Essentially what students mean when they make that statement is that the test has content validity. The items seemed to be representative of the total universe of possible items that could have been included in the test. Obviously, there is also an element of face validity argument in this kind of statement. As with face validity, it is a good idea to have a panel of experts rate the test we have constructed for content validity.

Criterion-related Validity. As discussed earlier, our concern continues to center on consistency. When developing an argument for **criterion-related validity** the researcher attempts to demonstrate that the results obtained with his or her measurement procedure are consistent with another criterion measure. Thus, if a researcher is trying to develop a new measure of listening ability, he or she might want to correlate the results of the new test with the results of another already-accepted test. If the correlation is high the researcher might then claim to have established the criterion validity of the new test. There are two ways of establishing criterion-related validity: "concurrent validity" and "predictive validity."

CONCURRENT VALIDITY is established by correlating the results from a new measurement procedure with the results of an accepted measurement procedure, with both measurements taken at the same point in time. For example, a college might have an entrance exam it gives to entering freshmen which has been found to predict performance in college quite well in the past but which is excessively long and expensive to use. It it were to develop a new, less expensive test, it might wish to establish the concurrent validity of the new test by giving both tests to an entering group of freshmen and correlating the results. If the correlation of the two tests were high, most people would accept the new test as having concurrent validity because it correlated well with the criterion test.

Thus, it is possible, as was the case in establishing reliability, to establish a quantitative index of validity by correlating a newly-developed measurement procedure with one that has already been established and accepted as valid. There are two problems with this approach to validity. First, we must assume that the earlier-developed test we are using as a criterion measure is valid in the first place. If the earlier-developed test has not been established as valid there is not much point in correlating a new test with it.

The second problem with this form of validity is that by correlating a new measurement procedure with an old one we are, practically speaking, doing something very similar to what we do when we correlate two alternate forms of a test in order to establish reliability. In other words, the difference between validity and reliability, at least when we are considering concurrent validity, becomes somewhat blurred. The parallel forms, or alternate forms, approach to the establishment of reliability seems in practice very similar to concurrent validity. Both are based on a quantitative assessment of the consistency of responses between two tests or two forms of a test intended to measure the same phenomenon.

PREDICTIVE VALIDITY is established by comparing the results of a new measurement procedure with a criterion that occurs sometime in the future following the administration of our new test. This is the most pragmatic/applied form of validity because it is based on the purpose for which the measurement procedure was developed. Some scholars consider this a content-free form of validity (Bowers and Courtright, 1984). Carmines and Zeller (1979) state the extreme view of this argument for validity when they suggest all that really matters is that there be a correlation between the measure and the criterion. For them, a measure is valid if it correlates with a criterion whether there is a theoretical connection between the measure and the criterion or not. Nunnally (1967:77) went so far as to state, "If it were found that accuracy in horseshoe pitching correlated highly with success in college, horseshoe pitching would be a valid measure for predicting success in college."

Although this is a commonly accepted view of predictive validity it would seem that this has less to do with the question of whether or not a measurement procedure measures a construct of interest than it does with the validity of a prediction from one variable to another. Given Nunnally's extreme horseshoe example, it must be obvious that there is no concern with *what* horseshoe pitching might be measuring. To be sure, if one variable will predict another, as in Nunnally's example, we will make use of it whenever we need to predict the second variable; however, this does not seem to this author a question of measurement validity.

It is the position of this author that for the predictive validity approach to be used to argue that a measurement procedure has measured a construct of interest the measure being validated *should be theoretically related to the criterion measure*. That is, if we are trying to measure a construct such as "academic ability" with a college entrance exam it would not make sense in the first place to attempt to measure this construct by quantifying horseshoe pitching skill. Rather, keeping in mind the importance of consistency to our inferences, we would select two measures that we believed were theoretically related to the construct of academic ability.

For example, the school measuring "academic ability" at the beginning of a student's entrance into college, could later correlate the grade point average of students with the scores on the new test of academic ability. If the correlation were high, they would have established an argument for good predictive validity of the college entrance exam.

To establish predictive validity there must be some kind of a performance criterion the researcher attempts to predict using a measurement procedure. If the performance criterion is successfully predicted by the results of a measurement procedure the procedure is said to have high predictive validity. The primary difference between concurrent validity and predictive validity is that the criterion score or performance with which we correlate our measurement procedure occurs simultaneously with the administration of our test in concurrent validity and occurs at a different point in time when we are trying to establish predictive validity. Another difference is that concurrent validity is established through correlation of a new procedure with an established procedure whereas predictive validity is established through correlation of a new procedure with a behavior we believe should be theoretically predictable by the construct our new procedure measures.

There is a problem with predictive validity arguments similar to those in concurrent validity. We must be assured that the criterion score for performance with which we correlate our measurement procedure is theoretically linked to the construct we are attempting to measure. Relative to college entrance exams, it is usually assumed that achievements in verbal and mathematical areas are predictive of performance in college. This may not be the case. Theoretically, we could make the case that factors such as motivation and interpersonal effectiveness affect college performance as much as the mathematical and verbal achievement usually measured. If this is true, then an entrance exam that measures only math and verbal skills may not be theoretically linked to college performance as tightly as we would wish. How we answer the question about this theoretical link could cause us to change either the criterion we select for validation purposes or to include items in our entrance exam that test the other factors that might affect college performance.

Whenever attempting to establish criterion-related validity the researcher should be aware that the selection of the criterion is of prime importance. When establishing concurrent validity, the researcher should always present evidence that supports the validity of the criterion measure being used. Even if this is a long-used test, past validation data should be presented that justifies use of the test as a criterion measure for the new test. When establishing predictive validity, the researcher should determine the logical linkage between the criterion behavior and the measurement procedure in question. In addition, as with concurrent validity, the validity of the measure of the criterion behavior should be established. Without adequate support for acceptance of criterion-measures, criterion-related validity arguments are practically meaningless.

Construct Validity. Of all the approaches demonstrating the validity of a measure, the **construct validity** approach is the most theoretically based. If a researcher has developed a measure of a construct, the scores resulting from that measure should relate in a theoretically meaningful manner to *other variables* with which the construct is supposed to be connected. For instance, if a physiological measure of heartbeat is supposed to be indicative of communication anxiety, then it would be reasonable to expect people in high stress communication situations to have more rapid heartbeats (higher measured communication anxiety) than would be expected of people in low stress communication settings. If our "measure" of communication anxiety produces scores in the theoretically expected directions, we say it has high construct validity. If, on the other hand, there were no difference in the physiological "communication anxiety scores" in high and low stress communication contexts, then researchers would conclude that the "communication anxiety scores" had low construct validity.

A construct validity argument is based on the extent to which results obtained with a measurement procedure are consistent with theoretical predictions. If the theory underlying the construct itself permits predictions of other observable behaviors, and if a measurement procedure produces measures consistent with those predictions there is a strong argument for construct validity. This approach to validity may seem somewhat circular in nature and yet it is a strong argument because of the powerful theoretical base underlying it. It would be hard to argue against the kind of evidence in the example concerning communication anxiety.

SUMMARY

This chapter has considered the history and importance of measurement in social science research. Measurement procedures were shown to be a potential weak link in many studies. Both the functions of measurement and the difficulty of measuring hypothetical constructs were discussed. It was pointed out that many variables in behavioral science research are unobservable and must be inferred.

The process of measurement was shown to produce four levels of measurement: nominal, ordinal, interval, and ratio scales. It was pointed out that nominal and ordinal data should be analyzed using nonparametric statistics whereas parametric statistics can be used to analyze interval and ratio data. Finally, the importance of establishing high reliability and validity was considered. It was noted that we can only argue for acceptance of the reliability and validity of our measurement procedures. The types of reliability arguments discussed were the test-retest, parallel test, split-half, and internal consistency methods. The types of validity arguments discussed were the face, content, criterion, and construct methods. While some scholars treat these as methods of "computing" reliability and validity, in this chapter they have been presented as arguments for gaining acceptance of measurement procedures.

STUDY QUESTIONS

1. Is the notion of a hypothetical construct any more important for behavioral scientists than for physical scientists? If so, why? If not, why not?
2. Consider any measurement instrument/procedure with which you are familiar and critique its face, content, criterion-related, and construct validity. What are its strengths and weaknesses in terms of these arguments for validity?
3. Which do you consider to be the strongest argument for the validity of a measurement procedure—and why?
4. Of what importance is the concern researchers have relative to the question of whether or not attitude scales are interval or ordinal scales?
5. Why are the procedures for constructing a measurement instrument more important than the instrument itself? How might the importance of procedures relate to the

common practice of one researcher "borrowing" an instrument created for another study by another researcher?

6. Consider any measurement instrument/procedure with which you are familiar and attempt to determine whether it produces nominal, ordinal, interval, or ratio data.

7. If you were going to develop the data to argue for an instrument's reliability which strategy would you follow, test-retest, parallel test, split-half, or internal consistency—and why?

8. Of what use is the notion of the "operational parallel" and how is it different from an operational definition?

9. What are the similarities and dissimilarities between predictive validity and construct validity?

10. What is the difference between the reliability and validity of a measurement instrument/procedure?

ANNOTATED READINGS

Babbie, E. R. (1986). *The practice of social research* (4th ed.). Belmont, CA: Wadsworth.
    This book has an excellent section on conceptualization and measurement. Babbie focuses on the nature of the hypothetical construct and the link between measures and constructs.

Blalock, H. M. (1982). *Conceptualization and measurement in the social sciences.* Beverly Hills, CA: Sage.
    This book is for the more advanced student. It does present an excellent discussion of Blalock's auxiliary measurement theories. An important book for anyone more than casually interested in measurement.

Carmines, E. G. and Zeller, R. A. (1979). *Reliability and validity assessment.* Beverly Hills, CA: Sage.
    This is an excellent introduction to classical measurement theory. Although there is some mathematical treatment most senior level college students will understand this material.

Kaplan, A. (1964). *The conduct of inquiry.* San Francisco: Chandler.
    This classic may be difficult to find but it is worth the search. Kaplan writes clearly and understandably for the beginning student as well as thoughtfully for the advanced reader. His comments about measurement are still thought-provoking more than twenty years after publication.

Kibler, R. J. (1970). Basic communication research considerations. In P. Emmert & W. D. Brooks (Eds.), *Methods of research in communication* (pp. 9–49). Boston: Houghton-Mifflin.
    Kibler's discussion of hypothetical constructs not only stands the test of time, it is still one of the best explanations available.

CHAPTER 6

Scaling Techniques

By William E. Arnold,
Arizona State University

As indicated in the previous chapter, **measurement** is vital to the development of communication theory as it provides a way to classify and define objects under study. It is the basis for all quantitative research in communication. You also considered the levels of measurement in that chapter.

If you want to measure how long a person talked to an audience, you could turn on a timer to determine the length of the message (ratio data). If you want to know the number of visual aids a speaker used, you could watch the live presentation or a video tape and count the visual aids used (nominal data) and/or rate the effectiveness of their use (ordinal data). If you want to know if the speaker was nervous, you could use electronic recordings of galvanic skin response or of heart rate to determine physiologically how the speaker was behaving (interval data). If you want to know if one speaker is better than another, your task becomes more complex and will probably require the use of some form of a rating scale (ordinal or interval data).

Measurement provides us with the tools to go beyond counting or simple enumeration. Knowing that a speech was listened to by 500 people gives us little evidence of the effectiveness of the message unless they all walked out halfway through the presentation. In this chapter we will consider a critical component of measurement—scaling.

INTRODUCTION TO SCALING

Gorden (1977) provided a good definition of scaling as the process and/or techniques used to validate the existence of a property of an object or event. It also aids in the establishment of an operational index of the relative magnitude of the property. While counting told us in the previous example that 500 people listened to the speech, we could use rating techniques to tell us whether they liked what they heard. If the speaker was at a political rally, we could use scaling techniques to determine which listeners were Republican or Democratic. Counting or looking at the 500 would not tell us either of these potentially useful pieces of information. Scaling techniques could even be used to tell us how much the audience like the speech.

In this chapter we will describe the purposes of scaling for communication research. We will also consider the characteristics of scaling techniques. We will look at scale development but not at attitude scales like Likert or semantic differential scales, which are considered in Chapters 7 and 8 respectively. Although you know about **reliability** and **validity** as applied to measurement, we will review them relative to various scaling techniques.

This chapter serves as the foundation for the chapters that follow. Without an understanding of what scaling is or how to use it, you would not be able to apply Likert or Guttman attitude measures, including the semantic differential. Even psychophysiological and nonverbal measurement involve scaling procedures.

PURPOSES OF SCALING

Why would you use scaling procedures in a research project? Babbie (1986) describes three uses for research methods which parallel the three uses of scaling. His categories are:

- Exploratory
- Description
- Explanation

In exploratory research you check out hunches and develop ways of measuring the object under study. Scaling offers the method by which you can measure both your independent and your dependent variables. The purpose at this exploratory level is to determine if the variable can be scaled and how to best accomplish it. If we were interested in speaker apprehension, we would explore the ways that we might scale apprehension so that we could tell if there are different levels of the construct. If we were looking for a simple scale to rate the number of gestures in a given communication, we might try to develop single item scales like the following:

- Number of gestures: Too many   About right   Too few
  or
- Number of gestures: Many   Some   Few   None

Levels of Listening

		1	2	3	4	5
	Empathy					
	Self-Disclosure					
Core	Confrontative					
Conditions	Respect					
	Genuine					
	Immediacy					
	Concrete					

Figure 6.1. Carkhuff's Listening Model

Once we had developed the scale we might try it out on a sample speaker and speech to see if it was feasible. The early work by McCroskey on speaker credibility (1966) or communication apprehension (1978) began as exploratory and quickly moved to the second purpose.

The second purpose of research and of scaling is to describe. We would not be testing a hypothesis but trying to describe the data set for the scale that we were using. For example, we might analyze data collected on a listening scale that was designed to measure Carkhuff's (1969) five levels of listening. We are making no predictions but are trying to determine the level of listening for a given population. We could describe each of Carkhuff's seven core conditions—empathy, self-disclosure, confrontative, respect, genuine, immediacy, and concrete as they relate to listening. We could look at age, sex, and relationship differences on each dimension and for each core condition that might fit the scale listed in Figure 6.1.

Finally, the third type of research is explanation and hypothesis testing. Scales are used in the testing of hypotheses. We use the results of scales as both independent and dependent variables. If we measure how liberal-conservative a group of subjects are, we could use the results as the independent variable in the study of political persuasion. We could also measure changes in subjects' liberal/conservative scores and use the data as a dependent variable. In both cases we are using the scale scores for hypothesis testing.

In the 1960s and early 1970s, we relied on scales to measure attitudes and credibility, to test hypotheses on fear appeals, message structure, and evidence. We tested hypotheses using scales to determine the impact of highly credible sources, reluctant testimony, and fear messages on attitudes toward issues and toward the speaker.

As you can see, scaling can serve a variety of purposes, depending on the nature of your research and the questions you are attempting to answer. It is important to understand these purposes when you start your research project.

CHARACTERISTICS OF SCALING TECHNIQUES

Regardless of what the researcher is scaling or who is doing the scaling, several characteristics must be considered to ensure precision in measurement.

What is Scaled

The first characteristic is what is being scaled. You can scale people, stimuli/objects, or both. Attitude measurement relies on the scaling of people in order to determine how the individual feels about a given topic. For example, you may ask individuals to describe their attitudes toward drug use in order to test the effectiveness of a series of messages designed to reduce drug use. In this example we would be scaling the individuals in response to the attitude instrument.

Scaling of individuals is widely used in communication research as we attempt to understand the impact of communications on people. We measure attitudes, values, and interests not just to understand that person as psychologists might, but to determine communication impact.

Using the above example, we could ask the individuals to rate the persuasiveness of a series of antidrug messages on a scale from 1 (most persuasive) to 10 (least persuasive). In this example we are scaling the objects or messages (stimuli) rather than the individuals. Every time we go to a shopping mall or grocery store, someone is asking us to rate a new soft drink, diet product, or food. We are accustomed to rating objects but we may not have seen the relationship to scaling at the time we were asked. Our responses to these ratings provide the manufacturer with information that can be scaled to determine product viability. In nonverbal communication, we use scaling techniques to rate gestures, eye contact, touch, and spatial relationships.

When we scale objects or stimuli, we can be asked to consider those things that are observable or abstract. In nonverbal research we may rate the effectiveness of eye contact by participants in a videotape of a job interview. We could actually observe the amount of eye contact and provide a rating on two scales like the following:

- Amount of eye contact   Great   1   2   3   4   5   Little
- Effectiveness of eye contact   Very   Very
                                Good   1   2   3   4   5   Poor

The measure of effectiveness is more abstract than the amount of eye contact because we do not have a concrete observable definition of effectiveness. On the other hand we may have to evaluate the organizational climate of a company, which would be even more abstract. We might have to ask questions like:

- The communication in this organization is very open.
- My supervisor seeks my opinion on work issues.
- I seldom get communications from the top manager.

We could ask the employee to respond on a scale from *strongly agree* to *strongly disagree*. These organizational issues are more abstract and less observable.

We can combine objects or stimuli with people and ask a person to rate a stimulus that would give us an understanding of their own attitude. If we ask a person to select the presidential candidate he/she prefers and then select the best statement from a series of statements that best represents his/her views on the issues, we have a rating of the stimulus and the person. Another example may make this point clearer. We could also ask subjects to rate the ideal teacher and then rate a series of teachers on the same scales. This would give us a comparison of the subject's own attitude about what constitutes an ideal teacher as well as a rating of the specific teachers.

As a corollary, we are sometimes asked to provide scaling information about ourselves and at other times about others. If we were to complete an empathic listening scale about our own listening, we would be scaling our perception of our own abilities. This approach would fall in the first category of scaling people. We could use the same scale and rate the empathic listening ability of our best friend. This would fall into the second category of scaling stimuli even though we are rating a person. The important distinction is what is being rated or scaled. If we were to fill out a scale on job satisfaction, it would provide information about us. If we filled out another scale on organizational climate, it would tell us something about the object or in this case the organization. For research purposes we might do both in order to determine the impact of organizational climate on personal job satisfaction. Likewise we may be interested in studying the relationship of perceived listening skills of our best friend with our perception of our own skills.

Types of Data

A second fundamental characteristic of scaling techniques is the type of data provided. Coombs (1964) suggests the existence of four types of data. The first type he calls preferential data because we make a choice by ranking some object according to some criterion. We might be asked to rank our favorite colleges according to their academic standards. Becker (1970) called this approach the rank order method of rating. If we ask several people to rank the colleges we would know the relative ranking but we would not know how much better one college is over another.

Rank order causes problems for researchers if the criterion is not specified.

We could have similar objects ranked differently or vice versa. We could also face reliability and validity issues if we had to rank order a large number of items. Miller (1956) discussed perception and the magic number seven plus or minus two. Following his advice we could rank from five to nine items or objects.

If we selected a single stimulus, we would have a second type of data. For example, we could ask individuals to rate a single university or college. We are not comparing colleges. If you recall our discussion of the first characteristic (what is scaled), we would be scaling an object, the college or university, rather than an individual.

We can have single stimulus data but we do not have to have a single rating. As you will see in the next chapter on Likert attitude scaling, we can scale attitudes on a single stimulus like balancing the federal budget or U.S. foreign military aid using a number of scale items. All discussion of the appropriateness of using a number of scale items appears later in this chapter in the Likert scaling in the next chapter.

The third and fourth types of data developed can be combined into comparison/contrast. In essence you compare sets of stimuli for their differences or for their similarities. For example, you might present a research subject with two speech samples and ask for the most humorous one to be selected. You could introduce a variety of samples until you would place the stimuli (speech samples) on a continuum of humorful to humorless. The fourth type could take the same samples and ask which ones are most similar. In both types you are taking a stimulus approach to measurement.

Again, Becker (1970) discussed similar types when he presented paired comparison and comparison with examples that possess attributes of the criterion. Paired on comparison means just that, we compare x number of objects two at a time. If we had eight objects, we would have 28 comparisons to make. To illustrate the formula for the number of comparisons we would need for four objects, use the information in Figure 6.2.

	A	B	C	D
A		1	2	3
B			4	5
C				6
D				

Figure 6.2. Paired on Comparison

We would need six comparisons. A simple formula is (n) $(n-1)/2$ where n equals the number of objects. How many comparisons for 10 objects? If you said 45, it is correct $[(9 \times 10)/2]$.

If we were to compare different pictures of room arrangements for discussion, we could move quickly. If we had to compare 10 speeches as paired comparisons, it might take 20 hours if each speech was 10 minutes long. Not only would it take a long time but we could lose our ability to discriminate after hearing each speech so many times.

Becker's comparison with examples fits this type of data. Each rater is given a set of standard objects like five speech samples with different degrees of nasality. New samples are compared to the standard set of five.

A variation of this approach was used in a study of convention-going behavior by Arnold and Lee (1973). Convention attendees were given reasons for attending a convention. Each subject placed the reasons in one of nine categories from most important to least important. This process, known as Q sort methodology, produced three types of convention attendees. As suggested earlier we can compare objects or stimuli and use the data to compare people. data to compare people.

Dimensionalism

The third characteristic of scaling techniques is an issue of dimensionality. Essentially we can approach scaling from a **unidimensional** or **multidimensional** perspective. In the 1950s and 1960s researchers were busy studying the impact of communicator credibility on attitude change. Early studies looked upon credibility as a unidimensional concept. Therefore a speaker could be rated on a scale of high to low. As we developed methodological sophistication, we soon realized that credibility existed on several dimensions. There is a character dimension as well as an expertness dimension. While additional research produced other dimensions, the point is, we were assuming unidimensionality when the concept was multidimensional. We needed to look at the contribution of each dimension of credibility to attitude change. Sure enough, researchers discovered that the character dimension made a difference in some circumstances and expertness in others.

While it would be nice to think that creating dimensions would solve the problem, it is not that easy. With the credibility example, the dimensions of character (C) and expertness (E) each have their own properties. Each does not act alone but in conjunction with the other. By way of illustration, we are saying the following:

$$5C + 3E \neq 3C + 5E$$

While the total (8) may be the same, the component parts are different. As we use scales like those used to measure credibility, we are combining a number of

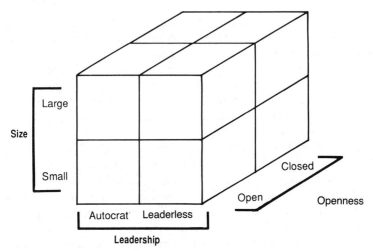

Figure 6.3. Organizational Culture-Multidimensionality

unidimensional scales to create the construct. True multidimensional scaling differs.

Multidimensional scales allow for the unique position of each scale and response in relationship to each of the others. In fact, multidimensional scaling is like three dimensional tic-tac-toe while unidimensional scaling would be like tic-tac-toe without an opponent.

To illustrate, using organizational communication culture as the construct, we would have the following dimensions, just to name a few:

- Openness   Organizational size
- Leadership   Organizational climate

A multidimensional approach would relate each to the others in this space. Perhaps Figure 6.3 will help you visualize this concept using just three of the components, size, openness, and leadership. Given just these three dimensions, they can be located throughout the model depending on each score.

Since most of our research approaches scaling from the unidimensional perspective, refer to the references at the end of the chapter for more detailed discussion of multidimensional scaling (See Kruskal and Wish [1980]). Since multidimensional scales offer greater power and flexibility, we should see more researchers developing the skills necessary to use them in research.

WHERE TO USE SCALING TECHNIQUES

We have completed an overview of scaling and the specific characteristics of scales. We have considered some of the ways that scales can be used. In looking at the characteristics of scaling, we indicated that you could scale people, stimuli, or both. We would like now to be more specific and describe where to use scaling techniques in communication-related research.

When we are trying to measure a person's view on a concept, whether it is an attitude held on a given subject or a measure of a personality trait, we are using scaling techniques. If we are measuring attitude change, we will need an attitude scale on the topic(s) being presented. Suppose a friend is running for student body president, he/she may want to know students, interests on a variety of topics like tuition and fees, governance, and other topics that could be measured on attitude scales. We make widespread use of scaling for this type of research.

Second, we use scaling techniques for behavioral ratings. We could rate the amount of a given behavior on a simple scale or use the scale to compare behaviors on a given topic. For example, a researcher may want to know which speech of a series of speeches is the most humorous. To determine an evaluation of humor, a panel of judges could be asked to rate the humor of each speech on a scale like the following:

- Rate the humor of speech #——— on a scale of one (1) to ten (10) with ten being the most humorous.

A comparison of the ratings will tell us which of the speeches was rated as the most humorous.

The above example also demonstrates where we use scaling to provide quality judgments. We assess whether something or someone is better or worse, more or less effective, and other such quality statements. Whether you seek a quality judgment, a scale for behavior, or a scale to measure attitude, your research question determines which you will use.

SCALE CONSTRUCTION

The first step in scale construction is to determine if a previous researcher has already developed a scale that would meet your needs. Why reinvent the scale if there exists a valid reliable measure that could work for you? It is not our intent to consider all sources of scales that exist. All of these sources fall in two categories. First, many published research reports present scales that have been used in studies. Even if the scales are not listed in an article, one can usually write the author for a copy.

Second, there are published volumes of scales that have been used in a number of studies (see Shaw and Wright [1967] and Buros' *Mental Measurement Yearbooks* [1985] to name just two). These sources will give not only the scales but provide other information like reliability estimates and how the scales were administered.

When we cannot find an existing scale to meet our needs, we must construct one. First and foremost, as we said before, you must have your purpose clearly in mind as you begin development. If we have developed a theoretic position on a concept, then we should make certain that our scale reflects that position.

Recall, for a moment, the earlier example of organizational culture. To develop a scale to measure organizational culture, we have to create a series of statements that reflect the concept. We must make certain that our concepts or constructs are clear. We must clarify whether we are talking about the value system of an organization or the process by which members are socialized to the value system. One way describes content while the other describes a process. The same scale could not effectively measure both.

Second, we need to test our scales to determine their relationship to the object of our study. As we cited (Babbie 1986) earlier, we have three purposes for research, and one is to help in scale development. We are at a point now where we pilot test the scale and statistically analyze the results using factor analysis. Thus we have discussed the construction of a scale from a generic perspective.

In Chapters 7 and 8 we consider the development of very special scales to measure attitudes. In Chapter 9 we present measurement research that requires scaling for content analysis, nonverbal behavior and psychophysiological studies. While much of this research may require attitude scales, we should consider a class of scales that can be used in measurement studies—rating scales.

Rating Scales

The name, **rating scales** provides the best clue for what they are. As we said in the beginning of this chapter we can scale people, objects, or a combination. We use a rating scale when we ask a person to rate, judge, or evaluate another person, stimulus, or object.

Guilford (1954) presented five broad forms of ratings that vary in their usefulness for communication research. Numerical scales use a sequence of numbers applied to a series of descriptions. For example, the following numerical scale might be used to measure visible speaker apprehension.

1. Extremely Apprehensive
2. Very Apprehensive
3. Moderately Apprehensive
4. Mildly Apprehensive
5. Non-Apprehensive

Kerlinger (1986) described a variation of the numerical scale which he called a category rating scale. If we removed the numbers from the above scale, we would have a categorical rating scale. Needless to say, we need the numbers for data analysis, but a respondent does not need them to rate apprehension.

Categorical and numerical scales are used in communication research for overall effectiveness ratings, self-rating of listening and speaking skills (Arnold, 1985), and communication comforting behaviors (Meyer, Hecht, and Arnold, 1987) to name but a few studies. To further elaborate on the last study, subjects were asked to rate how comforting a response was to a communication on a numerical scale from 0 to 9. This rating was then used to predict how empathic the listener was perceived to be.

Graphic rating scales do not appear to be used in communication research. This form requires that the respondent be given a line on which to indicate the rating. For example, we could rate speaker enthusiasm on the following graphic scale:

Very   No
Enthusiastic   Enthusiasm

The respondent would then mark on the line an enthusiasm rating. The following composite might serve as ratings for four speakers.

	A	**B**	**C**	**D**	
Very					No
Enthusiastic					Enthusiasm

Scoring for data analysis requires placing a grid with numerical categories over each graphic scale. You can see from a logistic point of view why this approach has been abandoned.

Guilford's (1954) fourth form of rating scale, the standard scale, is called comparisons with examples by Becker (1970). Becker's definition of standard scales is really a variation of numerical or categorical rating scales. Becker describes a standard rating scale as one in which raters are given labels such as excellent to poor. If you wish to pursue the material provided by Guilford (1954) and Becker (1970) you should note the confusion of terms. Guilford (1954) distinguishes the standard form by the fact that raters are given a preestablished set of standards. Raters might be shown five videotapes of speaker eye contact. Each standard could be described as high eye contact, moderate, modest, minimal, and none. Raters could judge other speakers, using these standards. You can see the amount of preparation required to develop such a standard rating scale.

The final form, the forced choice rating scale, was considered earlier in our discussion of the generic scaling approaches of comparison/contrast. An example of forced choice is as follows:

- Please check one:
  _____ An effective speaker uses at least three examples per speech
  _____ An effective speaker uses at least five examples per speech

By selecting one or the other, the rater is being forced to make a choice. You have probably filled out such a scale when you were given guidance counseling. Would you rather clean test tubes or garden? Responses to such questions indicate potential career preferences. As a form of rating scale, it is seldom used in current communication research because of the difficulty in developing a valid reliable scale.

Before we leave rating scales to consider reliability and validity sources, we should look at the unique problems of rating scales. There are three major issues that emerge in measurement literature which require us to plan carefully when we use rating scales.

First we have the problem of central tendency. When a rater is given five, seven, or any number of choices, the rater tends to avoid using the extreme categories. If a seven-point rating scale is used the rater uses categories three, four, and five and not one and seven. In fact McCroskey, Arnold and Pritchard (1967) determined the end points on a semantic differential were further from the points next to them than the other points were from each other. Usually it would look like this:

$$\text{GOOD} :\!—\!: \quad —\!:\!—\!:\!—\!:\!—\!:\!—\!: \quad —\!: \text{BAD}$$

Kerlinger (1986) suggests that this occurs where the raters are unfamiliar with what is being rated, while we could also conclude raters just avoid making extreme judgments.

Two parallel problems, severity and leniency, involve raters being too harsh or too easy on what is being rated, Kerlinger [1986]. We have all had college teachers whom we would accuse of being too hard or too easy. We take courses from the latter and avoid the former. Guilford (1954) called both of these leniency—positive and negative.

Finally rating scales suffer from a halo effect. For example, if you have just rated a very humorous speech, there is a carry-over effect (halo) to the next one that you have to rate. If the previous speech was bad, that can also impact the next one to be rated.

The halo effect also works in a different way. If you have just rated a speaker as attractive, it might carry over into a positive rating on fluency. Thus, the effect can be from two ratings on the same object being rated, or it can carry over from one object to another.

These are the major problems we face when we use rating scales in our research. We can avoid them by first making sure there isn't a better way to measure the object, person, or stimuli. Second, we can make sure that our raters are well trained in using the rating scales and are knowledgeable on what is being rated. Third, we can make sure that our rating scales are clear, relevant, and precise. Finally we can make sure that the categories used for rating fit what is being rated and offer differences. For example, we deliberately used extremely, very, moderately, and mildly enthusiastic earlier. Is moderately more than mild and less than very? We would need to know before we used them.

Rating scales form a subset of scaling techniques just like attitude scales. They are a viable part of finding answers to hypotheses and research questions. Their use should be guided by our awareness of the problems we have highlighted and by their appropriateness to the research task.

In a previous chapter you have been introduced to the concepts of validity and reliability. One answers the questions, "Does the scale measure what it was supposed to measure," and, "Will it consistently show the same results over time?" Both of these concepts are important to scaling because you are asking someone to rate themselves or someone else. We will consider the unique problems of reliability and validity as they relate to scaling.

Reliability

There are several problems related to reliability of scaling techniques. First, you must face the issue of intrarater reliability. This concerns the agreement of a rating taken at different times on the same object by the same rater. We are considering what happens to one person's rating if it is taken many times. We are now asking, Am I consistent? If we ask the same question over a period of time, is the response the same, assuming that nothing has happened to change the rating? So, for example, suppose we see if the rater who must assess the speaker's persuasive effectiveness on a 1 to 10 scale is consistent. Suppose we get the following rating of the same speech on three different occasions.

Time 1	Time 2	Time 3
8	4	9

We could conclude we have low intrarater reliability.

We can enhance intrarater reliability by first training the rater. As we said earlier, if the rater is unfamiliar with the object being rated or with the scale we will get low consistency or reliability.

Becker (1970) suggests ways in which we can modify the rating scale to increase intrarater reliability. Essentially, he suggests more rating choices

(1–7 instead of 1–5); forcing use of all rating choices; and measuring components of an attribute instead of the entire attribute will enhance reliability.

Second, you have the issue of consistency of the people doing the rating. Returning to the earlier example of humor ratings, you would want to be certain that your raters have a fairly consistent view of humor. If not, you will have low interrater reliability. If you rate one speech with a 1 (low humor); I rate it with a 10 (high humor); and other raters are spread across the ten-point scale, we have low interrater reliability. By increasing the number of raters, you can increase the reliability. Of course, your reliability is not doubled just because you go from two raters to four raters. If you get a reliability of .45 for four judges, it will not necessarily jump to .9 for eight judges or raters. Becker (1970) cites research where raters increased from 5 to 10 to 20 and reliability went from .66 to .83 to .91.

Interrater reliability can be enhanced by following earlier suggestions for intrarater reliability. Both Becker (1970) and Guilford (1954) point to numerous reasons why raters may not agree on their ratings or scale scores. One example, (Clevenger, 1963) found the sex drive of male judges affected their ratings of female speakers.

The study of general semantics provides a basis for the third type of reliability, which Becker (1970) calls intraobject reliability. General semantics says that an object or event changes from one moment to the next. What you see now is not the same thing you will see in a few moments. Subtle changes in the behavior being studied could have an impact on reliability.

All three of these types of reliability are important as you assess previous scales or in the preparation of your own scale. You need a highly reliable scale to allow you to test hypotheses and make generalizations.

Validity

While you are already familiar with validity as an important component of research, it is integral to scaling. Whether we are scaling attitudes or trying to measure the amount of nonverbal behavior using a rating scale, we must be concerned with validity.

If our pocket calculator gives us the answer four every time we add two plus two, we can say it is consistent or reliable. Since four is the correct answer it is also valid. If our calculator consistently (as some do) gives us the answer five it is reliable but hardly valid. We must have reliability with validity but not necessarily the reverse.

We do not have measures of validity per se, but we can seek content, concurrent, predictive, or construct validity. In each case, we are saying that our scale is valid if it meets one or more of these standards.

When we examine our scale and determine that it covers the topic we conclude that it has content validity. This could also be labelled as face validity.

If we know that Carkhuff (1969) developed five levels of listening and seven core conditions for each, and our scale addressed all 35 combinations, we might conclude we had content or face validity.

On the other hand, if we had found a scale to measure empathic listening in the literature we could compare our scale with it. If our subjects scored approximately the same on both scales, we would have concurrent validity.

If we could use scores on the rating scale to predict behavior, we would have established predictive validity. Since this involves prediction, it may take time to establish this form of validity.

Finally we have construct validity. In Chapter 1 you learned about constructs so you are aware of how difficult it is to explain. If our scale measures some aspect of our construct, we say it has construct validity. Of course, you may also have to establish the validity of the construct.

A Special Concern

In addition to issues of validity and reliability, there is another concern that you must look out for as you develop your own scales. That is, a single item does not a scale make. For example, if you were to develop a Likert scale to measure empathic listening, you would need more than the following:

My best friend is an empathic listener.
Strongly agree   Agree   Neutral   Disagree   Strongly disagree

Research has demonstrated that one item is very unreliable (Clevenger, 1964). You might add several items like the following to the one above:

- My best friend listens with concern.
- My best friend provides respect to me while listening.
- My best friend is genuine in response while listening, etc.

Where would the research on credibility and communication apprehension be if we used a single item for each?

ANALYSIS USING SCALES

A complete statistical treatment of scaling techniques will not be presented here. Review Chapter 2 for a thorough discussion of data analysis. As we began this chapter we gave examples of scales and the type of measurement that would be appropriate to each. Once you have decided that you are using a scale based on **ordinal** data, you must select statistics that are appropriate for it. Just as you are concerned with the validity and reliability of your scales, you must make certain that you analyze the results with the appropriate statistics.

SUMMARY

In this chapter we have looked at one of the essentials of measurement—scaling. We described the characteristics of scaling as well as when and how to use scaling. We focused on generic scales rather than the specific scales to measure attitudes, which are discussed in the next two chapters. We also looked at rating scales as a special form of scaling. These three chapters should provide you with a basis for the development of scales appropriate to your research questions and design.

STUDY QUESTIONS

1. What are the types of rating scales?
2. When would you use scaling procedures for research?
3. How can you enhance the reliability of a scale?
4. How can you determine the validity of a scale?
5. Under what circumstances might you want to use forced choice rating scales?
6. What type of scale would you use if you wanted to determine how candidates for an office compared to the ideal? Why?
7. Why would the paired comparison approach be less than ideal for evaluating numerous persuasive speeches?
8. You have been asked to interview a dozen people for a position. What form of scale would you use to evaluate the candidates? Why?

ANNOTATED READINGS

Babbie, E. R. (1986). *The practice of social research.* (4th. ed.) Belmont: Wadsworth.
    This text provides excellent information on all aspects of research from design to the advanced statistics. It is very handy for the researcher who needs to brush up on various aspects of quantitative research.
Coombs, C. H. (1952). *A theory of scaling.* Ann Arbor: University of Michigan Press.
    An excellent historical overview of the principles of scaling in the social sciences is provided by Coombs. The book will be too technical for the novice researcher.
Davies, P. M., and Coxon, A. P. M. (Eds.) (1982). *Key texts is multidimensional scaling.* Exeter: Heinemann Educational Books.
    This book is good for the advanced researcher who is interested in multidimensional scaling techniques.
Gorden, R. (1977) *Undimensional scaling of social variables.* New York: The Free Press.
    A good introduction is provided by Gorden on scaling theory. He includes a discussion of Likert, Thurstone, and Guttman scaling approaches.
Guilford, J. P. (1954). *Psychometric methods.* (2nd. ed.) New York: McGraw-Hill.
    This book offers an excellent historical perspective on scaling methods. Like other such books, it is not designed for the novice researcher.

Kruskal, J., and Wish, M. (1980). *Multidimensional scaling*. Beverly Hills, CA: Sage.
Part of the Quantitative Applications in the social science series, this book is a short concise overview on multidimensional scaling.

McIver, J., and Carmines, Edward G. (1981). *Unidimensional scaling*. Beverly Hills, CA: Sage.
Part of the Quantitative Applications in the social science series, this book is a short concise overview on unidimensional scaling.

Robinson, J. P., and Shaver, P. R. (1969). *Measures of social psychological attitudes*. Ann Arbor: Michigan Institute for Social Research.
This volume, while dated, gives the reader numerous examples of scales that have been used in social science research.

Shaw, J. E., and Wright, J. M. (1967). *Scales for the measurement of attitudes*. New York: McGraw-Hill.
Like the above book, this is another good source of existing scales for attitude measurement.

CHAPTER 7

Attitude Measurement

Philip Emmert,
University of Wyoming

Attitude continues to be one of the most frequently studied variables in the behavioral sciences, usually serving as a dependent measure in research. Initially, the concern with attitude probably resulted from a desire to predict behavior. These two interests were linked because most scholars believed that something called attitude caused behavior. In fact, Lemon (1973:2) suggests that the need for the concept of attitude "... arises only from the need to explain and predict conduct." Given the prominent role of the attitude construct in the social and behavioral sciences it must be clear that it is important to know how to measure this construct.

HISTORY

Early researchers contented themselves with asking subjects in their studies if they favored or opposed a policy, behavior, or a position. There was an assumption that an attitude was basically an "either-or question." A person was for or against, liked or disliked, or accepted or rejected something. There was basically no middle ground that allowed for attitudinal positions between the extremes of "agree" and "disagree." This approach to measuring attitudes may have had the effect of creating a corresponding theoretical view that people had attitudes either "for" or "against" things. In other words, the construct of "attitude" just as easily could have resulted from the measurement procedure as the procedure may have resulted from the theory.

The conceptualization of attitudes has been profoundly influenced by attitude measurement. Early discussions of measurement compared attitude scales to scales of physical phenomena, in keeping with the psychophysicists' approach discussed in Chapter 5. Thurstone and Chave's (1928; 1929; 1931) early work was based on a transfer of the notions of just noticeable differences in the perceptions of physical stimuli to comparative perceptions of psychological states (Dawes, 1972). The measurement of attitudes was considered similar to the measurement of physical phenomena such as length, weight, and speed. These comparisons and analogies imply that such a thing as an attitude exists which can be located as a point on a continuum just as a physical phenomenon can be located on a linear continuum.

Thurstone was the father of attitude measurement. His development, with Chave, of the **Method of Equal Appearing Intervals** reconceptualized the attitude construct and made possible the development of data that was at least ordinal and, possibly, close to interval. This method, now most often referred to as "Thurstone scales" brought about a view of attitude that included a continuum of positions relative to an issue, rather than total acceptance or rejection of an issue. This was an important change in the theoretical view of attitude.

In the late 1920s and 1930s the mainframe, mini-, and microcomputers we take for granted today were not available to researchers. Since Thurstone's method was relatively complicated computationally and procedurally (and because of other questions about the unidimensionality of Thurstone's scales and the effects of judge biases), Likert (1932) developed an alternative (and simpler) method that produced results that were highly correlated with the results produced by Thurstone's method. Likert's **Method of Summated Ratings**, generally referred to as "Likert scales," was quickly accepted and incorporated into research in all of the behavioral sciences. To this day, this method (or variations of it) is probably the most widely used procedure for the measurement of attitude. It is also one of the most misused methods, as will be discussed later in this chapter.

A major question about both Thurstone and Likert procedures concerned the unidimensionality of the scale items produced by the procedures. One assumption made by both Likert and Thurstone was that all of the items used in their scales belonged on a single continuum concerned with an attitude object. Guttman (1944) felt that neither Thurstone's nor Likert's procedures provided persuasive evidence that this was the case. For a scale to exist, according to Guttman, a response to one item on a test should tell the researcher what the responses to all other items on that test would be.

The assumption of unidimensionality is parallel to an assumption that a cake is composed of only one ingredient. Thus, if you find out how much of that one ingredient is present you have "explained the cake." It must be obvious with cakes that they have more than one ingredient. You must know how much flour, milk, eggs, shortening, etc., there is to "explain the cake." Likewise, with hypothetical constructs it is possible to assume that they are composed of multiple ingredients, or are **multidimensional**. If this assumption is made, then one cannot assume that an attitude can be represented by a single continuum like one attitude scale. Rather, one would assume that a procedure is needed that would provide a multidimensional/multicontinua view of the attitude construct. One major procedure for obtaining this kind of information is factor analysis. This will be discussed later in this chapter and in Chapter 8.

The ability of items to predict responses to other items is a defining characteristic of **Scalogram Analysis, Cumulative Scaling,** or as it is frequently called, Guttman scaling. For example, if you are responding to a series of items concerning your preference for ice cream we know that if you respond negatively to an item such as "I like ice cream," you are not likely to respond positively to an item such as "Ice cream is a great party treat." As will be discussed later, the items on a Likert scale do not predict responses to other items—they only predict the total score on the questionnaire.

Although Guttman scaling has been used extensively in the social sciences (especially in political science), Edwards (1957) has indicated that it is not really a procedure for constructing an attitude scale. This author wholeheartedly concurs with that position. While it may be an excellent tool for scaling voting behavior in legislative bodies, its usefulness in developing attitude question-naires is limited, at best, to the exploratory selection of items from a large set of items (McIver and Carmines, 1981).

The next major development in attitude measurement was the development of the **Semantic Differential Technique** by Osgood, Suci, and Tannenbaum (1957). Although Osgood et al. were attempting to develop a measure of "meaning" they indicated that one set of scales (those measuring the evaluative dimension) could be used to measure attitude. Since they published the scales resulting from their factor analyses, researchers began to use their evaluative scales extensively. These scales are still in widespread use today.

Probably the most theoretically based procedures for measuring attitudes are those developed by Sherif, Sherif, and Nebergall (1965). These procedures, the **Method of Ordered Alternatives** and the **Own Categories Procedure,** were based on the **Social Judgement-Involvement Approach** to attitudes and attitude change. This approach, which focuses on the role of ego-involvement as it relates to attitudes and attitude change, is rich theoretically, though the measurement procedures leave much to be desired. Unfortunately, the data produced by these measurement procedures is ordinal at best, and very likely nominal. This means that the data are not appropriate for analysis by parametric statistical methods. There were many studies in the behavioral sciences that investigated the theory and methods of the Social Judgment-Involvement Approach in the 1960s and early 1970s, but scholarly interest in this approach appears to have waned. This may be unfortunate as the present author feels that if the methodological problems were solved this approach could become fruitful indeed.

It should be evident that there is a long history of attitude measurement, with roots that extend back to psychophysics. Although each development has resulted in an extension or modification of the attitude construct, there appear to be some commonalities that are worth considering. In 1935, Gordon Allport (1935) indicated that "attitudes today are measured more successfully than they are defined." This probably is as true today as it was over half a century ago, but in order to discuss attitude measurement intelligently we must consider the nature of the construct to be measured.

WHAT IS AN ATTITUDE?

Given the discussion in Chapter 5, it should be evident that the term "attitude" is a hypothetical construct. There is nothing observable that we call "attitude." We must admit that we cannot see a person's attitude, but rather must infer and assume its existence. Although we cannot see an attitude the term/construct is useful for talking about what we are able to observe in certain kinds of behaviors.

If you observe a friend frowning whenever the president's name is mentioned, putting up editorial cartoons that criticize the president, and making critical remarks about the president in various contexts, how would you describe your friend's behaviors? Of course it would be possible to talk about the consistencies in those behaviors, the negative aspects of those behaviors, and the different contexts in which they occur, but wouldn't it be a lot easier simply to say "My friend doesn't like the president"? A statement like this is a verbal "summing up" of the observed behaviors, along with an inference about your friend's state of mind—his or her "attitude." The construct "attitude" is also a shorthand way of talking about (and explaining) a relatively complex set of observed behaviors and the inference we make about a person's cognitive state based on our observations of those behaviors.

Scholars have defined attitudes in many different ways. Some samples include the following:

"An attitude is a relatively enduring organization of beliefs around an object or situation predisposing one to respond in some preferential manner. (Rokeach, 1968:112)

"An attitude is defined as a relatively enduring predisposition to respond favorably or unfavorably toward an attitude object." (Simons, 1976:80)

"Generally we take the word *attitude* to mean a particular predisposition to respond in a given social situation. (Bostrom, 1983:39)

The above definitions, while varying slightly, all have in common six characteristics, according to Littlejohn and Jabusch (1987). They suggest that all attitudes are (1) implicit, (2) composed of predispositions to respond, (3) predispose people to respond in a preferential manner, (4) directed at something, (5) relatively enduring, and (6) learned. Attitude measurement procedures are not directed at characteristics (1) and (2) because these cannot be observed. We cannot yet measure ideas or emotions in someone's brain (as discussed in Chapter 13.) Likewise, without a long-term opportunity to observe someone and a procedure that incorporates time into the measurement we cannot measure characteristics (5) and (6). Thus, we are left with characteristics (3) and (4) as the objectives of most attitude measurement procedures. How we attempt to measure a person's "preferential response which is directed at something" depends on the logic underlying the measurement procedure. In order to better understand the logical bases of these procedures we will now consider the five major approaches to attitude measurement.

OVERVIEW OF MEASUREMENT PROCEDURES

As was mentioned earlier, major methods of attitude measurement include the Method of Equal Appearing Intervals, the Method of Summated Ratings, Scalogram Analysis/Cumulative Scaling, the Semantic Differential Technique, and Social Judgment-Involvement Procedures. This chapter will provide an overview of all except the Semantic Differential Technique, which will be discussed in Chapter 8 and the method of Summated Ratings, which will be considered in greater detail in this chapter because of its heavy use today.

Method of Equal Appearing Intervals

Also known as "Thurstone scales," this method is based on the notion that the psychological phenomenon of attitude can be scaled as can physical phenomena.[1] The logical assumption of this method is that an average of group perceptual ratings of attitude statements can be used to create a scale of statements with equal intervals between them and that this scale corresponds to a cognitive attitude continuum within all our minds. This method represents an early attempt to scale individual items for use on an attitude questionnaire in a manner that permits the ordering of attitude statements along an 11-interval continuum.

In order to accomplish this a large number (at least 100) of attitude statements (frequently on cards) are sorted into 11 piles according to the degree of favorableness the statement on each card expresses toward the attitude object of interest. The researcher then assigns a value to each statement based on the mean or median value the statement has received through the sorting procedure. The statement values are then used to construct a questionnaire of about 22 items, with the items corresponding to each of 11 intervals on a continuum. Because of the method of assigning values to the statements the assumption is made that the intervals between statements are equal.

Once the questionnaire is constructed it is administered to subjects who are instructed to indicate the statements with which they agree. An average of these statements is then the "attitude score" on an 11-interval scale. Attitude scores derived through this procedure have been relatively reliable, but the validity of the statement values appears to be significantly affected by prior attitudes of the subjects used in the initial sorting of the statements (Babbie, 1986; Emmert, 1970; Hovland and Sherif, 1952, 1961). Highly ego-involved subjects tend to perceive statements very differently from subjects of moderate-to-low ego involvement. This can distort placement of the statements during the sorting procedure. This method has never enjoyed wide use, even though it is the method from which most other attitude measurement procedures are descended. This is probably because it is such a time and energy consuming procedure.

Scalogram Analysis/Cumulative Scaling

Often referred to as "Guttman scales," this procedure is based on the premise that the items on a questionnaire should be ordered in such a way that if a person finds one item acceptable it is possible to know that person's response to all other items (Guttman, 1944).[2] For instance, if a person agrees with the statement, "I would vote for candidate X for president," then it would be likely that this subject would also agree with the statement, "Candidate X is an honest person." In other words, like the Thurstone procedure, this procedure is based on the *pattern* of responses to items on a questionnaire. It is different from many attitude measures in that this procedure makes a deliberate attempt to order items on a scale (not unlike Thurstone's objective) whereas many other procedures such as the Likert procedure and the semantic differential procedure attempt to place respondents on a continuum.

This method is used throughout the behavioral sciences and is especially useful for scaling votes of legislators by political scientists. In this application it is possible to categorize and scale the legislators themselves reliably and validly according to their political predispositions. As a method for developing attitude questionnaires, however, this approach is time consuming and labor intensive compared with the more popular Likert and semantic differential procedures, which will be discussed later.

Social Judgment-Involvement Approach

The Method of Ordered Alternatives and the Own Categories Procedure[3] were developed to permit the measurement of latitudes of acceptance, rejection, and noncommitment (Sherif, 1967b). These concepts were central to an approach to attitude change behavior which suggested that an attitude should not be represented by a single point on a continuum. Rather, it was suggested that to understand the attitude change process it was necessary to conceptualize

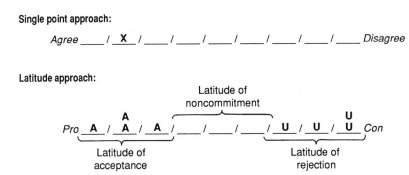

Figure 7.1. Attitude Pictured as a Single Point and as a Latitude of a Continuum

attitudes as including latitudes rather than being single points, as pictured in Figure 7.1.

In the Method of Ordered Alternatives subjects are instructed to indicate all statements they agree and disagree with from a continuum of nine statements. The statements chosen are then labeled as latitudes of acceptance, rejection, and noncommitment, with the number of statements in each being the measure of the latitudes. In the Own Categories Procedure subjects are permitted to determine the number of intervals in the continuum and the latitudes are measured by the number of statements in each latitude.

Although these approaches appear to have considerable theoretical richness, statistical analysis of the results from these procedures is limited because they produce nominal data. In addition, more work is needed relative to the reliability and validity of the methods. A promising recent effort to measure the constructs of the Social Judgment-Involvement Approach is the **attitude pie** procedure of Lull and Cappella (1981). Rather than employing linear graphic scales as a response mode they used circles, that subjects could "slice" as one slices pieces of pie, to indicate their evaluations of items on a questionnaire, as well as the salience of each item for them. This is accomplished by asking subjects to divide a circle that represents all their feelings about the attitude object in question into pie-like slices, as in Figure 7.2. They are instructed to label one slice with a + sign to represent favorable feelings, another slice with a − sign to represent unfavorable feelings. The area in the circle left unmarked would then represent noncommitment. The researcher can use a protractor to measure the size of the angles of the "slices." This permits ratio level measurement from zero to 360 degrees. These areas correspond to the latitudes of acceptance, rejection, and noncommitment set forth by Sherif et al. (1965).

The procedure was compared with Likert scale and semantic differential "look-alikes," though the Likert and semantic differential procedures for scale construction were not followed. Although the reliability coefficients were computed using the test-retest method they were not significantly different from the reliability coefficients of scales employing the agree-disagree scales similar to

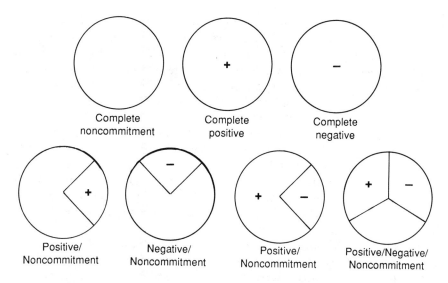

Figure 7.2 Seven Essential Categories of Attitude Structure as Represented by the "Attitude Pie" Method (Reprinted by permission of the Eastern Communication Association (*Communication Quarterly*, vol. 29, no. 2, 1981).

Likert's and bipolar adjectives like a semantic differential. Results, based on the Multitrait-Multimethod technique (a method of developing arguments for construct and concurrent validity), were less definite, yet encouraging, concerning the validity of this approach. Had the item analysis procedures of Likert and Osgood et al. been followed in the development of the measures we would have a better notion of the reliability and validity of this new procedure. One of the chief advantages of this approach is that the method produces ratio data reflecting latitudes of acceptance, rejection, and noncommitment. Further refinement of this procedure could result in a significant advance in attitude measurement.

Semantic Differential Technique

When Osgood, Suci and Tannenbaum (1957) published *The measurement of meaning* their intent was to present a method they felt enabled researchers to quantify meaning. Their procedure resulted in bipolar scales which were factor analyzed into three major dimensions of meaning, the evaluative, potency, and activity dimensions. Researchers were quick to use the scales, though not so quick to develop their own scales, because of the wide applicability and ease of administration.

Of the three dimensions, the evaluative dimension was said by Osgood et al. to be appropriate as a measure of attitude. Persuasion and attitude change researchers made extensive use of the evaluative scales developed by Osgood et al. as attitude measures. The logic underlying the use of these scales to measure attitudes was fairly straightforward. Since bipolar scales such as "good-bad," "like-dislike," and "valuable-worthless" were among the scales used to measure responses to attitude objects the face validity argument was fairly clear. When subjects responded to one of these scales they were, in Littlejohn and Jabusch's terms, indicating their preferences toward some attitude object. In addition, these scales were highly correlated with other measures of attitude, thus establishing an argument for criterion-related validity.

There were problems, however. The problems with concept-scale interaction suggested the need for construction of a new set of scales with each attitude object to be measured (Darnell, 1966; Cronkhite, 1976). As discussed in Chapter 8, a given bipolar scale is not necessarily appropriate for use with all concepts/constructs/topics. For instance, a "hot-cold" scale might work very well with the topic "weather," but not at all well with the topic "capital punishment."

In addition, research indicating that attitudes are multidimensional (Emmert and McDermott, 1976), may mean that all three of the Osgood et al. dimensions should be used rather than just the evaluative dimension. These problems do not negate the possibility of the use of semantic differential scales for attitude measurement, but this does suggest that care should be taken to follow the procedures discussed in Chapter 8 in the construction of scales rather than simply "lifting" scales from previous studies.

Method of Summated Ratings

Although the Method of Equal Appearing Intervals preceded the Method of Summated Ratings as mentioned earlier, Likert's approach to attitude measurement has enjoyed the greater popularity. Since its development by Likert (1932) it has been used to a greater extent than the Thurstone scales. The reasons for its popularity, though not quite as valid today as they were 50 years ago, were discussed by Edwards and Kenney (1946), who suggested that Likert scales appear to take less time to construct than Thurstone scales, are at least as reliable as Thurstone scales, if not more so, and yield results comparable to Thurstone results. The amount of time it takes to construct the scales is no longer as important as it was then, since the accessibility of computers makes it possible to perform the computation necessary to construct a Thurstone scale with far greater ease than when the method was first developed. Because of the reliability of Likert scales and because this method is less time-consuming even with the availability of computers, Likert scales have been widely used in persuasion studies.

Unfortunately, many researchers have equated the linear, graphic "agree-disagree" format with the procedure itself. It is not uncommon to read studies in which **Likert-type** scales have been used. This usually means that the researcher wrote items for a questionnaire, placed "agree-disagree" five-or seven interval graphic scales beneath each item, did no **item analysis** procedure, and called it a "Likert-type" measurement instrument.

This author feels this aproach does a disservice to Likert. As emphasized in Chapter 5, it is the *procedure* for the construction of a measuring instrument that is critical to questions of reliability and validity. If one does not follow the item analysis procedures developed by Likert (or their contemporary equivalents) then one does not have a Likert scale. Furthermore, to say that one has a "Likert-type scale" simply because it looks like a Likert scale does not confer validity on it—except, possibly for a questionnable level of face validity. If publications in behavioral science journals are any indication, however, many other researchers appear to take the appearance, or form, of the questionnaires for the substance of the procedure.

The procedures for constructing Likert scales are critical to the development of scales whose validity is defensible, even though the Likert format is so easy to respond to that acceptable reliability coefficients are often obtained without going through the item analysis procedures (Lull and Cappella, 1981). Keep in mind, however, the discussion in Chapter 5 which points out that a measurement instrument can be reliable without being valid. It may be that many researchers are assuming that the ease of use and the reliability of the Likert format automatically produces valid measures of attitude, even without following the item analysis procedures. It is possible that "Likert-type scales" are valid sometimes, but they should be viewed with suspicion if researchers have not used legitimate item analysis procedures or otherwise provided evidence of validity.

Procedure for Constructing Likert Scales

1. Gathering statements. The first step in constructing a summated rating scale is to develop a large number of statements about the attitude object that meet Likert's (1932) criteria for items: (a) The statements should be an expression not of fact but of desired behavior or of value; (b) conciseness, clarity, and straightforwardness should always be goals in formulating the items; (c) the statements should be worded so that reactions to them will be toward both ends of the continuum. Likert did not require statements to which the responses are at the extreme ends of the continuum; and (d) the statements should be so worded that about half of the items are positive toward the attitude object, while the order half are negative. These two kinds of statements should be distributed on a random basis throughout the questionnaire.

2. Formatting the statements. Each of these statements is assigned to a graphic scale of either five, seven, or nine intervals on a continuum ranging from "agree" to "disagree." Likert originally indicated that these should be five-interval scales but, given Miller's (1967) comments about the information

Horizontal Likert scale:

There should be more women in our government.

STRONGLY   X___:___:___:___:___:___:___   STRONGLY
AGREE   DISAGREE

Vertical Likert scale:

   ①   STRONGLY AGREE
   2
   3
   4   NEITHER AGREE NOR DISAGREE
   5
   6
   7   STRONGLY DISAGREE

Figure 7.3. Sample Graphic Likert Scales

processing capabilities of people we could probably conclude that scales ranging from five to nine intervals can yield reliable and valid results. Though many who use "Likert-type scales" religiously use Likert's five intervals, seven- to nine-interval scales have been found to be better, especially in situations in which subjects have well-developed attitudes (Flamer, 1983; Ryan, 1980).

These continua can be arranged so that they run horizontally or vertically beneath the statements. They typically look like the examples in Figure 7.3. Notice that you can provide blanks for subjects to check or place an "X" in or you can provide numbers for the subjects to circle. It is also possible to label the middle position, though the meaning of this position on the scale is somewhat ambiguous, as will be discussed later.

3. *Scale administration.* Subjects are instructed to indicate the extent to which they agree or disagree with each statement by placing a mark in the interval or circling the number on the scale which shows how close to either the "strongly agree" or "strongly disagree" end of the continuum they feel they belong. Edwards (1957, pp. 156–157) suggests that scores derived with the Method of Summated Ratings should not be interpreted independently of the distribution of scores of a defined group. If there is a strong bias on an attitude topic, item responses, and thus the item analysis and subsequent scale construction, would be valid for the group used in the item analysis, but there would be no guarantee that other groups would respond to the items selected in the same way as did the original group. Thus when constructing the scale one should always use subjects as similar as possible to those who will ultimately respond to the finished scale (Bardo, 1976; Emmert, 1970; McIver and Carmines, 1981). In fact, Nunnally (1967, pp. 514–588) suggests that all circumstances surrounding the initial

preparation of the Likert scale should be as similar as possible to those in which the completed scale will be used. He even suggests that if the responses in the final situation will be anonymous, the responses of the judges in the initial step should also be anonymous.

4. Scoring Likert Scales. In the case of a seven-interval scale, the end of the continuum that is "unfavorable" toward the attitude object is commonly scored as "1", while the "favorable" end is scored as "7". Thus, if a subject chooses the "very strongly agree" interval on a scale that has been paired with a statement worded favorably toward socialized medicine, and if we are measuring his attitude toward socialized medicine, then this response would be scored as "7".

Sometimes, a researcher's own bias on a topic may cause him or her to perceive a statement as being unfavorable to the attitude object when, in fact, most people perceive it otherwise—and vice versa. This may result in the researcher scoring items inappropriately. Although researchers must go with their own perceptions the first time through, the correlation-based item analysis procedures discussed in the next section make it possible to determine more appropriate scale directions for each item based on subjects' perceptions. Once items have been correlated with the total score, or after factor analysis of responses to all items, the positive and negative correlations and loadings of items with the total score or with derived factors are indications of the degree of favorableness or unfavorableness of each item toward the total or factor scores. This then permits a rescoring of responses to each statement relative to the results of the correlation-based item analysis. If the analysis indicates that an item is favorable toward an attitude object, then disagreement with the statement is scored as a "1". If the analysis indicates that a statement is unfavorable toward an attitude object then disagreement with the statement is scored as a "7".

The individual item responses are then summed to produce a total score for each subject. Then each total score usually is divided by the number of statements on the questionnaire to produce a mean score for each subject, which permits placement of all the subject's responses—i.e., his attitude—on the seven-point continuum.

5. Item analysis. In order to determine which statements to keep for the final questionnaire, the experimenter performs an item analysis. There are at least three major approaches to item analysis for a Likert scale: t-tests, item correlation with the total score, and factor analysis of responses to all items.

One type of item analysis is accomplished by dividing the subjects into the top and bottom quartiles in terms of their total scores. The researcher then compares the mean scores for the high and low group on each of the statements. If the mean response for a statement is significantly higher for those in the high group than for those in the low group, the experimenter keeps that statement.

The determination of significance is achieved by use of a t-test. The logic underlying this procedure is severalfold. First, the total score is a composite score produced by items that have only one thing in common—evaluative responses to the attitude object. Second, dividing subjects into top and bottom quartiles based on the total composite score should produce one group of subjects extremely positive toward the attitude object and another group extremely opposed to the attitude object. Third, any item that discriminates between these two groups at a statistically significant level must be an effective discriminator (measure) of feelings toward the attitude object and should be retained for the final questionnaire.

A second approach to item analysis is to calculate the correlation coefficient for the responses on each statement for all subjects with the total composite scores for all subjects. This approach has the advantage over the t-test method of making use of data obtained from all respondents rather than just the two extreme groups. Those statements that have a high positive correlation with the total score are retained for inclusion in the final questionnaire. One obvious problem with this approach is that, since the total composite score contains all items, each item that is correlated with the total is partially contributing to the total score. This means that a part of the correlation computed (although a small part) is a correlation of the item with itself. Thomas and Petersen (1982) suggest that this problem can be solved by correlating each item with the total score only after the raw item score has been removed from the total.

Given the earlier comments about the total composite score being composed of items with only the subjects' evaluations of the attitude object in common, it logically follows that items that correlate highly with this score should be strong indicators of those evaluative feelings. Statements correlated negatively but strongly with the total score should have the values reversed and rescored. Statements with low correlations should not be used on the final attitude test, since a low correlation should be an indicator of a lack of relationship with the total score, or the attitude the total score is supposed to indicate.

The third method of item analysis is the use of factor analysis to determine which items among all items "clump together." Based on the intercorrelations among all items, factor analysis is ideal for developing a "clean" set of items to measure an attitude object. All items that load strongly on a single factor would be retained for the questionnaire. In addition, the use of factor analysis enables the researcher to discover the multidimensional structure of the attitude discussed earlier, if one exists.

It is possible, also, that we should not assume that the attitude of interest is unidimensional, as do the other two analysis techniques—and as do the measurement procedures of Thurstone (1928), Guttman (1944), and Sherif, Sherif and Nebergall (1965). Rather, especially with relatively abstract or complex attitude objects, it may be more reasonable to assume multidimensionality of the construct in question (Thomas and Petersen, 1982). Granted this assumption, it would be more valid to use all scales from a semantic differential rather than just the evaluative scales and, likewise, it would be reasonable to expect Likert scales to be composed of multiple factors, with some items loading on some factors and other items loading on other factors. All of the factors could be considered indicative of the attitude object.[4]

All three procedures assume that some common factor—the attitude under investigation—causes statements to discriminate between the high and low groups as in the first procedure, to correlate highly with the total score for all subjects as in the second procedure, or to cluster together in a single factor (or multiple factors) as in the third procedure. Thomas and Petersen (1982) have determined that the most discriminating of the item analysis procedures are the correlation-based procedures. Both the item-to-total score and the factor analytic approaches accomplish the deletion of poor items. Factor analysis appears to eliminate the most items, so the researcher may have to balance the desire for the greater discriminatory power of factor analysis against the likelihood that this procedure may produce too few items to construct a questionnaire. If this is the case, then the item-to-total score correlational procedure may be preferable. For the construction of the final test approximately 20 to 25 items should be chosen.

Edwards (1957, p. 155) suggests that approximately half of the statements retained should be worded so that they are favorable to the attitude object, with the "very strongly agree" response having a value of "6" or "7", while the other half of the statements retained should be worded unfavorably toward the attitude object, with the "very strongly agree" response having a weight of "0" or "1". This minimizes the possibility that subjects responding to the scale might acquire a response set in which they respond to all items in the same manner without thinking because the items are worded either favorably or unfavorably.

Reliability and Validity of Likert Scales

Reliability. The reliability of Likert scales has been a source of some controversy, largely because of some early studies comparing the Thurstone and Likert methods. Likert (1932) himself began the controversy. His study seemed to indicate that a scale could be constructed using Thurstone's approach, and then most of the selected items could be used according to the Likert approach, with resulting reliability coefficients as high or higher than they were with the original Thurstone scale.

Others later attempted to examine the same question with diverse results (e.g., Ferguson, 1939; Edwards and Kenney, 1946). Only Edwards and Kenney actually used the two separate methods to construct attitude scales "from scratch"; the other studies all used one basic method and then attempted to adapt statements chosen with the first method for use with the second method. When reporting their results, Edwards and Kenney concluded that "the coefficient of .92 between the Likert and one of the Thustone scales is surely sufficiently high to establish the fact that it is possible to construct scales by the two methods which will yield comparable scores" (p. 82). Edwards (1957), after reviewing the work in this area, went a little further when he concluded that "there is no reason to doubt that scales constructed by the method of summated-ratings will yield reliability coefficients as high as or higher than those obtained with scales constructed by the method of equal-appearing intervals" (p. 162).

Bardo (1976) suggests that unless a Likert scale has been constructed using appropriate item analysis procedures, with subjects like those the final scale will be administered to, reliability may be questionable. It is also likely that this problem would be true for any measurement procedure which must first be constructed with one group of subjects and then administered in its final form to a second group. Bardo (1976:416) strongly cautions against using prebuilt scales in research because ". . . there is no way of knowing if it is applicable to the population under study . . . without retesting for internal consistency."

Bardo's (1976) study also suggests that the Likert procedure, when conducted with appropriate item analyses on the appropriate population, continues to be a highly reliable procedure, with reliability coefficients ranging from .814 to .945. Even "Likert-type scales" attain reliability coefficients ranging from .759 to .916, depending on the method of reliability computation (Lull and Cappella, 1981). All things considered, if one follows the procedures just discussed for constructing a Likert scale it would seem that a reliable measurement instrument is possible to attain.

Validity. A major validity problem with Likert scales (and other attitude measures) concerns the equality of units of the scale. This was alluded to in Chapter 5 in the discussion about types of data produced by measurement procedures. Although most researchers assume that measurement procedures such as Likert scales produce interval data, the likelihood is that this is not the case. Hovland and M. Sherif (1952) suggested that the distortions and displacements observed in their research might have been caused by the individual judges' perceptions of the size of the category intervals in Thurstone scales. This problem would very likely be equally true of the Likert procedure.

Subjects who hold extreme views on a topic or who are ego-involved with it may perceive the equality of units in any attitude scale on the topic as unequal (Sherif et al., 1965). This is one of the reasons Shaw and Wright (1967) have suggested that Likert scales "probably should be treated as ordinal scales" (p. 24). Lull and Cappella (1981) make the point that we should not assume equivalent intervals with traditional linear continuum scales. This should give cause for exercising caution when interpreting results from Likert and any other linear attitude scales that deal with highly involving topics and topics on which people are likely to have extreme views.

A second problem concerns the assumption that the middle interval of the scale represents either an undecided or no opinion. Actually, it is possible to interpret a middle position as "undecided," "don't know," "neutral," "no opinion," "don't care," or "none of your business" (Ryan, 1980). Whichever assumption one makes cannot be supported very forcefully. Lull and Cappella (1981) provide impressive evidence that suggests that the middle position on a Likert scale is extremely complex, involving considerable variance in topic salience for subjects who mark the middle position. That subjects who mark this position are very different should not come as a surprise, but it does call into question the validity of a scale that measures different constructs with different subjects—at least insofar as the middle position of the scale is concerned.

A third problem in validity can result when appropriate item analysis procedures have not been followed. Given that items have not been appropriately analyzed the following scenario could occur. A subject could mark the interval that has a vaue of "7" on half the items and the interval with a value of "1" on the other half, thus producing a total attitude score of "4". An experimenter might conclude that the subject had "no opinion" on this particular topic, when, in fact, the subject had very definite attitudes that didn't show up because responses to items counterbalanced each other. This is certainly an extreme example and probably would not happen if the item analysis procedures previously discussed were carefully followed. Certainly, the process of item analysis should eliminate all but a very remote possibility of this occurring.

Finally, a problem that can affect the validity of Likert scales, and all other attitude scaling procedures, concerns the population on which the instrument is developed. The comments above suggest that the biases and perceptions of the subjects affect the perception of the size of the intervals. In addition, Bardo's (1976) study suggests that the item analysis and the reliability of questionnaires varies with the population to whom the items are administered. Finally, Warland and Sample (1973) discovered that the certainty with which subjects held views affected their responses to items. It only follows that researchers should refrain from using Likert scales developed by other researchers, using subjects from other populations. It would also seem prudent to try to match the population that is used to develop a questionnaire with the population for which the questionnaire has been constructed. It would especially be desirable if the sample that served to construct the questionnaire and the sample to whom the final questionnaire is administered were drawn from the same population. The two samples should certainly be as much alike as possible.

Studies Using Likert Procedures. As was stated earlier, social science journals are full of studies using Likert or "Likert-type" scales. One of the advantages of the Likert procedure is that it can be adapted to measure many different kinds of attitudes. It is not just suitable for the measurement of attitudes toward social issues/policy. Eadie and Paulson (1984) conducted a study in which they employed the Likert procedure to construct a measure of communication competence (they actually appeared to measure attitude toward the communication behavior of communicators in written dialogues). In this study they used items that had been developed by other researchers, but quite appropriately conducted their own item analysis of 46 items by correlating each item with the total. Having conducted their item analysis, they retained 20 items which, when administered, had a reliability coefficient of .89, using Chronbach's alpha method of internal consistency. Although face validity was a primary form of validity established in this study, subsequent factor analysis of the items suggested a structure which added weight to the argument for the construct validity of the measure.

Another study, which has been referred to several times in this chapter, is that by Lull and Cappella (1981). This study has the potential to expand/modify our conceptualization of attitude along lines similar to those of Sherif et al. (1965). Their "attitude pie" method permits the development of the notion of people simultaneously holding both positive and negative attitudes toward a topic. This is a potentially rich procedure for attitude theory and research. Although this study has much to contribute, the researchers, unfortunately, did not follow Likert's procedures in constructing their questionnaires. The items were chosen from other studies and were never analyzed by any of the methods discussed above. The study makes a significant contribution as it is, but had the authors conducted an appropriate item analysis this study could have been strengthened significantly.

Advantages and Disadvantages of the Likert Procedure. A primary advantage of the Likert procedure is its ease of use. Not only was it easy to use in 1932 when Likert developed it, computers today make it an even more efficient procedure. It is almost difficult to understand why any researcher would want to short-cut the procedure by not using the item analysis methods, given their computational ease today.

A second major advantage of this method is that the item analysis procedures can be conducted on the same sample that is being studied. If the initial number of items is not too great there is no reason why they could not all be administered to the target subjects. After administration it would be possible to perform the item analysis, choose the final items to be retained, and then compute scores based on the retained items. This would eliminate the need for two separate groups of subjects, but even more importantly, it would eliminate the problem of population differences affecting the results. The group used for item analysis would not just be from the same population as the group ultimately tested, they would be the same people.

Finally, this technique is especially adaptable to many different purposes. It is obviously possible to use it for the measurement of social attitudes, but it is also possible to measure attitudes toward communicative competence, language appropriateness, and even communicator credibility (McCroskey, 1966; Cronkhite and Liska, 1980). Researchers should feel free to follow their creative inspirations, so long as they also follow the Likert item analysis procedures.

A major disadvantage of the Likert procedure is that it characterizes attitude as a single point on a continuum. By reducing all of a subject's responses to statements on a questionnaire to a single number the procedure oversimplifies and trivializes the construct. It is evident from our earlier discussion that many attitudes are multidimensional. This would suggest the desirability of using the factor analytic approach to item analysis to at least develop multiple continua, each of which is measured by a single point. A combination of the "attitude pie" approach with the Likert approach might be better yet in that it could provide latitude measures on more than one dimension.

A second major disadvantage, which was discussed earlier, concerns the questionable assumption of equal intervals with the procedure. The data produced by this procedure is likely quasi-interval at best (Kachigan, 1986). This would suggest that the use of parametric statistical procedures during item analysis and subsequent analysis is questionable.

SUMMARY

This chapter has provided an overview of the methods of attitude measurement, beginning with a definition of the construct of attitude. It is evident that we cannot measure attitude directly, but rather must infer its existence indirectly through our measurement procedures. Among the procedures discussed were the Method of Equal Appearing Intervals, Scalogram Analysis/Cumulative Scaling, the Method of Ordered Alternatives, the Own Categories Technique, the Attitude Pie Method, the Semantic Differential Procedure, and the Method of Summated Ratings (Likert scales).

Although each has strengths and weaknesses, the one in use the most today is the Likert procedure. Critical to the validity and reliability of this method of measurement are its procedures for item analysis, the most effective being correlation-based. So long as these item analysis procedures are followed, using similar populations to construct questionnaires to those ultimately measured, the method can produce reliable and valid measurement procedures.

NOTES

1. For complete and detailed discussions of the procedures for creating Thurstone scales see Edwards (1957), Emmert (1970), and McIver and Carmines (1981). In addition, for those interested in a computerized approach for computing values for equal appearing interval attitude scales, see Hoffman (1976).
2. For a complete explanation of the procedure for creating Guttman scales see Edwards (1957) and McIver and Carmines (1981).

3. For a complete explanation of the Method of Ordered Alternatives and the Own Categories Procedure see Lemon (1973, Chap. 7), Emmert (1970), Sherif and Sherif, (1967b), and Sherif, Sherif and Nebergall (1965).
4. Emmert and McDermott (1976) found multiple factor solutions for nine different attitude objects, with some loading on an evaluative dimension for all Likert items. This would suggest dimensions of attitude that are not purely evaluative, but which nevertheless have an evaluative aspect that may reflect our feelings toward attitude objects.

STUDY QUESTIONS

1. Given that "attitude" is a hypothetical construct, how can researchers presume to "measure" something that may or may not exist? Specifically, how does any one of the procedures discussed in this chapter *measure "attitude"*?
2. What are the major differences between the Thurstone procedure and that developed by Likert as improvements over the Method of Equal Appearing Intervals?
3. What is the chief advantage of the factor analytic approach to item analysis in the Likert procedure over the t-test procedure?
4. What is the chief drawback of the Method of Ordered Alternatives and the Own Categories Procedure? How does the "attitude pie" procedure address this problem?
5. How might the Semantic Differential Procedure be used more validly to measure attitudes than it has in the past?
6. Why should researchers be careful to construct questionnaires using subjects from the same population as that to which they intend to administer the finished questionnaire?
7. Of what importance is the question concerning the equality of intervals of attitude measurement procedures?
8. What is the problem with using "Likert-type" scales rather than using the item analysis of the Likert procedure?
9. What implications are there of using a multidimensional measure of attitude via the Likert procedure or the Semantic Differential procedure as compared with a unidimensional approach?
10. What are the theoretical implications for the attitude construct of the "attitude pie" approach to measurement?

ANNOTATED READINGS

Babbie, E. R. (1986). *The practice of social research.* (4th ed.). Belmont, CA: Wadsworth. An exceptionally readable book concerned with many issues in behavioral science research. The section on attitude scales and indexes is well written and provides a perspective that is somewhat different from the one in this chapter.
Bardo, J. W. (1976). Internal consistency and reliability in Likert-type attitude scales —

Some questions concerning the use of pre-built scales. *Sociology and Social Research*, *60*, 403–420.

An excellent study to read relative to the issue of using pre-built Likert-type scales. This chapter has suggested that this practice is unwise and Bardo's study provides ample reason for following this suggestion.

Edwards, A. L. (1957). *Techniques of attitude scale construction*. New York: Appleton-Century-Crofts.

Although some of the material in this book is outdated a surprising amount is still relevant to today's concerns. This book is especially useful for gaining a historical perspective on attitude measurement. The treatments of Likert, Thurstone, and Guttman procedures are very useful.

Emmert, P. (1970). Attitude scales. In P. Emmert and W. D. Brooks (Eds.), *Methods of research in communication*. Boston: Houghton-Mifflin.

A very applied treatment of Guttman, Likert, and Social Judgment-involvement Procedures. The chapter provides a step-by-step explanation of each approach to attitude measurement.

Lull, J., and Cappella, J. (1981). Slicing the attitude pie: A new approach to attitude measurement. *Communication Quarterly*, *29*, 67–80.

The major presentation of the research underlying this approach to measurement. The "attitude pie" approach has potential in behavioral research. It is well-written, complete with illustrative material as well as substantive for the methodologically sophisticated reader. The reader should, however, be critical of the method used to construct the Likert and Semantic Differential Scales for validation purposes.

McIver, J. P., and Carmines, E. G. (1981). *Unidimensional scaling*. Beverly Hills, CA:

A very readable, yet methodologically substantive book. It is deceptively short in that it does manage to cover most of the major issues concerning scales purported to be unidimensional. The treatment of Likert and Guttman procedures is an excellent expansion of the material in this chapter.

Sherif, C., Sherif, M., and Nebergall, R. (1965). *Attitude and attitude change*. Philadelphia: W. B. Saunders.

The vehicle for the first major presentation of the Method of Ordered Alternatives and the Own Categories Procedures. Although not written for the novice, it is a complete presentation of these procedures, as well as the data concerned with the construct validity of the methods.

Thomas, C. W., and Petersen, D. M. (1982). Methodological issues in attitude scale construction. *Journal of Social Psychology*, *116*, 245–253.

An excellent study and discussion of methods of item analysis in the Likert procedure. Though some of the issues discussed are complex, it is well worth the effort for the novice to tackle.

CHAPTER 8

Bipolar Scales

James C. McCroskey,
West Virginia University
Virginia P. Richmond,
West Virginia University

One of the oldest methods of measurement, which currently remains very popular, is bipolar scaling. The essence of this method is the establishment of concepts that are opposite of one another, with degrees or steps between these extreme poles.

Every student has been subjected to the most basic of bipolar scales—the true-false test. This type of bipolar scale recognizes no degrees or steps between the opposing poles: the statement is either "true" or "false." However, the test-taker sees shades or degrees of truth or/and falsity, which makes choosing between the extreme polar options very difficult.

A similar problem occurs when we are asked to evaluate a policy or another person on a "good-bad" bipolar scale. Few policies (or people for that matter) are totally "good" or totally "bad." Thus, it is best to have a several-step scale between good and bad. We might, for example, have the following options: very good, fairly good, equally good and bad, fairly bad, very bad. These options form a typical five-step, bipolar scale. The number of options may vary substantially, depending on a large number of factors, but all bipolar scales are essentially similar to this one.

While most bipolar scales employ some type of verbal description of the opposing poles, and often include verbal descriptions of the intermediate steps, this is not an essential characteristic of this method. For example the poles can be identified by colors, with black and white being the opposing poles, and the steps in between can be represented by various shades of gray. Similarly, researchers have used drawings of smiling and frowning faces to establish bipolar scales when working with pre-literate children. The steps between the extremes are created by varying the degree of smile or frown on the face.

PROCEDURE

The development of measures based on the method of bipolar scaling is both extremely simple and very complex. It is simple in that any person of below average intelligence can slap a few bipolar scales together, assign numbers to responses on them, add up the numbers and claim to have a measure. Indeed, examples available in the published literature of the social sciences indicate this not only can be done but it is being done. On the other hand, developing a solid measure with this procedure is a fairly complex and often a time-consuming process.

The development of a measure employing bipolar scales involves three initial steps: (1) determining what is to be measured; (2) determining how many different concepts must be measured; and (3) determining the scales to constitute the measure. We will consider each of these in turn.

Determining what is to be measured. Measures of this type typically are designed to probe such things as feelings, perceptions, attitudes, and/or beliefs which people have. They may be self-reports of one's own internal feelings, beliefs, or attitudes. They may be self-reports of one's perceptions with regard to something or someone in the external environment. An example of the former would be Jack reporting how competent as a communicator he perceives himself to be. An example of the latter would be Jack reporting how competent as a communicator he perceives Bill to be. The critical test of the validity of the former is whether it measures what Jack really thinks about himself. The critical test of the latter, depending on what the researcher has decided he/she is trying to measure, could be whether it measures what Jack really thinks about Bill or whether it measures the degree of Bill's competence as a communicator. The same scale could be both an excellent measure of Jack's perceptions and a worthless measure of Bill's competence.

The importance of determining what is to be measured as the first step in the measurement process cannot be overestimated. If this task is done carefully, it removes the potential for a lot of confusion and error later. For example, if it is clear what is to be measured, it usually is clear exactly how the validity of the measure can be determined. Equally important, once it is clear what is to be measured it becomes possible to conduct a search of the literature to determine whether an appropriate measure already exists. It is totally wasteful of research effort to take the time to develop a new measure when an appropriate measure already exists. Exerting such effort will normally only be appropriate when there is need for more than one alternative measure of the same thing.

To exemplify, colleagues of the first author of this chapter have avoided the need to develop measures of attitude, belief, and credibility for many years because of parallel projects which the author conducted in the mid-1960s. After spending several months developing Likert-type attitude scales on two topics for a research project in persuasion, he became convinced there had to be a better way. After becoming familiar with the work on measurement of meaning

(Osgood, Suci, & Tannenbaum, 1957), he decided to attempt to develop a generalized scale to measure attitudes toward a wide variety of topics. This work, which need not be reported in detail here, involved 40 bipolar scales and 154 topics. The outcome of this project indicated that 6 of the 40 bipolar scales were among the ten judged best for measuring attitude for each of the 154 topics. In addition, the internal reliability (Alpha) of the six scales, presented in a seven-step response format and summed as a single measure, was above .90 for each of the topics. The six scales are good/bad, wrong/right, harmful/beneficial, fair/unfair, wise/foolish, and positive/negative.

These scales can be used for measuring general attitudes toward such issues as capital punishment, foreign aid, current speed limits, and the like, with considerable confidence that they will generate a reliable and valid measure of attitude that will correlate highly with other carefully developed and tested measures. In most instances, these scales may be used to measure people's attitudes without additional testing. Figure 8.1 illustrates how the measure could be presented to research subjects. Note that half of the items need to be reversed for scoring. The resultant scores may range from 6 to 42, with 24 representing the hypothetical neutral score. Higher scores represent more positive attitudes.

The scales presented in Figure 8.1 cannot, of course, be used to measure all kinds of attitudes and beliefs. The researchers determined they were not appropriate for measuring feelings toward belief statements such as "The U. S. should reduce taxes." For these kinds of beliefs, the following bipolar scales were found to produce a much more appropriate measure: true/false, right/wrong, yes/no, disagree/agree, correct/incorrect. A measure based on these scales was found to be highly reliable ($> .90$) when used with over 75 belief topics and thus can be used with confidence for such topics in place of the scales used in Figure 8.1.

To summarize this section, it is critical that the researcher planning to use bipolar scales determine at the outset precisely what is to be measured. Once this is done it may be determined that such measures already exist and are available for use. If, however, it is determined that no appropriate measure is available, the researcher should proceed to the next step.

Determining how many things are to be measured. Instruments may measure only a single variable or several variables. The former type is referred to as **unidimensional**, the latter as **multidimensional**. While bipolar scales may be used to develop either type of measure, it is of vital importance to know whether a measure is multidimensional or unidimensional.

To understand the concept of multidimensionality in measurement, consider physical space. We know that space has length, width, and height. Those are the three dimensions of physical space. Knowing any one of these dimensions of a space tells us quite a bit about that space. Knowing all three gives us a great deal of knowledge about the space. For example, if we know the

Directions: On the scales below, please indicate your feelings about
_____. Circle the number between the adjectives which best repres-
ents your feelings about _____. Numbers "1" and "7" indicate a very
strong feeling. Numbers "2" and "6" indicate a strong feeling. Numbers "3"
and "5" indicate a fairly weak feeling. Number "4" indicates you are
undecided or do not understand the adjectives themselves. Please work quickly.
There are no right or wrong answers.

Good	1	2	3	4	5	6	7	Bad*
Wrong	1	2	3	4	5	6	7	Right
Harmful	1	2	3	4	5	6	7	Beneficial
Fair	1	2	3	4	5	6	7	Unfair*
Wise	1	2	3	4	5	6	7	Foolish*
Negative	1	2	3	4	5	6	7	Positive

*Scoring should be reversed for these items.

Figure 8.1. General Attitude Scale

length of a room is 16 feet, this gives us some information. If we also know the
width of the room is 14 feet and the height is 8 feet, we have a much better
picture of the room. It becomes an average size room in our minds. If, however,
someone told us the size of the room was 38 feet (16 + 14 + 8), we really would
have no idea at all of what the room looked like.

The person describing the room size as 38 feet has no understanding of the
concept of physical space. He or she is adding length to width to height. That is
like adding five apples to seven oranges to four watermelons. We have 16, but
we don't know 16 what. The basic idea here is that we cannot simply add across
dimensions to obtain a score on a measure. Each dimension must have a
separate score. While there are complex mathematical methods for generating
meaningful numbers representing composites of numerous dimensions, simple
addition is not one of those methods. Thus, determining the dimensionality of a
construct prior to developing a measure for it can greatly reduce the problems of
measurement development.

Consider, for example, the concept of "interpersonal attraction." This has
to do with how much we are attracted to another person. Many researchers
have treated this concept as unidimensional, and several have used bipolar
scales to measure it. Based on the substantial theoretical work of others,
McCroskey and McCain (1974) demonstrated that this concept definitely is *not*
unidimensional. Although they did not use bipolar scales in their research, the
approach they used illustrates what researchers need to do when they suspect
the concept they want to measure is multidimensional.

Based on the work of other writers in the area of interpersonal attraction, McCroskey and McCain (1974) decided that there probably were three dimensions of interpersonal attraction—physical, task, and social attraction. They reasoned that we see some people as beautiful or handsome, but would really not like to be around them socially or work with them. Further, they presumed that we know some people we would like to socialize with because they are fun, but they are less than prize physical specimens and are goof-offs at work. Additionally, they presumed that we know some people who are very good to work with, but whom we do not want to spend time with away from work. While they recognized that some people are positively attractive to us on all three dimensions and some are repulsive on all three, it is quite possible to be attractive on one or two dimensions and repulsive on one or two others at the same time. Thus, these dimensions may operate independently.

McCroskey and McCain (1974) proceeded to construct scales to measure each of the hypothesized dimensions of interpersonal attraction (in this case they used Likert-type scales rather than bipolar scales, but the rest of their procedure is appropriate for either type of scale). After developing the scales, they randomly placed scales from all three presumed dimensions on a single instrument and had subjects respond to the scales in terms of a person with whom they interacted in a study. They then analyzed the data by means of a statistical procedure known as "factor analysis." The results confirmed the existence of the three presumed factors of attraction and the scales that had been created formed three distinct, but related, measures.

Factor analysis is a very sophisticated form of data analysis and we will not attempt to explain it fully here. For our purposes it is enough to say that factor analysis determines what groups of scales are substantially correlated with each other but not highly correlated with scales in other groups. These "groups" of scales represent the dimensions inherent in a measure. If there are no distinct groups, the measure is unidimensional. If there are two or more groups of scales, the measure is multidimensional.

Although in the McCroskey and McCain (1974) study, the factor analysis results supported the existence of the three dimensions they had presumed to exist, such supportive findings do not always occur. For example, in earlier research McCroskey (1966) had concluded from reading classical writers such as Aristotle and early social psychologists (Hovland, Janis, and Kelly, 1953) that source credibility (or as he called it at the time "ethos") was composed of three dimensions—competence (or intelligence), character (or trustworthiness), and good will (or intentions toward the receiver). After developing measures using bipolar scales as well as Likert-type scales and subjecting his data to factor analysis, he was forced to conclude the good will or intention dimension simply did not exist separate from the character or trustworthiness dimension. His findings, however, resulted in separate measures for each of the other two hypothesized dimensions (see Figure 8.2).

The importance of factor analysis in the process of developing a measure

Competence

Reliable	1	2	3	4	5	6	7	Unreliable*
Uninformed	1	2	3	4	5	6	7	Informed
Unqualified	1	2	3	4	5	6	7	Qualified
Intelligent	1	2	3	4	5	6	7	Unintelligent*
Valuable	1	2	3	4	5	6	7	Worthless*
Inexpert	1	2	3	4	5	6	7	Expert

Character

Honest	1	2	3	4	5	6	7	Dishonest*
Unfriendly	1	2	3	4	5	6	7	Friendly
Pleasant	1	2	3	4	5	6	7	Unpleasant*
Selfish	1	2	3	4	5	6	7	Unselfish
Awful	1	2	3	4	5	6	7	Nice
Virtuous	1	2	3	4	5	6	7	Sinful*

*Scoring should be reversed for these items.

Figure 8.2. Measures of Competence and Character

using the bipolar scaling methodology should not be understated. Many researchers have totally destroyed the value of their work by ignoring the dimensionality issue. Some have published research which treated every scale as an independent dimension, hence an independent measure. Single scales may be highly unreliable; thus the amount of error associated with a score on a single scale may be extremely high. Hence, differences between scores may be much larger or smaller than they appear by looking at the results generated by such scales. In contrast, some have published research in which they have summed data from scales representing several dimensions to get a single score (remember our apples, oranges, and watermelon?). Their scores, hence the entire results of their research, become instantly worthless. Imagine, for example, how you would interpret a score on interpersonal attraction that summed across physical, task, and social scales. You might decide to ask someone for a date, when he/she simply hoped you would make a job offer!

Determining the scales to include in the measure. The third and final step of the procedure for developing measures using bipolar scales is the "nuts and bolts" step. When we start this step we presume we know what it is we want to measure and its dimensions. We may discover the dimensionality of the measure is different than we presumed at the outset so that we must go through a major revision of the measure later. However, at this point we assume we know what it is we need to measure and that no appropriate measure currently is available.

Bipolar scales themselves are at the heart of the bipolar scaling methodology. On the face of it, bipolar scales seem extremely easy to construct. All you need is two words (pictures, colors, etc.) that are opposites. The rest is simple. You create some steps—3, 5, 6, 9, or whatever—in between them.

Unfortunately, it is not as simple as that, although numerous researchers have done exactly so—to the detriment of their later research. As communication teachers constantly stress to their students, words do not have meaning. Meaning is in the minds of people. Thus, concepts that seem to a researcher to be opposites of one another may not seem so to research subjects. What is the opposite of hard? To a researcher concerned with rocks, it might be "soft." To a student who has just completed an exam in another class, it might be "easy."

It is very tempting to select opposite words for scales by going to the dictionary or thesaurus. Both of these sources treat words as if they had meaning and are insensitive to context differences. Even one of the classic research efforts employing bipolar scales (Osgood, Suci, & Tannenbaum, 1957) was partially guilty of using this approach. Actually, the only way to be sure that words may be used appropriately to form bipolar scales is to be certain that research subjects, like those with whom the completed instrument will be used, will respond in opposite ways to the words.

The most direct method of determining this is to select a substantial number of words that appear to form bipolar opposites and appear to be related to whatever it is the researcher wishes to measure. Once selected, these words should be randomly placed to form an instrument like the one in Figure 8.3. You will notice the words are not placed in the form of bipolar scales but rather stand alone. The research subjects are asked to indicate on a five-point scale the degree to which each word describes the concept to be measured. Data on this working instrument from at least 100 research subjects (preferably 200 to insure stability of correlations) should be submitted to simple correlational analyses.

Words that have a perfect negative correlation (-1.00) are, of course, ideal for use in the formation of bipolar scales. Unfortunately, you are unlikely to find any such perfect correlations. As we noted before, single scales often are not very reliable and, consequently, cannot produce valid high correlations. As a rule of thumb, the correlation between words should be $-.50$ or stronger to qualify those words for use as the anchors of a bipolar scale.

If the observed correlation is smaller than $-.50$ it is an indication that one or more significant problems may be present. The most common is that different subjects are interpreting one or both words in different ways. Another is that the two words are generating responses to different things. In some instances, you may even find words you thought were opposites to be *positively* correlated. When this occurs it almost always indicates one of the words is being interpreted differently than intended. If "good" and "bad" are positively correlated, the subjects may be responding to "baaaaad" not "bad!"

Once you have selected your bipolar opposites, you must determine how many steps you want to place on your scale between them. It is customary to

Directions: Please indicate the degree to which you think each of the following words apply to _____ on a continuum of 1 to 5. Presume "5" represents *very well* and "1" represents "*very poorly*." The numbers "4," "3," and "2" represent the steps in between these extremes.

_____ good

_____ right

_____ harmful

_____ fair

_____ negative

_____ foolish

_____ beneficial

_____ wrong

_____ bad

_____ unfair

_____ wise

_____ positive

Figure 8.3. Preliminary scale items

use seven steps, although some research conducted by the present authors has indicated five steps produces the same results. There is no reason to expect major differences if one uses nine steps. Although in some instances researchers have even used 100 steps successfully, too many steps can generate false precision. It is doubtful that many people can make a distinction between 42 and 43 on the continuum between good and bad!

In general, adults and better educated subjects can handle more steps. Young children often can handle only three—each pole and "I don't know." Surveys conducted by telephone also may suffer from a large number of steps— the respondents may not be able to remember them all. In general, our advice is to use seven or five steps unless there is some very good reason to use some other number.

The final concern in developing the initial instrument is how many scales to include. Within limits, the general rule is the more the better. Of course, people will get exhausted if you ask them to respond to too many scales at one time, and your data will be worthless. Hence, it often is important to reduce the number of scales. The issues to be considered in determining how many scales must be included are primarily the *intervality* of the score on the measure and the *internal reliability* of the measure.

The use of parametric statistical analyses requires the assumption that scores analyzed are at least at the interval level. While visual examination of a bipolar scale makes it appear obvious that such scales have equal intervals, research indicates clearly that the individual scales do not (McCroskey,

Prichard, & Arnold, 1968). In fact, the two steps at the extreme poles are seen in the minds of respondents as twice as far from their neighbors as any other two steps. Thus, a single seven-step scale should probably be scored 1, 3, 4, 5, 6, 7, 9 rather than 1, 2, 3, 4, 5, 6, 7 as usually is done. This is not a serious problem, however, since this same research indicates summed scores for six scales do meet the intervality assumption. Thus, if you make certain you have at least six scales, that will be sufficient to meet the assumption of parametric statistics.

The second factor of concern is that of internal reliability. In general, measures based on the bipolar scaling approach have very high internal reliability. It has been our experience in working with bipolar scales for over 25 years that there are some very consistent patterns of association between the number of scales and the internal reliability of scores representing a summation of those scales. In general it appears that two or three scales will produce reliability of .5 to .7; four or five scales will produce reliability of .6 to .8; six to seven scales will produce reliability of .7 to .9; and eight or more scales will usually produce reliability above .9.

Mathematically, number of scales and internal reliability must be positively related if other things are equal. If you obtain reliability below the range noted above for your given number of scales, it most likely is an indication that you have multidimensionality in your measure. This is a sign that you must return to step two of this procedure; you probably have added apples and oranges to obtain your score.

Exactly how high you require your reliability to be before you are satisfied with your measure is a matter of judgement. The lower your reliability, the lower the precision in your instrument and the more likely you will have so much error in your data you will draw a false conclusion. In our view, there seldom is reason to accept internal reliability below .80 when using the bipolar scaling approach. It is simply too easy to improve the measure and thus raise the reliability. This rule should not be universally applied, however. In some cases, for example, increasing the number of items to gain better reliability might lead to exhaustion of the subjects when many measures are being completed. By adding more scales in such an instance one would simply be trading one source of error for another. Obviously, that would serve no useful purpose.

RELIABILITY OF METHOD

Reliability relates to consistency of measurement. Two types of consistency are of concern. One relates to consistency across time—if we administer the measure today and again next week, will we obtain similar (consistent) scores? This is often referred to as test-retest reliability. The second type of consistency relates to consistency within the measure. Is the score on one subset of scales within the measure highly correlated (consistent) with the score from another subset of scales? This usually is referred to as internal reliability.

The type of reliability with which a researcher may be concerned will depend on the purpose for which the measure was developed. In some cases it is assumed that what is being measured is something likely to be highly stable across time, such as a person's attitudes on some public policy questions. In other cases, it is clear that what is being measured is subject to substantial change from time to time, such as a person's mood.

When the item to be measured is subject to frequent change, the only type of reliability with which we are concerned is internal reliability. This type of reliability may be assessed through **split-half** techniques or analysis of variance procedures. But whichever method is used, internal reliability of measures employing bipolar scales, if developed properly, usually is very good. Reported reliabilities above .80 are common. Those above .90 are not unusual.

Determining the reliability across time of measures based on bipolar scaling is more complex, as it is with other types of measures. The actual computation process is easy—a simple correlation is computed. This may be between two scores on the same instrument obtained at two different times or it may be between two scores on two different, but presumably equivalent, instruments collected at two different times. The latter often is referred to as "alternate forms" reliability. Either method will provide a good estimate of the reliability of the measure if it can be established that there is no good reason to think the item measured would have changed over time. This method of measuring reliability is useless if the target of the measure is changeable, since the fact that two scores may have a low correlation may be a function of either unreliability of the measure or change in what is being measured, and there is no way to sort out these contributing factors. Although bipolar scaling has been used more commonly to measure things subject to frequent change, such as feelings and perceptions, when used to measure stable characteristics the reliability across time generally has been good.

Before leaving the topic of reliability, we should consider the placement of scales on a measure, because such placement can impact reliability. In the early development of a measure, when multidimensionality is suspected, scales should be randomly assigned to positions on the measure. This will reduce the possibility that a false "dimension" will be produced by factor analysis simply because several somewhat related scales were answered sequentially. Later, after the question of dimensionality has been settled, items on a given dimension should be grouped together. In this way respondents can focus on one thing at a time. Doing so will tend to increase reliability somewhat.

In this regard, you are cautioned to avoid one type of scale assignment that will appear to increase reliability, but will not actually do so. If you turn back to Figure 8.1 you will notice that some scales have the "good-positive" pole on the left and some have it on the right. If you put all of the positives on one side and all of the negatives on the other, reliability estimates are likely to go up. Unfortunately, this probably is a function of what is known as "response bias" rather than increased reliability. When people are responding to this type of measure they tend to get into a pattern and may not even pay attention to the individual scale to which they are responding.

The authors have seen this error made on instruments used to measure students' evaluations of classroom teachers in several universities. Unfortunately, when this is done, however the student responds to the first few items will predict with considerable accuracy how he/she responds to the later items. To break this response bias, approximately half the scales should have the "positive" pole on the left and half on the right. While this might slightly reduce the reliability estimate for the measure, it will not reduce the real reliability and might actually increase it.

VALIDITY OF THE METHOD

As noted in chapter 5, validity of a measure has to do with whether it actually measures what it is supposed to. Assessing the validity of measures based on bipolar scaling often is very difficult. This difficulty stems not from the measuring procedure but from the nature of what is being measured. Attitudes, feelings, perceptions, and the like exist in people's minds. They cannot be observed directly. Hence, measures, such as ones based on bipolar scaling, often are used to estimate them. Once such measures are developed, researchers commonly try to validate them by observing people's behavior. Such an approach often is overly simplistic.

Consider the question of attitude measurement. As noted in the previous chapter, attitudes are not always consistent with behavior. Thus, if scores on a measure based on bipolar scales do not correlate highly with observed behavior, we might be tempted to say the measure is not valid. Such a conclusion could be completely false. If a behavior is not related to an attitude, the fact a score based on a measure of that attitude does not correlate with the behavior is quite meaningless. It tells us nothing about the validity of the measure.

While we do not want to discount completely any consideration of the correlation between scores on a measure and observable behavior as a method of estimating validity, such data often will be inconclusive or misleading. Thus, it usually is necessary to consider other data in making validity judgements.

Content or **face validity** frequently are important to consider. For example, we should be able to tell something about the validity of a bipolar scaling measure just by looking at the bipolar scales employed. Which of the following scales would you think might be appropriate to measure a person's attitude toward his/her mother? (1) kind-cruel, (2) wise-foolish, (3) hot-cold, (4) timely-late, (5) good-bad, (6) fast-slow. If you picked 1, 2, and 5 your choices have been supported by research (Osgood, Suci, & Tannenbaum, 1957). If you would say those three should be better than the others, you are suggesting a scale using those three would have "face" validity—they look like they should be related to attitude toward one's mother. While it would be dangerous to base all decisions on the validity of a measure of this type on such "face" concerns, this often is a good place to start.

Concerns with **concurrent validity** are very common among researchers using the bipolar scaling methodology. Often there are complex measures already available of something of interest, which have been determined to be valid. The concern of the research may be the development of simpler measures. Bipolar scaling often is used when researchers desire simpler measures. If the bipolar scaling measure correlates well with the more complex, and previously validated, measure, it is concluded the bipolar scaling measure also has validity.

In general, bipolar scaling measures are very reliable. Any reliable measure is a valid measure of *something*; the question is whether it is a valid measure of the factor the researcher wants to measure. If the procedures described earlier in this chapter are followed, the odds are good the resulting measure will be valid for its intended purpose.

ADVANTAGES AND DISADVANTAGES OF PROCEDURE

There are two major advantages to the use of measures based on the bipolar scaling approach. First, they tend to be highly reliable and valid if properly developed. Second, they consume little subject time so that more items can be measured at one sitting without exhausting the subjects. The first advantage is a concern of all researchers. The second is particularly important to those researchers who must measure a substantial number of items at one sitting. When subjects are asked to fill out too many scales, their later responses may be little more than random.

The major disadvantage of measures based on the bipolar scaling approach is that they appear so easy to use many researchers succumb to the temptation to take shortcuts and become very sloppy. Instead of carefully designing and pretesting their measures, they may simply slap some bipolar scales together and call them a measure. They administer the "measure," add the scores across the scales, and analyze the results. As a result they may be adding across several dimensions of response, have inadequate reliability, and have no validity at all. Or they may even take every single bipolar scale as an independent measure and analyze scores for each scale separately. As noted previously, such scales typically do not even represent interval scaling, hence are not amenable to the statistical analyses to which they are typically subjected. The weakness of the bipolar scaling approach is that shoddy researchers can use it. It is not an exaggeration to say measures based on the bipolar scaling approach are no better nor worse than the researcher using them.

SUMMARY

This chapter has reviewed one of the oldest methods of measurement, the bipolar scaling technique. The three initial steps in the development of a measure employing bipolar scales are determining (1) what is to be measured, (2) how many different variables must be measured, and (3) the scales to constitute the measure.

Determining what is to be measured involves questions of validity. A measure is only of value if it measures something of importance. Once that "something" is identified, the literature must be surveyed to determine if appropriate measures already exist. This developmental stage is critical in that it establishes at the outset whether the measure ultimately developed will be of any value to researchers.

Determining how many variables are to be measured primarily involves the distinction between unidimensional and multidimensional constructs and measures. While determining unidimensionality and multidimensionality initially is considered conceptually, ultimately it must be determined empirically as well. Factor analysis frequently is employed in this process.

A decision on the scales to include in a measure presumes the researcher knows what it is she/he wants to measure, and its dimensions. Bipolar scales themselves are at the heart of the bipolar scaling methodology. The researcher must determine empirically that the scales truly are bipolar and decide how many steps will be employed between the bipolar extremes. Next, he or she must determine empirically the dimensionality of the measure, obtain estimates of the reliability and validity of the measure, and repeat these processes until the completed measure is acceptable for research purposes.

STUDY QUESTIONS

1. Describe the bipolar scaling technique. Discuss its advantages and disadvantages for social scientific research.
2. Discuss why the authors suggest, "the importance of determining what is to be measured as the first step in the measurement process cannot be overestimated."
3. Review the work of Osgood, Suci, and Tannenbaum. Describe the significance of their research for the field of communication.
4. Distinguish between "unidimensional" and "multidimensional." Identify why this distinction is necessary in bipolar scaling. Review the McCroskey/McCain interpersonal attraction measure and discuss the nature of the measure.
5. Explain why it is necessary for the researcher to determine clearly the dimensionality of a measure before using it in studies. Discuss consequences if this procedure is not followed.
6. Review the various methods of determining the words (pictures, etc.) which are used to form bipolar scales. Discuss the issues related to each method.

7. Discuss how a researcher might determine if he/she has found a useful bipolar scale.

8. Discuss the "sophistication" of the measure when administering it to adults versus children.

9. Review and discuss the reliability and validity issues as related to bipolar scaling. Discuss the issue of "scales must have equal intervals."

10. Explain why content or face validity are important to consider in bipolar scaling. Identify some bipolar scales that might be used to measure your attitude toward your teachers.

ANNOTATED READINGS

Kerlinger, F. N. (1973). *Foundations of behavioral research* (2nd ed.). New York: Holt, Rinehart and Winston.

    This text is designed to assist the student in understanding the nature of scientific behavioral research. It is specially designed for persons in the sciences and education. It is divided into the following section: language and approach of science; sets, relations, and variance; probability, randomness, and sampling; analysis, interpretation, statistics, and inference; analysis of variance; designs of research; types of research; measurement; methods of observation and data collection; multiple regression; and factor analysis.

Kerlinger, F. N. (1979). *Behavioral research: A conceptual approach.* New York: Holt, Rinehart and Winston.

    The purpose of this book is to assist students in comprehending scientific research and its components. It looks at research and applies scientific principles from a wide array of fields. It reviews the following topics: nature of science; scientific concepts; forming hypotheses; relations and explanations; probablity; design; experimental versus nonexperimental; multiple regression; factor analysis; canonical correlation; and concludes with misconceptions and controversies.

Osgood, C. E., Suci, G. J., and Tannenbaum, P. H. (1957). *The measurement of meaning.* Urbana, Ill., University of Illinois Press.

    This book is a report on the authors' research program on measurement of meaning. It discusses their ongoing program of research and reviews more than fifty studies. It is the text which introduced the field to semantic differentiation through the use of bipolar scaling. This is the most extensive single research program based on bipolar scaling extant in the literature.

CHAPTER 9

Survey Research

By Deborah A. Barker,
Windward Communications, Inc.
Larry L. Barker,
Auburn University

A young married couple has just moved to a new city and plans to open a professional videotaping service. Their immediate target audience includes realtors, lawyers, and physicians in the area. Two problems which they must address, however, are how to determine the community's need for these professionals concerning their service, and how to "educate" the community regarding the value of video, if a need is not perceived.

A large subsidiary of a corporation has had administrative problems for the last three years. In fact, the top administration has turned over at least five times. Finally, the parent corporation decides that something must be done. They have learned, in recent weeks, that net profits of the subsidiary are plummeting, and that the job turnover rate at lower levels is on the rise.

What do these scenarios have in common? Had we asked you this question in person, you might have replied, "Very little!" However, for the consulting firm which has just been contacted by both clients to gather information, several commonalities emerge. First, both clients are in need of information albeit at different levels. Second, several research methods may be used to gather data for each. Of greater interest in this chapter is that both clients could benefit from the use of a survey to collect the data in which they are interested. Although each survey instrument would differ in purpose and, ultimately, in form, the method itself could easily be adapted to suit the needs of both clients.

In the following pages, a variety of survey topics will be explored that are applicable to these and other scenarios. First, we will address the purposes and methods employed in survey research—as well as how to select the best survey method. Second, we will briefly address the selection of survey respondents. Included as topics in this discussion will be four basic sampling designs and the actual procedures that are used in generating a sample. Third, we will focus on how to design an effective survey instrument, including how to write questions, how to construct the final questionnaire, and how to improve your instrument all along the way. Finally, we will discuss how to prepare for the data entry and analysis stages of a survey. Because of the space limitations a chapter (rather than a textbook) imposes, no discussion of data analysis procedures will be included.

SURVEY RESEARCH: PURPOSES AND METHODS

Researchers across the social sciences use surveys for a variety of reasons. In fact, it probably would be safe to say that there are as many purposes for doing survey research as there are survey researchers who do it. For example, surveys have been used to describe characteristics of graduate programs in speech communication—as well as to compare these programs on a number of criteria. Radio and television stations have commissioned surveys to determine listener and viewer habits and to find out what motivates people to listen/watch at a given time. And, of course, politicians and advertisers rely heavily on surveys for information—as well as to provide them with an index of voter or consumer preferences and attitudes.

As you can see, the list could go on and on. However, underlying each possible reason is one of three primary goals or objectives (Babbie, 1973): description, explanation, and exploration. Each of these purposes will be addressed in the following paragraphs.

Purposes of Survey Research

Whenever a researcher (or client of a researcher) is interested in determining the characteristics of a specific population, or in comparing the attributes of several groups, programs or events, his or her primary aim is that of *description*. In such instances, the researcher is not interested in "why" these characteristics exist. Rather she is interested in simply describing such things as beliefs, attitudes, values, motives, etc. As an example, description is the primary aim in public opinion polls. In addition, it is the goal of election polls and consumer market studies.

While all surveys are partially descriptive in nature, others target *explanation* as their primary aim. For example, a research team may be interested in explaining specific consumer habits, such as *why* some househusbands prefer scented over unscented cleaning products. Or a corporation might hire an outside consultant to assess why job satisfaction in the company is at an all-time low. Such explanatory objectives as these require the use of a different set of analyses (generally multivariate in nature) and, as we will discuss later, a different level of measurement.

Finally, surveys are useful for *exploring* uncharted territory—or some topic which the researcher is only beginning to investigate. For example, after the explosion of the space shuttle Challenger in 1986, many researchers became interested in the perceptions of Americans concerning the space program, overall, and in assessing the impact of the destruction of a national symbol. Surveys were one means by which the topic was explored.

These three purposes or aims are the basic objectives of any survey. However, as we implied at the beginning of this section, any or all combinations of the three may be employed. Given a clear understanding of the goals of the survey researcher, we now turn to a discussion of the three primary data collection methods used in survey research.

Data Collection Methods

Survey data may be generated in several ways, depending on the survey's purpose, the targeted population, the time frame of the study, and the number of available resources. The three primary data collection techniques that are used are: (1) face-to-face interviews, (2) telephone interviews, and (3) postal questionnaires. Because each of these techniques is discussed at length in several current survey research texts (Babbie, 1973; Backstrom & Hursh-Cesar, 1981; Fowler, 1984; de Vaus, 1986), this discussion will focus on the appropriateness of their use and the advantages and disadvantages of each.

Face-to-Face Interviews. Whenever a researcher makes a decision to employ the survey as a tool, he also must decide which survey method is the most appropriate. Face-to-face interviews may be one of his primary options. Generally, this method is used when:

a. complete or detailed answers are desirable;
b. a high response rate is needed;
c. respondents may have difficulty in reading, understanding, or interpreting questions;
d. assurance is needed that respondents do not collaborate with others when answering questions;
e. spontaneous reactions are desired;
f. observations and recording of nonverbal behaviors are desired; and/or
g. greater amounts of time are required to collect the data (Tucker, Weaver, Berryman-Fink, 1981, p. 104).

For example, when gathering data from low income groups about their knowledge of nutrition and child care, the researcher might find the interview format produces the most valid and reliable results. The primary reason is that such groups may respond more willingly and truthfully in a face-to-face interview.

Advantages of face-to-face interviews include the ability to answer respondent questions, to probe inadequate answers, and to build rapport and confidence whenever necessary. Additionally, longer interviews can be conducted when the meeting is face-to-face. As a result, this type of interview usually results in more complete, usable data.

Face-to-face interviews also have several distinct disadvantages. Because a trained staff of interviewers will be needed to complete the survey, the costs of conducting the overall study will be higher. Furthermore, this data collection procedure requires a more extensive time frame, given the need to carefully train and monitor interviewers. Problems also arise when researchers attempt to schedule the interviews. Finally, the researcher is generally more limited regarding the geographical distance covered, since budgets for most surveys do not carry an unlimited expense account.

Telephone Surveys. The second data collection procedure that the researcher may use is the telephone interview. Like face-to-face interviews, telephone surveys are useful when (1) high response rates are needed, and (2) more complete or detailed answers to questions are required. Like face-to-face interviews, using the telephone also allows the interviewer to put the respondent at ease.

The distinction between face-to-face and telephone interviews, however, is in the added advantages associated with the latter method. First, more geographically distant populations may be included in the survey at a lower cost, since the interviewer is only required to pick up the phone. Second, the data collection period usually is shorter, thereby providing additional time for the researcher to complete other phases of the study. Third, the staffing and management of interviewers is generally easier, and quality control is potentially higher.

Telephone surveys also have their own unique disadvantages. First, random digit dialing (despite its sampling advantages) often produces higher rates of nonresponse than do face-to-face interviews. Thus, additional time is needed to increase the overall response rate. Second, telephone surveys cannot reach respondents who do not have telephones; therefore, the representativeness of the sample may be limited. Finally, this data collection method may be less appropriate for personal or sensitive questions, especially if no prior contact has been established.

Postal Surveys. This third data collection method involves the transmission of a questionnaire through the mail, accompanied by a letter of explanation and a return envelope. Respondents then complete the questionnaire and return it in the mail, using the envelope provided. (See Babbie, 1973, for a more complete discussion.) Generally, this data collection technique is appropriate for regional or national surveys, especially when time and money are important factors. For example, a public relations firm might be interested in the effectiveness of a campaign it is conducting across several regions. Using a postal survey would allow the firm to make such an assessment, especially if a high response rate is not of central concern.

The advantages of using a postal survey are several and include the ease of presenting questions requiring visual aids, of asking questions with long or complex response categories, or of asking batteries of similar questions (Fowler, 1984, p. 71). Additionally, the respondent can choose not to share answers with the researcher, thus alleviating some of the respondent's apprehension. Third, when compared with either the in-person or telephone interview, the mail survey offers reduced costs and minimal staffing as advantages. Fourth, a wider geographical sampling of the targeted population may be achieved, including those respondents who might be difficult or impossible to interview. Finally, by its very nature, a mail survey gives respondents additional time to reply—as well as to provide more complete and thoughtful answers (Fowler, p. 71).

At least three disadvantages exist when using mail surveys, however. First, depending on the respondents who are targeted, the overall response rate will be low. As a rule, the "success" rate of most mail surveys is less than 35 percent. Second, the questionnaire must be designed with both skill and care, with as few open-ended questions included as possible. The latter is especially important, given that the researcher is not present to exercise quality control. Third, the researcher must be sure that she has targeted a population with good reading and writing skills. If they are not endowed with such abilities, validity and reliability of the survey may be reduced. In addition, respondents' poor writing skills can make data coding and entry more difficult.

As you can see, many options exist regarding survey objectives and methods. Whether the researcher is attempting to determine the popularity of a political candidate or the effectiveness of an ongoing ad campaign, employing the appropriate methods and techniques will allow him to compile an effective final report. To conduct the final survey, however, the researcher will need to rely heavily on his knowledge of sampling designs and procedures. It is to a discussion of these topics that we now turn.

SELECTING THE SURVEY SAMPLE

One way a researcher can gather information about a specific group of people is to ask everyone in that group to complete a survey. However, if that group is extremely large, the time and costs involved will be prohibitive. One alternative way she can gather the necessary data is to collect information from only some members of the group—but to do so in such a way that their responses will be representative of the group overall. Common sense should tell her that this procedure is less costly, faster and easier than collecting data from all group members. This process of collecting data from a portion of a group is known as **sampling**.

Before we begin a discussion of particular sampling procedures, it may be useful to define some of the technical terms associated with "sampling." Whenever a researcher collects data from every member of a group, she is conducting what is known as a **census**. The group of people from which she would be gathering such information represents the **population** in which she is interested. A **sample**, then, is obtained by collecting data from only a portion of that population, or from specific **elements** involved (i.e., people, families, social clubs, or corporations). Additionally, in survey research, an emphasis is placed on obtaining a **representative sample**, or a sample that accurately reflects its overall population (de Vaus, 1986, p. 52).

To ensure that a sample indeed is representative, the researcher must be certain that particular types of people in the population are not systematically excluded. For example, if a researcher completed a telephone survey during the hours of eight to five on a weekday, not only would he be excluding those members of the population who do not have telephones, but also those who work at eight-to-five jobs. Such a sample would be **biased** rather than representative and, as a result, the conclusions could not be generalized to the entire population—at least not without appropriate statistical adjustments (de Vaus, 1986, p. 52).

Before beginning to draw a sample, the researcher also must decide whether the sample will be a probability or nonprobability sample. A **probability sample** is one in which every member of the population has an equal and known chance of being selected. A **nonprobability** sample is one in which some members have a greater chance than others of being selected. To ensure the representativeness of a sample, the ideal is to choose a probability sample. The best way to create such a sample is to use the principle of **random selection**, which involves creating a *sampling frame*, or a list of all members of the population, and either "pulling their names out of the hat" (termed the *lottery method* of selection) or using a random number table to generate the sample (de Vaus, 1986, pp. 52–53). Each of these methods will be discussed more completely in the following pages.

Although using a probability sample will increase the chances that a sample is representative, some differences—by chance alone—will emerge between the sample and the overall population. These differences are due in part to **sampling error**, or inaccuracies that were generated throughout the measurement process. Fortunately, because most random samples produce estimates that are close to those in the population, a statistic called **standard error** can be used to estimate the sampling error generated in a particular study. The computation of standard error allows the researcher to estimate the accuracy of his or her statistics, and provides a **confidence level** regarding the degree to which the description of the sample matches an accurate description of the population, could such a description be obtained (de Vaus, 1986, p. 53).

Sample Size

Although deciding what type of sample will be used is indeed an important factor, another variable of concern is that of sample size, or the number of elements to be included in the final survey. Ideally, this number is determined by the statistical model employed, by the number of items or questions that have been generated for the survey, and through the use of statistical power tables, which are designed to take the guesswork out of determining sample size (Tucker, Weaver, & Berryman-Fink, p. 159). An example of a power table is included in Figure 9.1. However, in actual practice, time and budgetary constraints may limit the sample size selected. Likewise, the pool of qualified respondents may be limited, and some of the desired respondents may object to participating in the study.

How then does the researcher decide how many elements to include in a given survey? Ultimately, the answer is based on (1) an estimation of the population size, (2) the number of subgroups that must be represented within that population, and (3) the percentage of respondents that must be contacted in order to ensure representativeness. Because each of these variables will vary from survey to survey, so, too, the necessary percentage of respondents will change from study to study. For example, if the population of interest equals one million and you are conducting a radio listenership survey, 3 to 5 percent of the population may be an adequate sample size. However, if the targeted population is 100 families of children stricken by AIDS, and that population varies across a number of ethnic, social, and economic levels, you may need to aim for as high as a 50% sample size. As desirable as a single percentage might be in determining every sample size, such a suggestion at this point would be highly misleading. At all times, the representativeness of a given sample should be the primary criterion.

Types of Sampling Designs

To this point in the discussion, we have treated populations as if they were generally homogeneous, and all samples as if they were simple random samples. In reality, neither is true—a fact that has produced several sampling designs from which the researcher may choose. In the following pages, four basic sampling designs will be discussed. Included are those that utilize: (1) simple random samples, (2) systematic samples, (3) stratified samples, and (4) multi-stage area or cluster samples.

Simple Random Sample (SRS). Five basic steps are used to generate a simple random samples:

1. Create a complete sampling frame.
2. Assign a unique number to each element, beginning with the number one (1).
3. Decide on the required sample size for the survey. .
4. Select that many numbers through either the lottery method or through the use of a random number table.
5. Survey the elements which correspond with the numbers randomly selected (de Vaus, 1986, p. 53).

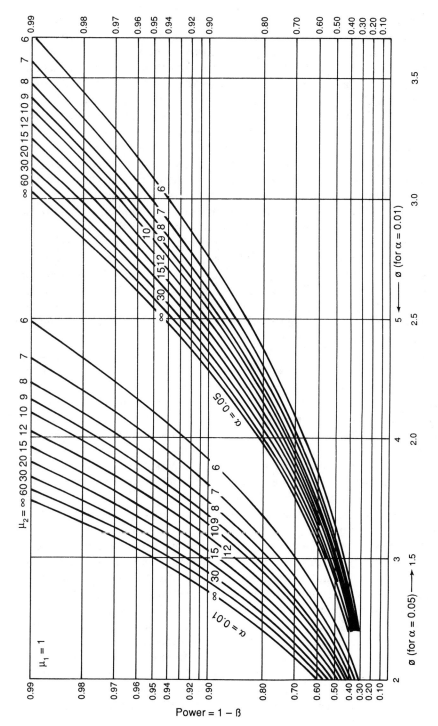

Figure 9.1. Sample Power Table (Reproduced with permission from E. S. Pearson and H. O. Hartley.)

175

As we have stated here and in an earlier section, random numbers may be generated through a variety of methods. The two methods used most often, however, include the use of a lottery procedure or random number table.

When using the lottery method, the researcher assigns each element a sequential number, as suggested above. The corresponding numbers are written on separate slips of paper and are placed into a revolving drum or closed container. The numbers are then tossed; a single slip of paper is selected; the number is recorded; and the slip of paper is tossed back into the drum to be tossed, again. *Note: The slip of paper must be returned to the pool in order to ensure an equal and known chance of each respondent being selected.* Should the same number be selected twice, the second drawing is ignored; the number is returned to the pool; the drum is tumbled again, and another number is selected and recorded. Drawing and tumbling continue until the number of slips drawn and tabulated equals that of the predetermined sample size. Thus, if sample size = 25, 25 numbers should be selected and recorded (Leedy, 1980, p. 112).

Although the lottery method is sometimes used by researchers, the most frequently used method for random selection involves a table of random numbers. Figure 9.2 presents a portion of a table of random numbers. (Complete tables of random numbers may be found in most statistics textbooks, and computer programs are available to generate their own series of random numbers and to print out the list of elements selected.)

When using the table of random numbers, the researcher may enter at any point, and numbers may be selected by moving horizontally or vertically within the chart. Thus, with the predetermined sample size in mind, the reseacher selects (and records) the corresponding number of random numbers by moving systematically from row to row or column to column within the table until the process is complete. If the sample size is less than 100, only two-digit numbers are selected; if it is less than 1000, only three-digit numbers are selected. If a number comes up twice or is larger than the designated sample size, the researcher should simply ignore it and continue to move through the table according to the fixed pattern. Once the appropriate number of random numbers is recorded, those elements with corresponding numbers are then selected for the sample.

Although simple random sampling is the simplest sampling procedure to employ, it is the least sophisticated of all sampling procedures. Perhaps its greatest weakness is that the design overlooks heterogeneity among population subgroups. Thus, it should not be used when important subgroups of a population must be represented. Another problem of simple random sampling is that it requires a comprehensive and accurate sampling frame, which sometimes is difficult to obtain for larger populations such as a city, state, or country. Likewise, when populations are drawn from large areas (e.g., a region or nation), conducting personal interviews based on this sampling procedure becomes prohibitive. In short, simple random sampling is best when the researcher has an excellent sampling frame, when postal rather than other data

5	27	115	453	1681	6007	913	1414	272	8905
978	5727	5559	1811	836	8715	4761	135	7959	6544
7628	6876	2602	3730	8958	176	436	1033	2278	4371
5722	4993	8461	5823	8794	358	2996	4757	1576	6648
5700	4366	4903	118	6584	8440	1385	2353	1654	8744
7576	6760	2378	3429	9176	4193	2572	7699	3045	8979
6467	7993	9753	6577	1689	939	429	4130	914	8315
1665	5155	5946	9286	2201	9629	7968	1148	5174	713
7710	9840	9655	9364	9291	1475	5228	8090	1489	6131
3379	5097	172	5161	9421	75	5657	3273	8721	2873
8745	6613	972	6319	9166	8126	6261	4426	211	1431
6686	7241	3270	4450	7272	3584	6055	4070	9927	2930
8239	3058	4200	7677	8265	494	8585	7057	5082	6977
6122	3941	8550	5832	8044	5776	2264	1600	9221	925
2560	7032	9153	1634	7426	9848	2255	4900	9104	521
1195	2475	4099	2319	7022	1261	4369	4862	9851	5348
3430	2450	3831	937	1139	8404	174	5411	895	6671
1971	1792	3013	1945	4558	9840	8020	9560	5179	5039
3623	6385	5700	6733	9100	4002	2109	6640	858	5383
4577	9018	2918	6344	1801	3714	6073	3011	3409	3358
9461	6550	4149	5943	8318	6415	3632	4056	1643	3360
5371	1981	3551	3468	8863	1965	2021	4444	8475	855
8854	5426	2870	8391	4513	1558	8733	8377	1662	4584
2543	4001	1119	702	4144	8545	3973	6936	5859	2729
3639	7276	906	9953	1568	9827	4854	679	391	6234
3883	7197	8230	4610	3589	38	7931	7243	2078	7278
4968	4305	1121	7976	7771	4839	9094	1012	4227	6252
9471	556	8097	3581	8610	9435	9113	9768	6592	1636
489	8209	4848	5206	7611	8806	4339	6782	1640	8800
8037	9022	1800	9606	1437	2168	73	924	4888	1012
2077	3357	1450	8485	7861	801	4061	7154	6372	3849
5748	9846	7346	5457	6631	675	4368	131	1480	7696
2856	7878	1561	8461	6719	4168	4538	9711	7428	7170
6165	2459	9271	3495	7528	3713	4521	3713	1584	6089
2279	8876	2741	6569	4739	9316	3248	5643	4624	6956
117	8100	7547	2379	6351	6699	3036	7923	217	9990
7992	8040	6313	5521	6308	8161	2189	9687	8421	3340

Figure 9.2. Portion of a Random Number Table

collection methods are employed, and when the population of interest is geographically concentrated (de Vaus, 1986, p. 56).

Systematic Sampling. Much like simple random sampling, systematic sampling requires five basic steps:

1. Generate a complete sampling frame.
2. Assign a unique number to each element in the frame, beginning with the number one (1).

3. Divide the desired sample size by the population size to determine the sampling interval (or the distance between elements to be selected).
4. Select a starting point in the sampling frame by choosing the initial number from a random number table.
5. Choose every Nth number after that one from the sampling frame, using the sampling ratio (or the proportion of elements in the population to be selected, calculated by dividing the desired sample size by the population size).

To illustrate, if a researcher's population size is 200 and her desired sample size is 50, the sampling ratio for her survey would be equal to 1/4. Thus, she would select every fourth element from her sampling frame, given a sampling interval of N = 4. To ensure a random start, however, she would first consult a random number table to select the initial number. If the number she selected was nine (9), she would include that number in her list, and then select every fourth element after that one.

Perhaps the greatest advantage of this sampling method is convenience: the resulting sample can be obtained much more easily than is possible with other methods. Additionally, if the elements of the sampling frame are randomized in advance of actual sampling, systematic samples drawn from that list indeed are random. However, one inherent danger exists if the sampling frame is not randomized in advance, or if the arrangement of the list involves some cyclical pattern. To illustrate consider a sampling frame comprised of a list of married couples, with the husband's name listed first followed by that of the wife. If the sampling interval is equal to four and the initial number chosen is equal to 5, the final sample would be comprised of only males (de Vaus, 1986, pp. 56–57). The term used to describe this danger is **periodicity**. It can be overcome by carefully examining the sampling frame and by taking steps to counteract any cyclical ordering (e.g., through the use of randomization).

Stratified Sampling. Although SRS and systematic sampling are both useful to the researcher, at times they may restrict the degree of representativeness he can achieve in a given survey. Consider, for example, a case in which an outside research team is hired by a large company to conduct a communication audit. Among the tasks the consultants have been asked to accomplish is a survey to determine overall level of job satisfaction. Although the survey format will be useful to this research team, they realize that employees may be more or less satisfied, depending on the department and level of management in which they work. How do they overcome the problem of surveying too few administrators and too many lower-level employees? (Note: Simple random sampling or systematic sampling could produce this result.) The solution lies in organizing the population into homogeneous subsets (or strata) before the survey begins, based on any important variables of specific concern (e.g., department and management level). By first identifying any important **stratifying variables** such as these, the consultants can better ensure correct representation in the sample.

As we stated, for the research team described above, department and management level are at least two highly salient stratifying variables. Thus, before conducting their survey on job satisfaction, the researchers will group their potential respondents based on both of these variables. Then, on the basis of the relative proportion of their population represented by each group, they will select—either randomly or systematically—the number of employees from each group that constitutes the same proportion of their desired sample size. For example, if supervisors across all departments in the company constituted 10 percent of the total population, and the research team desired a sample of 800 employees, the team would select 80 supervisors to complete their final survey. In this way, the researchers could *ensure* representativeness for this group and any others they surveyed through the use of stratification. In addition, this sampling method would give them two additional options; they could use either a random sample or a systematic sample.

To this point we have discussed three primary sampling methods researchers use to generate a representative sample. However, with each of these methods come several distinct disadvantages, including the need for a comprehensive sampling frame and the necessity of geographical concentration if face-to-face interviews are conducted. The final sampling method that we shall discuss reflects an attempt to overcome these problems. That method has been termed multistage "area" or "cluster" sampling.

Multistage Area or Cluster Sampling. This method of generating a final sample involves a series of two basic steps, each of which is used over and over until a final list of survey respondents (or elements) is obtained. To describe this sampling method, an example is provided. Note the (1) listing then (2) sampling sequence that is used.

1. Generate a complete list of areas or regions, from which the final sample will be drawn. (Usually this list will be comprised of such elements as geographic areas, census districts, electorates, etc.)
2. Using simple random sampling, draw a sample of those areas to be used to help construct the next primary sampling frame. (Generally larger samples are selected first, and then, progressively, smaller areas are chosen.)
3. Compile a sampling frame of elements located within the areas generated in #2 above.
4. Select a random sample of those elements comprising the frame in #3 above.
5. Continue this process until the elements comprising the final sampling frame are the specific list of elements that you are targeting.
6. Select a random sample of elements, who will complete the survey.

To illustrate, a small computer company is interested in the openness of U.S. colleges and universities to a new computer software package—a package which, for example, could cut student registration time in half! (Oh, don't we wish?) As you might guess, to set up face-to-face interviews (desired by the company) in every college and university in the United States could be prohibitive, especially to a company that has just invested almost everything in the package it wishes to market. To overcome this problem, the company might begin by compiling a list of states, while at the same time carefully grouping states by geographic region. (In this instance, stratification would be necessary to ensure regional representativeness.) Once this list was compiled, the company could draw a random sample of states and compile a list of all colleges and universities within those states. The company could then select a random sample of specific institutions to be contacted by its marketing department. In this way, the computer company could ensure representativeness, while at the same time limiting the personal contacts that it needed to make.

Although this example is admittedly farfetched, it does illustrate the steps used in multistage cluster sampling. As implied above, this sampling method has several distinct advantages. First, it does not require a comprehensive sampling frame at the onset. Second, larger geographic regions can be covered, while minimizing the costs of final interviews or mail surveys. Finally, when coupled with stratification, this method optimizes the chances of obtaining a representative sample, a primary goal of any survey researcher. One distinct disadvantage, however, has been associated with the method as well. Because both listing and sampling occur at several stages, inaccuracies (i.e., sampling error) invariably will creep in at each successive stage. Hence, the fewer the stages that are used, the more accurate will be the final results and overall conclusions.

To this point in the chapter, we have discussed several purposes and methods used in survey research. In addition, we have addressed in detail sampling designs and procedures. We now turn to the nuts and bolts of every survey: the design and construction of the final survey instrument.

DESIGNING THE SURVEY INSTRUMENT

Once a researcher knows that she is going to use a survey format and has decided on the population to be sampled, her next task is to actually construct the survey instrument. Although other aspects of survey research may be highly technical, this phase requires a subtle blend of creativity and skill—in order to frame questions that will tap what they are designed to tap.

When you begin to design a survey instrument, three major variables should be taken into account. First, you must consider the method by which the data will be collected—i.e., whether you will use an interview format (either face-to-face or telephone) or whether you will employ a mail (or postal) survey. Second, based on the purpose of the survey (i.e., description, explanation, or exploration), you must consider the level of measurement that is required. Third, and of equal importance, you should take into account the means by which you ultimately will process the data. Each of these factors are considered as follows.

Data Collection Method

If we were to show you a sample of three basic survey instruments, each constructed for a different data collection method, you probably would perceive very few differences at first glance. The reason is that certain principles of good question wording apply to all questionnaires. (In a later section of this chapter, we will discuss these basic principles.) However, if you were to examine each instrument more closely, you probably would discern a number of differences. Generally, these differences emerge as a function of the amount of control the researcher has over respondents' exposure to questions, the manner in which technical subjects are handled, and the way in which demographic items are approached (Backstrom & Hursh-Cesar, 1981, p. 177).

For example, think for a moment about the nature of face-to-face inteviews. Because the interviewer has access to a variety of verbal and nonverbal cues, he can ask more lengthy, in-depth and complicated questions. He can also probe responses that are either incomplete or vague. As a result, face-to-face interviews allow the inclusion of a greater number of highly personal, and technical questions. They also provide an excellent format for open-ended, contingency or follow-up questions.

As with face-to-face interviews, telephone interviews allow a greater number of questions to be asked. However, telephone interviews generally are briefer because (1) respondents have the option of hanging up the phone, and (2) the costs of the survey may escalate if long-distance calls are necessary. With telephone surveys, questions generally are less technical, since the interviewer has only verbal cues to interpret. They also tend to be less personal, since respondents can again hang up the phone at any time. (Note: For this reason, demographic questions are usually asked at the end of the survey). In addition, respondents tend to give more lengthy and rapid replies to open-ended questions. As a result, a greater number of closed-ended questions usually are used (Backstrom & Hursh-Cesar, 1981, p. 180).

When comparing mail surveys to the two methods discussed above, the "control" variable becomes particularly salient. Indeed, with this data collection method, the researcher loses *all* control over subject responses. Given this problem, she must be prepared to have her questionnaire answered by someone other than the respondent selected, thrown away upon initial reception, or trashed at the first sign of a threatening or embarrassing question (Backstrom & Hursh-Cesar, 1981, p. 83). As a result, assuming that she can get her foot in the door, the researcher must word each question in a straightforward and diplomatic way. She also should avoid highly technical jargon, any threatening or potentially embarrassing questions, or any questions that may seem irrelevant to the respondent. In addition, the more brief the survey instrument is, the greater the likelihood that it will be returned. As a result, mail surveys generally employ a greater number of closed-ended questions and, as a rule, are no greater than two to three pages in length.

Level of Measurement

Another variable the researcher must take into account when designing a survey instrument is the type of data analysis to be conducted. More specifically, he must determine whether or not he can measure a given variable of interest and, if so, how he can do so in such a way to permit the required analysis. For example, if a purely descriptive analysis is the goal, he may use questions that reflect less vigor regarding the measurement process. However, if explanation is his goal, he must construct questions that allow for more accurate measurement.

In this section, we will address the four primary levels of measurement that must be considered during questionnaire construction. Included in the discussion are nominal, ordinal, interval, and ratio level variables.

Survey questions reflecting the **nominal level** of measurement merely allow the researcher to distinguish among categories of a variable. For example, sex, religious or political affiliation, college major, and race are nominal level variables. Generally, the categories which comprise such variables are mutually exclusive in nature (i.e., a member of one category cannot be a member of another) (Babbie, 1973, p. 138).

Variables reflecting an ordinal level of measurement usually take the form of "rank order" variables. In other words, they reflect some type of order on an index or scale. Three examples of ordinal-level variables are social class (lower, middle, and upper), university class or status (freshman, sophomore, junior, and senior), and rank (private, sergeant, corporal, major, and general). Although ordinal measures indeed reflect ranking and may correspond with increasing (or decreasing) scales, these numbers have no actual meaning other than as an indication of rank order. Thus, while members of a higher socio-economic class may be wealthier than members of a lower socio-economic class, ordinal measures would not indicate how much more wealthy they are (Babbie, 1973, pp. 138–139).

One step up from ordinal level is the interval level of measurement. Although interval level variables also have numbers associated with them, the distances between each number have real or actual meaning. Perhaps, the most common example of such a variable is the Fahrenheit temperature scale. On this scale, the difference between 70 and 80 degrees is the same as that between 90 and 100 degrees (Babbie, 1973, p. 139).

If we structure a question at the ratio level of measurement, we have done so with the maximum amount of vigor in measurement possible. In addition to knowing that the distances between the numbers on a scale are actually meaningful, with ratio level measures, we also know the true zero point. Such measures allow for direct comparison since knowing the zero point alows us to multiply, divide and perform other complex functions (Backstrom & Hursh-Cesar, 1981, p. 135). Examples of variables operationalized at this level include average income, height, weight, and length of time that you have owned an automobile.

Data Processing Considerations

A third major factor that should be taken into account when constructing a survey instrument is the type of data processing to be ultimately used. This factor is essential to consider if data from the questionnaire are to be entered directly into the computer. To ensure a minimum of problems at this later stage, it is useful to construct a code book of all variables, variable names, and the columns into which a given datum will be entered into the computer. Once such a code book has been constructed, notations concerning column assignments can then be placed on the questionnaire itself. Figure 9.3 illustrates this form of questionnaire precoding.

A second way in which data processing can be facilitated at the question-naire construction phase is to use numbers rather than letters or words themselves to indicate each possible response. For example, when asking respondents to indicate a range within which they fall regarding income, the following format would facilitate later coding and/or data entry.

X. What would you estimate your present income range to be? (Check one)

_____ (1) Less than $20,000
_____ (2) $20,000–$40,000
_____ (3) More than $40,000

Such numbering of ALL responses in the questionnaire will reduce coding and data entry headaches at a later point.

Once a researcher has considered the survey method to be used, the level of measurement that he wishes to ultimately obtain, and the method by which he will process the final data, he is ready to begin the process of questionnaire construction. The following discussion presents the types of questions that he may use and examples of each.

Writing Questions

In constructing a survey instrument, primarily two types of questions are used: open-ended and closed-ended. With **open-ended questions** the respondent is asked to provide her own answers. The question is asked and a space is provided for the response. **Closed-ended questions**, on the other hand, ask for a response

---

The first set of questions that we would like to ask concerns Radio Stations in the _____county area.

(7)   1. First, do you ever listen to the ratio?   (1) Yes (2) No
            ***If yes, continue survey.
            ***If no, go to page 6, question #17.

(8)   2. Do you ever listen to AM radio?   (1) Yes (2) No

(9)   3. Do you ever listen to FM radio?   (1) Yes (2) No

(10–16) 4. What time of the day would you say that you listen to the radio most often?

      _____ (0/1) 6 am to 9 am   _____ (0/1) 1 pm to 5 pm
      _____ (0/1) 9 am to 12 pm   _____ (0/1) 5 pm to 6 pm
      _____ (0/1) 12 pm to 1 pm   _____ (0/1) 6 pm to 10 pm
                                   _____ (0/1) after 10 pm

(17)   5. Do you ever listen to the radio while at work?   (1) Yes (2) No

(18)   6. Do you ever listen to the news on the radio?   (1) Yes (2) No

---

(19)   6a. Which do you prefer: local or national news?
                   _____ (1) Local
                   _____ (2) National
                   _____ (3) Both
                   _____ (4) Neither

---

(20)   7. Do you ever listen to the radio for emergency broadcasts, including weather warnings?   (1) Yes (2) No

*Note: Number in parentheses beside each question is the card column(s) associated with each question. Number in parentheses beside each possible response is the code to be entered into the computer.

Figure 9.3. Sample from a Pre-coded Questionnaire*

---

to be selected from a predetermined list provided by the researcher. The respondent reads the question and corresponding responses and then selects the appropriate response. Open- and closed-ended questions, however, may be divided into several different categories, as discussed in the following paragraphs.

Open-ended Questions. Open-ended questions may be categorized into one of two major types: (1) fill-in-the-blank questions, and (2) written statements asking for either a paragraph or short essay. Fill-in-the-blank questions are used to elicit information that is unique to each respondent and must be non-threatening in content. Examples might include:

7. Number of years you have worked with the company: _____

8. Position that you currently hold: _____

A request for a written paragraph or essay is usually used when a researcher is attempting to determine general feelings or to assess the reasons behind a specific attitude or opinion. For example, two follow-up questions that might ask for a paragraph or essay, given earlier negative responses, are:

15a. Why do you feel that your work is unsatisfying?

      _____

      _____

      _____

19b. What variables do you feel caused the climate in your office to change?

      _____

      _____

      _____

      _____

Closed-ended Questions. Closed-ended questions may be categorized into one of five major types: (1) dichotomous, (2) multiple-choice, (3) check list, (4) ranking, and (5) attitudinal scales. Generally, closed-ended questions are easy to use because the interviewer or respondent may simply check off or circle the appropriate response. They are also easy to work with at the data processing and analysis stages.

Dichotomous questions are "either-or" questions. They are asked to determine if respondents "agree" or "disagree" with certain statements, or whether they do or do not think, act, believe or feel a certain way. Also considered to be dichotomous are "yes-no" questions. Two examples might be:

1. Have you ever participated in the Model _____ (1) Yes _____
    U.N. Program at your college or _____ (2) No
    university?

    If Yes:

    1a. Did you approve or dis-   _____ (1) Approve
         approve of the way   _____ (2) Disapprove
         the program was run?   _____ (3) No opinion

Although the "No Opinion" category in #1a above provides a third, alternative response, the question would still be categorized as dichotomous in nature. The inclusion of the latter response category simply allows respondents with no definite opinion to avoid being placed in a forced choice situation.

Multiple-choice questions, on the other hand, generally include three or more possible responses, and are usually placed in a list from which the respondent is asked to choose. Both dichotomous and multiple-choice questions should be worded in such a way that the respondents will be compelled to select one and *only* one answer. Examples might include:

15. About how long have you lived in Lee County?
     _____ (1) 0–5 years   _____ (4) 16–20 years
     _____ (2) 6–10 years   _____ (5) more than 20 years
     _____ (3) 11–15 years

22. Do you feel that WQED is doing an *excellent* job, a *good* job, a *fair* job, or a *poor* job regarding public service in the Auburn area?
     _____ (1) Excellent   _____ (3) Fair
     _____ (2) Good   _____ (4) Poor
              _____ (5) Don't Know

As you can see, multiple-choice questions should provide a set of response categories which are mutually exclusive (i.e., which compel the respondent to select only one response). In addition, the set of potential responses should be as exhaustive as possible.

Checklist questions are another form of closed-ended question. However, with these questions, the respondent is allowed to select multiple responses. Consider the following example:

4. Do you subscribe to any news-
    paper(s) on a delivery basis?   _____ (1) Yes   _____ (2) No

---

4a. To which paper or papers do you subscribe?

_____ Auburn Bulletin   _____ Birmingham News

_____ Opelika/Auburn   _____ Montgomery
          News   Advertiser

_____ Atlanta Constitution _____ USA Today

_____ Wallstreet Journal   _____ Other (Please specify):

Because multiple responses can create difficulties for the researcher at the data entry and analysis stages (the number of responses to be tabulated will equal more than 100 percent), he should be certain that the question is of great importance and that it could not be asked in such a way as to produce mutually exclusive categories. However, if the question must be asked in checklist form, the researcher can partially overcome data entry problems by (1) treating each possible response as a separate variable (i.e., giving it a separate punch column), and (2) entering "0" if the response was not selected and "1" if the response was chosen.

A fourth type of closed-ended question is the rank-order question. The researcher asks the respondent to rank-order categories or items, such as those presented in the following example:

9. Please rank (from 1 to 5) the items below in order of their present importance to you as a member of the Olympic Health Club.

    _____   Aerobics classes

    _____   Weight room

    _____   Swimming pool

    _____   Racquetball courts

    _____   Indoor track

As you can see, the criterion of mutual exclusivity is not in force with this form of multiple-choice question either. Thus, as with the checklist question discussed above, data entry and analysis of responses will be more difficult. However, if inclusion of such a question is necessary, analysis is possible.

The final multiple-choice question we will discuss at this time is the attitudinal scale. These scales are designed to measure attitudes through expressed opinions, and are usually operationalized in the form of Likert scales. The general approach is to ask respondents to indicate how strongly they agree or disagree with a given statement. The following example illustrates this question-form.

GENERAL INSTRUCTIONS: Please circle the number which most closely represents your response to the following items.

5 = Strongly Agree (SA)
4 = Agree (A)
3 = Not Applicable or No Opinion (N)
2 = Disagree (D)
1 = Strongly Disagree (SD)

	SA	A	N	D	SD
1. I receive adequate information concerning my job performance from my immediate supervisor.	1	2	3	4	5
2. I receive adequate information concerning L & M Electric's plans, policies and activities.	1	2	3	4	5
3. My orientation to my job at L & M Electric was adequate.	1	2	3	4	5

As you can see, attitudinal scales consist of a list of statements that require a response in terms of how a subject feels about a problem, issue, or solution. They may include from three to seven points of reference, but most often include five points. To develop a set of attitudinal scales, the researcher begins by generating a number of statements about a subject or issue, which reflect opinions that realistically could be held by the targeted population. Each statement should reflect a definite favorable or unfavorable position, and the final list should include an equal number of favorable and unfavorable responses. Before the questions are used, however, they should be carefully pretested to identify any weak or ambiguous statements. (Note: *All* items used in a final questionnaire should be pretested. A more complete discussion of pretesting is included in a later section).

To this point, we have discussed two major types of questions that may be used in constructing a survey instrument. In addition, we have described and given examples of seven subtypes of questions. In the following section, we will briefly address ten Do's and Don'ts of questionnaire design. Armed with these, the beginning researcher should be able to construct a more effective and efficient questionnaire.

Guidelines for Effective Questionnaire Construction

When attempting to construct an effective survey instrument, the researcher will benefit from applying ten major rules. These rules can be divided equally into a set of "Do's" and "Don'ts," as discussed in the following paragraphs.

DO'S: Effective questionnaires should always be:
1. Brief
2. Clear and unambiguous
3. Organized
4. Relevant
5. Attractive

1. *Be brief.* Whenever a researcher constructs a questionnaire, she should always try to be brief. This criterion applies to the length of both the questionnaire and the individual items. Ideally, the final instrument should be no longer than two to three, $8\frac{1}{2}$ by 11-inch pages (front side only). The respondent should be able to listen/read each item quickly, to understand the researcher's intent, and to provide an answer with little if any difficulty. Generally, short instructions and items (i.e., questions) are the best.

2. *Be clear and unambiguous.* Generally, this criterion applies to both the survey's purposes and instructions, as well as to the questionnaire items. To maximize clarity, always keep the questions and word choice simple. Be concrete and define any technical words that are used. Avoid questions the respondent must take time to think about at any length. Finally, limit the number of open-ended questions whenever possible.

3. *Be organized.* This rule involves organization of topics within the instrument itself as well as individual items within each topic. To aid the respondent in moving through the instrument quickly and effectively, group items by topic and use headings to section off each of the topics (especially important when the instrument is to be self-administered). Within each topic, begin with the more general questions and conclude with the more specific ones. To help ensure that respondents will complete the instrument once they have started, place budget and monetary items at the end of the questionnaire. Demographic items also are usually placed toward the end of the instrument.

4. *Be relevant.* Whenever a researcher constructs a survey instrument, she should include only items that are relevant to her purpose. In addition, the questions should be relevant to those being surveyed. Not only will unrelated questions (or those in which you have only a casual interest) lengthen the survey. Their inclusion will reduce the probability that the respondents will complete it.

5. *Be attractive.* This may be one of the most important rules of survey design, for how your survey looks on the printed page will influence respondents either to complete it or to throw it away. To construct a questionnaire that meets this criterion, always leave plenty of white space on the page. Margins should be uniform; headings should be clearly indicated; and sufficient space should be left for respondents to respond. Once completed, the instrument should be professionally printed and, if possible, should utilize different type styles and faces. The highest quality of paper that is affordable should be used for duplication. Finally, if the survey is to be mailed to respondents, it should be folded and stamped neatly, and labels (if used) should be placed on the envelope "straight."

Although the researcher should follow these rules in designing and constructing the questionnaire, he also should take into account several "Don't Rules" of instrument construction.

DON'TS: To construct effective questionnaires, the researcher should NOT:
1. Use double-barreled questions.
2. Ask leading questions.
3. Ask irrelevant, personal questions.
4. Use negation in questions generated.
5. Use "biased" or "loaded" items and terms.

1.   *Avoid double-barreled questions.* Double-barreled questions are those which ask for a single answer to more than one question. Evidence of such questions may be found in the use of such words as "and" or "or." For example, consider the following question: "Do you believe that Mayor Jingleheimer is fair and impartial when appointing city officials?" Although one respondent may agree that the mayor is both fair and impartial, another respondent may believe that the mayor is fair but not impartial or vice versa. With only "yes" or "no" as response categories from which to choose, the latter respondent will be placed in a bit of a bind. As a rule of thumb, then, if a researcher is tempted to use "and" or "or" within a given statement, she should break the sentence into groups and create a separate item for each time the conjunction "and" or "or" is used.

2.   *Avoid asking leading questions.* Leading questions are those that suggest there is only one "right" answer. Usually they begin with such phrases as "Don't you agree that . . .?" or "Wouldn't you say that . . .?" Such questions should be avoided at all costs, since disagreeing with them could require some amount of courage on the part of the respondent. In short, the researcher should ensure that all questions reflect neutrality.

3.   *Avoid using irrelevant, personal questions.* Essentially this rule of thumb applies to ANY questions that tap personal data irrelevant to the study. For example, if income level isn't needed, *Don't* ask the respondent to provide it. In

one telephone survey we conducted, several respondents reacted with hostility when a question concerning income level was asked. In several instances, when this question was asked, targeted respondents actually hung up the phone. The sad part was that the income item was last on the questionnaire. However, with each hang-up, the interviewers had to discard the entire questionnaire and replace it with that of a different respondent.

4. *Avoid using negation.* When generating items, the researcher also should avoid using words such as "not" or "but." The problem with a negative sentence structure is that respondents may read over the "not" and answer the question as if the word did not exist. An example of such a statement might be: "Our city should not maintain the 'city council' as its form of government."

5. *Avoid using "biased" or "loaded" items and terms.* Biased or "loaded" questions take on a variety of forms. They may (1) use unfair wording which reflects the researcher's position on an issue, (2) link an attitude or position with a prestigious person or group, thereby influencing responses, or (3) distort meaning through the use of emotionally charged words. For example, if a researcher asks respondents to agree or disagree that the U.S. Congress, indeed, was wrong in its handling of the 1987 "Contra Affair," he would be guilty of #1 listed above. If she asks respondents to agree or disagree with the current president's position on the "Star Wars Defense Initiative," she is overlooking the bias that can creep in with #2 above. Finally, if a researcher requires respondents to state the extent to which they agree or disagree that a U.S. senator is "racist" or "defrauding" the American public, he also may be charged with biasing or loading the given question (Backstrom and Hursh-Cesar, 1981, pp. 140–143).

As you can see, the ten rules we have discussed indeed can help a researcher to more effectively construct and design a questionnaire. However, as with all survey writing projects, both the individual items and the overall instrument can be improved along the way. Two specific ways in which we can increase the quality of a survey are through the use of pretests and pilot studies. Each of these methods will be briefly addressed in the following paragraphs.

Pretests and Pilot Studies

Whenever a researcher begins to construct specific items for a questionnaire, he can maximize quality by using **pretests** all along the way. Pretests involve the initial testing of each item on the questionnaire, the questionnaire as a whole, or any other aspects of the survey that is being conducted (e.g., the sample design, interview formats, data entry, or statistical analysis). When pretesting any aspect of the questionnaire or study design, either the entire process or a portion of it may actually be tested. For example, if a researcher decides to replicate an earlier study, she may use some of the original questions as well as new ones of her own. In this instance, she would probably only pretest the new items, once they are generated.

To pretest a set of items to be used in a questionnaire (or the survey instrument overall), the researcher may (1) ask interested colleagues to complete the items in question, or (2) select several individuals similar to those to be surveyed in the final study. In either instance, the subjects who are asked to be "guinea pigs" simply complete the items and provide feedback concerning possible oversights or ambiguities. However, no matter what phase of the survey is being pretested, it should be pretested in the manner in which it will be conducted in the final study (see Babbie, 1973, pp. 205–211 for a more complete discussion).

Another way in which the researcher may increase the quality of a survey is to conduct what has been termed "a pilot study." A **pilot study** is a "miniaturized walkthrough of the entire study design" (Babbie, p. 205) that allows the researcher to detect any problems before the final study begins. Pilot studies involve a test of the survey design—from sampling to final analysis. As such they involve the actual selection of a representative sample of the target population, administration of the final survey instrument to those subjects, and the coding, entry and analysis of data that are generated. Because a pilot study should differ from the final survey only in scale, it is of great value to the researcher before she invests time, energy, and money into a design that may not "fly."

PREPARING DATA FOR ENTRY AND ANALYSIS

As we stated at the beginning of this chapter, time and space limitations do not allow for a discussion of data analysis procedures as a whole. Entire books are written about the subject and should be consulted before or at the time a survey begins. However, in order to provide you with the information you will need to prepare for data analysis, the following six suggestions are offered.

1. *To determine and effectively use local conventions for data formatting, consult with a member of the computer facility that you plan to use.* Although this suggestion should be followed at the questionnaire construction phase of a study, it is particularly important to visit the statistician, keypunch operator, or computer facility that you will employ before you punch or enter your data. To do so will provide you with important information concerning how your data should be coded and how its actual formatting should ultimately be completed. Many statistical consultants and keypunch operators can tell war stories about projects on which this suggestion was not followed. In the best instances. *not* following it costs the researchers time, money, and energy. In the worst cases, the majority of the data simply may not be usable.

2. *Construct a codebook and present it to the appropriate individuals before beginning data entry.* As we stated earlier, a codebook is a directory of all the variables (and accompanying variable names) used in a study. In addition, it includes the column numbers associated with each variable. However, the codebook should also contain additional information, including any special codes to be used for *missing data* (i.e., questions which are not answered) and for which "Don't Know" is selected by respondents. Although such a codebook should be constructed and used at the questionnaire construction phase, it must be created prior to data entry and analysis. The reason is that the person who will be entering data (yourself or a professional keypunch operator) will need the codebook to enter the data quickly and accurately. Thus, the codebook should be presented at the time the data is delivered and should be provided to any statistician and/or keypunch operators whom you plan to employ.

3. *Once the data are collected, place the appropriate identifying information on EACH questionnaire.* The "identifying information" includes respondent identification number (i.e., a serial identifier for each respondent) and any (computer) card or project identification to be included during data entry. If data are to be entered directly into the computer from the questionnaire, this suggestion will be especially helpful. Following it will allow the person who is entering the data to use only that information recorded on the questionnaire itself.

4. *Scan each questionnaire before data entry to ensure that any decisions are made prior to this stage.* Many times, researchers leave major decisions to keypunch operators, once they have delivered the data to be entered. As a result, inaccuracies may accrue if the operator is not highly skilled or cognizant of the implications of improper coding. To maximize the chances that the data will be entered correctly, the researcher should make all decisions about how EACH questionnaire should be coded. For example, scanning the data prior to its entry will allow her to correctly code any missing data. In addition, it will allow her to code any additional respondent comments, if such coding is necessary.

5. *Create an appropriate coding scheme for open-ended questions, and hand-code questionnaires if open-ended responses are to be entered into the computer.* Although this suggestion is relatively straightforward, the coding process itself is much more complex. In fact, the researcher who uses open-ended questions must make a number of decisions. For example, he must determine the number of categories to be utilized as well as the criteria to be used when categorizing responses. In addition, he will have to determine how to best tabulate results. Once again, given the space limitations that a chapter offers, the reader is directed to current textbooks that address the construction of coding schemes. Several relevant sources are presented in the "Annotated Readings" section that accompanies this chapter.

6. *Once the data are entered onto cards or tape, they should be verified, or "cleaned," before data analysis.* This suggestion includes the need for data fields to be checked to (1) ensure that only legal codes are used and (2) eliminate any inconsistent data that may have been entered. (Note: **Data field** is defined here as the specific column or columns associated with each variable.) *Data cleaning* may be accomplished in a number of ways: from "eyeballing" a computer print-out of the data to using computer software that informs the operator of an inappropriate "punch" at the time the data are entered. For example, an operator may use computer software to set parameters on the range of each variable, and to program the computer to "BEEP" if the parameters are exceeded. However, no software to date allows the operator to discern a mistake within the appropriate parameters. Thus, additional methods of data cleaning should be utilized.

SUMMARY

In this chapter, we have discussed a variety of topics associated with survey research. First, we discussed three major purposes: description, explanation, and exploration. Then, we described three primary data collection techniques: face-to-face and telephone interviews, and mail or postal surveys.

At this point we moved to the overall topic of sampling. We addressed the subject of appropriate sample size as well as four specific sampling designs.

Next, we proceeded to a discussion concerning effective questionnaire construction. Here we included three considerations to take into account before beginning, talked briefly about how to write more effective survey questions, and presented ten do's and don'ts of instrument design. We concluded this section with guidelines on how to improve the survey instrument by effectively using both pretests and pilot studies.

Finally, we focused on six suggestions to be used in preparing for data analysis. Included were suggestions concerning data formatting, coding, and verification.

Hopefully, on completing this chapter, you have learned a few basics of survey design. At the very least, we have provided a broad outline of topics. Given the vast number of readings that are available regarding survey methods, we heartily encourage you to continue reading in the area. As our introductory comments suggested, you *never* know when a survey might be needed.

STUDY QUESTIONS

1. Identify and briefly discuss the three purposes of survey research.
2. Compare and contrast the advantages and disadvantages of the following: (1) face-to-face interviews; (2) telephone interviews; and (3) postal or mail surveys.

3. Distinguish between a census and a survey. Then, discuss briefly the concept of sampling.

4. Identify the major difference(s) between representative and biased samples. Discuss why standard error and confidence levels are of great help to the researcher.

5. Describe briefly the four major sampling designs. Discuss the advantages and disadvantages of each.

6. List and discuss three considerations that should be taken into account before questionnaire construction begins.

7. Identify and define the four levels of measurement.

8. Compare the advantages and disadvantages of closed- versus open-ended questions. List and provide examples of at least three types of closed-ended questions.

9. List and briefly explain the ten do's and don'ts of questionnaire design.

10. Distinguish between the roles of pretests and pilot studies. Discuss briefly their value to the researcher.

11. List and briefly discuss the six suggestions provided regarding preparation for data entry and analysis. Explain why they are important (as a whole) for the researcher to follow.

ANNOTATED READINGS

Babbie, E. R. (1973). *Survey research methods.* Belmont, CA: Wadsworth.
    A classic survey methods text. Included in its contents are comprehensive discussions of survey designs, sampling procedures, instrument conceptualization and design, and survey analysis. This text is highly readable and less "dry" than some survey textbooks currently on the market. For both beginning and experienced researchers, it is an excellent reference book.
Beed, T. W., & Stimson, R. J. (Eds.). (1985). *Survey interviewing: Theory and techniques.* Boston: George Allen & Unwin.
    An excellent edited volume addressing survey interviewing, specifically. Of particular note are the chapters that address various aspects of telephone surveys, the use of simulation games as a data collection technique, and improving response accuracy. As a resource book, the text is both interesting and enlightening.
de Vaus, D. A. (1986). *Surveys in social research.* London: George Allen & Unwin.
    An excellent basic text concerning survey research. Includes a very complete discussion of survey analysis (for a book its size) as well as an interesting discussion of the scope of survey research. The book would serve as an excellent resource for beginning researchers.
Fowler, F. J., Jr. (1984). *Survey research methods.* Beverly Hills, CA: Sage.
    A popular survey textbook in the field of speech communication. Both its comprehensiveness and level of readability would be attractive to the beginning researcher. Of particular interest are Fowler's address of the topic of "nonresponse" and his brief discussion of ethics. He also has constructed an excellent discussion of sampling and questionnaire design.
Rossi, P. H., Wright, J. D., & Anderson, A. B. (Eds.). (1983). *Handbook of survey research.* New York: Academic Press.

An outstanding reference book concerning survey research. Contributors represent some of the best survey researchers in the business. In addition to some of the more basic topics addressed are discussions of sampling theory, applied sampling, response effects, computer usage, causal modeling and trend analysis. The book is a "MUST" for the bookshelves of the serious researcher. However, its level of readability makes it approachable for the beginner as well.

CHAPTER 10

Content Analysis

By Lynda Lee Kaid,
University of Oklahoma
Anne Johnston Wadsworth,
*University of North Carolina
at Chapel Hill*

Since its recognition as a major research technique early in this century, content analysis has been an increasingly popular methodology for communication researchers. Actually, many researchers would argue that the roots of content analysis can be traced back to historical and theological analysts who have long applied content analysis, albeit in sometimes informal ways, to written and spoken messages. Modern content analysis developed primarily as a way of analyzing mass communication messages. Certainly its evolution as a scientific method of inquiry was accelerated by the propaganda analysis projects of Laswell and his colleagues in the 1940s (Laswell & Associates, 1942, 1949).

Today's researchers not only adhere to well-defined procedures, but they pursue an expanded realm of questions. Spurred by the development of new conceptual frameworks, advances in statistical tools, greater variety of available communication content, and the use of computers, content analysis is now one of the most frequently used communication research methodologies. For instance, a survey of journal articles on political communication in 1978–79 reported that content analysis was the most used method, employed by one-third of all studies surveyed (Jackson-Beeck & Kraus, 1980).

CHARACTERISTICS OF CONTENT ANALYSIS

Although a few researchers, such as Kerlinger (1964, 1986) see content analysis as merely a form of data-gathering, most users see content analysis as a set of full-blown research procedures. The most widely accepted definition of *content analysis* is that offered by Berelson. "Content analysis is a research technique for the objective, systematic, and quantitative description of the manifest content of communication" (Berelson, 1952, p. 18). Two key elements in this definition are *objective* and *systematic*. The need for objectivity has been rarely questioned by content analysts. It is well accepted that the lack of bias is an inherent characteristic of any specific research methodology. This differentiates content analysis from other analytic approaches such as literary criticism or critical theory with its ideological overtones. Likewise, there is little controversy over the need to be systematic, to apply consistent criteria in a rigorous and careful way.

To the need for objective and systematic inquiry, Holsti (1969) adds the need for *generality*, arguing that simple descriptions of content are of limited worth without comparisons and relationships drawn from theoretical concerns. Thus, a researcher could objectively apply systematic criteria to a list of titles of communication research articles from the past twenty years and generate a listing of topics covered. Such a list would not be a content analysis by Holsti's interpretation unless the procedure also projected some relationship between or among topics. A trend analysis comparing the development of certain topics in communication research from 1940 to 1960, for instance, might serve to prove or disprove some projection.

Two aspects of Berelson's original definition have generated considerable controversy among communication researchers. Krippendorff (1980), for instance, posits an approach which defines content analysis as a "research technique for making replicable and valid inferences from data to their context" (p. 21). This definition, while embodying the need for objectivity and consistency in its requirements of repl.cability, challenges the **manifest content** and *quantification* notions.

In rejecting the need to rely only on manifest content, Krippendorff suggests the desirability of viewing communication messages as symbolic content emanating from a source and from which a receiver draws inferences, and of considering the context in which the content exists. On the surface, a willingness to draw inferences about a receiver's interpretations of message content and an openness to consider a communicator's context seem desirable. Even conservative content analysts exhibit concern for "inferences" which can be drawn from communication content but caution, as does Holsti (1969), against dependence on a method which requires an understanding of the motives and intent of the source. The problem with allowing one's self to look very far beyond manifest content is that someone must decide what is latent within a message, what is implied, what motives were behind the communication, etc. The politically moderate researcher who approaches the propaganda documents of the National Conservative Political Action Committee (NCPAC) will undoubtedly bring certain values and predispositions to the judgment of the source's purposes and motives. If such a researcher extends his/her analysis beyond manifest content, it is likely that the essential content analytic ingredient of *objectivity* will be compromised. Thus, researchers who wish to go beyond manifest content in their application of content analytic methods must be particularly careful to avoid contamination of their findings.

The second challenge to traditional content analysis is the question of whether or not content analysis must be a **quantitative** undertaking. Holsti has argued that the "case for content analysis based on exact counts of frequency is a powerful one" (Holsti, 1969, p. 599) because quantification increases the degree of precision of one's conclusions and permits a more accurate description of covariance between elements.

However, the assumption that numerical counting and summing are the only ways to characterize communication content may seem unreasonable. It is not difficult to invoke classic examples where an item's importance may far exceed the frequency of its occurrence. An analysis of two hours of children's television programming might turn up twenty incidents of "helping" behavior, seventeen incidents of "friendly" conversational exchange, and two incidents of violence. However, one of the violent episodes may be so dramatic and emotionally explosive that it encourages viewer imitation or related aggression. A researcher who engages in counting alone might incompletely describe the programming content as well as miss the chance to correlate content with communication effects. On the other hand, quantification guards against the problems of allowing novelty to substitute for importance, a trap into which practicing journalists frequently fall.

There is no easy resolution of this problem. The content analyst must decide the extent to which the questions being asked require quantitative or qualitative analysis or perhaps some combination. When qualification is involved, researchers should then take special care to insure that the objective and systematic goals of content analysis are not violated. Researchers who are particularly concerned with these issues may be well served by attention to efforts which seek an accommodation between the quantitative and qualitative dimensions of content analysis (Sepstrup, 1981).

PROCEDURES

Any application of content analytic procedures includes at least seven steps. The researcher must:

1. Formulate the hypotheses or research questions to be answered.
2. Select the sample to be analyzed.
3. Define the categories to be applied.
4. Outline the coding process and train the coders who will implement it.
5. Implement the coding process.
6. Determine reliability and validity.
7. Analyze the results of the coding process.

This presentation of steps implies that each step follows the step before it. While this may be generally true, the discussion of each step makes it clear that overlap among steps can be expected.

Formulating the Hypotheses

This step in content analytic procedure is common to most empirical research endeavors. Ideally, hypotheses are generated from sound theoretical perspectives or are suggested by previous research in an area of interest to the researcher. In content analysis, many research hypotheses simply suggest a particular description of a message. For instance, a researcher might hypothesize that persuasive speeches contain substantial amounts of emotional proof or that women occupy low-status positions in television dramas.

A good research formulation suggests a relationship between communication variables. Examples of such hypotheses include:

1. Editorials in national newspapers are more favorable to Democratic than to Republican candidates.
2. The amount of violence in prime-time television programming has increased during the past two decades.
3. Conversational patterns of mentally disturbed children differ from patterns of normal children.
4. Propaganda messages of Arabic countries contain more appeals to religious values than do propaganda messages of the Soviet Union.

Such hypotheses imply fairly straightforward descriptions of communication context from which researchers may draw inferences about the relationship between content of a message and intentions of the source or effects on receivers. It is also possible to utilize content analytic procedures in testing hypotheses which relate content directly to receiver effects. There has been a paucity of studies which test the effects of message content on cognitive, affective, and behavioral responses of receivers (Holbrook, 1977), although Merton's (1946) study of Kate Smith's war bond appeals is an early exception.

Increasingly, researchers are recognizing the ability to use content analytic procedures to generate hypotheses which may be more explanatory and predictive (Mitchell, 1967). Examples of such research include the agenda-setting studies which link media content to receiver perceptions of important public issues (McCombs & Shaw, 1972) and media cultivation (enculturation) research which links television violence to viewer passivity (Gerbner, Gross, Morgan, & Signorielli, 1980).

At early stages in a content analytic study, the precision with which hypotheses can be stated may be limited. Sometimes a researcher must formulate categories before detailed relationships can be specified. Thus, Bowers (1970) suggests "reformulating general hypotheses" as an important step in content analytic procedures. The usefulness of such an approach is apparent. Suppose the researcher formulates the initial hypothesis that one political candidate received more favorable camera treatment during a televised debate. When formulating categories, several ways of looking at "camera treatment" might be devised. For instance, one could examine long, medium, and close-up camera angles. Assuming the favorability of close-up shots, the reformulated hypotheses then can provide the researchers with a way of relating the hypotheses more directly to the specific measures to be used in the study.

Selecting the Sample

The researcher must identify the universe of content to which the hypotheses apply. Usually, the hypothesis suggests in general terms what the universe of communication content would be—prime-time television programming, newspaper advertising, job interview dialogues, etc. While some content analytic researchers decry the use of any sampling (Bowers, 1970), pragmatic concerns often make it essential. In determining if African nations have received positive or negative treatment on network television news programs in the past decade, it would be infeasible to examine every newscast during the 10-year period. One must devise a method of obtaining a sample which is (1) representative of the universe from which it comes and (2) of sufficient size to adequately represent that universe.

Representativeness presents the greatest problem, although the problem is not unlike that faced by researchers who wish to do survey research. Ideally, representativeness can be satisfied by the application of random principles so that the content which makes up the universe has an equal chance of falling into the sample. In some cases, such principles are easy to implement. If the researcher wishes to compare feminist language in the weekday editions of the *New York Times* and the *Washington Post* during 1972 and 1982, a purely random method of sampling can be devised to represent the universe of content by simply arraying every weekday edition of each paper and using a random number table or a computer program to select a sample. While not purely random, systematic sampling (selecting every nth occurrence) often produces similar results, as long as the researcher is careful to avoid situations in which such a system may build a bias into the sampling mechanism. Systematic sampling can create bias if the order of the items on a list would create some lack of representativeness resulting from the selection process. Suppose the researcher were systematically selecting issues of a daily newspaper for analysis, and all the newspaper dates for one year were listed in chronological order. If every sixth issue were chosen, all issues would end up being Saturday issues and therefore unrepresentative of the sample as a whole. The use of a random starting point can often overcome such problems with systematic sampling.

Sometimes representativeness can be produced by other sampling approaches. A stratified sample might be necessary if the research question calls for comparisons that make divisions of the sample necessary. For instance, a research question might ask for a comparison of conversational patterns or phrases occurring in television newscasts in the Midwest, Southwest, Northeast, and West regions of the United States. In order to produce a representative sample for such a study, the researcher would first have to stratify according to the regional distributions and then devise a method for random selection of newscasts within each strata or region.

Multistage sampling may require several steps as in samples that rely on time frames where it might be necessary to select certain years, then months, then days. Cluster sampling involves selections from various groups that must be represented in the sample. Samples of media materials often present special problems that require full understanding of the characteristics of the medium being examined. An excellent analysis of such problems and possible solutions can be found in Stempel (1981), who suggests special considerations for days of the week in newspaper and television news sampling, for organizational aspects of the media, for availability, and for types of inferences that might relate to specific media characteristics (circulation, size, region, type, etc.).

Throughout the sampling process, the researcher must take care to avoid any selection process that might introduce bias or jeopardize representativeness. For instance, in comparing television network news coverage of Congress before and after the introduction of floor coverage in the House of Representatives in 1977, Kaid and Foote (1985) could not simply randomly select days in 1977 and 1978. The first and second sessions of the same Congress differ dramatically in the progress of legislation and the patterns of legislative activity. Instead, the researchers chose the same months in 1977 and 1979 since these represented the same time frames during the first sessions of the 95th and 96th Congresses. Thus, the researchers used a form of systematic sampling to ensure that comparable patterns of legislative activity were represented in the sample.

Overall, probably the most frequent misuse of sampling in content analysis is the use of what are sometimes called "convenience" samples, which means that the sample consists of materials readily available to the researcher. Examples of such unrepresentative samples abound in the communication literature. For instance, in examining newspaper and wire service leads during the 1980 campaign, a researcher arbitrarily selected seven events to check for coverage characteristics (Martindale, 1984). Little concern was shown for the possible bias that might have been introduced, either by the events themselves or by the researcher's interest in choosing them. Joslyn's (1980) analysis of political television spots is similarly flawed by a sample that included a number of ads selected by the author from those made available by a political consultant and a private collector.

Once a decision to sample has been made and a representative method is chosen, the *size* of the sample becomes an appropriate concern. Of course, there is no clear-cut guideline for sample size selection in content analysis. It has become generally well established in content analysis that larger is not necessarily better. Stempel's (1952) often-cited analysis compared samples of 6, 12, 18, 24, and 48 issues of one year of a daily newspaper with a complete analysis of all issues in that year and found that "... all five of the sample sizes do an adequate job and that increasing the sample size beyond 12 does not produce marked differences in the results" (p. 333). With television news, samples of less than 20 percent show declining reliability (Lichty & Bailey, 1978).

One method for determining sample size is the *split-half technique* described, although not advocated, by Krippendorff (1980). The researcher divides the sample in half. If both halves produce the same result, an adequate sample size is presumed. This procedure can be repeated, increasing sample size until an adequate level is reached.

A final consideration for sample size determination may relate to the statistical tests used to analyze the data. If a particular test requires certain sample sizes for satisfactory computation, then care must be taken at the sampling stage to produce an adequate sample size.

Defining Categories

No step in content analysis is more crucial than the formulation of **categories** and their units of analysis. The categories formulated by the researcher must be carefully devised to represent the concepts embodied in the research hypotheses/questions. Ideally, categories should be *exhaustive* and *mutually exclusive*. However, in practice, the necessity for exhaustive or exclusive categories may not always be essential to answer a particular research question.

Berelson (1952) divides categories for content analysis into two basic types, substance ("what is said") categories and form ("how it is said") categories. A substance category is often a subject matter category in which the researcher organizes the content according to the specific nature of the topics contained in the communication. For instance, agenda-setting studies categorize the issue content of the media into foreign policy, law and order, fiscal policy, public welfare, and civil rights (McCombs & Shaw, 1972). Directionality is also a widely used type of substance category. Researchers are often looking for pro-con treatment of a subject and seek to characterize content according to categories such as for-against, positive-negative, favorable-unfavorable, criticism-praise. Other substance categories may identify the source or referent of a message.

Categories that describe the form of a communication might differentiate among television news, game shows, dramatic programs, and sports shows or between switching and hesitation pauses in conversational turn-taking. An attempt to classify the types of logical fallacies contained in a persuasive speech would constitute another form of categorization.

Unit of Analysis. For every category or set of categories a researcher must select the appropriate **unit of analysis**. A unit of analysis may range from a word or phrase to an entire item (such as a book, a speech, a news story, a conversational exchange, a film, etc.). Krippendorff (1980) suggests five ways of defining a unit: (1) a physical unit (book, time, pages), (2) a syntactical unit (sentence, word), (3) a referential unit (objects to which unit refers), (4) a propositional unit (redesigning sentences and other units into propositional units which can be analyzed), and (5) a thematic unit (recurring elements).

Unit of Enumeration. Closely related to the unit of analysis is the way in which quantification is accomplished for each category and unit. Holsti (1968) calls this the **unit of enumeration**. The unit of enumeration may be as simple as a frequency count or a recording of the presence or absence of the classifications of a category. In newspaper content, column inches or other measures of space are common with the comparable unit for television and film being time. The unit of enumeration may involve a measure of intensity and include an assignment of weight. For instance, a researcher might ask coders to determine how positive a news story is by using a scale of $+3$ (very positive) to -3 (very negative). A rank ordering could be used in some cases.

The increased availability of video recording techniques has opened new opportunities for communication researchers. Not only has such technology provided easier access to data from television and film, but videotape has made the study of nonverbal and other visual elements of communication much more feasible. The availability of such content for research has created new problems in category formulation. Traditional formulations designed to analyze only verbal content (often transcribed to a printed format) do not encompass the nuances of nonverbal and visual communication. Researchers interested in television news content have made great strides in formulating appropriate categories for media content, and their works provide excellent guidelines (Adams & Schreibman, 1978). Graber (1985) has also recognized the necessity for more sophisticated category formulations which capture the impact of verbal and visual content on the television screen. Donaghy's discussion of the Bernese Time-Series Notation System and the Facial Action Coding System in Chapter 14 offers additional methods of coding visual content.

Outlining the Coding and Training Coders

Content analysis is designed to be systematic and objective, and to this end the training of **coders** is normally outlined by researchers. Usually a written **coding instrument** containing the categories to be used in analyzing the communication is constructed for coders. Coders may be asked to assess the communication according to sets of categories and subcategories, to respond to open-ended questions concerning their judgment abut some aspect of the message, or to "tally" the appearance of some category. Even if the coders will be responding to open-ended questions, it is necessary for them to have a structured guide to assist in their open-ended answers. Typically open-ended questions can be used in conjunction with the "closed" response questions. For example, a study may ask coders to code for the presence or absence of a particular symbol in a political ad, such as a flag. In addition, the researcher may ask coders to respond to an open-ended question such as "What other symbols of the United States appear in conjunction with the flag?"

In using open-ended questions, guidelines defining the exactness and specificity of the response are usually made clear to the coders on the coding instrument and are repeated during the training session. Responses to open-ended questions must also be "content analyzed" or categorized by the researcher or by a second set of coders. Whatever form the coding process will take, the researcher designs the code sheet to assist the coders in analysis of the communication and organizes it in such a way that it is easy for the coders to use.

To make the code sheet clear, several researchers (Bowers, 1970; Holsti, 1968; Krippendorff, 1980) suggest that a corresponding written **codebook** be given to coders in which each category and its components are described in detail. In this way, the researcher can explicitly define for coders what is to be included and excluded in the categories. This is probably most important where categories may require fine distinctions, and coders must know the boundaries for each category.

Researchers can specify on the code sheet and in the codebook if categories are to be marked according to their presence or absence in the communication or if they will be asked to choose from among subcategories the one which is "dominant" in the message. For example, in some instances, the researcher might want to analyze a product ad for the presence or absence of an appeal to a need in Maslow's hierarchy. In other instances the coder might code for the "dominant appeal" in selecting from the list of Maslow's hierarchy of needs the one which is dominant in the ad.

The accuracy and dependability of the coding process in content analysis is greatly influenced by the selection and training of the coders or judges. Normally, two or more coders are used in a content analysis. The single greatest problem in coder selection arises when a researcher does not use independent coders. As Krippendorff (1980) laments, "Probably the worst practice in content analysis is when the investigator develops his recording instructions and applies them all by himself or with the help of a few close colleagues and thus prevents independent reliability checks" (p. 74). If the researcher decides to code the material, Stempel (1981) suggests that some of the items be recoded at the conclusion of the coding process to check the consistency of coding or that a second person spot check the researcher's work from the beginning.

Selection of Coders. Another consideration for researchers is the type of coder to be used. Several researchers advise that coders should be experienced and from similar academic backgrounds (Stempel, 1981) and that reliability may be influenced by the coders' experience and training (Berelson, 1952) as well as their socioeconomic and linguistic backgrounds and educational differences (Krippendorff, 1980). Depending on the level of expertise that the coding requires, the researcher might want to include on the coding instrument the "type" of coder for which the coding sheet was designed (Krippendorff, 1980). More often the practice involves the researcher identifying the type of coder used (e.g., graduate students in a mass communication seminar) in the methodology section of the research report.

Coders should be trained so that their individual skills and judgments are secondary to a common orientation to the categories and the units of analysis, so that, ideally, they function as one judge. In other situations, however, the differential skill of an individual coder should be exploited (Andren, 1981). The researcher may want to use "experts" to code or at least assess the categories present in the content. An example of this use of "experts" is a study which used an expert panel or a Delphi panel of political science and communication scholars to list issue terms contained in a subsample of political advertisements (Shyles, 1983). This list of terms was used to form category divisions under which a variety of specific issues could be coded. A larger sample of ads was then coded by other coders using these same divisions. The use of experts to code in conjunction with another population of coders may also allow the researcher to test the validity of the instrument and of the study itself (Krippendorff, 1980).

Training of Coders. Whatever the type of coder used, the researcher should provide a structured training session for coders where procedures are outlined and the coding instrument is explained. The first step in training coders is to provide a session where the researcher explains the study, in general, and the coding instrument, in detail. In this session, definitions for each category or subcategory are presented, and coders learn the procedures for marking the coding sheets and the form their answers to open-ended questions should take.

Bowers (1970) suggests that definitions of categories be as explicit as possible so that coders know exactly how to use each category. By specifying what is to be included and excluded, the researcher may reduce disagreements among coders resulting from inadequate definition of categories (Stempel, 1981). In this part of the coders' training, the researcher provides many illustrations and examples of the categories (Bowers, 1970; Stempel, 1981). Coders might then be asked to code a sample of units similar to those which will be analyzed in the study, and the researcher can provide immediate feedback to the coders about their use of the categories (Krippendorff, 1980). This simulated training session allows the researcher to assess the clarity of the instructions, the explicitness of the category definitions, and the abilities of the coders in applying the categories. One result of the training session may be that the researcher revises or modifies definitions to accommodate the experience of the coders who are using them.

Besides inadequate definition of categories, disagreement among coders may result from failure to achieve a common frame of reference concerning the definitions of the categories and to oversights (Stempel, 1981). In some instances, disagreement among coders may be a result of the overlapping of subcategories within a particular category. In this case, the coders may be unable to make the fine discriminations in applying the subcategories. If the researcher decides that the fine discriminations are not vital to the study, the subcategories can be collapsed (Holsti, 1969). Often the training session will help to identify such problems and allow for revisions before the actual coding begins.

The final step of the training process is to have coders individually code a representative sample of the content to be analyzed. Several goals are accomplished by this step. One, the researcher can assess the **intercoder reliability** from this sample especially if the coders will not each be coding all of the units of the analysis for the study (and therefore, intercoder reliability cannot be computed for the whole sample). Second, it permits the researcher a further assessment of the ability of the coders to implement the analysis and to use the coding instrument. Finally, it allows the researcher to make any last minute modifications in the coding instrument, in the definitions of categories, and in the instructions to coders.

Implementing the Coding Process

Implementing the coding process should be straightforward. Usually, the researcher asks coders to work individually and to use the codebook strictly, adhering to its definitions, not their own definitions, of categories. Some researchers believe that discussion among coders should be reduced to a minimum (Krippendorff, 1980); however, if a particular coder has questions about the coding procedure, the researcher is typically the final authority on how the content should be coded. If each coder will not be coding every unit of analysis, then the researcher may want to randomly assign coders to the units or units to the coders.

The researcher may need to conduct "spot checks" on coders to see how the coding process is progressing and to check on item confusion. Conferences or discussions may be held if the instructions or definitions seem unclear. Whatever changes are made in the definitions or instructions should eventually be put in writing for the coders.

Coders should also know any time limits placed on their coding of information. If, for example, they are watching a video tape, then the researcher should decide if numerous viewings of the tape are needed to code all of the information or if a "first impression" on several categories is important and should let the coder know about these restrictions. It is probably best to have any televised or radio (video or audio) material taped so that the coders can go back to look in more detail if appropriate to the study.

Assessing Reliability and Validity

Reliability, which is discussed in greater depth in Chapter 5, is of great concern to most researchers doing content analysis. **Reliability** is typically viewed as the "objectivity" of the measuring instrument or "the degree to which data are independent of the measurement instrument" (Berelson, 1952). Typically, the researcher asks if different coders would come up with the same data using the same instrument. This definition implies the reliability (i.e., the objectivity) of the coders as well as the reliability of the categories, the nature of the coders, the preciseness of the coding rules, and the appropriateness of the examples used in illustrating the categories (Berelson, 1952; Krippendorff, 1980; Stempel, 1981).

Although the most commonly assessed reliability in content analysis is intercoder reliability, other forms of reliability have been addressed by scholars in this area. According to Krippendorff (1980), *three* forms of reliability exist: (1) stability (the same results could be produced at a future time); (2) reproducibility (the process conforms to a known standard or yields what it is designed to yield as decided by a panel of experts); and (3) intercoder reliability which is typically assessed in most content analyses as how two or more coders code the same set of data working independently using the same coding sheet. Another form of reliability is category reliability (Holsti, 1969) in which the researcher is interested in categories which are clear and free of confusion.

If one judge appears to be consistently in disagreement, some researchers advise "dropping" that coder (Holsti, 1969). Stempel (1981) advises dropping a coder if he or she is unable to apply the categories according to the definitions given in the codebook. In some instances, the categories may be the source of the unreliability, and judges may be unable to make the fine distinctions required by the categories. In this case the categories might be collapsed and refined.

Levels of reliability should be assessed initially on a subsample of the total sample to be analyzed before proceeding with the actual coding. Stempel (1981) suggests that a minimum standard would be to compare all coders' ratings of at least three items. When a very large sample is involved, a subsample of 5–7 percent of the total is probably sufficient for assessing reliability. Sometimes if each coder is coding every unit, the reliability can also be assessed on the entire sample at the conclusion of the coding process. Several other diagnostic forms of reliability tests are available to researchers to use before the actual coding begins. These include unit reliability (assesses the difficulty in coding the unit itself, which may cause disagreement about the coding); single-category reliability (assesses the difficulty in applying a category because of its similarity to other categories); individual reliability (assesses the ability of a particular coder to consistently apply the coding instrument); and conditional reliability (assesses reliability of subcategories of a particular category or variable which is difficult to code) (Krippendorff, 1980).

In assessing the level of agreement between coders or the intercoder reliability, there is no absolute standard. The method of reliability selected should be relevant to the purpose of the study, depending upon the researcher's goals. While the highest possible reliability should always be a goal, researchers can usually be satisfied with coefficients over +.85, while those below +.80 should be suspect (Kassarjian, 1977). The level of reliability considered acceptable is also related to the complexity of the categories. In some instances, categories that ask coders to code for the sex of newscasters are likely to have higher agreement than those that ask the coder to make finer discriminations such as age or nationality. However, the finer discriminations may provide more useful information than the simpler categories. The researcher usually decides the compromise to be made from including more complex, more difficult categories that provide very useful information at an acceptable level of reliability (Holsti, 1969; Krippendorff, 1980; Stempel, 1981).

Another way in which reliability can be examined is by its correspondence to some facts or truth (Andren, 1981). In this definition, the typical belief that validity indicates a correspondence to what is real is said to be the domain of reliability. That is, the raw data are reliable in the sense that they correspond to some facts or truth. Validity of a set of data can be described by the data's relevance to the problem or purpose of the study.

Several formulas exist for assessing intercoder reliability. Early formulas for assessing this type of reliability used coefficients based on a ratio of agreements among judges (or the number of agreements about categories) over the number of times the category is used (Holsti, 1968).[1] Stempel (1981) maintains that the appropriate reliability measure is simple "percentage of agreement between coders" (p. 128). Because these approaches are biased in favor of small samples and do not take into account the number of agreements that could be expected based on chance alone, they may not be appropriate measures of reliability (Krippendorff, 1980) in all instances. Other formulas correct for the number of chance agreements and also incorporate not only the number of ratings given or number of things rated, but the number of times a given category is used (Cohen, 1960; Fleiss, 1971).[2]

Another formula for intercoder reliability takes into account the complexity of the category system, the agreements expected by chance alone, and corrects for the number of categories and the frequency with which each is used (Scott, 1955). Scott's (1955) *pi* is a ratio of actual differences between obtained and chance agreement over the maximum difference between obtained and chance agreement.[3] Researchers may also wish to assess the agreement of judges on a particular category and can use tables designed to assist in assessing how judges are using the coding rules and not chance factors (Schutz, 1952), or can use contingency tables and chi-square tests to compare the reliability of pairs of coders, item by item (Stempel, 1955).

A final formula for intercoder reliability considers whether the categories use nominal, ordinal, interval, or ratio scales in the calculation of differences between categories or values of a variable (Krippendorff, 1980). This calculation of intercoder reliability is equal to Scott's *pi* when the number of coders is exactly two, the categories are nominal, and the sample size is very large.

Validity is not as easily assessed in content analysis as there is no convenient formula with which to calculate the validity of the study. **Validity** traditionally has meant asking if the instrument used was measuring what it was intended to measure. One could say that a study was valid if its inferences could be "proven" through corroboration from other outside evidence. In content analysis, the most common form of validity is face or content validity where the researcher may only need to ask (having insured good sampling techniques) that the results are plausible. Content validity is satisfactory if the researcher intends only to provide a description of a particular sample. If predictions or broader generalizations are to be made as a result of the data analysis, then the researcher may need to address other, more stringent, forms of validity. Several researchers offer detailed descriptions of and ways of assessing other forms of validity in content analysis such as data-related validity, predictive validity, concurrent validity, and construct validity (Budd, Thorp, Donohew, 1967; Holsti, 1968; Krippendorf, 1980). A more thorough discussion of general concepts of validity can be found in Chapter 5.

Analyzing the Results

This step in content analysis is usually dictated by the hypothesis and the research question. For example, a researcher may have posed a research question about the occurrence of a particular persuasive strategy used by a group leader. In this case, frequencies are obtained to show the occurrence of this and other phenomena. In some instances, the researcher may be interested in evaluating the relationship among or between variables. For example, the researcher may wish to look at the association between the type of persuasive strategy employed and the leadership style of the communicator. In this instance the researcher would obtain cross-tabulations between the variables and look at the differences in expected frequency in a particular cell and the observed frequency in that cell.

Researchers using cross tabs to analyze content analytic data can use **chi-square tests** to determine if the relationships among categories are statistically significant. Researchers using chi-square should be aware of evidence which suggests that the chi-square test requires an expected frequency of at least five in each cell (Stempel, 1981). Another way of analyzing content analytic data is to look at the associations or correlations between the categories. One problem with using tests of association, according to Krippendorff (1980), is that the categories from a content analysis are, by nature, associated, and testing for associations using correlational statistics may reflect this inherent association among the categories. To avoid this, Krippendorff (1980) advises looking at associations and correlations between data gathered from a content analysis and data gathered independently through a different methodology. Several other methods exist for analyzing data from a content analysis, including multivariate analyses, contingency analysis, and clustering (Krippendorf, 1980; Stempel, 1981).

Computers in Content Analysis. The increasing use of computers to assist in content analytic procedures is undoubtedly one of the reasons for the growth of content analysis as a research tool. Not only have computers served a valuable function in the data analysis process, but they can actually substitute for human coders in many research designs. Very simple programs that count words are an obvious application. However, far more sophisticated possibilities have been devised.

The best known of the more elaborate computer content analytic programs is the *General Inquirer.* Developed at Harvard University, the program uses dictionaries, such as the Stanford political dictionary, the Harvard psychosociological dictionary, and other special purpose dictionaries with tags attached to words in the dictionaries (Stone, Bales, Namenwirth, & Ogilvie, 1962; Stone, Dunphy, Smith, & Ogilvie, 1966). Some researchers have developed their own dictionaries designed to isolate content characteristics related to particular research problems. The SLCA-II program was developed to analyze characteristics of language (Cummings & Renshaw, 1976), and DICTION uses dictionaries derived to study the styles used by presidents in their "talk" (Hart, 1984, 1985).

The use of computers in content analysis has several advantages. Computers minimize the time needed for routine counting, produce high reliability, insure greater degrees of reproducibility, and lessen the problems of researcher bias. On the other hand, there are disadvantages such as the difficulty computers have in accounting for communication context. In addition, the typing necessary to input data in a form usable for the computer can be tedious. The increasing availability of optical scanners can reduce this problem if the researcher has sufficient financial resources.

Applying the Procedures

The application of content analytic procedures is no easy task. Many excellent researchers find themselves with problems in the search for answers to seemingly simple questions. Several such problems are exemplified in the study of network news coverage of Congress conducted by Robinson and Appel (1979). Beginning with the task to "find out what network news has been saying about the legislative branch" (p. 408), the researchers immediately encountered problems in the selection of a sample. They chose five weeks in early 1976. This initial decision was apparently arbitrary. While the researchers are to be commended for discussion of the aberrations created by the sample, foresight might have prevented a problem which hindsight could only rationalize.

The definition of categories was an easier one for the congressional coverage study. Categories such as network, date, length, position in newscast, committee type, etc., offered straightforward coding potential. However, for the much more ambiguous category of *slant* (positive, neutral, negative), the researchers offered no explanation of how the category was defined. The unit of analysis utilized in the study is not explicitly identified, although the reader can deduce that each news story was considered a unit. Since Robinson and Appel elected to code the news stories themselves, they left their study open to suspicion about objectivity of the coding process. Also, no rationale is provided for why one coder used written abstracts and the other the actual videotapes of the newscasts. No details are given regarding the actual coding process. Questions such as how many times each coder read or watched the stories or whether a written codebook guided the efforts remain unanswered. The determination of reliability is also a problem here. Robinson and Appel report that they "reached agreement on over 90 percent of our coding decisions" (p. 408), but no explanation for the procedure or formula used to calculate this number is given. Despite their somewhat sketchy methodological precision, the authors did a nice job of presenting and analyzing their results.

In contrast, an excellent study by Tiemens (1978) used content analysis to assess the visual components of television in the 1976 presidential debates. In order to facilitate coding and to make it as objective as possible, Tiemens developed a category system and a coding instrument that carefully defined the limits of the categories and described how material was to be coded. The unit of analysis was each camera shot, which was numbered and timed prior to the actual coding. The code sheet consisted of categories such as shot length, type of camera movement, horizontal and vertical screen placement of candidates, camera framing of candidates, primary vector orientation of persons shown (direction they were facing), primary vector target of candidates, vertical camera angle on person speaking, eye contact of speaker with camera, and facial expression of candidates. The categories were selected according to past research production aspects of television and film.

To facilitate coding, a grid with vertical and horizontal lines was placed over the monitor where the camera shots were shown to help coders determine screen placement. In addition, drawings or visual aids were used on the coding form to assist coders in assessing such factors as camera framing, vector orientation, and camera placement.

Tiemens (1978) reports several types of reliability. In addition to assessing intercoder reliability on eight categories requiring coders' judgments (e.g., horizontal screen placement, camera framing), the researcher also computed the reliability of several different categories measuring a single dimension. The results were clearly displayed and explained, providing a good overall model for the application of content analytic methods.

CONCLUSION

Content analysis is an increasingly popular technique for objective, systematic, and usually quantitative description of communication content. The process begins with the formulation of hypotheses, sample selection, and careful definition of categories. The implementation of a coding process with trained coders then allows the assessment of reliability and validity and appropriate analysis.

Despite the popularity of content analysis, there are several disadvantages to the method. One disadvantage is that content analysis is limited to examination of recorded communication (Babbie, 1986). This is probably most problematic for researchers who wish to look at communication that has occurred in the past and must rely on some form of written or recorded material for their sample. Even in studies about the present, the communication must usually be recorded in some form so that coders can review the material a number of times and so that the researcher can spot check coders or recode incorrectly coded material.

The limitation of recorded material is related to a second problem with content analysis—the difficulty of drawing inferences about the intentions of sources or of isolating effects. A third disadvantage is that the rigidity imposed by careful category selection and definition may cause the researcher to overlook important insights.

Other disadvantages to content analysis come from the difficulty of implementing all of its steps in an ideal fashion. Sometimes it may be impossible to randomly sample the materials needed for a study. For example, the researcher may have available to him or her a specific number of items. In this case, the researcher may need to decide the usefulness of the sample available and exercise caution in making any inferences to larger populations. Related to this is the fact that sometimes a researcher may not wish to randomly sample but instead prefer to analyze an entire population. In their book on agenda-setting during a presidential election, Weaver, Graber, McCombs, and Eyal (1981) argue that sampling news stories during a particular event may not be feasible because "major news events are not randomly distributed" (p. 13).

The determination of reliability and validity present other problems. As this chapter indicates, there is much disagreement about acceptable techniques and levels of reliability and the way in which validity can be assessed.

Overall, however, content analysis offers communication researchers several advantages. First, content analysis provides procedures for dealing with large amounts of material. Second, materials for content analysis are usually readily available. Content analysis can also be done fairly quickly and without substantial financial resources (Babbie, 1986). The gathering of materials, the setting up of the study, and the training of coders are usually more quickly implemented than the procedures involved in carrying out a survey or field experiment. Related to this advantage is the increased objectivity and speed of computers. Third, content analysis can provide information on processes and messages occurring over time and is particularly useful in retroactive measurement. For example, an analysis of presidential political ads from 1952 to 1984 provided a look at the trends in the use of strategies and styles, various issue appeals, and negative advertising during those 32 years (Wadsworth, 1986). By looking at the evolution of messages from similar sources or the same source, researchers can gather information about the changes and adjustments made in these messages over time.

A fourth advantage of content analysis is the fact that it is an unobtrusive technique for data collection and analysis. Thus, it usually does not interfere with the operations of the sample to be measured. Consequently, bias is easier to deal with than bias in other methods such as experiments or surveys. If, for example, a coder has talked with other coders during some actual coding of material, the researcher can have the material recoded by another coder. The same is true if the researcher discovers through a spot check that coders have not been applying the categories correctly. In this case, an additional training session can clarify the categories and the content can be recoded. In other words, a researcher can usually correct or eliminate intervening variables so that there is little danger that the coding, and subsequently the study itself, will become contaminated. Finally, content analysis is easily combined with other research techniques.

These advantages, and the controllable nature of most disadvantages, make content analysis an appealing communication research methodology. Its applicability to many modern communication settings will undoubtedly result in its increasing utilization.

NOTES

1. Holsti's formula for computing reliability:

$$R = \frac{(C_{1,2})}{C_1 + C_2} \qquad \begin{aligned} C_{1,2} &= \text{\# of category assignments both coders agree on.} \\ C_1 + C_2 &= \text{total category assignments made by both coders.} \end{aligned}$$

Given for two coders; can be modified for any z of coders.

2. Reliability formulas by Cohen and Fleiss:

Cohen (1960)

$$R = \frac{N \sum_i x_{ii} - \sum_i x_{i+} x_{+i}}{N^2 - x_{i+} x_{+i}}$$

x_{ii} = # of agreements about category i
x_{i+} = # of times judge used category i altogether
x_{+i} = z of times other judge used category i
N = of ratings given or z of things rated

Fleiss (1971)

$$P_j = \frac{1}{N_n} \text{ times } \sum_{i=1}^{N} n_{ij}$$

N = total # of subjects
n = number of ratings per subject
i = subjects; j = categories
n_{ij} = number of raters who assigned the ith subject to the jth category.
P_j = proportion of all assignments which were to the jth category

3. Scott's (1955) formula for intercoder reliability:

$$pi = \frac{P_o - P_e}{1 - P_e}$$

P_o = (observed percent agreement) = % of judgments on which the two judges agree when coding the same data independently
P_e = percent agreement to be expected on the basis of chance
(Total probability of chance agreement is equal to the sum of probabilities of agreement on each of categories taken individually)

STUDY QUESTIONS

1. Define content analysis. What elements of traditional definitions engender the greatest controversy?
2. What are the seven steps in a content analysis procedure?
3. Discuss the major concerns in selecting a sample of content to be analyzed.
4. What are the most common types of categories used in content analysis? Give several examples of each.
5. Define a unit of analysis and explain how it is used in content analysis.
6. What are the most important parts of coder training?
7. Review the various ways in which reliability can be assessed.
8. Discuss the advantages and disadvantages of using computers in content analysis.
9. Overall, what are some of the advantages of content analysis as a research technique? What about disadvantages?

ANNOTATED READINGS

Adams, W. J., & Schreibman, F. (Eds.). (1978). *Television network news: Issues in content analysis*. Washington, D. C. : George Washington University Television and Politics Study Program.
   In addition to material on the availability of television news data, the book has good chapters on the application of content analysis techniques to the verbal and visual aspects of television.
Berelson, B. (1952). *Content analysis in communication research*. New York: Hafner.
   An important early book on content analysis where the rationale and the steps for using the method are described. Also contains a bibliography of studies through 1950 which used content analysis.
Budd, R. W., Thorp, R. K., & Donohew, L. (1967). *Content analysis of communications*. New York: Macmillan.
   An early book on content analysis with detailed treatment of categories and analyzing direction content. The book also includes a chapter on the types of analyses that can be done with content analysis data.
Gerbner, G., Holsti, O. R., Krippendorff, K., Paisley, W. J., & Stone, P. J. (Eds.). (1969). *The analysis of communication content*. New York: John Wiley.
   This book contains a series of articles on differing approaches to content analysis. Some chapters deal with applications of computer technologies and with methodological issues, while other chapters are devoted to explanations of how content analysis procedures have been adapted to specific research questions.
Holsti, O. R. (1968). Content analysis. In G. Lindzey & E. Aronson (Eds.), *The handbook of social psychology* (Vol. 3, pp. 596–692). Reading, MA: Addison-Wesley.
   This chapter provides a good, short version of Holsti's position on content analysis as a quantitiative and qualitative technique.
Holsti, O. R. (1969). *Content analysis for the social sciences and humanities*. Reading, MA: Addison-Wesley.
   Classic text on content analysis, including considerable information on the rationale and use of the technique. The book gives examples of types of research and studies which could benefit from content analysis and contains extensive chapters on developing category systems and on computers in content analysis.
Krippendorff, K. (1980). *Content analysis: An introduction to its methodology*. Beverly Hills, CA: Sage.
   A textbook on content analysis that can serve as a handbook for researchers actually using the method. Includes an extensive discussion on reliability and offers a formula for assessing intercoder reliability. Also includes discussions on various types of reliability and validity and how to assess these factors, a chapter on use of computers in content analysis, and one outlining the practical steps that a researcher takes to do a content analysis.
Laswell, H. D., & Associates (1942). The politically significant content of the press: Coding procedures. *Journalism Quarterly, 19*, 12–23.
   In this early work on the application of content analysis to political media, the authors consider such problems as frequency of presentation, prominence, weighting, etc.
Pool, I. (Ed.). (1959). *Trends in content analysis*. Urbana: University of Illinois Press.

A collection of chapters authored by different scholars on application of content analysis in studying emotional states, linguistics, biography, and history, as well as a discussion of the state of content analysis as a method (at that time).

Stempel, G. H., III., & Wesley, B. H. (Eds.). (1981). *Research methods in mass communication*. Englewood Cliffs, NJ.: Prentice-Hall.

Contains two chapters that represent a practical guide to content analysis methods, particularly as related to media studies. Good discussion of sampling problems in media.

CHAPTER 11

Interaction Analysis

By Victoria J. Lukasko Emmert,
University of Wyoming

Frequently the terms interaction, communication, discourse, and conversation are used synonymously. We are all taught that if we call a set of dialogue "a conversation" in one sentence it is better to refer to the same dialogue in the next sentence as "an interaction." This gives our writing variety and reduces the monotony of reading or hearing the same word over and over again. As a consequence, when you see a chapter titled "Interaction Analysis" you might logically expect it to concern the analysis of human conversation.

INTRODUCTION

Interaction analysis covers a variety of methodologies which are concerned with the "systematic study of behavior streams" (Bakeman & Dabbs, 1976, p. 335). Therefore in the broadest perspective interaction analysis is not limited to human communication. Studies of social aggression in groups of monkeys, the mating rituals of birds, mother-child expressive displays, as well as husband-wife conflict negotiation fit this definition. Some definitions do suggest an emphasis on the study of human communication: "Interaction analysis historically has focused upon the flow of 'acts' in the course of classroom, small group or dyadic interaction" (Hatfield & Weider-Hatfield, 1978, pp. 44–45); interaction analysis refers to "any systematic method of classifying verbal and nonverbal behavior" (Poole & McPhee, 1985, p. 124).

A final perspective suggests that who is studied is not nearly as important as the type of analysis of the behavioral stream which is undertaken. The purpose of interaction analysis is "to identify sequences, patterns, and repetitive cycles of behaviors . . . between pairs or larger groups of subjects" (Sackett, Ruppenthal, & Gluck, 1978, p. 13.). Some interaction analysts (Bakeman & Gottman, 1986; Fisher & Hawes, 1971; Weick, 1969) suggest that the most important criterion in defining interaction analysis is that the dynamic process of "interaction" be studied. Birds defending their territory, unhatched chicken calls and mother hen responses, mother and infant primate touching and vocalizations as well as husbands and wives communicating, children developing friendships with one another, and small groups engaged in decision making—all of these use behaviors which are sequenced in time. It is this study of the dynamic process itself, of the actual behaviors as they unfold through time, which characterizes the most stringent definition of interaction analysis.

Suppose we are interested in a conversation between two people, A and B. Simply examining the speaking turns we can code the behavioral stream into:

A	B	A	B	A	B
1	1	2	2	3	3

Each individual behavior we are coding, in this case each speaking turn, is called an "**act**." Two contiguous acts are called an "**interact**." $A1/B1$, $B1/A2$, $A2/B2$ are successive interacts. The minimal unit of behavior which is analyzed in the most stringent definition of interaction analysis is the interact. "Given that interdependence is the crucial element from which a theory of organizations is built, *interacts* rather than acts are the crucial observables that must be specified" (Weick, 1969, p. 33). This is because when we code the relationship of one message to another we are attempting to study the interdependence between messages and/or communicators. Some interaction analysts believe that a triad of messages, corresponding to a stimulus-response-reinforcement sequence ($A1/B1/A2;B1/A2/B2$) is necessary to analyze certain patterned aspects of the behavioral stream (Bateson & Jackson, 1964; Rogers & Millar, 1982; Sluzki & Beavin, 1965).

The patterns of behavior which are examined using interaction analysis may be **concurrent** or **sequential**. Concurrent behaviors occur simultaneously, while sequential behaviors occur one after the other. Suppose we are interested in examining some relationship between verbal and nonverbal behavior in the behavioral stream. Speakers (A1, B1) communicate both verbally (V) and nonverbally (NV) while listeners (B-A1, A-B1) are sending only nonverbal behaviors. Our coded behavior stream might look like this:

	A1	A-B1	A2	A-B2	A3	A-B3	A4	A-B4
Person	V	NV	V	NV	V	NV	V	NV
A	NV		NV		NV		NV	

	B-A1	B1	B-A2	B2	B-A3	B3	B-A4	B4
Person	NV	V	NV	V	NV	V	NV	V
B		NV		NV		NV		NV

Concurrently, we can study how some nonverbal communication of listeners affects some nonverbal or verbal communication of speakers (B-A1NV/A1V, NV; A-B1NV/B1V, NV). Sequentially, we might examine the association between the nonverbal communication of contiguous nonverbal messages of the two different speakers (A1NV/B1NV; B1NV/A2NV). Or we might examine how earlier messages of a speaker affect later messages of the same speaker (B1V/B2V; B2V/B3V). We use the term interact always to refer to the sequential study of the behavioral stream. Concurrent interaction analysis studies occur less frequently than sequential ones, although there are a few (Adamson & Bakeman, 1985).

In addition to interaction analysis there are other ways to study conversational behavior: **conversational analysis** and **discourse analysis**. Conversational analysis uses ethnomethodology to examine how conversation is constructed so that it is coherent to its participants. Conversational analysis is concerned with "the description and explication of the competences that ordinary speakers use and rely on in participating in intelligible, socially organized interaction" (Heritage and Atkinson, 1984, p. 1). A conversational analyst might examine the rules for taking turns in a conversation (Sachs, Schegloff, & Jefferson, 1974; 1978) or face-saving through the use of politeness in conversation (Brown & Levinson, 1978) but the conversational units that are examined may be as short as two or three exchanges long. These are chosen because they typify the conversational rules which are hypothesized to exist as part of the speaker's competences. A conversational analyst would not be interested in the overall frequency of "politeness exchanges" in 60 dyadic interactions among strangers who have been manipulated in a laboratory into spilling drinks on one another. The competences involved might be described by using only three or four typical examples of such exchanges. An interaction analyst might use this frequency information to determine that "the greater the number of politeness exchanges, the more satisfaction participants will report concerning the interaction."

Discourse analysis examines conversation from the perspective that "discourse is highly organized and amenable to analysis using traditional linguistic concepts such as sequential and hierarchical organization, system and structure.... This is a powerful procedure and is standard in phonology and syntax" (Stubbs, 1981, p. 107). Coulthard, Montgomery, and Brazil (1981), for example, described the hierarchical structure of classroom, doctor-patient, committee meeting, and BBC broadcast discussion interaction. The structure of classroom interaction was theorized to consist of four hierarchical levels (in descending order): Lesson, Transaction, Exchange, and Move. Lessons are made up of transactions, transactions of exchanges, and exchanges of moves. This hierarchical order was then used to analyze the other three types of interaction. Labov & Fanshel (1977) also provided an extensive discourse analysis of the therapeutic interview. Discourse analysis focuses on the linguistic structure of conversations and is closely related to the study of language.[1]

Many different researchers from a variety of disciplines have contributed to the history and development of interaction analysis. Sociobiology, education, psychology, communication, and sociology, all use interaction analysis to examine behavior streams.

HISTORY AND DEVELOPMENT OF INTERACTION ANALYSIS

Most interaction studies trace their historical roots to work by scholars in various fields in the late 1920s and 1930s. In education, Anderson (1937a, 1937b, 1939a, 1939b) was examining the dominative and integrative behavior of children and teachers. Later Flanders (1960) developed a coding system for categorizing the teacher-pupil interaction in the classroom which others (Amidon & Hough, 1967) revised and expanded.

What has come to be called the Palo Alto group (Wilder, 1979) has had a strong influence on the interaction analysis system called "relational communication." As early as 1936, Bateson was developing a theory of complementary and symmetrical interaction exchanges which has been applied to the "command" or relational level of interaction (Sluzki & Beavin, 1965). In **relational analysis,** the "content," or what is said, is distinguished from the "relationship level," or how something is said (Ruesch & Bateson, 1968; Watzlawick, Beavin, & Jackson, 1967; Wilder, 1979). "All such relationship statements are about one or several of the following assertions: 'This is how I see myself . . . this is how I see you . . . this is how I see you seeing me' . . . and so forth" (Watzlawick, Beavin, & Jackson, 1967, p. 52). "Relational messages are those verbal and nonverbal expressions which indicate how two or more people regard each other, regard their relationship, or regard themselves within the context of the relationship" (Burgoon & Hale, 1984, p. 193).

Relational analysis is closely associated with **pragmatics** (Morris, 1938), the study of the relationship between signs and language and their interpreters. The control dimension of relational communication has been the most researched, but other relational aspects have been proposed (Burgoon, Buller, Hale, & deTurck, 1984; Burgoon & Hale, 1981, 1984). Early theory development in relational interaction analysis by Bateson (1958), Jackson (1959, 1965), Haley (1963), Sluzki and Beavin (1965), Watzlawick, Beavin, and Jackson (1967), Watzlawick and Weakland (1977) has influenced the development of several interaction coding systems of relational control (Ellis, Fisher, Drecksel, Hock, & Wertel, 1976; Erickson & Rogers, 1973; Folger & Puck, 1976; Mark, 1971; Rogers & Farace, 1975; Sluzki & Beavin, 1965). These all originated from the same theoretical perspective, and each of the others is an extension or refinement of Sluzki & Beavin's (1965) work. Rogers and Farace (1975) review eight observational systems as a preliminary introduction to their relational control interaction analysis coding scheme, in addition to citing the early work by Carr (1929) and Thomas, Loomis, and Arrington (1933).

Bales' (1950) Interaction Process Analysis (IPA) coding system, and several revisions have been used extensively by those studying small group communication decision making and are still used in validity comparisons for other interaction systems (Poole & Folger, 1981b; Stiles, 1980).

Using a rhetorical perspective, Austin (1962) first classifed **illocutionary acts** in his 1955 William James lectures at Harvard University. An illocutionary act "denotes the role which an utterance plays in the interpersonal relationship between speaker and hearer as social actors" (Streeck, 1980, p. 134). Classifications such as question, command, and assertion are illocutionary acts. If you issue a command to another person, you see your role as one who gives commands and the other person as one who is obligated to take commands. Searle's (1968, 1976) revised taxonomy of illocutionary acts formed the theoretical basis for Stiles' (1978) intersubjective verbal response mode (VRM) coding system.

Interaction analysis also has roots in the study of information processing. Gottman (1979a) cites Shannon and Weaver's (1949) influence on Ruesch and Bateson's (1951) early work. The development of more sophisticated systems for analyzing interaction data such as those discussed by Bakeman and Gottman (1986) also can be traced to Sackett's work (1978; 1979; 1980; Sackett, Holm, Crowley, & Henkins, 1979) in measurement and to Rausch, Barry, Hertel, and Swain's (1974; Hertel, 1968) early application of Markov chains to interaction.

INTERACTION ANALYSIS PROCEDURES

Although each of the following steps will be considered separately they are not completely independent. Hypotheses and research questions are generally derived from a field of study. This field of study may also suggest appropriate categorizing systems, coding techniques, behaviors to be analyzed and even statistical analyses. Certain types of data are available only from some categorizing systems and not others. Each decision in the procedural steps affects, or has consequences for, the possible decisions made at any other step.

Formulation of Hypotheses and Research Questions

Two types of hypotheses are common in interaction analysis. The first type relates different categories of acts to individual members of the interaction or to end-products, such as roles, cohesiveness, consensus, leadership, effectiveness and satisfaction. An example of such a hypothesis is that high status members in a dyad are more presumptuous than low status members (Cansler & Stiles, 1981). Another example is that verbal behavior directed toward a high power individual will differ significantly from verbal behavior directed toward a low power individual (Bradley, 1978).

The second type of hypothesis relates interacts or other behavioral sequences to dyads or groups, or to end-products such as satisfaction and knowledge of the other. One example of such a hypothesis is that dyads composed of paired internal-locus-of-control individuals will be characterized by competitive symmetry; dyads composed of paired external-locus-of-control individuals will be characterized by complementarity; mixed dyads (one of each) will be characterized by transitive patterns (Emery, 1982). A second example is that in dyadic conversations characterized by multiple conversational lapses (three or more 3-second or more periods of silence during turn-taking), behavior sequences most likely to occur subsequent to the lapse will contain question/answer adjacency pairs (McLaughlin & Cody, 1982).

Many studies using interaction analysis are descriptive in nature. The theoretical constructs are explained, the coding system is described, a type of interaction is chosen for study, and the results of the analytical procedures are given and explained relative to the theoretical constructs. Specific hypotheses are not generated in these studies although research questions may be asked (Bergan & Tombari, 1975; Courtright, Millar, & Rogers, 1980; Hawes, 1972; Rogers, Courtright, & Millar, 1980). A sample research question was, "Which sets of categories form a pattern of rises and falls over the following 25 subsequent messages [Putnam, 1982]?" Another research question was, "Will similar verbal sequential patterns emerge in the negotiation processes of nonclinical, normal-functioning marital couples situated at different levels of marital adjustment [Ting-Toomey, 1983]?"

Constructing the Category System

Many decisions are involved in constructing a category system. First, a researcher can choose a specific theoretical approach such as a **logical/deductive approach**, a **theoretically based/discourse analytical approach** or an **inductive/ grounded theory approach**. Second, a researcher chooses a categorizing system which matches the aspect of interaction which is to be examined. Stiles (1978), for example, differentiates among three aspects of interaction each of which has its own categorizing system: **content categorizing systems, intersubjective categorizing systems** and **expressive categorizing systems.** Each of these aspects may be examined using any of the three approaches mentioned in the first step.

Theoretical Approaches

Logical/Deductive Approaches. The construction of a category system generally follows one of three major theoretical approaches: a strict logical/deductive approach, a theoretically based/discourse analytical appraoch or an inductive/ grounded theory approach. The logical/deductive approach is based on "testing hypotheses generated by logical deductions from *a priori* assumptions" (Fisher & Hawes, 1971, p. 444). In this approach the categories are created using previously developed theory to create the decision rules about how particular behaviors are to be classified by the categorizing system.

Stiles' (1978, 1980, 1981; Cansler & Stiles, 1981; Russell & Stiles, 1979) verbal response mode (VRM) categorizing system is a good example of a coding system for verbal interaction derived from logical/deductive theory. VRM codes messages on the basis of answers to three questions: (1) whose experience is the topic of the utterance (speaker or other); (2) whose viewpoint is used in the utterance (speaker or other); and (3) does the speaker presume or does the speaker not presume to have knowledge of the other's experiences and frame of reference? This 2 × 2 × 2 classification system creates eight basic modes of verbal interaction: disclosure, edification, advisement, confirmation, question, acknowledgment, interpretation, and reflection.

Each of these speaker intentions has a characteristic grammatical structure or form associated with it. For example, "Disclosure concerns the speaker's experience in the speaker's frame of reference . . . without necessarily presuming knowledge of the other. Disclosure form is first person singular (I) or first person plural (we), where the other is not the referent (i.e., where 'we' refers to the speaker and some third party)" (Stiles, 1978, p. 695). "I'd like to ask her out," would be classified as self-disclosure in both intent and form. "That really bothers me," would be classified as edification in form and disclosure in intent, a mixed mode (Stiles, 1978, p. 697). The resulting classification system has eight pure modes in which both form and intent are classified identically and fifty-six mixed modes in which the intent is expressed in a noncharacteristic grammatical form. Categorizing systems developed from the logical deductive approach are internally logical and the coding is often relatively easy because the decision rules for coding clearly specify how a particular message is to be coded.

Theoretically Based/Discourse Analytical Approaches. These involve the compilation of categories which code the relevant functions in the discourse field being studied. This can be based on a theoretical perspective such as the one underlying the relational communication coding systems (Ellis et al., 1976; Erickson & Rogers, 1973; Folger & Puck, 1976; Mark, 1971; Rogers & Farace, 1975; Sluzki & Beavin, 1965). The categories originally developed by Sluzki & Beavin (1965) "correspond more or less to the basic grammatical forms (interrogative, declarative, imperative), with the addition of some metacommunicational categories (agreement and negation)" (p. 79). The latter two codes were response modes. The theorized relationship between grammatical form, response modes and relational control has been maintained directly or indirectly in later relational coding systems (Ellis et al., 1976; Mark, 1971; Rogers & Farace, 1975).

Bales' (1950) IPA is another example of this type of a theoretically based/discourse analytical coding system. The IPA was developed from the theoretical perspective of a differentiation in task and socio-emotional leadership. Coding categories in the IPA reflect this distinction. Coding schemes that are developed using a theoretical approach, but still responsive to the type of discourse being studied, have the advantage of being adaptable to special types of discourse, such as Donohue's (1981) adaptation of Roger and Farace's (1975) coding scheme to negotiation tactics. They also have the advantage of sharing a theoretical base so that eventually they can allow for more abstract meta-theories of interaction to be developed. A disadvantage is that their coding decision rules are not as clearly explicated or as easily followed as the completely theoretical, deductive approaches.

Inductive/Grounded Theory Approaches. "Generating a[n inductive, grounded] theory from data means that most hypotheses and concepts not only come from the data, but are systematically worked out in relation to the data during the course of the research. Generating a theory involves a process of research" (Glaser & Strauss, 1967, p. 6). Hawes' (1972) study of physician-patient interviews is an example of an inductive, grounded theory approach. He used stimulated recall in which his subjects, doctors and patients, separately watched a videotape of their interview which was stopped at regular intervals. During this time the viewer was asked to recall thoughts and feelings about the sequence and to describe the effects of the other's verbal behavior on the viewer's own behavior. Eleven of the thirteen categories used to analyze the data were generated from this process and the remaining two were derived from previous research.

Grounded theories have the advantage of being able to examine the data from the meaning-perspective of those who produced it. However, each new context, type of interaction, and group of participants may generate a new coding system which bests fits "their" data. This makes it very difficult to produce coherent theories and predictions about communication that are not completely group-interaction-context specific.

Each of these approaches generates different research questions and answers to those questions. Areas of study that have been more thoroughly explored are better suited to generate logical or discourse analytical theoretical approaches.

Categorizing Systems. Many types of categorizing systems can be created from the theoretical approaches just discussed. For example, Russell and Stiles (1979) distinguish among three types of categorizing systems for studying three different aspects of verbal interaction: content, intersubjective, and expressive categorizing systems.

Content Categorizing Systems. The first categorizing system consists of "... *content* categories, such as *mother* or *death anxiety*, [which] concern denotative or connotative semantic content" (p. 405). These categories are similar to content analysis even though they are applied to verbal interaction because they focus on the "manifest content" of the interaction, as was discussed in chapter

10. For example, suppose a coder is classifying the following conversation between a mother and daughter:

> MOTHER: How late do you think you will be out tonight? I really think you ought to come in early since we will be leaving on vacation tomorrow and you promised to drive part of the time.
> DAUGHTER: It all depends on how long the party lasts. Don't worry. I'll keep the driving in mind.

The researcher might be interested in the content category "time management" so that every occurrence in the content that refers to time management would be counted. In the conversation above, both mother and daughter would receive one count for the content category "time management."

Intersubjective Categorizing Systems. The second categorizing system consists of "*intersubjective* categories, such as *self-disclosure* or *question*, [which] concern syntactically implied and other relationships between the communicator and recipient" (Russell & Stiles, 1979, p. 405). This type of category system is often referred to as "relational analysis" or a "pragmatic categorizing system" in interaction analysis studies. In the previous conversation between mother and daughter, the mother asks a question and the daughter answers it. This suggests that the mother-daughter relationship in this conversation is one in which the mother has less control than in other possible mother-daughter relationships, such as one in which the daughter asks, "How long can I stay out?" or one in which the mother commands, "Be in by 10 o'clock or you don't get to drive."

Expressive Categorizing Systems. The expressive categorizing system consists of "*extralinguistic* categories, such as *pauses* or *laughing* [which] concern vocal noises, tonal qualities, and temporal patterning of speech, defined independently of semantic content and syntactic structures" (Russell & Stiles, 1979, p. 405). This is a categorizing system for examining the nonverbal characteristics of verbal interaction. In the previous mother-daughter conversation the mother's question might have sounded as if she were simply asking for information, or it could have sounded as if she were angry and upset. The daughter's response could have sounded unsure about the time and reassuring about the promise to drive, or it might have sounded angry about even being asked the question about time and sarcastic about the promise to drive. The vocalics or the emotional impression of the responses can also be coded.

Russell and Stiles (1979) theorize that each of the three categorizing systems examines a different feature of the communication system. This is a good example of Emmert's suggestion in chapter 5 that methodology is never entirely separate from theory. These researchers suggest that "the content channel carries information pertaining to the speaker's psychodynamic process and personality structure, ... the intersubjective channel carries information pertaining to the quality of the speaker's relationship with the other, and . . . the extralinguistic channel carries information pertaining to the speaker's emotional state" (Russell & Stiles, 1979, p. 404). For this reason Russell and Stiles (1979) suggest that the three categorizing systems be kept separate and not mixed together so that greater clarity can be achieved in exploring a theoretical approach to interaction analysis. While Russell and Stiles (1979) strongly deplore combining of categorizing systems into one coding system, other systems such as Bales' (1950) Interaction Process Analysis (IPA) combine the expressive and intersubjective categorizing systems because the creators of these systems do not make the same theoretical connection between the methodology and the categorizing system (Heyns & Zander, 1953; Russell & Stiles, 1979).

Choosing Coding Systems. Cutting across the three theoretical approaches (logical/deductive, theoretically based/discourse analytical, and inductive/ grounded theory) and three categorizing systems (content, intersubjective, and expressive) are two coding strategies that may be used separately or combined within a given system of analysis.

Classical Coding Strategy. In a *classical coding* "strategy, categories describe characteristics of the text (or some other record of the communication)" (Russell & Stiles, 1979, p. 405). For example, in Shimanoff's (1985) study of affect words used in conversation she counted the number of affect words and indirect references to emotions in conversations. Both Stile's (1978) VRM and Rogers and Farace's (1975) relational communication coding procedures code the grammatical form of the utterance which is a characterization of the text.

Pragmatic Coding Strategy. In a **pragmatic coding** "strategy, categories describe characteristics of the communicator, such as his or her internal state, intentions" (Russell & Stiles, 1979, p. 405). Coders using a pragmatic strategy often infer the intent of the communicator from syntactic features of the discourse. Russell and Stiles (1979) call their pragmatic code an "intent" while Rogers and Farace (1975) refer to their pragmatic code as a "metacommunication response of the message relative to the statement that came before it" (p. 228). Both Stiles (1978) and Rogers and Farace (1975) have developed intersubjective categorizing systems which combine classical and pragmatic codes.

Rating Coding Strategy. A rating coding system for messages may also be used in which coders rate each message using a set of Likert scales. A message might be rated on the adjective "self-centered" on a 1–7 point scale—not at all to very much (Stiles, 1980). Rating scales do not give as much detailed information about how the behaviors performed relate to one another (Bakeman & Gottman, 1986).[2]

Choosing Behavioral Units of Analysis. The behavioral units you choose to code relate to your research question in that the complexity of your coding system is partially determined by the complexity of the behavior you wish to observe. Bakeman and Gottman (1986) suggest that a slightly finer level of analysis may create more reliable data by breaking up events into more specific parts, may support the theoretical lumping or splitting of categories, and may suggest other research questions. Unfortunately many beginning researchers become fascinated with the finer and finer distinctions they can make when coding the behavioral stream. They expect that lumping the data into broader categories later will solve the problem of the level of analysis to use when analyzing their data. The final level of analysis should be related to the conceptual level of your research question (Bakeman & Gottman, 1986; Hartup, 1979; Suomi, 1979). Bakeman & Gottman (1986) particularly caution that the development of a coding system is more profitably guided by clearly stated research questions than by the ability to create finer and finer distinctions in the behavioral stream. Two types of behavioral units can be distinguished: **events** and **time intervals** (Bakeman & Gottman; 1986).

Events. An event is a single occurrence of the behavior in the behavioral stream. Events can be the type of play a child is engaged in, an utterance or a message. An utterance, for example, can be defined as "each independent clause, each term of address, or acknowledgment, each element of a compound predicate, and each nonrestrictive dependent clause" (Stiles, 1979, p. 54). A message can be "defined as each verbal intervention by participants in a dialogue" (Rogers & Farace, 1975, p. 228), such as a speaking turn. When that particular event occurs it is coded.

Events are often chosen so that they are contiguous, so that no gaps remain in the behavioral stream where noncoded behavior occurs. When behaviors are coded so that there is some code for every behavior, the coding system is said to be **exhaustive.** This type of coding is necessary for sequential analyses to be performed. Sometimes only a subset of an interaction is coded, such as questions and answers (Folger & Ruck, 1976) in what are called "**sieve codes**" (Guetzkow, 1950, p. 48). Whether codes need to be exhaustive depends on the research question and the type of data analysis to be performed.

Ideally, the categories should also be **mutually exclusive.** That is, the categories should be created so that any given behavioral event in the behavioral stream is associated with only one code (Lazarsfeld & Barton, 1951; Holsti, 1969; Russell & Stiles, 1979). Bakeman and Gottman (1986) suggest that for all practical purposes there are strategies for making almost any coding system mutually exclusive. Many coding systems do this by establishing a decision tree of priorities for the codes so that if a given message or utterance can be coded into more than one category, it is coded into the category with the highest priority. Other coding systems recognize the multifunctions any given behavioral unit may play in an interaction by cross-classifying behavioral units on more than one dimension (Bakeman & Gottman, 1986). Even in a multifunctional approach, each dimension represents only one function and the coding system for that dimension is mutually exclusive.

Time Intervals. Time intervals are created by coding what occurs every 10 seconds, or 2 minutes—whatever unit of time is chosen. Bakeman and Gottman (1986) suggest that if the time interval chosen is shorter than the average event to be coded during the time interval, there is probably little distortion due to interval coding. Time interval coding is particularly risky, however, because more than one coding event may occur during a time interval no matter how carefully the time interval is chosen. Time interval coding is always questionable when sequential analyses are performed because there is no way to tell if the same event is of a sufficiently long duration to occur over more than one time interval, or if two separate events have occurred within the behavioral time stream.[3]

Choosing the Sample

The questions concerning sampling that were discussed in chapter 10 also apply here. It is important to achieve as representative a sample as possible from the population suggested by your research question. Some common questions about sampling in interaction analysis concern the representativeness of the individuals whose communication is to be studied, the representativeness of the types of messages sampled from those individuals, and the representativeness of the behaviors sampled from the messages.

The first two sampling problems are common to most communication methodologies. Studies in interaction analysis describe the subjects in the study so that readers may judge their representativeness. They also describe how the behavioral stream was generated so that it can be analyzed. Most interaction analysis studies give the participants a task to perform and then record their interaction while they complete the task.

One methodological problem which studies in interaction analysis often fail to examine is the nature of that task. In studying marital interaction, for example, researchers often make the inference that couples produce interaction using a structured discussion on some problem that is equivalent to the interaction they would produce if they were discussing a real marital problem together spontaneously (Gottman, Markman, & Notarius, 1977). This same methodological issue should be confronted in all interaction studies. The discussion topic, or instructions, and the decision-making task must produce a behavioral stream that is consistent with the aims of the study and is a representative sample of the interaction the researcher wishes to examine.

The representativeness of the sample of behaviors chosen from the generated behavioral stream is also of some importance to the interaction analyst.[4] Random sampling of the behavioral units is frequently frowned on in interaction analysis because it does not allow the dynamic processes in the behavioral stream to be studied. The use of time interval units of analysis is a sampling technique that allows the researcher to "sample" the behavioral stream every so often (determined by the length of the time unit). It is particularly vulnerable to questions of representativeness because "some behaviors occur very frequently, whereas others are relatively infrequent. Some behaviors have fairly long and variable durations, whereas others are moment-ary and go on and off quickly" (Sackett, Rupenthall, & Gluck, 1978, p. 7).

Selecting and Training Coders

Choosing and training the coders follows the format discussed in chapter 10, so you might want to review this material. Using coding manuals and training sessions that do not alert the coder to the hypotheses or research questions being tested is very important. Coders may also need periodic retraining sessions to make sure they continue to code consistently within the coding system.

Several common coding strategies are included in interaction coding manuals to make training more effective and efficient. One is a coding strategy in which the coder makes either-or classifications to a series of categories such as Stiles' (1978, 1980, 1981; Cansler & Stiles, 1981; Russell & Stiles, 1979) VRM, discussed above, or Shimanoff's (1985) pleasant-unpleasant valence, past-present-other time frame, speaker-other experiencer, object/event-person source. The **binary decision tree** is another common coding strategy in which a sequence of yes-no questions are asked for every behavioral unit. When the answer is "no" another question is asked. When the answer is "yes," the behavioral unit is coded (Anderson, 1983; Rogers, 1979). Finally, the use of coders from similar backgrounds is particularly important for interaction analyses based on inductive, grounded theory approaches.

Determining Reliability

When different individuals are used to code behavioral units we need to be sure that they consistently assign the identical codes to the data. "We need to calibrate observers with each other, or better yet, calibrate all observers against some standard protocol" (Bakeman & Gottman, 1986, p. 72). Intercoder reliability is a measure of the consistency with which coders agree with one another. If one coder's answers, such as the researcher's, are used as criteria for the other coders' answers, then the consistency being measured is against a standard protocol. Generally, reliability is assessed using some subsample of the entire data set. The types of coder reliability that are usually examined in interactional analysis studies include **unitizing reliability** and **categorizing,** or **interpretative reliability.**

Unitizing Reliability. Unitizing reliability is "the consistency with which coders selected the same amount of verbal behavior to be classified in each category" (Hawes, 1972, p. 95). When categories such as thought units, or utterances, are used we should determine that all coders perceive both the same number of units and the identical units to be coded. Using the same transcript, two coders might not agree on the same number of units to be classified. For example, "How late do you think you will be out tonight? I really think you ought to come in early since we will be leaving on vacation tomorrow and you promised to drive part of the time," might be coded into four units by one coder, /How late do you think you will be out tonight?/ I really think you ought to come in early/ since we will be leaving on vacation tomorrow/ and you promised to drive part of the time/, while another coder might see only three units, /How late do you think you will be out tonight?/ I really think you ought to come in early since we will be leaving on vacation tomorrow/ and you promised to drive part of the time/. Coders can also agree on the number of units without the units being identical or coterminous. Two coders might create three units as in the following, but only the final unit is identical: /How late do you think you will be out tonight?/ I really think you ought to come in early since we will be leaving on vacation tomorrow/ and you promised to drive part of the time/ vs. /How late do you think you will be out tonight? I really think you ought to come in early/ since we will be leaving on vacation tomorrow/ and you promised to drive part of the time/. Formulas for examining unitizing reliability can be found in Guetzkow (1950), and Bakeman and Gottman (1986, pp. 70–99). Hawes' (1972) study of physician-patient interviews solved the first unitizing problem by dividing verbal flow into ten-second units, and using Guetzkow's (1950) formula for estimating coder accuracy in unitizing a given segment.[5]

Unitizing reliability is "particularly crucial under three conditions: if the index of interpretative reliability is low and one needs to locate the source of the problem; if the units of analysis are conceptually independent of the coding system ('turns,' for instance); if the units themselves are interesting phenomena in their own right" (Folger, Hewes, & Poole, 1984, p. 119). Bakeman and Gottman (1986) and Folger, Hewes, and Poole (1984) also suggest that unit-by-unit reliability checks rather than general overall agreement in the number of units are necessary when subjective codes, or codes that are not exhaustive, are used, or when sequential analyses are to be performed using the codes.

Categorizing or Interpretative Reliability. Categorizing, or interpretative, reliability is "the proportion of units of behavior which the coders classified similarly" (Hawes, 1972, p. 95) using the categories in the coding system. When a researcher is training coders he or she should be concerned with categorizing reliability at the level of the individual codes. "Casual inspection immediately reveals which codes are often confused and which almost never are" (Bakeman & Gottman, 1986, p. 83). The codes that are confused with one another may suggest codes for which coders need to be retrained to improve clarity or may suggest improvement in the coding categories themselves if some codes are confused with other codes. When researchers report categorizing reliabilities for the study, they should be most concerned with reliability at the conceptual level of analysis being used. These two levels, the codes which the coders generate and the final conceptual codes used in the analysis, are not necessarily the same, as combined codes are often used in the final analysis procedures.

Guetzkow's (1950) P and Cohen's (1960) kappa are the two most common measures of categorizing reliability used in interaction analyses. They are measures which summarize the general reliability of a coding system. Bakeman and Gottman's (1986) "inclination, based on using kappa with a number of different coding schemes, is to regard kappas less than .7, even when significant, with some concern, but this is only an informal rule of thumb. Fleiss (1981), for example, characterizes kappas of .40 to .60 as fair, .60 to .75 as good, and over .75 as excellent" (p. 82). Ting-Toomey (1983) suggests that the standard criterion for kappa is .75.

Bakeman and Gottman (1986) and Folger, Hewes, and Poole (1984) caution that these measures are not sufficient if hypotheses which predict differences in the distributions among the categories for different groups of people are being tested or if sequential analyses are being performed on the codes. They suggest a set of procedures to test reliability category by category for systematic bias introduced into the data from varying reliabilities within a coding system relative to how individual categories are used. Bias is introduced into the data when some codes are used more frequently than others (particularly if the number of codes in the coding system is small). This bias may result from observers having a perceptual set that causes them to overuse a particular code, or when some categories are easier to perceive. Also, it may result when some codes occur less (or more) frequently in the behavioral stream being examined. Another type of bias occurs when some codes are misclassified as other codes more often than the latter codes are misclassified as the former codes.

If some misclassifications are considered more serious than others Cohen (1968) suggests the use of a weighted kappa as a solution. When sequential analyses are used it is also necessary to examine interact reliability between coders. Gottman (1980) suggests that if coders produce similar patterns of sequential transitions then they are reliable even if their category-by-category reliability is low.

Reliability Decay. **Reliability decay** or **coder drift** is a decrease in an individual coder's consistency over time. It is not unusual to discover that there is a gradual decay in reliability in coders compared to their training level (Johnson & Bolstad, 1973; Romanczyk, Kent, Diament, & O'Leary, 1973; Taplin and Reid, 1973). This is a particularly important problem in studies in which coding occurs over a long period of time. Bakeman and Gottman (1986, pp. 72–74) suggest some methods for reducing this problem. They include practices such as the use of one coder as a reliability checker who codes a sample of each coder's work and who retrains coders to the original standard, and the use of coders as reliability checks on one another periodically throughout the coding process. Since infrequently used codes are the greatest reliability problem, they also suggest that reliability coders should code a sufficient amount of acts or interacts to check the least frequently used codes.

Determining Validity

A measure is valid to the extent that it measures accurately what it was intended to measure. This means that what a measure is designed to do determines to a certain extent what criteria are used to judge its validity. Folger, Hewes, & Poole (1984) suggest that there are three approaches to studying interaction. Each of these approaches requires a different set of criteria for validation. One approach is to study interaction solely from a theoretical perspective which is not concerned with the interpretations of participants in the interaction. They call this the "**experienced mode.**" Researchers may also be interested in the shared meanings for interaction among the members of a particular culture. They call this the "**experiencing mode.**" Finally, researchers may be interested in the idiosyncratic meaning of interaction for those participants actually involved in the interaction. They call this the "**experiencer mode**" The approach a researcher takes determines what validation criteria are appropriate for the coding system.

Experienced Mode

Face Validity. The experienced mode requires evidence of both "face" and "construct" validity. Evidence for face validity comes from the researcher and others working in the theoretical area of interest. For face validity the researcher creates a logical analysis of the concept of interest and relates the categories in the coding system to that concept. One face validity concern in coding systems is bias in the coding system.

Any time interaction is reduced to a set of classifications, a certain amount of bias which reduces the validity of the coding system will likely be introduced by the coding process. All coding simplifies the natural complexities in the discourse by making an **equivalence assumption** that may reduce the coding system's validity. "Typically, every time a behavior is placed in a category there is the assumption that it is equivalent to every other behavior placed in that category" (Weick, 1969, p. 423). In addition, the more general a coding category is, the more added meaning which may be introduced, since all utterances coded into a category are regarded in the analysis as having all aspects of that category when they may have only one or a few. Creators of category systems try to balance the need for extensive category systems with the need for manageable systems in their search for valid category systems. The categorizing reliability estimates discussed earlier are sometimes used to argue that the categories are clearly defined and therefore valid because they are coded consistently. Whether this is an argument for validity rather than a restatement of reliability is questionable.

Complete and extensive coding rationales are important for other researchers to check the face validity of coding systems, and coding systems that do not provide sufficient rationales are criticized (O'Donnell-Trujillo, 1981). Ayers and Miura (1981, pp. 160–163) examine six relational coding instruments for their theoretical match to the Palo Alto group's original concepts. Their logical analysis is an example of face validity concerns.

Predictive Validity. The researcher may also attempt to establish the predictive validity of the measuring instrument. A hypothesis, or set of hypotheses, is generated which links the concept that the coding instrument operationalizes to another concept, often called the *criterion*, such as group differences in understanding, satisfaction, etc. (Refer to previous sample hypotheses.) For example, in Ayers and Miura's (1981) study they found the Rogers and Farace (1975) relational coding instrument was best able of the six instruments examined to predict compatible and incompatible dyads by coding the symmetrical exchanges in the dyads.

Folger, Hewes, and Poole (1984) criticize the use of predictive validity in arguing the validity of a measuring instrument. If no relationship exists between the two concepts tested, the coding system associated with the first system may be valid but no relationship will be found to exist. This is somewhat analogous to the horseshoe and academic achievement example used in chapter 5. The researcher may have a valid measure of horseshoe throwing ability and a valid measure of academic achievement, but there may be no relationship between the two measures because horseshoe throwing ability and academic achievement are not related.

Even if a relationship is discovered the coding system may still be invalid because it also measures a third concept which does have a relationship with the predicted concept. Folger and Poole (1982) suggest, for example, that Rogers and Farace's (1975) coding scheme may code hostility/affiliation as well as dominance/submission and it may be a reciprocity phenomenon associated with the former which creates the large number of symmetrical interactions found between spouses rather than the hypothesized relationship that the spouses are vying for relational stances relative to one another. "Predictive validity alone does not guarantee explanatory adequacy" (Poole & Folger, 1981a, p. 27) because "in a pure sense, . . . predictive validity is independent of the content of the measure" (Bowers & Courtright, 1984, p. 120).

Construct Validity. Construct validity is the degree to which an operationalization produces results that correspond to the theoretical construct it is supposed to measure. While it "refers to *empirical* relationships between the constructs (as tapped by the coding system) and other observables that are predicted by the observer's theory" (O'Donnell-Trujillo, 1981, p. 103) it goes beyond simple prediction because it "seeks to understand what underlying constructs account for patterns of relationships between the measure in question and other variables" (Bowers & Courtright, 1984, p. 120).

Construct validity may be measured by **convergent validity**, according to Ayers and Miura (1981). The reasoning is that instruments which measure the same construct should (theoretically) correlate highly with one another. Ayers and Miura (1981) found the convergent validity of six relational coding instruments (Ellis, Fisher, Drecksel, Hock, & Wertel, 1976; Erickson & Rogers, 1973; Folger & Puck, 1976; Mark, 1971; Rogers & Farace, 1975; Sluzki & Beavin, 1965) better for coding complementary interactions (one-up moves followed by one-down moves, or one-down moves followed by one-up moves) than for coding symmetrical interactions (one-up moves followed by one-up moves, or one-down moves followed by one-down moves). This would suggest that these coding systems are more valid measures of the construct "complementary interactions" than they are for the construct "symmetrical interactions."

In another study, O'Donnell-Trujillo (1981) examined the act-by-act convergence of the Rogers and Farace (1975) and the Ellis et al. (1976) relational coding systems. He found that the act-by-act validity was poor because of the differences in the two systems. Unitizing created one problem. (Rogers and Farace's (1975) system allows for two codes for each utterance, one as a response to the preceding utterance and one as a stimulus for the following utterance, while Ellis et al. (1976) allows for one code per utterance.) Ellis et al. (1976) use only a response mode, which is a pragmatic code, but include a measure of response intensity. Rogers and Farace (1975) use a grammatical form and a response mode, a combination of content and pragmatic coding, and do not include a measure of intensity. Studies of convergent validity often must deal with the difficulty of having to ignore subtleties of coding which make significant differences in how each coding instrument relates to the construct it is designed to measure. One solution to this problem is to return to face validity in which the proponents for respective coding systems create logical/analytical connections between their coding system and the construct.

Another indication of construct validity is **discriminant validity** according to Ayers and Miura (1981). The reasoning is that concepts and their operationalizations should be distinct from the original concept and the coding system which operationalizes it. For example, "two measures should not correlate highly with one another if they measure different traits even though a similar method is used" (Helmstadter, 1964, p. 143). Ayers and Miura (1981) found the discriminant validity of the six relational coding instruments better for complementary exchanges than for symmetrical exchanges. This again suggests that these coding systems are more valid measures of the construct "complementary interactions" than they are for the construct "symmetrical interactions."

Experiencing Mode

Representational Validity. Folger, Hewes, and Poole (1984) argue that the only solution to the validity problems discussed above is to recognize that coding systems for communication interaction represent culturally shared interpretations to some extent. This suggests that the coding systems should be validated from the perspective of the experiencing mode. "Coding requires the inference and assignment of meaning to utterances; it attempts to duplicate the outcomes of human interpretative processes, to identify the conventional meaning of utterances. Therefore a valid coding system also meets the requirement of **representational validity**—its categorization should reflect the meaning of utterances in the culture" (Poole & Folger, 1981a, p. 26). "Evidence for representational validity would demonstrate that the particular constructs or functions identified by the coding system are part of the common meanings ascribed to the interaction by participants" (Poole & Folger, 1981a, p. 27). Representational validity is a type of predictive validity in which the "criterion" is the meaning ascribed to the interactions by individuals from the same culture as the participants. To the extent that "the researcher can give convincing theoretical reasons for those successful predictions" (Bowers & Courtright, 1984, p. 120) representational validity can also be considered a type of construct validity.

Folger and Poole (1982) argue that the relational or pragmatic perspective implies that individuals interpret the control function of messages and do not just respond to the messages themselves and therefore the experiencing mode is appropriate when intersubjective category systems are examined for validity. And "representational validity is the *sine qua non* of coding systems in the experiencing mode" (Folger, Hewes, & Poole, 1984, p. 145). Rogers and Millar (1982) strongly disagree. They argue that "The pragmatic researcher asks 'how behavior means' rather than 'what the performer means' by the behavior (Scheflen, 1974, p. 181) and attempts to answer this question by describing redundant, stochastic behavioral sequences and pattern of sequences.... We simply disagree with the implicit hierarchy that 'perceptions' and 'interpretations' of interaction are somehow more 'valid' or 'real' or 'true' than the 'level of mere behavior' (Heyman & Shaw, 1978, p. 231) and, therefore, should be given more theoretical weight in theory development" (p. 250). The focus on examining behavior sequences as meaning without reference to the common cultural meaning/interpretations of participants of both Ellis et al. (1976) and Rogers and Farace (1975) places these researchers (from their own perspective) in the experienced mode and not subject to the requirements of representational validity.

Folger and Sillars (1980), however, have examined the representational validity of Erickson and Rogers' (1973) coding system to see if certain specific message categories were perceived by untrained observers as dominant or submissive as they were coded. In addition, they broke down some of Erickson and Rogers' (1973) categories into new subcategories based on previous research with those subcategories. Their results suggest that some of the subcategories are not consistent with the overall category rating of one-up, one-down, one-across control functions as they are used in Erickson and Rogers' (1973) coding system. For example, Erickson and Rogers (1973) code all questions as one-down, submissive movements while naive observers code closed questions and questions in which the listener is fed the answer as much more dominant than other question types which are perceived as somewhat neutral in tone. Folger and Sillars (1980) demonstrate that Erickson and Rogers' (1973) coding system is not consistent with naive subjects' perception of domineering and submissive messages, particularly because naive observers perceive almost any verbal participation as nonsubmissive in nature.

In an examination of the representational validity of his verbal response mode coding system (VRM), Stiles (1980) had naive observers rate each participant in ten different dyadic interactions which had been used in previous research on twelve adjectives associated with the dimensions used in his VRM coding system or with Bales' (1950) interaction process analysis (IPA) coding system. He discovered that the roles conceived by the coding systems and the roles as they were perceived by the raters were consistent with one another. Even though the raters were not using the same language as the coding systems, they were apparently using the same basic information in making their judgments.

Poole and Folger (1981a) had naive observers rate the dissimilarity of pairs of passages on a nine-point Likert scale for all possible paired comparisons for eleven passages of seven utterances, each from a dyad decision making interaction. The pattern of these ratings was then compared to the ratings expert judges made, based on three different schemes for coding interaction (Bales' IPA (1950), Fisher's (1970) Decision Proposal Coding System and Mabry's (1975) Pattern Variable Coding System). The multidimensional scaling procedures they used allowed them to make judgments concerning the relative weight subjects placed on particular dimensions in making their judgments, the most representational features of each coding system analyzed, and a comparison of which coding system or combinations of coding systems were most representational. They found that overall, the Bales and Fisher coding systems had greater representational validity.

One problem with representational validity is that it should be demonstrated for each new type of interaction and for each new group of people being studied. Another problem is that naive observers use all the cues available when rating the general impact of a message, not just the words alone. For example, they use paralinguistic and non-vocal cues in rating the dominance/submissiveness of messages (Folger & Sillars, 1980). In addition, individuals seem to be attuned to the interactive nature of communication. Even when rating only one participant in an interaction, they apparently rely on how that person is being treated by the other participant in making their judgments (Stiles, 1980). This means that coding systems, such as Bales' (1950) IPA, which contain a mixture of the content, intersubjective, and/or expressive categorizing systems probably have a greater potential for representational validity than those which focus on one categorizing system. Also, representational validation studies which allow observers to use cues that are not available within the coding system being examined may find the coding system not as representationally valid as other measures (Folger & Sillars, 1980). Keeping coding systems theoretically pure and using multiple coding systems, each of which codes a particular concept or function, would allow researchers to discover the relative weights individuals use when interpreting messages. Rogers and Millar (1982) and Stiles (1980) also argue that only by keeping the study of social behavior and the study of participants' interpretations of social behavior separate can we examine the interdependence of the two.

Watzlawick, Beavin, and Jackson (1967) and Wilder (1979) also suggest that relational definitions may be achieved outside the conscious awareness of participants. Some participants may be more aware of the criteria they use in interpreting messages than others. For example, Burggraf (1985) proposes that individuals' subjective interpretations of their communication and their relational definitions are based on cognitive schema, such as self-perception. She suggests that not all individuals, for example, are equally aware of controlling cues and therefore they are not all equally qualified to judge relational control implications. "People with an explicit schema for relational control should be more consciously aware of such cues when displayed by others, while those with no schema for relational control may not even notice those controlling cues. . . . Aschematics for relational control would miss the controlling intent of messages and would process the same message for some other type of information relevant to a different self-defined schema domain (friendliness, perhaps)" (p. 15).

Males and females may, for example, have different schema regarding interpersonal interactions. Thompson, Hatchett, and Phillips' (1981) study of male-female differences in the interpretation of interpersonal relational words and Krueger's (1985) study of egalitarian (equal) decision making in dual-career couples support the premise that coding systems may be used differently by men and women in interpreting messages. Coding systems based on the sole criterion of a general representational validity would not allow these differences to be clearly examined. Poole and Folger (1981a) do, however, suggest using the dimensional weights generated by multidimensional scaling techniques for each subject to judge if different interpretative schema are being used by the individual raters in representational validation studies.

Experiencer Mode. Validation in the experiencer mode requires that the researcher generate "evidence that the participants *in the interaction being studied* would assign the coded function to the messages in the exchange" (Folger, Hewes, & Poole, 1984, p. 152). Hawes' (1972) study of physician-patient interviews mentioned earlier is an example of a study in which the actual participants viewed their interaction and reported their thoughts and feelings. If the actual participants had also rated or coded their own interaction using the coding system then evidence for validity in the experiencer mode would have been generated. Some studies suggest that there is not much difference between observer and actual participant ratings as long as both are from the same culture (Gouran & Whitehead, 1971; Schneider, 1970).

Analysis of Data

Many types of measures can be utilized in examining communicaton interaction behavior such as: frequency, latency, intensity, duration, and sequences (Hartup, 1979). Frequency is the number of times an act (or a given interact) occurs. Relative frequencies, the number of times an act (or a given interact) occurs divided by the total number of acts (or interacts), are often used as a measure of intensity when acts or interacts are related to roles or groups of individuals. For example, the number of one-up moves initiated by an individual in an interaction may be defined as that individual's domineeringness (Rogers-Millar & Millar, 1979). The VRM has also been used to classify speaker roles by determining the ratios or proportions of different types of utterances made by different speakers. Speakers are attentive if their utterances mainly focus on the other's experience and informative if they mainly focus on the speaker's experience. Speakers are acquiescent if they use the other's frame of reference and directive if they insist on using their own frame of reference. Speakers are presumptuous if they presume they have knowledge of the other and unassuming if they do not (Stiles 1981). And Rogers-Millar and Millar (1979) used the ratio of one-up/one-down statements as a measure of the relative pattern of assertion and submission for an individual.

Latency is the amount of time before a behavior is manifested. Capella's (Cappella & Planalp, 1981) measure of between-turn reaction time in talk and silence sequences is a latency measure. When one speaker stops vocalizing the amount of time before another speaker begins vocalizing is the latency of the second speaker's behavior.

The intensity or magnitude of a behavioral response is difficult to measure, which is why relative frequencies are often used. Rogers, Courtright, and Millar (1980) have developed a measure of message intensity by creating weights for each code based on its theoretical distance from the other codes and multiplying the resulting rank distances for the grammatical codes by the rank distances for the response modes. For example, the least intense of the five grammatical codes is a noncomplete utterance (with a rank of 1) and the most intense is a talkover (with a rank of 5). The least intense of the ten response modes is support (with a rank of 1) and the most intense is disconfirmation (with a rank of 10). A talkover which is also coded a disconfirmation has an intensity rank of 50 (5 × 10) while a talkover which is also coded as support has an intensity rank of 5 (5 × 1). Using these message intensities, the authors are able to code the "distances" (intensities) between any two contiguous messages or interacts. A talkover/disconfirmation (50) followed by a noncomplete/talkover (10) has an intensity distance of 40 (50–10). Donahue (1981) has developed a similar intensity measure for his negotiation interact coding system called relative advantage.

Duration measures how long an act occurs. Frequencies are sometimes used as a measure of duration. The relative number of words used by each speaker is a rough estimate of duration of speech, but it does not take into account the rate of speech. Some people speak faster or use more pauses between vocalizations within their utterances. Recoding onset and offset times for a category (Bakeman & Gottman, 1986) gives you a measure of duration for that category.

Sequencing measures the relationship of one category of behavior to another in a stream of behavior. For example, in a conversation people exchange speaking turns. Some characteristic of A's message behavior may affect or predict some characteristic of B's message behavior. "Sequences may be studied within the ongoing behavior stream of single individuals or within two or more behavioral streams involving many individuals" (Hartup, 1979, p. 19). Data coded at the level of the interact (Rogers & Farace, 1975) is a sequencing measure.[6]

Many sequence interaction studies also do not use the message codes directly. They combine the codes into more useful groups which are theoretically interesting to the researcher. Hawes (1972) combines his codes into three categories: message inputs which facilitate, maintain, or impede information processing by the communication system. Rogers and Farace (1975) combine their grammatical and response codes into one-up, one-across, and one-down classifications which represent the control directions of these messages. These classifications are in turn combined so that the interacts or relationships between contiguous messages can be classified. For example, competitive symmetry is a one-up message followed by a one-up message.

Even more complex measures can be created: the comparative dominance of the members in a dyad can be measured by "the difference between the percentage of one-up complementarity ($\uparrow\downarrow$), indicating compliance, and the percentage of one-up symmetrical ($\uparrow\uparrow$), indicating resistance" (Rogers-Millar & Millar, 1979, p. 241) messages. This is, however, still a descriptive analysis at the proportion/ratio level of interacts. "Ratio measures of frequencies of . . . behaviors do contain a relational component, but with all aggregated data produced by summing single behavioral events across individuals and dyads, the temporal contingent quality of the discourse has been removed" (Rogers, Millar, & Bavelas, 1985, p. 181). **Lag sequential analysis** (Sackett, 1978, 1979, 1980), **Markov**, and **semi-Markov models** (Hewes, 1979; Manderscheid, Rae, McCarrick & Silbergeld, 1982), **log-linear** and **contingency table models** (Bakeman & Gottman, 1986) are methods for finding the probability of one category of behavior in a behavior stream being associated with other categories of behavior even when they are not contiguous.[7] These very powerful analytical tools produce a description of the patterns in the behavioral stream, but the theoretical frameworks which generate the hypotheses being examined provide the explanations for why the particular patterns are meaningful.

Interaction analysis yields a variety of analyses: (1) a descriptive pattern of the individual acts, interacts, and more complex behavioral sequence patterns generated by the interactants; (2) a descriptive pattern of recurring interacts which constrain the flow of communication such as phases in small group interaction research; (3) a descriptive pattern of repetitions of interact, and more complex behavioral sequence patterns or cycles in which phases recur; (4) correlates of act, interact, and more complex sequences of acts with various types of interactants; and, (5) correlates of interact, and more complex behavioral sequence patterns with hypothetical constructs such as cohesiveness, power, leadership, consensus, role strain, marital satisfaction, communication satisfaction, rigidity, understanding and gender (Courtright, Millar, & Rogers-Millar, 1979; Fisher, 1983; Hawes, 1972; McCarrick, Handarscheid, & Silbergeld, 1981).

Interaction Analysis Studies

Many early studies using interaction analysis contained some of the methodological problems which have been discussed in this chapter. Kohen's (1975) study of "The Development of Reciprocal Self-Disclosure in Opposite-Sex Interaction" is an example of some of the difficulties in using interaction analysis. Her study focuses on "how self-disclosure levels change during interaction ... the development of reciprocity of self-disclosure among individuals interacting in opposite-sex dyads" (Kohen, 1975, p. 404).

The behavioral "unit of disclosure was defined as the smallest segment of behavior to which the observer could assign a classification" (Kohen, 1975, p. 406) and intercoder reliability coefficients were computed for the three 5-minute intervals used in the study. These were probably interrater agreement reliabilities, although how the unitizing reliability coefficients were arrived at is not clear. These reliabilities also served as categorizing reliabilities since the number of units, a frequency measure, also serves as the measure of self-disclosure. Coders, then, agreed on the number of self-disclosure units within each 5-minute interval. This does not mean that they agreed on what constituted each specific unit. The agreement index also does not take into account the amount of agreement which is a function of chance. Cohen's (1960) kappa could be used to correct this problem.

The "verbal statements were defined as self-disclosing when the subject mentioned biographical data, attitudes toward family, dating, self, school, the research situation and/or partner, personal possessions, hobbies, past or future behavior, and feelings and emotions" (Kohen, 1975, p. 406). This is a very broad single category and it is difficult to believe that it fulfills Weick's (1969) equivalence assumption discussed earlier. A finer level of coding would have been helpful in examining the validity of the coding system.

Finally, the concept of reciprocity requires the analysis of contingent behavior (Dindia, 1982; Gottman, Markman, & Notarius, 1977). "Reciprocity of self-disclosure is defined conceptually as mutually contingent self-disclosure. This means that A's self-disclosure to B causes B's self-disclosure to A and vice versa" (Dindia, 1982, p. 506). Kohen (1975) analyzed the relationship between the number of self-disclosure units by using correlations. These indicate that the partner's self-disclosure was related but not that one partner's self-disclosure was contingent on the other partner. One partner's self-disclosure may be dependent on the other's, but the other's may not be dependent on the first individual's self-disclosure. Both partners may have similar predispositions for self-disclosure and respond with the same number of units categorized as self-disclosure but these units are randomly interjected into the interaction and are not contingent on the other's behavior. "It is easier to see this if we consider nonsocial behaviors, such as eating or typing. A husband may eat or type at a rate similar to his wife's without any contingency between these two activities; they may, for example, have similar physical tempos. In this case we would merely report that eating or typing took place at similar rates, not that they were reciprocal" (Gottman, 1979a, p. 65). Measuring input and output variables and inferring that a process accounts for the obtained relationship is not the same as examining the process itself (Fisher & Hawes, 1971). Lag sequential analysis is one alternative which could demonstrate reciprocity of the self-disclosing behavior.

In all fairness to this study, it should be noted that Rausch's early work in Markov chains (Rausch, Barry, Hertel, & Swain, 1974) had been published only the year before Kohen's (1975) study, and Sackett's (1974) early work in lag sequential analysis was still an unpublished manuscript. Interaction analysis is being influenced theoretically as well as in the sophistication of its analytical procedures by the development of new methodologies.

Manderscheid, Rae, McCarrick, and Silbergeld's (1982) study of "A Stochastic Model of Relational Control in Dyadic Interaction" exemplifies one of the more complete approaches to interaction analysis.

The study is clearly based on a theoretical model of negotiation processes which takes into account the contingency of one individual's behavior during a negotiation on the behavior of the other individual in the negotiation. The authors clearly relate the theoretical assumptions underlying their model of negotiation to the use of Markov models as their analytical tool. This is one of the major strengths of this study.

The authors hypothesize a behavioral response sequence "because *re*defining relational control implies a sequence consisting of (1) A's setting the stage, (2) B's responding with his/her definition of the relationship, (3) A's responding with *his/her* definition of the relationship, and (4) B's redefining the relationship based on (1), (2), and (3)" (Manderscheid et al., 1982, p. 65). This sequence is a third-order Markov structure and by predicting this structure the authors answer Hewes' (1979, p. 70) criticism that Markovian models are simply descriptive of behavioral chains if these chains cannot be explained within a theoretical framework.

The authors specified how the couples were chosen so that their representativeness as a sample can be judged by the reader. Mean age and marriage length, racial and occupational composition are given as well as a screening process described which excluded those who had previous therapy, were currently in therapy, or who had other mental or physical illnesses.

The authors used naturally occurring streams of behavior. "Prior to and following each of seven consecutive meetings with the psychiatrist, each couple was instructed to record a 10-minute dialogue reflective of feelings" (Manderschied et al., 1982, p. 65). One problem with the methodological description is that it is not clear whether the tapes were produced immediately prior to the meeting under controlled laboratory conditions or whether they were produced by the participants at home at their convenience.

The authors used the Ericson-Rogers (1973) Relational Coding system which they related theoretically to the negotiation process. In other words, they did not just adopt the coding system because it had been used previously in research. Unfortunately, as is typical in many interaction analysis studies, the authors rely on the interrater reliability reports from Roger's (1973) dissertation. They do not provide unitizing and categorizing reliabilities, or examine reliability decay. Unitizing reliability is probably not very important since those who use the Ericson-Rogers (1973) coding system typically use the uninterrupted speaking turn as the unit and these are typically identified with a high degree of reliability. Unit-by-unit categorizing reliabilities, however, should have been provided since the analyses to be used were Markov chains which are sequential analyses.

It might also be argued that the authors should have supplied evidence of representational validity since they base their concept of negotiation on Handel's (1979) description of the negotiation process as one involving "actors" who adapt to others and who evaluate and change their strategies based on the responses to others.

Finally, the results are displayed in a diagraph, a graph which pictures the transition probabilities from one message sequence to another. This makes the results easier to read since they are often complex. And the results are related theoretically to previous research in a straightforward manner.

Advantages and Disadvantages of Interaction Analysis

The major advantage of interaction analysis is that it allows behavior in the communication process to be examined directly. Patterns of behavior can be categorically described and related to theories about these patterns without reference to the interpretations of the participants themselves. It is also possible for the participants' interpretations to be related to these categorized patterns of behavior. Various inputs and outputs related to these behavioral processes can also be examined.

The communication process is very complex. By developing interaction analysis categorizing systems which examine separate aspects of this process and using these systems cojointly to describe interactions, we can begin to clarify and understand communication more thoroughly. Folger and Sillars (1980), for example, found that message cues which are not considered by the Erickson and Rogers (1973) system, such as paralinguistic cues, account for more of the naive subjects' perceptions of relationship definitions than the message cues that were coded by the system. This means that nonverbal interactional categorizing systems should be developed for use in conjunction with verbal categorizing systems if we are to attempt a more complete understanding of the communication process.

One of the criticisms concerning interaction analysis is that it does not take the context of the interaction into consideration. "For example, suppose a husband says, 'Let's spend Christmas at your mother's,' and the wife responds, 'You always get tense at my mother's.' Most coding systems would categorize the wife's statement as a disagreement since it *functions* not to support the husband's proposal of how to spend the vacation" (Gottman, Markman, & Notarius, 1977, p. 462). The wife might simply be trying to be supportive and understanding of her husband and the message might imply that she would understand his not wanting to spend their vacation time somewhere where he would be tense. The previously established relationship might affect how the message would be interpreted by the participants. This is true, however, of all studies of communication except those in the experiencer mode which ask for the idiosyncratic interpretations of those involved in the process. Even in that mode it might be helpful for the wife to recognize that her "understanding" comment is in a grammatical and response form which theoretically, or representationally, suggests disagreement. The context of the type of relationship is, after all, an input to the interaction which ought to be examined for its relationship to the behavioral stream.

Another criticism of interaction analysis is that people and their behavior fluctuate. "People are able to maintain stable conceptions of a relationship despite fluctuations in interactions" (Planalp, 1983, p. 9) so that what interaction analysis of the behavioral stream tells us is relatively insignificant when we are trying to understand and predict certain outputs, such as satisfaction or relational control. One important feature of Markov models is that they examine this indeterminacy. The overall pattern of behavior may be consistent even though individuals may vary widely (Hewes, 1975; Leik & Meeker, 1975; Manderscheid et al., 1982).

The major disadvantage to using interaction analysis is the time and effort involved. Gottman et al. (1977), for example, report that 28 hours of verbatim transcribing of the interaction and coding of the transcript were required for every hour of interaction. This does not include coder training time. When coders are paid, and many are, the expense can be prohibitive for scholars working without financial support for their research.

A second, and minor, disadvantage of using interaction analysis is that until very recently statistical programs for doing lag sequential analyses and Markov analyses were not readily available. Even now there are relatively few sources for the "advanced" beginner to consult to begin to understand the theory and application of these procedures. One notable exception is Bakeman and Gottman's (1986) book *Observing Interaction: An Introduction to Sequential Analysis*. The importance of studying the actual behavior involved in communication makes the struggle worth it for those involved in interaction analysis.

SUMMARY

Interaction analysis covers a variety of methodologies that are concerned with systematically examining behavior streams and how the behavior of one individual influences the behavior of another individual. Many disciplines have influenced the development of interaction analysis including education, psychology, communication, and information processing.

Researchers utilize interaction analysis to examine hypotheses and research questions about behavioral streams by developing coding systems. These coding systems may be derived from a logical/deductive approach, a theoretically based/discourse analytic approach or an inductive/grounded theory approach. Coding systems can categorize content, intersubjective, or expressive elements in the behavioral streams, utilizing classical or pragmatic codes or rating scales. Two types of behavioral units are commonly used in interaction analysis, events and time intervals. The units are generally chosen so that they are exhaustive and mutually exclusive. Sampling problems include the representativeness of the individuals, the interactions, and the behavioral units chosen from the interactions.

Coders are trained in applying the coding system to the behavioral stream, and unitizing and categorizing or interpretative reliability is examined. When coding occurs over an extended period of time, coder drift or reliability decay is also examined.

The validity requirements of coding systems vary with the perspective chosen by the researcher. Three different perspectives, the experienced mode, the experiencing mode, and the experiencer mode, were discussed. Face validity, predictive validity, construct validity, and representational validity are used to examine interaction analysis coding systems.

Many types of measures can be derived from data generated by interactional coding systems: frequency, latency, intensity, duration, and sequences of behavioral units. These measures can be used to describe the pattern of individual, dyadic or group acts, interacts, and even more complicated behavioral sequences. These patterns can then be related to communication processes and outcomes of interaction.

Two studies which used interaction analysis were examined. Interaction analysis allows behavior in complex interactions to be examined directly although it may fail to take the relationship and context of the interaction into account directly. It is time-consuming, sometimes expensive, and statistical procedures for analyzing the data produced are just beginning to be developed.

NOTES

1. See Levinson (1983), chapter 6, for a comparison of conversational analysis and discourse analysis.
2. Cairns and Green (1979) examine the differences in rating and category coding schemes.
3. See Bakeman and Gottman (1986) for a more detailed analysis of the problem of choosing the behavioral unit.
4. Bakeman and Gottman (1986, pp. 137–143) suggest that the number of necessary interacts which must be coded (sampled) for sequential analyses is greater when adjacent codes can be the same, when the coding system contains a larger number of codes, and when the analysis requires longer sequences, such as the message-response-reinforcement sequences discussed earlier. They offer several formulas for discovering the minimum number of behavioral units which should be sampled under these various conditions.
5. See Folger, Hewes, and Poole (1984) for a more complete analysis of the problems associated with unitizing reliability.
6. For example, while Stiles' (1978) coding system is derived from a clear theoretical perspective, it has not been used to study interaction as a dynamic process since it has been used to code acts rather than interacts (Cansler & Stiles, 1981).
7. Suppose you want to find out what happens in the behavioral stream after a "coaxing" message. Coaxing becomes the criterion and is called lag 0 in lag sequential analysis. Lag 1 is the next message, lag 2 the message following lag 1, etc. Ting-Toomey (1983) found that when coaxing was used as the criterion category, dyads in the high marital adjustment group had a significant sequence of coaxing messages at lags 2, 4, and 5. No such pattern was discovered in low marital adjustment dyads. Since odd numbered lags (when the lags represent speaking turns) are the other person and even-numbered lags are the same person as the criterion, this means that in high marital adjustment dyads an individual who sent a coaxing message (criterion, lag 0) was likely to respond with a coaxing message to the other individual's next two messages (lag 1 and lag 3) and the other person was likely to respond with a coaxing message at the end of this stream of behavior (lag 5).

STUDY QUESTIONS

1. What is interaction analysis?
2. How is the broadest definition of interaction analysis different from the most stringent definition?
3. Distinguish among interaction analysis, conversational analysis, and discourse analysis.

4. Discuss some historical contributions to the development of interaction analysis.
5. What is relational analysis?
6. What are two types of hypotheses examined using interactional analysis? Give an example of each. What often substitutes for hypotheses in interactional analysis studies? Give an example.
7. Differentiate among the logical/deductive, theoretically based/discourse analytical, and inductive/grounded theory approaches to the construction of interactional analysis coding systems.
8. Which three aspects of interaction are examined using content, intersubjective, and expressive categorizing systems?
9. What is the difference between a classical and a pragmatic coding system? How do these differ from rating coding systems?
10. Explain the difference between an event and a time interval behavioral unit.
11. What characteristics does an "exhaustive" coding system have? a mutually exclusive categorizing system? Do sieve codes have both of these characteristics?
12. Discuss some sampling problems in interaction analysis.
13. What are some common coding strategies used in interaction analysis training manuals?
14. Define unitizing reliability. When is it particularly important?
15. What is categorizing, or interpretative reliability? How is it most commonly computed? What are typical standards for these measures? Are these procedures sufficient for sequential analyses of interactional data?
16. What is reliability decay or coder drift?
17. Name the criteria for validity in the experienced, experiencing, and experiencer modes.
18. Explain the differences among face validity, predictive validity, construct validity, and representational validity. Differentiate between convergent and discriminant construct validity.
19. What are some of the methodological problems associated with each type of validity? Give examples from the studies discussed.
20. What are the common measures generated by interaction analysis? Give an example of each.
21. What type of analyses of interaction can be generated using interaction analysis?
22. Discuss the major advantages and disadvantages of interaction analysis.

ANNOTATED READINGS

Ayres, J., & Miura, S. Y. (1981). Construct and predictive validity of instruments for coding relational control communication. *Western Journal of Speech Communication, 45*, 159–171.
  Good examples of face validity, predictive validity, and construct validity comparisons in interaction analysis.
Bakeman, R., & Gottman, J. M. (1986). *Observing interaction: An introduction to sequential analysis.* Cambridge: Cambridge University Press.

Easy to read for a fairly complete introduction to methodological concerns in interaction analysis.

Folger, J. P., Hewes, D., & Poole, M. S. (1984). Coding social interaction. In B. Dervin & M. Voight (Eds.), *Progress in the communication sciences* (pp. 115—161). New York: Ablex.

Advanced reading in reliability and validity of coding systems.

Folger, J. P., & Poole, M. S. (1982). Relational coding schemes: The question of validity; and Rogers, L. E., & Millar, F. E. (1982). The question of validity: A pragmatic response. In M. Burgoon (Ed.), *Communication Yearbook, 5* (pp. 235–247; 249–257). New Brunswick, NJ: Transaction Books.

These two articles combined are a good example of the influence of theory on methodological issues.

Folger, J. P., & Sillars, A. (1980). Relational coding and perceptions of dominance. In B. Morse & L. Phelps (Eds.), *Interpersonal communication: A relational perspective* (pp. 322–333). Minneapolis: Burgess and Poole, M. S., & Folger, J.P. (1981a). A method for establishing the representational validity of interaction coding systems: Do we see what they see? *Human Communication Research, 8,* 26–42.

Both articles examine representational validity. The Folger and Sillars article is easier to understand.

Hawes, L. (1972). Development and application of an interview coding system. *Central States Speech Journal, 23,* 92–99.

Exemplifies inductive/grounded theory approach to interaction analysis.

O'Donnell-Trujillo, N. (1981). Relational communication: A comparison of coding schemes. *Communication Monographs, 48,* 91–105.

Good example of some of the difficulties in comparing coding schemes to determine their validity.

Rogers, E., & Farace, R. (1975). Analysis of relational communication in dyads: New measurement procedures. *Human Communication Research, 1,* 222–239.

A good example of a theoretically based/discourse analytical approach to interaction analysis. Differentiates the content and relational aspects of communication.

Rogers, L. E., Courtright, J. A., & Millar, F. E. (1980). Message control intensity: Rationale and preliminary findings. *Communication Monographs, 47,* 201–219.

Good example of measure of intensity in interaction analysis which is more sophisticated methodologically than the relative frequency of messages.

Russell, R. L., & Stiles, W. B. (1979). Categories for classifying language in psychotherapy. *Psychological Bulletin, 86,* 404–419.

Exemplifies a logical/deductive approach typology of three category systems by two coding strategies for verbal interaction. Also exemplifies the relationship of theory to methodology.

Sacket, G. P. (Ed.). (1978). *Observing behavior* (Vol. 2), *Data collection and analysis methods.* Baltimore: University Park Press.

Easy to read introduction to interaction analysis.

CHAPTER 12

Unobtrusive Measures

By Janis W. Andersen,
San Diego State University

HISTORY

The ingenious book that introduced unobtrusive measurement as a systematic research procedure was almost called *The Bullfighter's Beard and Other Nonreactive Measures*. The authors (Webb, Campbell, Schwartz, & Sechrest, 1966) created that title from an observation that bullfighters' beards are longer immediately before a bullfight than they are on any other day at that same time. The authors thought this observation might be a measure of anxiety level. Unsure of the causal mechanism, they suggested that perhaps the anxiety of the upcoming bullfight actually causes a beard to grow faster or perhaps the shaky hand of a bullfighter produces a poorer shave. Either way, beard length may be an unobtrusive indicator of anxiety. This observation and hundreds of similar indirect measures created the essence of their now classic measurement text.

A second title they almost used was *Oddball Research, Oddball Measures*. According to the authors, the "occasionally bizarre content of the material" made that title a natural. However, a fear that librarians might put the book in the sporting section or some other inappropriate place caused the authors to reconsider, choosing a more scholarly title. The book's eventual title, *Unobtrusive Measures: Nonreactive Research in the Social Sciences*, entrenched the term "unobtrusive measurement" so solidly in social science literature that its use today is often in nonitalicized lower case print. This everyday usage of a once technical term reflects an unobtrusive acceptance of the term. Today the label unobtrusive measurement is so commonplace that its origin need not be acknowledged (Sechrest, 1975). It is interesting to speculate about whether *Oddball Research, Oddball Measures* would have had the same impact.

The term **unobtrusive measurement** refers to methods of studying social behavior that do not affect or distort the behavior. The researcher is a distant observer, a clever detective, a hidden film maker, or an archivist searching previously collected data for new information. Obviously, unobtrusive measurement existed before Webb and his colleagues labeled, catalogued, and explicitly identified the technique. It was their book, however, that defined the research methodology and began the campaign to make unobtrusive measurement an important tool for those who conduct social science investigations.

Today it is more than 20 years since unobtrusive measurement was introduced as a labeled research tool. Currently there is widespread agreement about the advisability of using unobtrusive measurement techniques. Most researchers believe that the understanding of communicative processes will be richer if at least some of the data gathering techniques are minimally distorting and unobtrusive. Unfortunately, relatively few communication studies have used such measures. This lack is partly explained by a lack of awareness. Individuals who are not trained in methods courses abut unobtrusive measuring techniques often ignore this approach. This chapter is an attempt to help provide this training.

UNOBTRUSIVE MEASURES DEFINED

Unobtrusive measures, also called **nonreactive measures**, are research tactics that allow data collection without interference in the process being studied. Data collected through interviews, questionnaires, self-report instruments, semantic differential scales, and psychophysiological apparatus are obtained in obtrusive ways. That is, the communication activities are stopped or altered in order to assess causes, effects, patterns, and trends. Unobtrusive measures glean data from historical accounts, physical traces, statistical data banks, and unnoticeable observations. Unobtrusive measures are taken without the knowledge of the interactants.

Unobtrusive measurement or nonreactive research challenges the researcher to be an investigative detective. Like Sherlock Holmes, the researcher seeks to uncover the mysteries of the communication process by observing what people do, what they surround themselves with, and what they inadvertently leave behind them. Both the social scientist and the detective must hypothesize causes and determine effects of specific behaviors. They do this partly by inferring past behavior, previous and present internal states, current predispositions and likely predilections. Additionally they do this by carefully observing behavior directly, noting its patterns and correlates. Finally they do this by observing outcomes, consequences, or products and finding the likely pathways that lead to a particular outcome. The detective searches for motives, deeds, and victims. The social scientist uncovers independent variables, mediating processes, and dependent variables.

Both the social scientist and the detective must find evidence. Often, they interview or interrogate participants both directly and by having them complete questionnaires. Obtrusively gathered informaton is often quite useful in helping them solve a mystery. But both the detective and the social scientist have available a wide array of other relevant clues. These clues may provide corroborating evidence for the interview data. Sometimes these clues are keys that by themselves unlock mysterious doors. The detective is trained to notice, collect, and interpret these hidden clues. Likewise the social scientist must learn to gather unobtrusive data to supplement the obtrusively collected evidence.

GENERAL EXAMPLES

Perhaps unobtrusive methods can be more clearly understood through a few general examples supplied by Webb and his colleagues. How might one assess the actual popularity of an exhibit at a museum? A researcher could create a questionnaire to assess attitude towards various exhibits. It is possible, however, that these questionnaire responses might indicate greater popularity for the more easily remembered exhibits rather than for the exhibits that are actually more frequently visited. One could conduct a poll but people might name the exhibits that make them look good somehow—more intellectual, serious, or fashionable. A researcher could stand and count the number of people at each exhibit, but this is time-consuming. Moreover, it is not totally unobtrusive since people might see the observer and that could affect their behavior. A more unobtrusive measure might be to note the replacement rate for various floor tiles near the exhibit. The selective erosion of the floor tiles can serve as a measure of the relative popularity of exhibits. Webb and his colleagues noted that the floor tiles around the hatching chick exhibit at the Museum of Science and Industry in Chicago wear out about every six weeks while floor titles surrounding other exhibits hold up for several years.

How could one determine just how much alcohol is surreptitiously consumed in a town which is officially dry? Questionnaires and interviews might produce a distorted picture. You can think of numerous reasons why people might not want to admit how much alcohol they consume. Even if information-gathering was conducted anonymously, and even if respondents trusted the anonymity, people might not even have sufficient self-awareness about this negatively sanctioned behavior to report their consumption accurately. Webb and his colleagues suggest that one simply count empty liquor bottles in trash cans.

The degree of children's excitement surrounding Christmas might be determined by measuring the comparative size of Santa Claus in children's drawings. Popularity of radio stations could be assessed by asking auto mechanics to check the button settings of the radios when automobiles are in for repair. Racial attitudes might be observed by noting the degree of intermingling or clustering between two racial groups. The amount of fear induced by a children's story might be estimated from the shrinking diameter of a circle of seated children. Each of these examples suggests that unobtrusive clues are available to the clever detective/scientist to provide answers to important or interesting questions.

TYPES OF UNOBTRUSIVE MEASUREMENT

Maybe these examples have stimulated your creativity such that you've begun to think of ways to use unobtrusive measurement in communication research. Since creativity is heightened by providing structure or springboards for mental imaging, the next section of this chapter will discuss various categories or typologies of unobtrusive measurement. There are no agreed upon, exhaustive listings of all the types of unobtrusive measures. However, there are at least five different ways of gathering unobtrusive data and each of these will be discussed separately.

Physical Traces

First, the researcher can collect, count, or measure the physical evidence that earmarks the occurrence of an activity. Webb and his colleagues discuss two kinds of **physical traces**: accretion measures and erosion measures. **Accretion measures** provide evidence based on the accumulation or deposit of materials. **Erosion measures** are created by observing the selective wear on some material.

When things are consumed the packages and containers are discarded. These items of garbage are referred to as accretion measures. Perhaps individuals who are more concerned with their personal appearance might dispose of greater numbers of cosmetic packages and containers. Maybe fashion conscious individuals would fill their wastebaskets with greater numbers of sales tickets and tags. Through accretion measures one might be able to determine the type of individuals who most recently inhabited an area. A gathering of runners after a ten-kilometer race might leave cups of empty yogurt, granola bar wrappers, and orange and banana peels. A large family reunion might leave chicken bones, containers of potato salad, potato chip bags, and beer and Coke cans. Examining the accretion of a child's birthday party held in a park would probably tell a great deal abut the social class, sex, and values of the birthday child. Thus if one were interested in discovering different play rituals or patterns of interaction across social class, the researcher might use the accretion measures of children's birthday parties to estimate social class as opposed to direct questioning of parents or children.

The second kind of physical evidence is an erosion measure. If one wanted to determine the most typical physical arrangement of family members, the researcher might observe wear and tear on furniture. Common pedestrian paths can be discovered by examining the condition of the grass or ground cover. In fact, functional landscaping is done by putting in sidewalks where the grass is consistently worn. When building new additions some universities seed the entire new area and then put in sidewalks a year later to correspond with barren paths.

In order to determine which sections of a basic text are considered most valuable a researcher could look at the condition of the pages of used books. Heavily used sections should look more worn. They should be dirtier, more torn, more smudged, and even more yellowed. Obviously, a survey questionnaire could be used to ask this same question. However, the detective warns researchers not to ignore the physical traces. A textbook examination could provide good corroborating evidence for the survey questionnaire or it could suggest how survey respondents might be biased. Furthermore, the survey could shed light on how to interpret the physical evidence. Perhaps a certain part of the book (like the first chapter) is heavily used but not reported to be useful. Maybe it is the physical placement in the book that creates greater use. This hypothesis could then be tested by looking at different books. Is your first chapter in this book more worn than other chapters? Is the first chapter in other textbooks you own more worn? If so, this suggests that even though material in the first chapter might not be rated as important on a survey, it is widely read.

Perhaps both the survey questionnaire and book examination could together uncover a less intuitively apparent pattern. The questionnaire responses might suggest that the first chapter is very important. After all, don't people believe that authors place their important material in the beginning and would't they be inclined to report that belief on a survey? But upon observation one might find that the first chapter of most books is barely worn. Maybe in reality most students and instructors treat the first chapter as introductory rambling that is best ignored. In any case the survey questionnaire and the unobtrusive measure work together to answer the question. Unobtrusive measurement often is a supplement, not a substitute for other methodology.

Examining Statistical Archives

The second general type of unobtrusive measurement involves the analysis of previously existing data. Our society has numerous **statistical archives**— repositories of statistical information that provide answers to interesting questions. As a society, we collect government records, institutional records, sales records, judicial records, political records, and personal records. In fact, with the advent of computers and easy data storage and retrieval, the mass of accumulated information is astounding. A clever detective simply needs to spend some time digging around in these statistical archives in an effort to interrelate this data in unique ways to answer new questions.

Perhaps the marriage/divorce statistics might be related to economic indices, sales records, charge card records, popularity of particular media shows, or political trends. A fascinating media effects study used existing statistical data to demonstrate that suicide rate was highly correlated with suicide on leading soap operas (Phillips, 1982). A year-by-year analysis of popular children's toys might provide interesting insights into values and patterns of child rearing in a changing society. As greater percentages of mothers work full-time, do families spend greater percentages of their income on children's toys? Are different kinds of toys purchased and what might this say about mother-child relationships? Statistics on the increases or decreases in the number of individuals living alone might be related to dollars spent in various categories of recreational activity to determine what we substitute for human interaction.

The sources of statistical data available for analysis are numerous. If you spend a half hour browsing library shelves in the government documents section you'll see firsthand the wealth of data available. Babbie (1986) argues that the single most valuable resource book for statistical aggregations of data is the *Statistical Abstract of the United States*, published annually by the U.S. Department of Commerce. Babbie (1986) also notes that a softcover commercial version of the book is available for less cost. The less expensive version is titled *The U.S. Fact Book: The American Almanac* and is published annually by Grosset and Dunlap. Obviously, not all statistical compilatons are equally good. Just as the careful detective is wary of relying on sloppy investigative methods that might yield misleading information, the careful researcher must be wary of poorly gathered statistical data that is readily available but misleading.

Content Analysis

A third kind of unobtrusive measurement technique is **content analysis**. Babbie (1986) includes content analysis in his discussion of unobtrusive measurement and suggests that content analysis methods are applicable to virtually any communication modality. Possible artifacts to content analysis include books, magazines, newspapers, songs, videotapes, tape recordings of conversations, films, speeches, letters and any components or collections thereof. Briefly, content analysis involves developing operational definitions (see Chapter 1) for key variables and then coding instances of each occurrence as operationalized. For example, if you wished to assess rhetorical themes that separate liberal congressional representatives from conservative representatives you would have to devise a scheme for coding rhetorical themes and you would need to develop a category scheme to separate liberal and conservative representatives. Then you would analyze the speeches in the *Congressional Record,* coding them for themes. You would also note the speaker and classify him/her according to liberal/conservative criteria previously established (e.g., favorable voting rating by liberal and conservative lobbying groups). This data could then be used to answer your question about how liberals and conservatives differ in their rhetorical themes when speaking before Congress. Since all of Chapter 10 of this text is devoted to content analysis more detail here is unnecessary. However, it is important to note that content analysis can be done on data collected either overtly or unobtrusively. In fact, questionnaire responses can be content analyzed. However, content analysis is a procedure that works very well in making sense out of unobtrusively collected physical, statistical, or observational data. Repositories of communication artifacts lend themselves well to content analysis techniques and are often unobtrusively gathered data.

Natural Observation

A fourth type of unobtrusive measurement procedure involves direct but discrete observation. In this kind of **natural observation**, the researcher is an unobserved hidden spectator watching and noting events as they naturally occur. Many clues are available to the careful observer about communication patterns and correlates. Are people's communication exchanges filled with greater positive affect on sunny days? Do people who wear bright colored clothing use more expressive gestures when interacting? Do men and women assume differing interactional postures, use different talk time ratios and patterns, and respond with differing levels of confirming cues? Are older citizens responded to with greater numbers of disconfirming cues while checking out groceries at the supermarket? Do physically attractive children receive larger amounts of stranger interaction than less attractive children? These are just a few of the potentially communication-related questions that might be addressed with unobtrusive observation methods.

Webb et al. (1966) present an interesting discussion of the use of unobtrusive measurement for observing language behavior. According to them, "language is a hoary subject for observation, with everything from phonemes to profanity legitimate game" (p. 127). Studies of conversation have been done by observers walking the streets catching bits of overheard conversation, by listening in train stations, taxis, buses, ferries, restaurants, stores, night clubs and a host of other public places. Crowded theatre lobbies lend themselves well to overhearing others' conversations. Interestingly, most of the studies done in this manner were completed in the twenties and thirties. This body of literature might be revisited, eyeing it for research possibilities with current twists.

Although a few aspects of verbal interaction are capable of being observed unobtrusively, most readily apparent unobtrusive observation of communication-related phenomena involves the observation of nonverbal factors. An observer has to be quite close to an interaction to overhear the verbal interaction while many nonverbal factors are readily visible at greater distances. Thus, the chapter on nonverbal observation in this book (14) is a nice companion to this section. Again it is important to note that not all observations of nonverbal factors are unobtrusive. However, it is relatively easy for much nonverbal observation to be unobtrusive and whenever possible unobtrusive observation is suggested as an important complement to more intrusive observations.

Hidden Hardware

Finally the fifth type of unobtrusive measurement occurs in contrived situations where there is **hidden hardware** or hidden experimenter control. Generally if cameras are pointed somewhere without any control or manipulation over the kind of activity that takes place in front of them, there will be a high **dross rate**— a high ratio of irrelevant data to relevant data. Collecting and sifting through large amounts of unwanted data is costly and time-consuming. Thus, scientists attempt to avoid research investigations with high dross rates. Sometimes the use of a planted assistant (often called a **confederate** in research investigations) to do something, say something, or solicit some assistance can improve the dross rate. In his early work filming Candid Camera. Alan Funt apparently filmed naturally occurring events (Webb et al., 1966). Shortly, however, he discovered he could get better show segments more efficiently if he somehow manipulated the environment to encourage the varieties of behavior he was interested in observing.

Suppose a researcher wanted to know the effects of physical appearance on strangers' compliance with requests. Instead of waiting for people of differing physical appearance to spontaneously utter requests to strangers, the researcher might more efficiently study this by dressing confederates in different ways and observing how successful they are in their requests. Obviously, this procedure limits the data to the kind of requests and physical appearances the researcher has created, but if the manipulations are valid and not suspected by those being observed, the data can be extremely useful. Certainly this approach would yield greater collection efficiency than the alternative procedure of observing naturally occurring conversations and waiting for requests to occur, while hoping that the various requesters have differing physical appearances. Control itself is not necessarily intrusive. In fact, Tompkins and Cheney (1985) are developing an interesting theory about the unobtrusive control that organizations exert over their employees on a daily basis. But control must be engineered in such a way that it seems natural and doesn't arouse suspicions if the research is to be unobtrusive.

This problem has been dealt with in clever ways by creating good laboratory cover stories, by filming subjects in waiting rooms as they're waiting to begin the experiment, and by training confederates to behave in specific believable and natural ways in public places.

TAXONOMY OF UNOBTRUSIVE MEASUREMENT

Unobtrusive measurement includes a collection of hundreds of specific techniques. Nothing about the structure or the format of the measurement makes it unobtrusive. Instead the essence of unobtrusive measurement lies in the process. If the data collection does not interfere with the phenomenon being studied, its

	Characteristics of Responses to be Observed				
	Frequency of Response	Magnitude or Vigor of Response	Choice Response	Guilty Knowledge Response	Biased Response
Interest or Involvement					
Value					
Ability					
Affective State					
Category Membership					

Purposes of Assessment (row-group label at left)

Figure 12.1. An Illustrative Matrix for a Generative Taxonomy of Unobtrusive Measures (Reprinted with permission of Jossey-Bass Inc., Publishers. © 1979 Jossey-Bass Inc., Publishers.)

an unobtrusive measure. The lack of unifying structure or format makes it hard to create new measures or to readily think of how to unobtrusively measure communication phenomena. Other measurement approaches are defined by a formal structure. Likert scales rely on sentences that allow an agreement or disagreement response. Semantic differential measurement relies on a stimulus target and bipolar adjectives. Without too much difficulty a trained methodologist can easily think of how to measure a phenomenon through Likert or semantic differential scales. Unfortunately, the same is not always true of unobtrusive techniques.

Sechrest and Phillips (1979) argue that this lack of a conceptual structure impedes more frequent and systematic use of unobtrusive measures. They tried to solve this problem by creating a taxonomy that might give direction to someone attempting to develop an unobtrusive measure. They created a matrix (see Figure 12.1) that delineated the characteristics of responses to be observed (across the top) and the purpose of the assessment (down the side).

Following this matrix across the top of the first row, if one were interested in assessing interest or involvement, the frequency with which individuals talk to each other could be observed. The vigor of the response could be measured by examining levels of expressiveness during interactions. The frequency with which pairs of individuals interact when presented with alternate interaction choices, such as when at a party, could be observed. A guilty knowledge response betrays interest because only those interested would have such knowledge. Thus an unusual familiarity with the person's schedule or an unusual awareness of his/her interests might be a guilty knowledge response.

Finally a biased response represents an exaggeration such that an overestimate of physical attraction, height, or skill might betray interest.

Following the matrix down the side, the second kind of assessment might be to determine value. Value refers to the positive-negative continuum of worth. Our previous example assumed positiveness in all observations of interest. It's possible that high frequency of interaction (talk for conflict), expressiveness (anger), choice (tell him off), guilty knowledge (know a lot to get even) and even bias (distortions in opposite direction) could indicate negative value.

Continuing down the side of the matrix, and following the third row across, ability or skill is of interest to communication researchers. Communication ability might be assessed by observing the frequency with which children are chosen as interaction partners. Depending on the context, highly expressive or very calm individuals might be judged to have excellent communication ability. Nevertheless, the degree of expressiveness is a second measure of ability. Individuals with good communicative ability might choose high interaction seats or extra speaking opportunities. Someone claiming a very shy demeanor might betray that claim by knowing too many individuals at the social gathering. Finally those with greater communicative ability might unobtrusively indicate this by manifesting harsher judgments towards less competent people.

The fourth row of the matrix refers to affective state or emotional state which is of concern to communication researchers. An unobtrusive measure of relational happiness might come from observing the choice time that relational partners spend together or by assessing their notions of "normal" relationship length. Finally, category membership (the fifth row) provides an interesting unobtrusive measure. We may wish to assess parent-child relational intensity by noting a mother's degree of identification with a parent label. Women who fail to identify with the parent label may overestimate the joys of parenting. On the other hand, women who bond successfully with their children may indicate this through their choice of parenting behaviors when faced with parenting choices.

This taxonomy isn't perfect but it's a step in the right direction. Currently, devising unobtrusive measurement is as much an art as a precise science. Perhaps as Sechrest and Phillips (1979) point out, that's true with other measurement procedures as well. Some people write better questionnaire items, others devise clever interview techniques, and still others have a knack for focusing on the most intriguing issues. The use of unobtrusive measures challenges your creative energies and this often comes as a pleasant surprise to those who think that creativity holds no place in science.

RELIABILITY

Reliability is an essential concern in establishing the viability of any measurement tool. Basically reliability is an estimate of the random error or variability operating within a measurement procedure. To say it another way, reliability refers to the degree of accuracy or consistency within data. The way to assess reliability is generally to show that a response is consistent from time one to time two. Often scales ask the same question twice to build in a time one and time two response. Sometimes researchers ask people a question on Monday and then again on Friday to create a time one and time two response. Either way, the assumption is that a response which is consistent across two questions or two days is a more accurate reflection of the phenomenon being measured. Thus the phenomenon is assumed to be measured with reliability.

However, most unobtrusive measures are single attempts to assess a response. This is unfortunate because single item tests or single item measures have unknown and indeterminate reliability and the reliability is suspected to be low. A response to any single item might be influenced by the semantic structure of the item, or a momentary fluctuation in feeling by a respondent. So, too, any single behavioral response is subject to extraneous random fluctuations.

The reliability of unobtrusive measurements needs to be a concern. In order to establish something akin to internal reliability, you need to use multiple unobtrusive measures of the same behavior. To create a reliability which is relatively similar to test-retest reliability, you need to unobtrusively measure the same phenomena at time one and time two. When using previously existing statistics, you could compare the statistical compilations of two different sources to establish reliability. Procedures for estimating interrater reliability are beginning to be well established for content analysis approaches. When using direct observation more than one viewer might observe the behavior firsthand and when examining physical traces and videotaped patterns more than one individual could be called upon to view the instance. Then the different data gathered by each individual observer could be compared to establish reliability for the findings.

Reliability is just as important in unobtrusive measurement as it is in other measurement procedures. Perhaps it is more difficult to gather reliability data in unobtrusive procedures because it basically means collecting the data for every study twice. It is easier and more convenient to ask people's responses to scale items twice than it is to collect physical data twice. But inconvenience or difficulty is not an acceptable excuse for omission. The assurance of reliability is essential to any scientific claim. In short, reliability refers to how well or how accurately something is measured. Before researchers can claim any meaning for their results they have to feel assured that things were measured accurately. Without high reliability there can be no validity and without validity the findings are worthless.

VALIDITY

Validity refers to the degree to which research findings are accurate reflections and interpretations of the general reality that one wishes to understand. Research is conducted so that people can better explain and understand their world. To the extent that the findings of a particular research investigation are attributable to the causes that are judged as responsible and to the extent that subjects behave like most of the population they represent, the researcher can claim valid findings. In short, validity refers to the degree to which a researcher is measuring what he/she thinks he/she is measuring on the population that he/she thinks he/she is studying. If researchers are not measuring what they think they are or if they are not measuring the effects on people who behave like the population they're generalizing their findings to, their research is worthless. Validity is the *sine qua non* of research—without validity there is nothing.

Invalidity sources — Traditional research. Unobtrusive measurement techniques were introduced as a way to reduce the **sources of invalidity** in other more traditional kinds of research. In most traditional research, people know they are part of a research investigation. To that extent they are likely to behave differently, creating some invalidity. One group of researchers (Selltiz, Johoda, Deutsch, & Cook, 1959) called this the guinea pig effect and argued that when people feel like guinea pigs in an experiment they behave differently to impress, facilitate, or hinder the researcher. A research experiment also calls forth a particular role that subjects play; this role may reflect a "true" self but it may not reflect the "true" self that the situation most likely would elicit were it not an experiment. These experimentation effects are sources of invalidity because the findings of the study are better explained by the experimental setting rather than the phenomena being investigated.

When research scales and questionnaires are used, the wording of the questions creates potential invalidity sources. Factors such as argument bias, yes response patterns, and overall response patterns cause subjects to respond differently to a concept depending on how it's worded. For example, most subjects are more likely to agree with a statement than to disagree with its opposite. Furthermore, interviewing techniques and individual interviewers create effects that are better explained by the techniques or the person rather than the variables being researched. Thus, these factors create additional sources of invalidity in traditional kinds of research.

Many traditional research designs use subject volunteers. In fact, current human subject guidelines require that those participating in experimental studies provide voluntary consent. Volunteers are probably not representative of the population that a researcher wishes to generalize to and this introduces an additional source of invalidity. Pointing to the problem of using only volunteer subjects for research investigations, Webb et al. (1966) argued:

> The curious, the exhibitionistic, and the succorant are likely to overpopulate any sample of volunteers. How secure a base can volunteers be with such groups overrepresented and the shy, suspicious and inhibited underrepresented? (p. 25)

These are only a few of the potential sources of invalidity in traditional experimental and quasi-experimental research. In fact, in a later work which became a bible for researchers on validity issues, Campbell and Stanley (1963) outlined 13 specific threats to internal and external validity in experimental and quasi-experimental research. Webb et al. (1966) used these threats as the foundation for their later work and used invalidity as their major argument for the necessity of unobtrusive measurement. They argued that when employing unobtrusive measurement, subjects don't know they are part of a research study. Physical traces, previously existing statistics, and direct observation of behavior don't require questionnaires or interviews. Subjects are not volunteers since their participation is not something they are even aware of. In short, unobtrusive measurement is not subject to the same sources of invalidity as is more traditional research.

Invalidity sources—Unobtrusive measurement. However, Webb and his colleagues were not so foolish as to deny potential sources of invalidity in unobtrusive measurement. In fact, they were quick to point out some potential validity threats. For example, in their discussion of response bias they pointed out that response biases occur not only for questionnaires or public opinion polls but also for archival records such as votes. Statistical archives may contain invalid statistics.

Erosion methods such as assessing carpet wear are subject to extraneous factors, so that greater wear doesn't necessarily mean a more interesting or attractive exhibit in a museum. There is a general right turn bias in entering a room, people drag their feet more as they get tired, and the placement of exit doors and restrooms alters traffic flow. All of these factors contribute to carpet wear and reduce the validity of carpet erosion as an accurate measure of exhibit attractiveness. Other erosion measures are subject to similar influences.

Accretion measures may also be biased. If researchers search trash containers for patterns of consumption, they must be certain they are looking for something that would be discarded in the subject's own container. For example, a researcher could monitor trash cans for evidence of disposable diapers as an indication of a child-rearing pattern or philosophy. However, I know a person who thought it was illegal to throw diapers in the trash can. Therefore she took all her diapers in trash bags to a local dumping area. Each person who behaved this way would be a source of invalidity in an accretion measure.

Direct observation is also subject to validity threats. If a researcher is interested in observing the effects of sunny days and cloudy days on people's interaction behaviors at an outdoor mall, the researcher must assure that the two days are as identical as possible except for the weather. If the sunny day was the last day of the public school year and the cloudy day was the first day of summer vacation, some of the observed behavioral differences might not be attributable to weather but rather to attitudes towards summer vacation.

Triangulation. Webb and his colleagues argue that unobtrusive measures may be subject to fewer threats to validity. Certainly, they are subject to different threats. Thus, what is needed for valid research is the use of multiple methods of investigation to allow comparisons across the studies. Back in 1966, Webb et al. argued for **triangulation** of research methods — an idea that has finally become popular in speech communication in the 1980s. Triangulation refers to the acceptance and embracement of multiple research methods, tactics, and strategies to address the same issue. Valid phenomena surface across a variety of studies. Findings that are uncovered regardless of research methodology are explained by the phenomena under investigation rather than by the questionnaire wording, the interviewer, the observer, or the interpreter. Findings uncovered through triangulation are valid findings.

> It is only when we naively place faith in a single measure that the massive problems of social research vitiate the validity of our comparisons. We have argued strongly in this chapter for a conceptualization of method that demands multiple measurement of the same phenomenon or comparison. Overreliance on questionnaires and interviews is dangerous because it does not give us enough points in conceptual space to triangulate. We are urging the employment of novel, sometimes "oddball" methods to give those points in space. (Webb et al., p. 34)

SAMPLE RESEARCH

Oddball methods have not been widely diffused into the speech communication literature. A 1979 book edited by Sechrest summarizes hundreds of research investigations that use unobtrusive measurement across the behavioral sciences but not one of the references is to journals edited by speech communication professionals. Examples of studies that use physical traces as data sources for communication research are nonexistent. The discipline has begun to use more direct observation of behaviors but most of this observation is still done in laboratory settings. Statistical archives are a virtually untapped source of information regarding interaction patterns and human relationships. Content analysis procedures are beginning to filter into communication research. A recent content analytic study examined courtship talk in Harlequin novels (Alberts, 1986). Popular literature, songs, television and movies offer potentially rich data sources on communication processes, expectations, norms, and probable outcomes. Changing perceptions of relationship development, male-female communication norms, and effective influence strategies await systematic analysis through the use of unobtrusive measures.

Communication research has virtually ignored unobtrusive measurement techniques. However, today's ignorance provides tomorrow's challenge. Creative thinking regarding data collection procedures will allow you to address interesting communication issues, contributing to the important and growing body of literature regarding human communication behavior. Bon voyage after a few final words regarding the ethics of using unobtrusive measurement.

ETHICAL CONSIDERATIONS

The book *Unobtrusive Measures* was written during a period in which social scientists paid little attention to the ethical consequences of their investigative techniques. Studies were conducted in the 1950s that could never be replicated today due to a much greater **ethical concern** for research subjects. The mood in the 1950s was characterized more as one where the ends (knowledge) justified the means.

Today researchers are more aware of ethical constraints regarding scientific investigation. Human subjects guidelines dictate appropriate and inappropriate research procedures and most universities have human subjects committees that approve research protocols. Researchers must be aware of any direct or indirect harm that a research investigation might cause subjects and they must actively seek to prevent the harm or find another way to do the study.

If *Unobtrusive Measures* were written today, the authors would have been more critical of some of the previously used methods of unobtrusive measurement (Sechrest & Phillips, 1979). The major ethical issue somewhat unique to unobtrusive measurement is the violation of individual privacy rights. In more traditional research, subjects must give their consent to be part of a research investigation. That consent ameliorates many privacy invasion concerns. When researchers use unobtrusive measures, however, consent is impossible. Subjects must not know they are being investigated; unobtrusive measures are characterized by their ability to not interfere with or distort naturally occurring processes. Thus, consent is impossible; consent destroys the rationale for the use of unobtrusive measures.

Ethical guidelines are not clearly articulated nor are they agreed upon. Some consensus exists that observations of individuals or their physical traces in public places in ways that do not intrude beyond what occurs normally are ethical. In other words, few researchers would consider it unethical for a researcher to overhear a conversation and code some aspect of it on the spot. As Sechrest and Phillips (1979) point out, a few more researchers might object on ethical grounds to a tape recording of the conversation that is later analyzed. Furthermore, if special hidden microphones were used to record conversations that might not be overheard without the device, many more ethical objections would be raised. Technological devices (like listening bugs and powerful binoculars) and special techniques (like peepholes and one-way mirrors) that give researchers access to private information have to be carefully considered from an ethical perspective. At the very least, the researcher needs to assure the anonymity of data gathered in surreptitious ways and is responsible for protecting the dignity and integrity of individuals—even strangers.

One of the more controversial studies of spatial invasion provides a concrete example of the ethical debate surrounding privacy rights. A group of researchers (Middlemist, Knowles, & Matter, 1977) studied time and micturation (how long it took males to urinate) in a public restroom when personal space was invaded by a confederate who pretended to be another bathroom user. They were attempting to support a physiological arousal effect of spatial invasion. This research was criticized on ethical grounds (Koocher, 1977). The researchers argued that since the location was a public place open to anyone and the kind of encounters they engineered were like those naturally occurring, there were no serious ethical problems. Sechrest and Phillips (1979) think that because they used a periscope to make their observations of micturation, the ethical controversy is heightened.

The issue of ethical conduct in research is important regardless of research method. However, when considering "oddball" data collection techniques, ethical concerns are particularly significant. The code of ethics of the American Psychological Association (APA, 1973) does not forbid "covert investigation in private situations" but warns that such investigations should be done "only after very careful consideration and consultations" (p. 32). The researcher is personally responsible for subject reactions and harms. Since most people don't respond favorably to eavesdroppers, trash snoopers, and electronic surveillance, researchers choosing unobtrusive measures must be especially sensitive to ethical issues. Indeed, careful consideration and consultation ought to precede any investigation employing unobtrusive measurement.

SUMMARY

This chapter provided a discussion of unobtrusive measurement procedures. The chapter began with a history of the label unobtrusive measurement, indicating that Webb et al.'s classic book labeled, classified, and explicitly identified the technique. Their book title became the name for the measurement procedure. Next, obtrusive measurement was defined as research tactics that allow data collection without interference in the process being studied. A researcher using unobtrusive measurement was likened to an investigative detective.

The chapter proceeded with general examples of unobtrusive measurement in order to give the reader a better understanding of the procedure. Then, five specific types of unobtrusive measure were outlined. Physical traces, including erosion measures and accretion rates, were detailed. Use of previously existent statistical data banks, content analysis, natural observation, and observation with hidden hardware were also discussed. Then, a taxonomy of unobtrusive measurement was presented in an effort to systemize the format of unobtrusive observations.

The last sections of the chapter discussed reliabilty and validity issues related to unobtrusive measurement. Triangulation of unobtrusive techniques with other measurement techniques was suggested as the best strategy for assuring high validity in research findings. The paucity of speech communication studies employing unobtrusive methods was lamented and the reader was challenged to rectify this situation. Finally the importance of considering the ethical implicatons of various unobtrusive techniques was discussed. The reader was urged to exercise ethical care and caution when using unobtrusive measures.

STUDY QUESTIONS

1. What do a bullfighter's beard, oddball measures, and unobtrusive measures have in common? How did unobtrusive measurement become a unified methodological perspective?

2. Define unobtrusive measures.

3. Compare the role of a researcher to that of a detective. Detail the different kinds of evidence that each needs.

4. Create an unobtrusive measure to be used for each of the following research questions:
   a) What classes do students like the most?
   b) What students are most popular in a classroom?
   c) What foods are consumed by college students?

5. What are the five different types of unobtrusive measures discussed in the chapter? Give two examples (one from the text and one original) for each type of procedure.

6. Imagine you are interested in studying relational development by examining communication at various relational stages. Using Figure 12.1, complete as many of the boxes as you can with a possible unobtrusive measure that might advance your research.

7. Define reliability.

8. How does a researcher create a reliable unobtrusive measure?

9. Define validity.

10. Discuss three threats to validity that are common in traditional research but absent with unobtrusive measures.

11. Discuss threats to validity that might exist in the following unobtrusive measures procedures:
   a) The researcher decides to measure relational satisfaction by noting how much couples touch while talking.
   b) The researcher measures extroversion of individuals by recording the color of clothing worn. The colors are classified as bright (extraverted) colors or dull (introverted) colors.
   c) A researcher analyzes the divorce statistics, using marriage data collected by the Mormon church.
   d) A researcher measures concern about physical appearance by recording how much time employees spend in the restroom.
   e) A researcher measures social class by noting how much food an individual leaves on his/her plate.

12. What is triangulation of research methods? Why is it a good idea?

13. Discuss the most important ethical concerns that researchers must consider before using unobtrusive measures.

ANNOTATED READINGS

Babbie, E. (1986). *The practice of social research* (4th ed.). Belmont, CA: Wadsworth.
   This is an excellent general research methods textbook that has a good chapter on unobtrusive research. Content analysis, the analysis of existing statistics, and historical/comparative analysis are detailed and discussed as unobtrusive research procedures.
Sechrest, L., & Phillips, M. (1979). Unobtrusive measures: An overview. In L. Sechrest (Ed.), *New directions for methodology of behavioral science: Unobtrusive measurement today*. San Francisco, CA: Jossey-Bass.
   This edited book overviews unobtrusive measures and updates the research and conceptualization. Following the first overview chapter, successive chapters cite examples of unobtrusive measures in treatment evaluation, field experiments in social psychology, crosscultural research, nonverbal measures, and trace measures. This is a valuable reference to hundreds of research investigations which have employed unobtrusive measures.
Webb, E. J., Cambell, D. T., Schwartz. R. D., & Sechrest, L. (1966). *Unobtrusive measures: Nonreactive research in the social sciences*. Chicago: Rand McNally.
   This classic and ingenious book created unobtrusive measurement procedures as a labeled research technique. The argument for unobtrusive measures is detailed. The use of physical traces, archival records, simple observations, and contrived observation involving hardware and control is explained and exemplified. This book is important reading for anyone wishing to fully understand and appreciate unobtrusive measures.

CHAPTER 13

Physiological Measurement

By Samuel C. Riccillo,
University of Wyoming

This chapter introduces the basic concepts of physiological measurement that may be employed in studies of human behavior. The relationship of physiological concerns to communication behavior has a fairly recent appearance. Methods, as well as theoretical assumptions, have been derived from basic psychophysiological literature. While many researchers have inferred relational activity to an underlying system, few have drawn a specific relationship to actual physiological responses (Benkhe, 1970; Bostrom, 1980).

Measurement in psychophysiology has evolved as a unified effort within the last 80 years. The advent of technological developments in electronic measurement has advanced many of the theoretical and cumbersome measures of the past. Instrumentation developed after World War II seems to be the major impetus for this advancement. With the sophistication of computer enhancement in the last 20 years, solid state equipment, and large numbers of well-trained technicians, expertise in using the equipment has been much easier to acquire and more available to a wide variety of researchers from many disciplines.

Some very basic theoretical considerations must be reviewed before considering measurement techniques. The very concept of behavior in psychophysiology has two perspectives: covert and overt (McGuigan, 1979). **Covert behavior** is not always directly observable and involves such activity as heart rate, respiration, or brain activity. **Overt behavior** is observable directly, such as vocalization, movement of the limbs, or other collective acts directly within the sense observation of the researcher. Covert behavior is generally mediated by some measurement device, but in some cases can be acquired by procedures that assist our observations. For example, a researcher could assess the heart rate of a subject by touch and count the pulse within a given time frame. Behavior in physiological measurement is a concept that includes both covert and overt references.

The study of both covert and overt behavior is essential for research in the behavioral sciences. While most research has relied on various paradigms involving overt behavior, much research is also concerned with the relationship of covert to overt behavior. Many models have characterized the relationship of processes relating covert and overt processes (Goss, 1982). Some scholars have characterized the processes that underlie covert behavior as intrapersonal processes, cognition, or elaborate information processing systems. Some have utilized the concepts of encoding and decoding to explain the covert processes involved in information processing.

Models of human behavior incorporating physiological perspectives require an understanding of the process of communication from more than a social perspective. Many theorists involved with the behavioral sciences have focused primarily on the social mechanisms invoking characteristics related to physiological processes. Concepts such as stimulus, response, or reinforcement have played major roles in theory. The fundamental bases of these concepts have their roots in psychophysiology. Few researchers have attempted to correlate observed behavior with covert processes to assess the interrelationship (see Bostrom, 1980; Stacks & Sellers, 1986).

It is obvious that various theoretical perspectives play a key role in methodological decisions. How one chooses to characterize the process directly affects the choices made for measuring and interpreting the phenomenon. The position taken in this chapter is that what has been characterized as a message phenomenon is not separated from its source or receiver in the behavioral process. The human behavioral process is studied physiologically for the purpose of discovering how the entire organism is involved in the production and consumption of the signals that are characterized as messages.

Physiological methods are guided by biological perspectives. These perspectives are then taken into the social context in an effort to explain and describe an organism's capacity to process complex stimuli through the various neurosystems. In fact, the origin and evolution of human behavior is rooted in the biological limits of the observed organism (Delbruck, 1986). Recent developmental studies on the human organism suggest that the functional integration of human behaviors is an interaction between the neural sophistication of the biological system and the corresponding social conditions of the environment. This theoretical position describes human behavior as a neurosocial evolutionary process (Riccillo & Watterson, 1984).

Physiological measurement procedures for the study of human behavior focus on both covert and overt behavior. It is concerned with the nature of the behavior and the corresponding mechanisms used for both generating and receiving complex stimuli in various contexts. This method of measurement recognizes that a wholistic perspective of the process can be best achieved by the manipulation of both social and physiological phenomena. These methods require a careful grounding in various related disciplines to insure adequate understanding of various processes. Many interdisciplinary groups are developing from sister disciplines, creating new perspectives and developing innovative methodologies. See Waid, 1984; Cacioppo & Petty, 1983.)

HISTORICAL PERSPECTIVES

The human organism is a highly integrated system. When a person is engaged in the act of reading a book, he/she can be processing verbal stimuli on one level and digesting food on another. The process of reading requires visual input, and conscious effort is required to focus attention on what is being read. Digestion on the other hand operates on a different system that does not require conscious effort. Once a meal is completed, the process of digestion begins and the food consumed is relegated to the automatic processes without effort. Several systems can be operating simultaneously. These two systems seem to be operating independently of one another without much interference. But suppose that same reader encounters a passage that somehow creates a disturbance, a passage that transmits a disturbing piece of information that the reader does not agree with. As the person continues to read the passage, the level of disagreement continues. Another sensation is emitted suggesting a mild disorder from the stomach region. As the reader continues to be disturbed by reading this passage, the normal process of digestion is also disturbed. What happens on one level of information processing is now associated with another level. Is there a relationship between the two levels and is that relationship triggered by information that was read or by the consumption of a poorly prepared meal? Can information processed at one level of the organism have some effect on other parts of the organism?

From everyday experiences, many people have drawn relationships between various experiences like the one described above. Certain overt activities seem to be related to other covert processes. Physiological events such as heart rate, respiration rate, or levels of moisture on the skin appear to be the direct result of various verbal stimuli or complex behavioral events. Certain message characteristics are capable of being observed as having some effect on an individual's state of arousal.

The effect of various stimuli on the internal state of the individual has been the concern of scholars since the time of the Greeks. The brain/mind issue may have had its origin in the writings of the ancient physician Hippocrates. He was reported to have written that the brain is the interpreter of conscious experience. He asserted that humans experience sight, sound, emotions such as joy or sorrow, and other mental processes through the organ of the brain (Penfield & Roberts, 1959). About a century later, Plato was concerned with the relationships between mental and physical characteristics of human experience. The philosophical connection was established which lingers today regarding the relationshiop between physiological and mental activity. Aristotle, however, three centuries later postulated that mental faculties resided in the heart (Andreassi, 1980).

While speculation abounded in the classical period, physiological investigation proceeded in various primitive forms. The twentieth century marked the rapid development of the earlier speculations primarily due to discoveries of the relationship of electrical response activity. (See Mesulam & Perry, 1972.) Bioelectric responses began to acquire many interested researchers. Instrumentation for analysis of this activity for most of the predominant measures was experimented with at the turn of the century. Einthoven constructed the string galvanometer and the first electrocardiograph. Berger developed the first measurement of brain waves and is responsible for labeling alpha and beta waves.

The basic principles from these discoveries have led to contemporary advances today. Revolutions in instrumentation after the Second World War led to more nonintrusive techniques, with little risk for subjects (Stern et al., 1980). Today, commercially available equipment has made the physiological measurement of human behavior much more accessible to a variety of researchers, who combine many interests regarding the physiological responses of the organism. The basic principles of these measurement techniques, however, have remained relatively constant.

BASIC PHYSIOLOGICAL PRINCIPLES

A brief review of physiological principles provides some insight into what is measured by various techniques employed. The basic process essential to understanding relationships between overt and covert responses is built upon the bioelectric activity that occurs in the individual cell. Regardless of the sophistication of the measurement technique employed, this bioelectric phenomenon is the basis of the measurement taken.

The bioelectric activity represents the covert response. This response is then related to some overt activity. Formal technique development preoccupied many of the early physiology laboratories of the twenties and thirties. While the basic principles had been observed in cell activity, the relationship to other overt behavior required solving many problems. The most obvious was the use of recording devices that often inhibited the experimental conditions. Major theoretical concerns made their entry following measurement simplification and elaboration of collection devices. As physiological measurement became less complex, more researchers from several disciplines began to learn these basic principles, employing them under a variety of conditions with various associated overt behaviors (McGuigan, 1979). These principles of basic cell biology could be employed to explain activity in the nervous system through devices that before were too obtrusive for many behavioral experiments. Covert activity then can be viewed as a measurement of bioelectric phenomena from living organisms operating on the simple principles of cell biology.

The assessment of nerve, muscle, and even gland cells can be made with the same basic principle: all cells are enveloped by membranes. In a resting cell there is a phenomenon called *electrical potential*. This potential is the difference between the electrical property of the inside of the cell and that of the outside of the cell membrane. The inside of the cell membrane is electrically negative relative to the outside. (For a more elaborate discussion of this process, see Geddes, 1972.) Therefore, when a stimulus is applied to a resting cell an electrical event called an **action potential** is generated. This action potential occurs primarily because the applied stimulus produces a localized **depolarization** that is dispersed along the entire cell. This depolarization occurs due to an exchange of **ions** through the opening in the cell's membrane.

The openings in a cell's membrane are large enough to allow the passage of the cell's smaller ions from the inside of the membrane to the outside of the membrane. The smaller ions may move from the outside to the inside. The cell's openings, of course, are too small to allow the larger ions to pass through. The size of the opening selectively controls the passage of the ions. The passage of the smaller ions from the inside to the outside or vice versa is called cell semipermeability. It is this activity that is electrically sensed by an electrode. Placing an electrode near a cell and placing another electrode away from this cell creates a field where this ionic activity can be sensed.

The exchange of ions by a cell or group of cells described above is referred to as *action potential*. When the action potential is recorded on a measuring device, it consists of three identifiable electrical characteristics. First, depolarization occurs when a small prepotential, or electrical charge, is followed by a discharge. The inside of the cell becomes positive relative to the outside. The cell then repolarizes on the inside and again becomes negative relative to the outside of the cell. At this resting state, the cell voltage returns to a resting potential. This movement from depolarization to **repolarization** is the electrical phenomenon that is sensed by the electrodes. This bioelectrical phenomenon of depolarization to repolarization is the basic unit of measurement in a variety of measurement procedures used in psychophysiology. Second, the speed with which various cells recover after depolarization is also a factor. Neural tissue recovers rapidly, whereas muscle tissue is relatively slow. And third, the placement of the electrodes in relation to the source of the action potential becomes extremely important. In some cases the closer or further the placement of the electrode over a cell area can retard or cancel out the recording of this response. The basic principles underlying cell physiology play an extremely important role in measurement. Simple electrical response activity is the basis of measurement. There are also basic principles surrounding the organization of the human nervous system that play a central role in psychophysiological measurement.

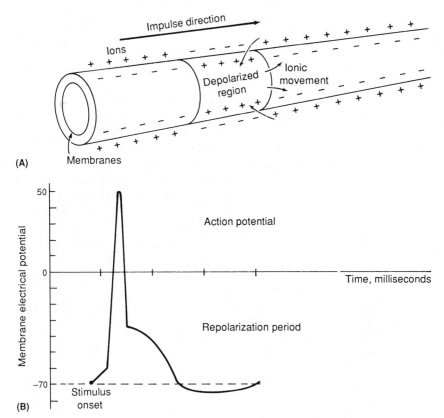

Figure 13.1.   A) Nerve conduction along a cell; B) an illustration of the action potential as it might appear on an oscilloscope

CENTRAL CONCEPTS IN THE HUMAN NERVOUS SYSTEM

In order to understand the basic processes involved in the human nervous system, it is necessary to review some selected concepts and their relationship to physiological processes. A general description of the human nervous system and its interrelationship is essential for understanding the various systems of measurement that are frequently encountered in the literature of physiological measurement. This review is a limited one, and serious students should consult more definitive works regarding each specific system that is discussed. (Some excellent sources to consult would be Andreassi, 1980; Martin & Venables, 1980; Brown & Wallace, 1980.)

The human organism is composed of two major systems for biological control: the nervous system and the endocrine system. The nervous system possesses the greatest speed and involves electrochemical processes which span nerve cells between the brain and the peripheral receptors and effectors. The endocrine system operates through the release of various secretions by glands into the blood stream. It is generally slower and more diffuse, especially when particular hormones are released outside of the brain. Neurophysiologists are carefully mapping the details of this system and its relationship to the central nervous system. The endocrine system will not be reviewed in any depth in this chapter. (See Brown & Wallace, 1980, for a careful and concise review.)

The transmission of information in the human nervous system is accomplished through various networks. Both internal and external stimuli are carried along the nervous system to the integrative structures of the brain. Information traveling to the brain moves along pathways referred to as **afferent pathways.** Instructions from the brain to various muscles or organs travel down **efferent pathways.** The signals transmitted along these pathways to and from the brain are of interest in basic physiological measurement.

Division of the human nervous system occurs in distinct segments. A schematic description of this division is provided in Figure 13.2. There are two major divisions of the human nervous system: the *central nervous system* (CNS) and the *peripheral nervous system.* The CNS represents the majority of the neural fibers in the human system. It is comprised of the brain and the spinal cord. The brain is housed in the cranium and the spinal cord is connected to the brain and located in the vertebral column along the back. The peripheral nervous system is that portion of the system that extends from the CNS to the outlying areas of the human body. The peripheral nervous system contains the *Somatic Nervous System* and the *Autonomic Nervous System* (ANS). Generally the somatic nervous system channels information to and from the external sense receptors. These receptors include the eyes, skin, skeletal muscles and proprioceptors such as those involved in muscle tension. This system is also responsible for the regulation of various bodily processes considered under voluntary control. The ANS, on the other hand, involves nervous system activity which is difficult to get under voluntary control (involuntary, such as heart beat or respiration; although it should be noted that it is possible to get heart rate or respiration under voluntary control. It is not *simply* involuntary). The ANS carries information to glands and smooth muscle. The ANS functions to maintain balance or equilibrium within the internal environment of the organism.

The ANS is further divided into two additional systems: the *Sympathetic Nervous System* (SNS) and the *Parasympathetic Nervous System* (PNS). (For a more descriptive account of these systems see Van Toller, 1979; and Gardner, 1975.) The SNS prepares the organism for "fight-flight-fright" responses. It activates, excites or mobilizes for operation. Changes in these physiological responses have been used to detect stress in the human organism. The very common instrument known as the "lie detector" or polygraph test, used commonly in industry, government and law enforcement, employs a method to measure SNS activation. Basically, it records blood pressure and changes in the

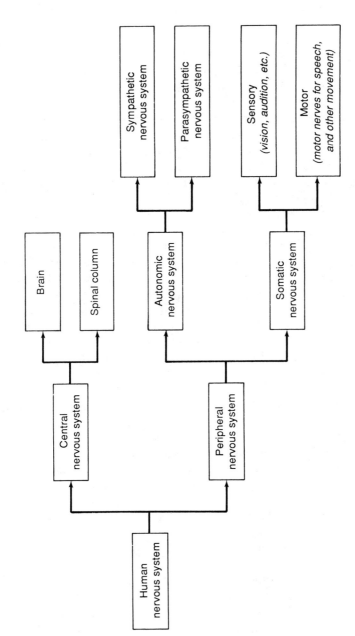

Figure 13.2. Graphic representation of the human nervous system

temperature and moisture levels on the skin. It is theorized that when a person lies, this stressful condition is capable of being recorded and is reflected in the activation of the SNS.

The PNS can be viewed as a system which repairs or activates at rest. This system usually activates a single organ at a time. Both systems can be operating simultaneously depending on the activity in which the organism is engaged. Nerve fibers which originate in the thoracic and lumbar portions of the spinal column are part of the SNS. The PNS is separated and focused at the top and lower regions of the spinal column. Generally, the PNS is viewed as a system which decreases neural activity when compared with the SNS.

The brain of course is considered the organizing center of neural activity. Considerable focus has been directed here in recent years with many theoretical accounts of its activity and with various measures. Numerous theories point to the brain as the center of cognitive activity. (For comprehensive reviews, see Pribram, 1971; Luria, 1973; Brown, 1975; Restak, 1979; and Delbruck, 1986.) The brain is viewed as a composite of three evolutionary structures: the hind-brain, midbrain, and the forebrain. (Figure 13.3 provides a graphic view. A systematic and graphic review can be gleaned from Ornstein et al., 1984). The hindbrain emerges from the spinal cord. The subcortical neural structures called the medulla and pons are included in the hindbrain. The majority of the cranial nerves are routed through this area and specific nuclei associated with the ANS, such as cardiac activity, respiration and various gastrointestinal activity. The pons is just above the medulla and serves as a relay center connecting the cortex, the topmost portion of the brain, with the spinal column.

The center portion of the brain, called the midbrain, is located just above the pons and retains the basic tubular form of the spinal column. It consists of neural tracts which connect the upper and lower areas of the brain. The upper portion of this structure houses the thalamus and the hypothalamus. Important relays are situated here for both the auditory and visual systems. Within the hindbrain and midbrain is a network of cell bodies and fibers which extend from the spinal cord to the thalamus. This network is called the Reticular Formation (often referred to as the Reticular Activating System or RAS). This formation serves the role of controlling the level of cortical excitation. Physiological arousal is theorized to occur in this region (see Lindsey, 1951). There is a growing body of literature, however, which cautions against generalizations about the role of this formation, suggesting that the structure is more complicated than once thought (see Van Toller, 1979).

The development of the forebrain seems to mark a distinct period in the evolution of brain structures (Delbruck, 1986). This structure covers the hindbrain and midbrain and is connected to these structures by numerous neuropathways. Most investigations of higher mental activity are associated with the forebrain. Processes characterized as perception, voluntary movement, thinking, learning, and memory are located in this area of the brain. The forebrain includes the thalamus, hypothalamus, limbic system, and the cerebral

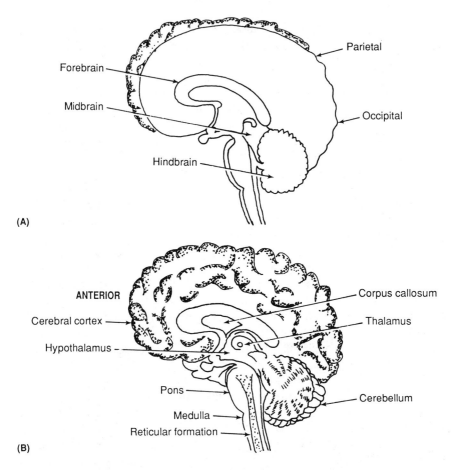

Figure 13.3. The human brain viewed medially. A) The tripartite brain; B) major structures of importance

cortex. The thalamus is located just above the midbrain. Acting as a sensory relay unit, the cells within the thalamus receive neural signals from the afferent pathways. These signals are channelled to specific areas in the cerebral cortex.

The hypothalamus is also a cluster of cells located above the midbrain beneath the thalamus. This system of neural structures exerts influence on the endocrine system through the pineal gland. As a system the hypothalamus influences feeding, fight and flight, sexual behavior, and many regulatory activities such as sleeping and temperature level. The hypothalamus is part of the larger system called the limbic system, which assists in the regulation of the ANS. The limbic system is also interconnected with the temporal and frontal areas of the cerebral cortex. Several functions are associated with this system, more importantly those attributed to suppression effects, for the hindbrain and midbrain areas. The limbic system derives its name from Latin origins, meaning

TABLE 13.1. THE HUMAN NERVOUS SYSTEM AND THE VARIOUS MEASUREMENT DEVICES ASSOCIATED WITH EACH SYSTEM.

CENTRAL NERVOUS SYSTEM

Electroencephalogram, Evoked Potentials

SOMATIC SENSORY NERVOUS SYSTEM

Electromyogram

AUTONOMIC NERVOUS SYSTEM

Electrocardiogram: Parasympathetic, Sympathetic

Electrodermal Responses: Sympathetic System Only

Electrooculogram: Parasympathetic, Sympathetic

Blood Pressure, Blood Volumn: Parasympathetic, Sympathetic

border. Lesions and electical stimulation of this area have shown various affects on emotional behavior. (See Brown and Wallace, 1980, for a complete review of these functions.)

The cerebral cortex is the top portion of the brain often referred to as the gray matter. Physiologists have divided the cortex into four regions called lobes: frontal, temporal, parietal, and occipital. Parts of the cortex have been mapped for specific functions. For example, the temporal lobe is associated with auditory percepts, while the occipital lobe is associated with visual percepts. The remaining areas of the cortex are generally referred to as association areas linking multiple operations: frontal lobe association areas are related to planning processes, whereas association areas of the temporal lobe are involved with language comprehension (Wernicke's Area). The cortex seems to be the epitome of evolution, providing a variety of form and function relationships. Researchers concerned with communication behavior are frequently interested in the cortex since much of the activity for information processing is traced to this region of the brain. From this simplified review, general association areas can be identified and focused on for various measurement devices. Realizing the interconnectivity of the nervous system, specific measurement devices have been developed.

Depending on the system of interest, measurement devices have been constructed and refined. Table 13.1 provides a list of devices and the principal system associated with each device. The choice of the system and the measurement device is based on activation potential that is of interest and the corresponding system. The next section reviews the basic concepts underlying these devices.

MEASUREMENT DEVICES

Earlier in the chapter, the action potential was identified as the covert behavior of interest in physiological measurement. This behavior provides the ionic signal that is the basis of measurement in psychophysiological inquiry. The

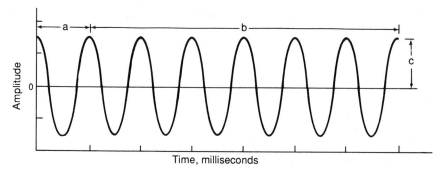

Figure 13.4. Wave form with its properties: a) cycle, b) frequency, and c) amplitude

signal is derived from the bioelectric activity of the cell through the basic measurement instrument called an **electrode**. This bioelectric phenomenon is an analog of the activity in a given cell or group of cells. Any signal derived from a cell can be described by three properties: **Amplitude, Frequency,** and **Wave Form** (see Figure 13.4).

The instruments that will be reviewed produce signals with these properties. Amplitude describes the magnitude of the signal. It is a reference recorded for a given wave and is the distance from a zero point to the highest elevation in the wave form. It can be a measure of distance created by a pen deflection on a polygraph recorder or the line signal produced on an oscilloscope. Each device can convert an electrical potential of a signal to a wave form that displays over a linear distance. It is advisable to become familiar with various wave forms so that the amplitude variations of given signals can be visually discernible. (Greenfield and Sternbach, 1972, provide an easily understandable review of instrumentation.)

Period and frequency of wave forms are measured at given points. A period of a wave form is defined in relation to time. It is a measurement of the length of time required to complete a cycle. All waves have patterns that can be regular or irregular. The movement of a given signal begins at a selected point and continues in a pattern. One complete cycle is the movement of this signal in a given pattern within a selected unit of time. Frequency is a measurement of the repetition of a given cycle within a given time period. The most general measure of frequency is cycles per second (cps). Frequency is usually described in hertz (Hz). A **hertz** is a unit of measurement for one complete cycle in one second, or 1 cps is equal to 1 Hz. A measurement of 10 Hz is a description of a wave that has a specific amplitude that completes a successive repetition of its pattern ten times in a given second. This is very slow electronically. Most signals are thousands of times faster and referred to as kilohertz (kHz).

The final characteristic of a signal is *wave form*. A wave form generalizes the shape of the wave recorded on a given instrument. There are many wave forms in bioelectric measurement with a variety of names that characterize their shape. Each measurement instrument has a characteristic wave that can identify it from any other. In various complex measurements the type of wave and its slope become important in selecting measurement units for analysis (See Martin and Venables, 1980) Amplitude, frequency, and wave form characteristics are difficult at first to recognize. However, with experience using a given instrument, the most novice user will be able to recognize these characteristics. Also, with the sophistication of devices available today, most measurements of these properties are processed electronically and computed for researchers in software packages that can be called up and viewed for analysis. The next section reviews common devices essential in the recording of bioelectric signals.

Electrodes

Between the action potential of the cell and the analysis of that potential are a series of devices that are extremely important. Each basic recording device requires electrodes. Electrodes transfer the ionic signal from the surface of the skin into electric potentials which are measured by various recording devices such as an EEG. The electrode itself does not come into direct contact with the skin. Most electrodes in current use today are encased in plastic on one side with a ridge of plastic around the edge of the recording side. On the exposed side, the ridge allows a small space between skin and receptor. Contact between the surface of the skin and the electrode is accomplished by conduction through an electrode paste or jelly. An electrode body is made of a precious metal such as silver-silver chloride (Ag-AgCl), and is commonly available through commercial manufacturers. Most manufacturers specify the paste specifications best for their electrodes. Resistance is checked before using the electrode in terms of ohms. The ohmmeter is essential in checking the reliability of the transference of the signal. Resistance requirements vary with the type of electrode and the type of measurement under consideration.

Polygraphs

The main component of any recording device is called a polygraph. Polygraphs today are pretty much self-contained units with couplers, amplifiers, and various display apparatus. The essential operations performed by a polygraph include conditioning of the signal, amplification of signals, and reproduction in various forms. Various filters are also included depending on the type of polygraph selected. Various polygraphs can also have a wide variety of couplers, amplifiers, and preamplifiers built in. Couplers generally condition the signal for various electronic modifications. Amplifiers take minimal signal voltage and increase it for various display or writing devices. Generally the weak signal from the action potential is multiplied in strength and converted electronically for various display devices such as a strip recorder or an oscilloscope.

Amplification is specified on the polygraph, and conversion factors are engineered by the manufacturer. Familiarity with specifications becomes important in assessing the recording reliability of the instrument. Manufacturers provide detailed summaries of their instruments, but calibration is essential for reliability. For example, the output of an EEG polygraph amplifier is approximately 1 volt. Since the bioelectric signal from the subject is in the microvolt range (millionths of a volt), this signal must be amplified a million times in order to be displayed by the polygraph. Because of the magnitude of amplification required to register these signals, interference can be a problem. Reliable polygraphs contain various filtering devices to reduce or eliminate unwanted signals. These filters reduce two types of interference: those below the range of a given measurement (called low pass), and those above the range (called high pass). Depending on the type of polygraph employed and the signal desired, attention to filtering is required. An instrument calibration measure should be performed before any data is recorded on any polygraph. (See McGuigan, 1979; and Martin & Venables, 1980.)

Computers

In the last few years, the sophistication of the polygraphs has been enhanced by microcomputers connected online in the actual recording session. The researcher has the option of display capacities ranging from raw data, analog display to relatively instantaneous analysis. Because of the potential volume of signals and various measurement analyses including spectral analyses of wave forms, a minimum of a 20-megabyte system is recommended. Almost all analyses that were once performed by hand can now be displayed and computed. Much more refined and accurate assessments are being performed by software which converts signals, quantifies and displays individual recordings. Needless to say, the use of spectral software has also provided new and interesting contributions to measurement concepts. These advances are expensive, but for programmatic research become almost essential if not required.

Recording devices are basic to physiological measurement. Their technology has been refined over the last 20 years, but their principles remain the same. The sophistication of measurement devices, however, has improved dramatically. A limited review of selected devices will be provided. The devices reviewed are by no means the most important. The serious student is directed to more expanded reviews in Martin and Venables (1980), and Cacioppo and Petty (1983).

Brain Measures

Electroencephalography (EEG) is a measure of small electrical potentials emitted by cells in the brain. They are detected by electrodes attached to the scalp of a subject. The electrical activity is small and ranges from 0.05 to 60 Hz.

The recording of this signal requires considerable amplification and filtering. The primary information provided by the EEG is derived from frequency measurement. Four frequency bands are commonly investigated in the literature: *delta,* 0.05–4.0 Hz; *theta,* 4.0–8.0 Hz; **alpha,** 8.0–13.0 Hz; and **beta,** 14–40 Hz. The discovery of these waves and the assignment of the Greek letters to represent them is attributed to Hans Berger in the early twenties, who first recorded alpha and beta waves. (See Andreassi, 1980, for both a historical and descriptive review of EEG.) As the sophistication of recording increased, more wave types were discovered and labeled with the Greek alphabet. Standard international placement procedures have also been agreed on and a numbering system called the "10–20 system" is used for placement of electrodes (Jasper, 1958).

Most EEG studies focus on the measurement of alpha and beta waves. Alpha is a measure of noncortical activity in contrast to beta waves. The beta wave is considered a measure of mental or cognitive activity. Alpha is a reference for a resting state or a relaxed state. If the frequency of the wave recorded shifts from an alpha range to a beta range, this shift represents a change from a relaxed state to a cognitive processing state. It is generally agreed among psychophysiologists that this shift from alpha to beta is a function of cognitive activation. As soon as a quiet relaxed person becomes involved in a cognitive act such as reading or doing silent math problems, the alpha wave changes to a higher frequency and a lower amplitude wave called beta (Ellingson, 1956).

The EEG is utilized by most researchers concerned about information processing. The left hemisphere of the human brain is considered the language center and hence the central area associated with verbal activation. The EEG provides an initial reference for exploring brain activation in this region. The right hemisphere is commonly referred to as the spatial, nonverbal area of the brain. This generalization holds for most right-handed individuals. The processing of verbal and spatial tasks has been the concern of many researchers utilizing the EEG.

Giannitrapani (1966) accelerated this research effort with a very basic study. His research effort was motivated by the general proposition that EEG waves would change during mental activity. Comparing both left and right frontal, temporal, parietal, and occipital regions, he measured the mean frequencies of his subjects in two states. He compared resting (alpha) sequences with mental (beta) activation caused by subjects computing simple multiplication problems. An increase in average EEG frequencies was observed. In addition, he observed a greater rate of EEG activity generated from the left hemisphere when compared to the right hemisphere for the frontal and temporal regions in both states of resting and mental activation. Giannitrapani hypothesized that the differential hemispheric activity may be associated with handedness, since there was no discernible interhemispheric difference.

Andreassi (1973) compared right and left occipital recordings during rest and during verbal activity. A significant amount of beta activity was recorded from both occipital hemispheres during mental activity when compared to the rest condition. That is, recordings of beta activity were observed on both sides of the brain. This research contrasts with that of Galin and Ornstein (1972). Their results suggested hemispheric asymmetry in the EEG patterns. Right hemispheric activity was greater in spatial tasks and left hemispheric activity was greater in verbal tasks. Can EEG waves be used to assess brain asymmetry, and could there be activation of beta on the right side of the brain during verbal stimulation?

These early studies set the stage for the discussions that exist today regarding EEG and brain **asymmetry**. In conducting EEG experiments, there are three variables that should be considered along with procedural requirements of a physiological nature. First, **monopolar electrodes** are more reliable than **bipolar** (two active electrodes placed over the same area) for asymmetry investigations. Bipolar leads tend to cancel each other out in the recording process. Placement of the grounding electrode on one side of the head or the other could influence the recording of the signal by shifting the balance to one side or the other. Grounding in the front of the head, or placing two grounding electrodes on each ear, can eliminate the shift.

Second, the type of mental activity selected for the subject to perform can also influence the movement from right to left hemispheres. And third, individual differences among subjects can create varying responses. Differences such as sex, age, and psychological state have impact on the responses that are recorded. These variables must be considered carefully in the selection of procedures when using the EEG. (See Gevins et al., 1979; Ray & Cole, 1985; Beaumont, Young, & McManus, 1984; and Sackiem, Wieman, & Grega, 1984.) Asymmetry, attention, and cognitive arousal are important areas for research using the EEG. (The sample study later in this chapter will provide further clarification.)

Peripheral Measures

The peripheral nervous system for the most part is not under the control of voluntary behavior. The previous section focused on stimulation and responses of the central nervous system. There are numerous measures for the peripheral nervous system. Physiologically, the measures are quite direct. The *electromyogram* is a measure of skeletal muscle activity that is independent of voluntary muscle contraction. The *electrocardiogram* is a measure of the heart activity, indicative of the muscle action of contraction over a period of time. The questions of relationship to behavioral factors and their concomitant structures persent theoretical problems. (See Stern, Ray, & Davis, 1980; and McGuigan, 1979). The measures independent of overt correlations under stimulus conditions present only minimal problems. Again, the sophistication of technological advances provides physiological sophistication. A brief summary of one of the measures will follow. In-depth elaboration of other measures can be reviewed in Martin and Venables (1980).

Electromyogram (EMG)

EMG is a measure of muscle activity. Typically it is used in psychophysiology as an indicator of anxiety or relaxation. This technique has been used with both surface or subcutaneous needles. The basic principle is to record muscle action potentials. The tracing of the muscle action potentials is recorded following some neural stimulation, not physical movement. The tension increase is recorded while the subject is in a resting position. The electrical activity is not the result of muscle contraction, but of stimulation generated through another system. The EMG is a bipolar recording system, with electrodes in close proximity to one another. A small electrical signal is passed between the electrodes. When the signal is interrupted by the cell bioelectric activity, a signal can be recorded. McGuigan and his associates have used the EMG to record subvocal speech activity (McGuigan et al., 1964); McGuigan & Baily, 1969; McGuigan & Rodger, 1968).

Other specific measurements of the peripheral nervous system have been studied in relation to the effects of stimulation and physiological responses. The electrocardiogram (EKG) has been of interest for some time as well as blood pressure and other cardiovascular issues. Measurement concerns with this instrument as well as others should be reviewed in detail. The interested student is directed to Andreassi (1980) for a complete physiological review. An excellent review of measurement problems and issues can be found in Cacioppo and Petty (1983) and Waid (1984).

INTERPRETATION PRINCIPLES

The review of physiological measures thus far has been restricted to the bioelectrical phenomenon that is measured as a result of ionic activity that is sensed through electrodes and recorded in some fashion by a polygraph. These empirical signals have to be related to hypothetical constructs associated with these signals. When confronting the issues that surround these concepts, researchers are faced with some theoretical concerns that must be addressed regarding interpretation of the recorded signals. While there is considerable controversy regarding the basic constructs surrounding these issues, one need not be overly concerned about which position is taken. Essentially, the issue faces all behavioral researchers regarding mental or material perspectives (see Chapter 5 in this volume).

Briefly, the issue concerns whether there are mental phenomena independent of physical phenomena; that is, whether there is a dualistic or monistic perspective. The dualistic perspective in physiological theory asserts that mental phenomena can exist independent of physiological limits; that is, for every corresponding physical phenomenon, there can be a mental phenomenon. This dualistic perspective recognizes that constructs such as symbolic behavior have impact on physiological processes. Since there has been no direct causal relationship established, an association is hypothesized between simultaneous events that are observed. It is important to remember that certain stimuli such as a list of words that have been labeled as having some cognitive intensity can be associated with certain measures of physiological changes. The relationship observed is one not of causality, but of correlation. (For an excellent review of this position, see Rosenbleuth, 1969.)

Monistic perspectives assert that mental phenomena do not exist. All that is capable of measurement is material or physiological. There are no mediating systems independent of the physiological mechanisms. Behavioral constructs are representative of relationships that are extensions of the material phenomenon. This perspective often restricts the questions under investigation, simply because the hypothetical constructs of materialism cannot admit phenomena of a mentalistic or cognitive nature. Relatively few researchers focus their investigations so narrowly.

Pribram (1986) recently addressed this issue and has developed a new construct called "neutral monism." Essentially his argument is that the issue is basically a philosophical one incapable of resolution. Since the two terms dualism and monism are restrictive sets that oppose each other, they are doomed as issues because of their paradoxical nature. Empirical issues and relationships simply cannot expand if limited to one perspective or the other. Hence, Pribram (1986) suggests that the limits of the constructs of monism and dualism should not prohibit the systematic investigation of relationships between physical and mental phenomena. A researcher designs investigations that clearly exhibit the observation and the inferred relationship that is constructed.

These constructions stem from careful measurement of such phenomena as brain waves, heart beat, and respiration rates and their careful association with measurements of behavioral phenomena such as information and other cognitive constructs. The resolution of philosophical differences will come only through systematic investigation in a scientific frame that recognizes limitations of its method and measurement schemes.

There are five strategic concepts that are related to psychophysiological research. These concepts are derived and associated with other behavioral measures that reflect relationships of covert and overt behavior. They are *activation or arousal*, **habituation,** *the Law of Initial Values*, **homeostasis,** and *autonomic balance*.

Activation

The concepts of activation or arousal are used interchangeably in the research. This is one of the oldest concepts utilized in the characterization of physiological change. Activation may be defined as an organism's preparation for "flight or fight." The origin of the concept can be traced to the work of Cannon (1915). Duffey (1957) extended this notion to include intensity aspects of human behavior. The use of the concept of arousal emerged from experiments that characterized the capacity of the organism to be physiologically aroused when emotional states such as fear or anxiety were inferred. Duffey (1962) hypothesized that the level of activation was associated with performance on the now famous "inverted U-shaped curve." As the level of performance increased, the level of physiological arousal also increased.

Not all measures of physiological activity increase and decrease in the same manner. For example, levels of heart rate, muscle potential and EEG asynchrony are associated with increased activation or arousal in the individual. Decreases in these same measurements are said to be levels of decreased activation. Generally, the level of performance rises with increases in the physiological activity of an individual up to a certain point. When that point is reached, performance begins to diminish. There is, then, some optimal point at which activation level and performance level maximize. The "inverted U-shaped curve" is thus an illustration of the relationship between the level of arousal and performance. An increase in heart rate or respiration would indicate an increase in the level of arousal or activation in the individual. In EEG activity, a change from slow synchronized activity (alpha) to rapid asynchronized activity (beta) would be an indication of arousal or activation in the brain.

Schachter and Singer (1962) related generalized arousal to emotions. They asserted that arousal or activation of an individual was closely associated with cognitive activity and that it was essential for emotional responses. Using several measures, both behavioral and physiological, they concluded that once a subject is at an aroused level, labeling plays a central role in determining the level of emotionality. They concluded that similar states of high physiological arousal could be labeled "joy" or "fury" or any number of emotional states. Activation, then, is an interpretive principle dependent on aspects of the situation and the labeling of the emotion of interest.

There is some controversy regarding arousal and how this concept is utilized in various research efforts. Activation and arousal refer generally to changes in physiological states. How these changes take place can vary in relation to the sources of stimulation. "False Feedback" studies have illustrated that telling subjects that a physiological change in their levels of arousal is taking place, when in fact it is not, has affected behavior. Arousal levels in the human can be observed on at least three levels of measurement: cortical, autonomic, and behavioral. (See Lacey, 1967; & Maslach, 1979a, b; Schachter and Singer, 1979.) At the cortical level, it can be induced by verbal or cognitive stimuli; at the autonomic, as a defense against physical harm; and at the behavioral level by situational factors induced by "false feedback."

Habituation

The concept of *habituation* refers to the cessation of behavior from repeated exposure to the same stimulus. It is as basic to physiological measurement as is activation or arousal. It is complementary to arousal in that arousal suggests excitation, and habituation suggests the cessation of responsivity to repeated stimulation. Habituation occurs, then, with continual repetition of the same stimulus over a period of time.

Time and intensity of the stimulation affect the response physiologically. The greater the time lapse between the stimulation, the slower the habituation. Similarly, the greater the intensity of the stimulation, the slower the habituation. Stern, Gaub, and Leonard (1970) have shown that as a subject anticipates a given stimulus, there is a relationship to the subject's habituation. When their subjects were exposed to electric shock, their expectancy affected the rate of habituation. Given 15 electric shocks, subjects' responses habituated by the time all 15 shocks were administered. In contrast, another group of subjects were given loud tones, but did not habituate over 15 trials. Intensity can vary the response of habituation. If the stimulus does not command the attention of the subject, repetition of the stimulus results in habituation.

Law of Initial Values

The law of initial values (LIV) was first proposed by Wilder (1958, 1967). The LIV predicts that when the prestimulus level of the subject is high, the smaller will be the response to stimulation; and that when the prestimulus level of the subject is low, the greater will be the response. Wilder (1967) considered the LIV to apply to all responses under the control of the ANS. However, not all experimental results indicate that the prestimulus level has effects on the responses of physiological systems. In some cases, the prestimulus level and the corresponding post-stimulus response do not show increases. Essentially, the LIV is, under some conditions, a good predictor of response level decreases, but not increases.

For example, Watterson and Riccillo (1983) explored the response behavior of infants in two states, "calm" and "crying," with a signal that has maximum impact on the basilar membrane (inner ear). They hypothesized that this signal would have the capacity to induce a reduction in overt crying behavior, which they confirmed. However, the same signal had no impact on the infant in the calm state. The prestimulus level of the infants under the first condition was altered from a high level during the prestimulus state, to a lower level of activity in the post-stimulus condition. The reflexive crying behavior changed as predicted under the LIV. During the calm prestimulus condition, however, no increase in crying behavior was observed. The LIV does not hold for all measures of physiological activity. (See Andreassi, 1980, for a review of several other studies using the LIV.)

The LIV is a concept that identifies the level of prestimulus activity for a physiological measure in order to assess the magnitude of response. Many experimental investigations have reported that certain physiological variables change in the predicted direction, while many variables do not change as predicted.

Homeostasis

The concept of **homeostasis** is a reference used in physiology that can describe both the state of the organism or various processes that can take place in the organism. In a general sense, it describes balance or stability. It is a reference about the internal environment of the organism. It would be difficult to characterize any biological organism as completely homeostatic; some systems may be more balanced than others.

The principle of homeostasis is based on negative feedback. It is a correcting device that returns imbalanced states to balanced ones. Metaphorically, a thermostat which controls the temperature in a room operates on this principle. As the room becomes colder, the thermostat activates the heat source and the room returns to a preset temperature. Biosystems like the human body operate the same way. Again, depending on the type of response to be measured, changes in the state of the organism such as temperature, heart rate etc. can vary. Assuming stability of the organism can invalidate a set of measures (see Stern, Ray, & Davis, 1980).

Autonomic Balance

Internal organs that operate on signals from the branches of the ANS are affected by autonomic balance. Essentially, internal organs such as the heart or lungs are regulated by the SNS and the PNS. The rate at which the heart beats is determined by both of these systems interacting with each other. When the two systems interact to maintain a steady heartbeat, a condition of autonomic balance is present. Earlier in the chapter, it was reported that the SNS activates various organs, and the PNS reduces or returns the organ to an even level of operation. Individuals may be dominated by either the SNS or the PNS.

Wenger and his associates (Wenger, 1966; Wenger & Cullen, 1972; and Wenger, 1972) are responsible for the concept of autonomic balance (referred to as A scores). They basically asserted that either the SNS or the PNS was dominant in any given individual. The degree to which the PNS or SNS was dominant could be determined by a derived score from several physiological measures. High A scores revealed that an individual was dominated by the PNS, while low A indicated dominance by the SNS. The importance of this test becomes significant when researchers utilize various measures of the ANS. The test can assure that relative dominance of the SNS or PNS is present in subjects exposed to various measures involving the peripheral nervous system.

Autonomic balance becomes a critical issue in studies dealing with multivariate measures involving the ANS. In univariate studies, the factors of SNS or PNS dominance usually will not play a role. (See Stern, Ray, & Davis, 1980.)

These basic principles assist researchers in determining the basic construct for measurement. A change in response is characterized by one or more of these principles, usually depending on what the investigator has determined to be the focus of the study. Essentially, these principles assist investigators by characterizing responses or change of states into viable constructs for measurement and analysis. The selection of the interpretive principle guides the researcher in determining the significance of the experimental findings.

Measuring physiological responses and relating them to hypothetical constructs is fundamental to psychophysiological methods. There is an inherent relationship between the selection of a particular measure and the corresponding interpretation of the findings. It is advisable to select measures and review the corresponding research literature to assess the various interpretive strategies that have been used. Two issues always confront the use of psychophysiological measurement. The first involves the careful assessment of the division of the nervous system that will provide the physiological data of concern; the second issue involves the interpretation of the data within a theoretical construct. A brief review of this format is provided in the sample study that follows. This study also focuses on communicative behavior as the basis for the investigation.

SAMPLE STUDY

There are numerous studies which can illustrate the methods that have been reviewed. The study selected for review in this chapter was chosen for its use of physiological measures as well as its use of communication behaviors. The study was conducted by Cacioppo, Petty, and Quintinar (1982). It is one of several studies utilizing physiological measures as well as social/cognitive variables of interest to scholars studying communication behavior.

Research Questions

Cacioppo et al. presented two basic research questions in this study. The first was concerned with whether or not there was lateral asymmetry in cognitive responses to persuasion stimuli. The second question focused on whether or not data could be identified regarding shifts in processing and how to manipulate the shift of processing using persuasion stimuli. There were three experiments in the study; the first two concerned the first research question, and the third concerned the second research question.

In order to answer the first research question, several methodological decisions had to be made regarding measurement issues. The first question focused on the activity of the CNS and was concerned with bioelectric activity in the brain. The selection of the EEG measure directed attention to cerebral activity in the brain. The wave of concern was alpha (8–13Hz). A continuous recording of this signal was made and as alpha activity was recorded, cognitive activity was inferred not to be occurring. If the alpha wave changed in frequency and amplitude to beta, then the subject was assumed to have shifted to an activated state.

To record this shift, Cacioppo et al. measured relative alpha abundance. That is, their EEG recordings were composed of amounts of alpha activity. The greater the amount of alpha activity over the test period, the less cognitive activation. The smaller the sum of alpha activity, the more cognitive activation in the subject.

This measurement also required the researchers to measure both hemispheres. Therefore, electrodes were attached to both the left (P3) and the right (P4) parietal regions of the scalp, and a reference point (Cz). A greater amount of alpha activity over the right parietal region suggested that more cognitive activation was occurring on the left; and a greater amount of alpha activity of the left parietal region indicated that cognitive activity was occurring on the right. A pretreatment or baseline was recorded before measures were taken under experimental conditions. Relative alpha was computed by calculating the ratio of the difference in alpha abundance at both the right and left regions over the total abundance of alpha evident at both the right and left parietal regions within the sampling period. This ratio was computed by the following formula: $[(P4 - P3)/(P4 + P3)] \times 100$. The larger the ratio computed with this formula, the greater the amount of alpha abundance. For example, if a large ratio were computed for the right parietal lobe (P4), the left side of the brain was more activated. This computational formula has been used frequently and successfully in other experiments involving hemispheric asymmetry.

The measurements were accomplished using computerized assessment of the EEG signals. The EEG signals were taken from the recording site and amplified, then filtered and sampled 100 times per second through the computer. Transformation of the signals was possible using computerized software that was programmed to provide the measurement of alpha abundance. Each subject's responses were monitored using an oscilloscope to assess artifacts that may have been present. In this fashion, artifacts resulting from a source, such as movement by the subject, could be edited. They reported relatively few during the recording sessions.

The stimuli used to induce activation were prerecorded persuasive messages on a computer-controlled recording system. This tape recording was played to the subject during the EEG recording. The computer-controlled procedure consisted of a 60-second baseline followed by a 195-second communication epoch. The communication epoch consisted of a 15-second forewarning of the topic and position of the impending message, a 60-second post-warning pre-message period of silence, and a 120-second presentation of a proattitudinal or counterattitudinal message. They provided the 15-second forewarning to allow subjects a brief time period to think about the attitudinal recommendation before receiving the external stimulus.

The significance of this stimulus condition rests on the fact that an entire message was being utilized. It has already been observed in many studies that semantic stimuli activate the left hemisphere. The construction of a message epoch was utilized to evaluate whether or not hemispheric activation was possible with a particular kind of cognitive stimulus, a persuasive message.

Dependent Measures of Cognitive Activity

It has long been theorized in persuasion literature that recipients of various persuasive messages have access to a variety of information beyond that which is contained in a given persuasive message. Persuasive messages can elicit individual cognitive responses that either contradict or support externally provided arguments (Festinger & Maccoby, 1964; Greenwald, 1968). Cacioppo et al. viewed their subjects as active contributors who were susceptible or resistant to the persuasive message on the audio tape. Theorizing from Corballis' (1980) results regarding functional cerebral asymmetry, they hypothesized that their subjects who were characterized by relative activation of the left hemisphere would respond in a more elaborative manner. Subjects who were characterized by relative activation of the right hemisphere would respond in a more message-dependent manner. To discover the response patterns of their subjects, they constructed a questionnaire instrument that was administered after each subject was exposed to the recorded persuasive message. The instrument measured two variables: affective polarization and affect-laden thought. The questionnaire was developed by Petty and Brock (1979).

Affective polarization of cognitive responses assessed the difference between the number of nonpredominant and predominant responses on the questionnaire. These responses yielded two possible scores: a proattitudinal score and a counterattitudinal score. The difference between these scores produced agreement indices that were either supportive or nonsupportive of the persuasive message. Affect-laden thought scores were a simple sum of the total favorable or unfavorable thoughts listed by each of the subjects. Manipulation checks confirmed that proattitudinal messages elicited more agreement when compared to the counterattitudinal responses.

Subjects

Two groups of male subjects were selected. One group was proattitudinal and the other was counterattitudinal. There were twenty subjects in each group. Right-handed males, with a history of righthandedness in their families, were selected to control for left-hemispheric dominance.

Results

Analyses performed by Cacioppo et al. (1982) revealed that individual differences in hemispheric activation during the period prior to the forewarning in the baseline measurement of the EEG, could not account for the variance in the two cognitive response measures. Expected results were confirmed for hemispheric activation that occurred during the period when the persuasive message was heard by the subjects. Subjects with relative right-hemispheric activation produced more polarized thoughts than did subjects with relative left-hemispheric activation. There was no significant relationship between subjects showing differences in relative hemispheric activation and listing favorable or unfavorable thoughts.

Second Experiment

In the second experiment reported in this study, Cacioppo et al. (1982) replicated the first experiment to assess the reliability of the effects obtained in the first experiment. They changed three procedures. First, they changed the topics of the persuasive messages, maintaining a controversial issue like the first message. Second, they altered the communication epoch for the EEG measurement into four separate periods: a forewarning period (15-seconds), a postwarning-premessage period of silence (45-seconds), the persuasive message period (the same as the first, 60-seconds), and the postmessage period of silence (15-seconds). Third, each subject was exposed to both proattitudinal and counterattitudinal messages, in an order randomly assigned.

Results

The results of the analyses revealed similar effects as were reported in the first experiment. Subjects characterized by relative right-hemispheric activation generated more polarized thoughts regarding the issues presented in the persuasive message when compared to subjects characterized by relative left-hemispheric activation. This effect emerged regardless of the period selected in the communication epoch. Relative hemispheric activation did not relate to the subject's self-generated lists of favorable or unfavorable thoughts.

Third Experiment

Reducing the sample size to seven males, the third experiment reported by Cacioppo et al. (1982) focused on affective polarization of topic-relevant thinking and interhemispheric shift patterns. The research question focused on whether subjects who thought longer about an issue would reflect a shift from one hemisphere to the other. In this case, subjects who were polarized toward an issue would, with additional thinking, shift back to the right hemisphere. The hypothesis was confirmed in a complex two-stage condition using the same EEG procedure as was reported in the previous two experiments. As individuals thought longer about an issue, there was a shift of relative hemispheric activation from the left to the right hemisphere.

The data reported from all three experiments suggest a reliable effect: Individuals who produce one-sided (polarized) profiles of cognitive responses to persuasive messages also demonstrate relative right-hemispheric activation in the parietal regions of the cortex. This study illustrates the effect of persuasive messages on hemispheric activation. In particular, complex message epochs rather than simple semantic signals are capable of eliciting hemispheric arousal in EEG activation measurement.

SUMMARY

This chapter has presented a brief review of psychophysiological measurement techniques and their relationship to communication behavior. The incorporation of perspectives from physiology requires investigators to be concerned with behavior that is covert as well as overt. Use of these techniques allows the researcher to consider activity that is beyond normal behavioral observations.

Physiological measurement has a history of achievements that go back in recorded time. Ancient Greek scholars were also intrigued and explored relationships involving covert and overt processes. The philosophical connection between mind and matter is an issue that has its roots in the classical writings of the past.

Basic physiological principles ground the exploration of psychophysiological measurement. Since the time that bioelectric activity was discovered, the basic tenets that guide research have remained in place. The concept of electrical potential is based on cell biology. Living organisms possess electrical potential that allows a system for movement or activation. It is the measurement of the action potential that is the common mechanism which is measured in various forms with various instruments.

The bioelectric activity of the human organism is organized into a sophisticated system. This system exhibits evolutionary sophistication, such that many of the mechanisms in the human nervous system are parallel to other biological systems. The human organism is composed of two major systems for biological control, the nervous system and the endocrine system. Only the nervous system with its two major divisions, central and peripheral, was reviewed. Either or both systems could be of concern in physiological measurement.

Each type of measurement device was designed to measure bioelectric activity in the system. There are specific measures associated with each part of the nervous system. A researcher's focus requires selection of specific devices and familiarity with the system under investigation. There are three properties of a signal that are identifiable: amplitude, frequency, and wave form. These properties are acquired through electrodes attached to the skin. The electrodes are connected to various polygraph instruments. Polygraphs can be simple or extremely complex, having couplers and amplifiers built-in. Computers are simplifying the recording of the signal with some systems having multiple operations and packaged software for various measurements.

Brain measures are concerned with activity in the central nervous system. The most common system is the electroencephalogram. Complex EEG's can record activity from the entire cortex and have specific regions for electrode attachment. The EEG is the most common instrument used for information processing, and is probably the most frequently used instrument in communication behavior. Lateralization and hemispheric studies focus on alpha and beta waves that are measured with the EEG.

Peripheral nervous system measurements are also of interest. While only the electromyogram was reviewed in this chapter, many other instruments are widely used. Heart rate, respiration, or moisture levels of the skin can also provide valuable insights on communication-related behavior.

Interpretive concepts are essential for relating covert and overt behavior. The historical paradox of mind/body dualism will be at issue for some time to come. Monistic perspectives do not rely on mentalistic concepts, whereas mentalistic phenomena have been viewed as important in raising theoretical concerns. The most frequent interpretive concepts reviewed were activation or arousal, habituation, the law of initial value, homeostasis, and autonomic balance.

The sample study provided a review of the work of Cacioppo, Petty, and Quintanar (1982). This study utilized the EEG in assessing the effects of persuasive communication on hemispheric activation. It provided evidence that individuals who produce one-sided (polarized) profiles of cognitive responses to persuasive messages demonstrate right-hemispheric activation in the parietal regions of the brain.

STUDY QUESTIONS

1. Psychophysiologists define behavior as having both covert and overt properties. How does the use of measurement techniques allow for this theoretical construct?
2. The concept of electrical potential is basic to the measurement devices used in psychophysiological measurement. What principles of cell biology support this?
3. Measurement devices are used to assess various bioelectric activities. What is the relationship of these devices to specific systems such as CNS, ANS, etc.?
4. Interpretive concepts play an important and instrumental role in psychophysiological measurement. Review each of the major concepts and determine the underlying hypothetical construct related to each of these concepts.
5. The sample study provided the use of a specific measurement device and focused attention on a specific issue: that the kind of message transmitted had an impact on the area of the brain utilized for receiving messages. Summarize in detail the specific methods used to select the kind of message and the procedure for determining which side of the brain was being utilized.

ANNOTATED READINGS

Andreassi, J. L. (1980). *Psychophysiology: Human behavior and physiological response.* New York: Oxford University Press.

    A beginning text in measurement written for the novice. It is well documented and takes the interested student through all of the basic measurement techniques at a level that is understandable and enjoyable.

Cacioppo, J. T., & Petty, R. E. (Eds.). (1983). *Social psychophysiology: A source book.* New York: Guilford.

    An excellent source book for the student who is interested in using physiological measurement with social variables. There are 25 chapters that review in detail programmatic research of interest to many facets of behavioral research employing covert and overt interactions.

Waid, W. M. (Ed.). (1984). *Sociophysiology.* New York: Springer-Verlag.
This text focuses on the biological basis of social behavior. It is an excellent edition of selected researchers who have incorporated physiological techniques in the description and explanation of human behavior. Physiological techniques employed in programmatic research dealing with social cognition, nonverbal behavior, learning, and communication are provided.

CHAPTER 14

Nonverbal Communication Measurement

By William C. Donaghy,
University of Wyoming

While it is very easy to find a multitude of examples showing the communicative significance of nonverbal behavior, it is extremely difficult to empirically
access this source of behavioral information. This dilemma is embedded in the
very nature of this mode of activity: nonverbal behavior owes its importance as
a means of expression to its dynamics, its complexity and its wealth of subtle
nuances. Yet these same features also cause enormous problems when any
attempt is made to actually document the complex stream of nonverbal
communication. (Frey, 1983, p. 63)

The list of individuals who have attempted to seriously study nonverbal
communication includes names such as Aristotle, Marcus Tullius Cicero,
Leonardo da Vinci, Johann Wolfgang von Goethe, Immanuel Kant, Sigmund
Freud, and Charles Darwin. Yet, until recently little of any real empirical value
has been learned. One of the greatest difficulties that has plagued the field is the
large and diverse number of research methodologies that have been developed
and utilized. This is an outgrowth, not only of the complex nature of the
phenomena, but also the number of disciplines and researchers interested in
studying nonverbal communication. With the growing awareness of the
importance of nonverbal communication, it has become a common research
procedure to begin a study by creating a high quality video (usually videotape or
film) record of the nonverbal behavior. Agreement ends, however, at that point.
Researchers, like the average observer, can easily see that important nonverbal
behavior is taking place, but they cannot agree on how to record what they see.
Ekman, Friesen, and Taussig (1969) make an important point when they state
that filmed or videotaped "records are not data. While records may be the raw

input for intriguing ideas and discovery, they must be converted into some digital form in order to be analyzed" (p. 298). Only recently have researchers begun to perceive the value of establishing comprehensive, benchmark recording methods which are capable of creating multi-user data pools and providing answers to questions arising in various disciplines.

The 1970 *Methods of Research in Communication* text included an excellent chapter by Larry L. Barker and Nancy B. Collins on "Nonverbal and Kinesic Research" (Barker & Collins, 1970). They called nonverbal communication a "frontier of communication research" (p. 343) and reviewed eighteen different classes of nonverbal studies: animal and insect; culture; environmental surroundings; gestural, facial expression, bodily movement, and kinesics; human behavior; interaction patterns; learning; machine; media; mental processes, perception, imagination, and creativity; music; paralinguistics; personal grooming and apparel; physiological; pictures; space; tactile and cutaneous; and time. If some of these types of nonverbal communication are unfamiliar to you, please take the time to read their brief but excellent discussion of each (Barker & Collins, 1970, pp. 344–353).

Since the publication of the Barker and Collins chapter, there have been a great many reviews of the nonverbal communication literature (Argyle, 1975; Bull, 1983; Burgoon, 1980, 1985a, 1985b; Burgoon & Saine, 1978; Crouch, 1980; Davis, 1975, 1979; Donaghy, 1980, 1984; Druckman, 1982; Ekman, 1973; Ellgring, 1984; Harper, 1978; Harrison, 1973, 1974; Henley, 1977; Heslin & Patterson, 1982; Kendon, 1981, 1983; Key, 1977, 1980; Knapp, 1978a, 1978b, 1984; LaFrance & Mayo, 1978; Leathers, 1976, Malendra & Barker, 1983; Mehrabian, 1972; Morris, 1977; Patterson, 1983; Scherer & Ekman, 1982; Speer, 1972; and vonRaffler-Engel, 1980). A large portion of the studies found in that literature, however, merely use standard *laboratory* measurement techniques but apply them to nonverbal communication. Hence, much of the previous research has very little **external validity**, i.e., it is almost impossible to relate it to nonverbal behavior as it occurs in everyday interaction. It is not the purpose of this chapter to add yet another similar literature review.

Barker and Collins elaborated on specific methodologies related to body movement and facial expression. They justified this limitation by saying that "gestural, facial expression, and other types of movement research are most closely related to speech communication ... " (p. 353). For that same reason, this chapter will also focus on two important contemporary research methodologies designed specifically to increase our understanding of body movement and facial expression. The nonverbal measurement approaches that will be discussed here are the *Bernese Time-Series Notation System (TSN)* and the *Facial Action Coding System (FACS)*. These two contemporary measurement techniques are leading nonverbal communication researchers out of the dark ages and into the 21st century. For each of these nonverbal measurement systems, you will find (1) a discussion of its theoretical approach, (2) a brief introduction to how one codes data, (3) a description of the available data analysis procedures, and (4) some examples of research studies that have employed the technique. In attempting to cover these two complex measurement approaches, it is impossible to avoid simplifying many complex issues and omitting a large number of important aspects of each methodology. Persons planning to engage in research using either of these systems should consult the specialized references listed at the end of this chapter. Before we explore these two excellent nonverbal communication research methods in detail, however, it might be useful to contrast them with other coding strategies that have been used in the past.

CODING STRATEGIES

Because, up to this poin., there have been no widely recognized, multi-user nonverbal communication coding strategies, most researchers have begun by developing a coding scheme designed to fit their own specific research questions. This has produced a huge number of notational techniques, most of which have been employed only by their creator and often used in only one study. Perhaps the best brief overview and critique of these coding approaches was done by Frey and Pool (1976). They classify all previous coding strategies into one of three types: generic, restrictive, and direct evaluation.

Generic Coding

Researchers using this strategy record data into categories, labeled with generic terms, which cover a number of obviously different behaviors. Common category terms that have been used in the past are "point," "illustrate," "gesture," "automanipulate," "forearm sweep," "walk," etc. This approach forces coders to ignore any movement variations that do not signify differences between categories. Behaviors coded in the category "gesture," for example, do not necessarily mean the coders did not see differences in the type of gestures which occurred. They were trained, however, to ignore these differences because the investigator did not believe them to be "relevant."

Frey and Pool point out that when investigators choose to ignore visually discriminable behaviors, several problems arise. First, since most studies of this sort use everyday language to label categories, they are necessarily limited to the types of behavior for which common terms exist. Common language usually focuses only on high impact behaviors which generally occur infrequently in normal conversation. How often, for example, do things like "hit," "push," "grab," "embrace," or "kick" occur in normal interaction? These were common generic terms used to code interaction in the early 1970s. Brannigan and Humphries (1972) developed one of the most elaborate generic coding systems with 136 categories, only two of which, "demonstrate" and "gesture," cover almost all arm and hand activity. The generic coding strategy cannot be significantly improved by simply adding more common terms. The real flaw is in the use of generic language in the first place.

A second problem with this coding strategy, according to Frey and Pool, is allowing heterogeneous behaviors to be grouped into the same category. An example of this might be coding a "smile" denoting happiness together with a "smile" of contempt. With this approach there is no way to determine how the various behaviors categorized together really relate to one another or to the independent variable. Two different behaviors, such as types of smiles, coded into the same category may be related to the independent variable in opposite ways and cancel each other out. A statistical test on such data would show nonsignificant results.

Research economy is the final problem with generic coding. If an investigator does not find systematic relations between the research variable and the nonverbal behavior, then he or she must redefine the categories and start all over again. Finding the best generic coding scheme is a time-consuming process, and one that must be started anew with each study since the strategy that is optimal in one study may be useless in another.

Restrictive Coding

Whereas the generic coding strategy usually tries to cover *all* nonverbal behavior, in restrictive coding "behavioral description is confined to the assessment of a small subset of specific movements which are well defined, easily observed and difficult to mistake" (Hirsbrunner, Frey, & Crawford, 1983, p. 7). The typical study of eye gaze is a good example. A researcher watches where subjects gaze and for how long, but does not record gestures, posture, facial expression, or any other nonverbal behavior. This approach overcomes the problem of putting visually different behaviors into the same category, but data homogeneity is achieved by severely limiting the amount of nonverbal behavior examined. Restrictive coding is adequate when only very specific types of nonverbal communication are of interest, but this means neglecting the interrelationship that all nonverbal behaviors have to one another. The more restrictive the coding the greater the number of behaviors that are neglected. Hirsbrunner et al. call this "data reduction by ignoring" as opposed to generic coding, which they describe as "data reduction by lumping" (1983, p. 8). Hence, the problems with restrictive coding are not fewer, but only different.

Direct Evaluation

Frey and Pool's final coding strategy is designed to circumvent the difficulties inherent in generic and restrictive notation by having coders directly ascribe "meaning" to the nonverbal behaviors or transform observations into the psychological dimensions in which the researcher is interested. The coder is asked, for example, to determine if a particular behavior indicates "extroversion," "anxiety," "defensiveness," "dominance," etc. Since there is thus far no common agreement on what meaning or psychological dimension is indicated by various behaviors, coders must use their own discretion. The main problem with this strategy is that the digital notation is skipped completely; hence both the reliability and validity of such studies can be questioned.

It is the contention of Frey, Pool, and their colleagues that, in the long run, any truly useful coding strategy must be based on the principle of time-series notation. They state that "time-series notation forms the methodological basis for literally every efficient approach to the registration and storage of audio-visual information" (Hirsbrunner et al., 1983, p. 3). The alphabet is an obvious example, along with music and dance notation. The following coding strategy will illustrate how the time-series notation principle is applied to the analysis of nonverbal movement.

TIME SERIES NOTATION SYSTEM

The form of time-series notation discussed here is the product of over ten years' development by Siegfried Frey, Hans-Peter Hirsbrunner, and their colleagues at the University of Berne, Switzerland (Frey, 1973, 1976, 1983, 1984; Frey, Hirsbrunner, & Bieri-Florin, 1979; Frey, Hirsbrunner, Pool, & Daw, 1981; Frey, Hirsbrunner, & Jorns, 1982; Frey, Hirsbrunner, Florin, Daw, & Crawford, 1983; Frey & Pool, 1976; Hirsbrunner, Frey, & Crawford, 1983). For that reason it is referred to as the "Bernese Time-Series Notation System." TSN is the newest and most powerful multi-user coding system in the field of nonverbal communication research. At the present time it is being widely accepted and used by European nonverbal communication researchers. That is due, in part, to the fact that most of the literature on TSN is still available only in German—see "References" at the end of the book.

Theoretical Approach

Like Birdwhistell's Kinesics Notation System (Birdwhistell, 1952, 1970 and described by Barker & Collins, 1970 pp. 356—363), Bernese TSN derives its basic theoretical approach from the time-series principles underlying speech notation. Both systems try to break down nonverbal activity piece-by-piece over time in the same way a linguist analyzes speech. The major limitation of the Kinesics Notation System (and other generic nonverbal measurement methodologies) is that Birdwhistell tried to create a different symbol for each individual movement pattern. This approach may be satisfactory where the object of study contains a limited number of meaningful variables. Nonverbal communication, on the other hand, has an unlimited number of meaningful positions and/or movement patterns. Learning to code nonverbal behavior using a unique symbol system is like trying to learn the Chinese writing system, which uses a different character for each word and barely achieves its objective with over 50,000 symbols.

Bernese Time-Series Notation employs the principles of the Roman alphabet which accomplishes the same objective as Chinese writing but with just 26 letters. TSN uses slightly over 100 dimensions to code almost all body movement. **Body movement** as defined by Frey is the change of body position over time (Frey & Pool, 1976). "Just as the complex pattern of speech can be resolved into a phonetic and a temporal component, the complex movement pattern can be resolved into their spatial and temporal constituents" (Frey, 1983, pp. 65). The heart of TSN is a fairly simple technique for coding the various body positions. Once a static position is coded, a new coding is made only when the position changes. This change from one point in time to another, not the original position, represents movement. The theoretical principle underlying Bernese TSN, then, reduces the problem of *movement* notation to the problem of coding static *positions*. This is a major advantage of TSN over most other coding strategies.

Coding Procedure

I have found it takes 10 to 20 hours to train a coder to use TSN although Frey claims he can do it in a day. The system is designed to code nonverbal behavior obtained from individuals sitting in a chair and conversing. If an investigator is interested in coding persons standing or walking and talking, many of the coding dimensions and reference points would have to be changed. Although no such system yet exists, the same basic coding procedure described below could easily apply. Table 14.1 gives an overall summary of the original TSN categories. Various researchers have modified the system to fit their own applications. In my laboratory, for example, I omit the "touch" dimension since it does not really indicate body *movement*. I have also added a dimension called "head depth" (see discussion below). Finally, I have found it is just as easy to code the head, trunk, and various dimensions of the upper legs and feet into seven rather than five units. This gives the system somewhat more accurate resolution without a great deal more effort. Most of these changes were originally suggested by Dr. Frey and are being added to updated descriptions of time-series notation.

To demonstrate how coding a body part is accomplished, take the head as an example. Figure 14.1 illustrates the **sagittal, rotational, lateral,** and **depth** dimensions of head movement.

Sagittal head position refers to whether it is up or down. If the head is tilted neither up nor down, then the sagittal position is coded as a number one ("1"). If the head is tilted back *slightly* (facing toward the ceiling), then a number three ("3") is used to represent the sagittal position. A *moderate* backward tilt is coded a five ("5"), and an *extreme* backward tilt is coded a seven ("7"). In the same manner a forward head tilt (facing toward the floor) is coded a two ("2")

TABLE 14.1 SUMMARY OF CODING SCHEME FOR THE TIME-SERIES DESCRIPTION OF NONVERBAL BEHAVIOR IN FACE-TO-FACE INTERACTION

Body Part	#Of Coded Dimensions	Dimension	Type of Scale/ # of Units	Type of Movement Defined by Dimension
(1) Head	3	Sagittal	Ordinal/ 5	Up/down tilt of head
		Rotational	Ordinal/ 5	Left/right rotation of head
		Lateral	Ordinal/ 5	Left/right tilt of head
(2) Trunk	3	Sagittal	Ordinal/ 5	Forward/backward tilt of trunk
		Rotational	Ordinal/ 5	Left/right rotation of trunk
		Lateral	Ordinal/ 5	Left/right tilt of trunk
(3) Shoulders*	2	Vertical	Ordinal/ 3	Up/down shift of shoulder
		Depth	Ordinal/ 3	Forward/backward shift of shoulder
(4) Upper Arms*	3	Vertical	Ordinal/ 8	Up/down lift of upper arm
		Depth	Ordinal/ 8	Forward/backward shift of upper arm
		Touch	Nominal/ 7	Upper arm contact with chair/body areas
(5) Hands*	9	Vertical	Ordinal/ 14	Up/down shift of hand
		Horizontal	Ordinal/ 9	Left/right shift of hand
		Depth	Ordinal/ 8	Forward/backward shift of hand
		x/y orientation	Ordinal/ 9	Angle of hand in vertical plane
		z orientation	Ordinal/ 5	Outward/inward sway of hand
		Turn	Ordinal/ 5	Up/down turn of hand
		Closure	Ordinal/ 4	Opening/closing of fist
		Folding	Nominal/ 2	Folding together of hands
		Touch	Nominal/ 52	Hand contact with chair/body areas

(6) Upper Legs*	3	Vertical	Ordinal/ 5	Up/down shift of upper leg
		Horizontal	Ordinal/ 5	Left/right shift of upper leg
		Touch	Ordinal/ 3	Contact between knees
(7) Feet*	7	Vertical	Ordinal/ 9	Up/down shift of foot
		Horizontal	Ordinal/ 7	Left/right shift of foot
		Depth	Ordinal/ 7	Forward/backward shift of foot
		Sagittal	Ordinal/ 5	Up/down tilt from ankle
		Rotational	Ordinal/ 5	Left/right rotation from ankle
		Lateral	Ordinal/ 5	Left/right tilt from ankle
		Touch	Ordinal/ 10	Foot contact with chair/floor/body areas
(8) Position on chair	2	Horizontal	Ordinal/ 3	Left/right position on chair
		Depth	Ordinal/ 3	Front/back position on chair

*Left and right coded separately. *Reproduced by special permission of the Department of Psychology, University of Bern, Switzerland, from Movement in Human Interaction: Description, Parameter Formation, and Analysis by Hirsbrunner, H. P., Frey, S., & Crawford, R. 1983, p. 12.*

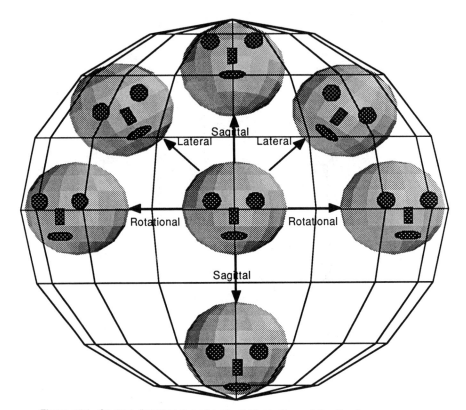

Figure 14.1. Sagittal, Rotational, and Lateral Dimensions of the Head

for *slight* forward tilt, a four ("4") for *moderate* forward tilt, and a six ("6") for *extreme* forward tilt. Odd and even numbers always refer to the same direction; that is, any even number indicates a forward head tilt and any odd number indicates that the head is in a backward position.

Rotation or left/right turn of the head is coded in exactly the same manner with one ("1") denoting *no rotation*; three ("3"—slight), five ("5"—moderate), and seven ("7"—extreme) indicating rotation to the *left* and two ("2"—slight), four ("4"—moderate), and six ("6"—extreme) indicating rotation to the *right*. In TSN "left" and "right" refer to the subject's right or left. For a coder looking at a picture or watching a television monitor, "left" and "right" would be reversed. Remember that when you try to code a head position later in this chapter.

The head can also move at a 45 degree angle, sometimes referred to as "cocking" or "tilting" of the head. Frey calls this the **lateral** head position. If the top of the head is inclined toward the left shoulder and the chin points toward the right shoulder the numbers to use would be three ("3"—slight), five

("5"—moderate), or seven ("7"—extreme), while a lateral head tilt in the opposite direction is coded two ("2"—slight), four ("4"—moderate), or six ("6"—extreme). If there is no tilt, the position is again coded as a one ("1").

It was mentioned earlier that I also code a **depth** dimension or forward extension of the head and neck. The depth dimension is very hard to see on videotape without a side view of the subject. This dimension does not appear in Table 14.1. I originally picked it up from Dr. Frey, who added it to his system late, after hearing suggestions from TSN users. He divided the depth dimension into five categories: normal (1), forward slightly (2), full forward (4), back slightly (3), and back full (5). I use these same five codes, not seven, since it is very difficult to differentiate seven positions in the depth dimension, especially if one has only a frontal view.

If I may digress for a moment, the preceding discussion of head depth is a good example of how TSN is constantly becoming more refined as increasing numbers of researchers use the system. Constant refinement is one real advantage of a multi-user measurement scheme. The other advantage, of course, is the possibility of sharing data and analyzing it for different purposes. At times these two advantages can come into conflict. Refinements in a multi-user coding system often require changes in the way in which data is recorded, and data entry alterations make it harder for others to utilize that data for their own purposes, especially if they want to use existing computer analysis programs.

By now you should have noticed the logic used in assigning numbers to head movement direction. For a coder facing a video monitor, all movement in the same direction is coded with the same numbers. Don't get fooled into thinking the different numbers somehow mean something different because they are odd or even. In coding rotational head movement, for example, the number "2" indicates exactly the same amount of head deflection in a forward direction as the number "3" indicates head movement in a backward direction. Instead of using a "3" Frey could just as easily have labeled the movement "backward slightly," and a "2" as "forward slightly," but this would have been awkward when recording and analyzing the data. Also, the movement distance between a "2" and a "4" or between a "4" and a "6" is exactly the same as that between a "3" and a "5" or between a "5" and a "7." The numbers are just convenient ways to indicate three different degrees of movement either in a backward or forward direction. The point here is not to think of the numbers as meaning anything other than the degree of backwardness and forwardness. This same principle applies to the coding of most body parts and saves both training and coding time. Many TSN users actually attach sheets of paper or cards with the appropriate numbers to the sides of a television monitor to help them remember whether a position is coded with an odd or even number. Figure 14.2 illustrates this shortcut.

At this point you may be saying to yourself, "This is too easy; why is TSN so much better than other coding strategies?" This is where the alphabet or time-series

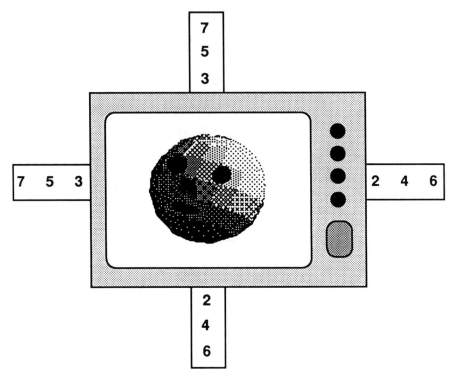

Figure 14.2. TSN Position Coding Monitor Setup

principle becomes important. By coding the head in the manner described above, using the sagittal, rotational, lateral, and depth head dimensions, a coder can accurately identify over 1,700 possible positions for this one body part alone. There is no other body movement measurement system that has anywhere near this degree of resolution. Can you imagine trying to develop 1,700 generic terms for the various head positions covered by TSN? The amazing part is how easy it is achieve this level of sophistication. From just the simple instructions already presented, see if you can code the head position pictured in Figure 14.3.

If you identified the sagittal position as "3," the rotational position as "5," the lateral position as "2," and depth position as "1" or "unknown" (since you cannot really see the depth), then you are correct. If your coding was only off by a single number, but in the *correct direction* (i.e., five instead of three or four instead of two), that's OK (for now) since novice coders often tend to see position variations somewhat differently until they have had a chance to practice coding and see all the possible positions. If you still miscoded Figure 14.3, go back and reread the discussion above until you understand what you did wrong.

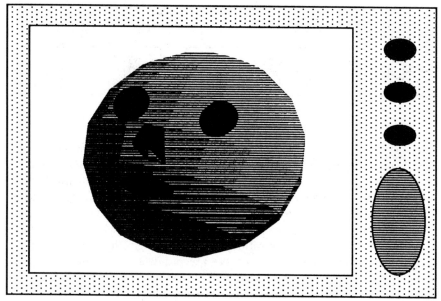

Figure 14.3. Practice Illustration for Head Coding

Sagittal   = _____
Rotational = _____
Lateral   = _____
Depth   = _____

Once you have completed this exercise, you have learned to code head position using Bernese Time-Series Notation. Congratulations!!! All you have to do now is learn how to code the other body parts!!! Actually that's not as hard as it sounds. The same basic approach employed for coding the head is also used to code all body parts. Refer back to the column labeled "Type of Movement Defined by Dimension" in Table 14.1 for a better understanding of the dimensions used to code all the various body parts. Obviously coding becomes a little more tricky when analyzing the hands and feet because they can move in several more dimensions (i.e., get into more positions) than the head. When using the seven dimensions listed in Table 14.1 for the hand, it is possible to distinguish almost a million different positions for *each* hand.

You will notice in Table 14.1 that TSN does not code all body parts. Lower arms/legs and fingers, for example, are not coded. If one knows the position of the upper arm and the hand, then there is only one possible position for the lower arm. Likewise it is impossible for the lower arm to move without moving the hand or upper arm. This also holds true for the lower leg. Coding these body parts, then, would be redundant. The fingers are not coded individually merely for simplicity. Movement of any individual finger or all fingers together is still

ID NUMBER				TIME						MOVEMENT CODES									SPEECH						
01	02	03	04	05	06	07	08	09	10	11	12	13	14	15	16	17	18	19	74	75	76	77	78	79	80
1	A	X	1		0	0	0	5		5	3	5	1	3	1	1	2	1	X	X	X	X	X		
1	A	X	1		0	0	1	0		5									X	X	X	X	X	X	

Figure 14.4. Coding form

coded as "hand" movement. TSN does, however, allow for special codes. Certain numbers are reserved in most dimensions for unusual positions. If a subject uses the "thumbs up" sign, for example, it could be noted with a special number in one of the dimensions for the hand, and this information would be communicated as a footnote to any other person using that data.

Most Bernese TSN researchers use an 80-column (IBM-type) work sheet or similar form to record position codes, although the development of microcomputers has made it just as easy to record data directly into a properly configured spreadsheet or similar program. A coding form such as Figure 14.4 would produce the first two lines of output found in Figure 14.5 for "Person B."

The typical coding form has a place for subject identification, time, one or two columns for each movement dimension, and a record of the speech. Using Frey's data recording procedure, for example, sagittal head position is coded in column 11 (labeled "Head — S" in Figure 14.5), rotational head position is coded in column 12 (labeled "Head — R" in Figure 14.5), lateral head position goes in column 13 (labeled "Head — L" in Figure 14.5) and so on.

Frey and his colleagues have examined both the reliability and validity of TSN position coding. In one study, retest and intercoder reliability were found to be over .90 after only a day's training (Hirsbrunner, Frey, & Crawford, 1983, p. 13). An interesting study (Frey, 1976; Frey & Pool, 1976) was performed to determine the validity of positional TSN coding. First, pictures of various individuals in 40 randomly selected positions were coded. Novice coders (one day's training) were then asked to place the head, hands, feet, etc. of a *live* model in what they believed to be the proper position using only the TSN position code. A picture was then taken of the live model's final position, and this picture was also coded. Frey reports that "over 98 percent of the 2,400 data items obtained from each set of photos were in agreement" (Frey, 1983, p. 13). Frey and Pool (1976) provide several samples of original and model pictures and the accuracy is astounding.

I tried a similar test comparing models posed by individuals using the actual (original) picture and those posed by trained coders using only the dimension numbers. I found the *latter* to be more accurate. That's right, TSN proved to be a more accurate method of posing a model than looking at the actual picture; the coded data appeared to force the posers to pay closer attention to the position (i.e, degree of tilt, turn, twist, lean, etc.) of each body part.

Up to this point, our discussion of TSN has focused primarily on the procedure for coding a body *position*. As stated earlier, in order to translate position coding into movement notation, one must add the temporal element. This is fairly simple once a high quality videotape or film with a visual time code has been made of subjects interacting. A high quality video record is produced by using good equipment and keeping all body parts in focus at all times. A visual time code is inserted on the picture using a special piece of equipment called a time code generator or timer which is placed in the video input line between the camera and the video recorder (see Figure 14.8 for an example). In order to analyze the video record, TSN coders either start with the opening frame or randomly select a starting frame and employ the following procedure:

> The video tape is set at the first time mark and put into "Stop Motion" mode to allow the coder to assess the position of a single part of the body in all its different coding dimensions. The video recorder is then set in "Normal Play" mode until a movement appeared in this part of the body. As long as there is no movement, the previous position code is simply continued. If there is motion in this part of the body, the tape is rewound a short distance and played back to find the exact time of the positional change. The new positions are then coded for each half second for the duration of the movement period. Then the video recorder is put back into "normal Play" mode for the duration of the new rest period (Hirstbrunner et al., 1983, p. 14).

TSN usually requires coding in no less than half second intervals to provide an adequate data base. With TSN, coding costs are tied directly to the amount of movement that occurs. If there is a lot of movement, a trained coder takes about two hours to code a single subject's movement for one minute. Where little movement occurs, a one-minute segment can be recorded in about a half hour.

Data Analysis

What is most important about TSN, however, is not necessarily how either position or movement coding is accomplished, but what can be done with the results. As you can see from Table 14.1, all of the coding dimensions (except touch) generate **ordinal data** — that is, the numbers represent rankings (from slight to moderate to extreme) — but there is no assumption that the differences between the various categories represent equal differences. Once the various movement dimensions of the body are coded in the manner described above, a series of multiple data strings are created which represent the behavior. When the data strings for each movement dimension for both communicators are combined using a common time code, a two-person data matrix is created. Figure 14.5 illustrates a typical data matrix. In this matrix the time code (in half second

Person   A

TIME	FOOT LEFT V H D S R L	FOOT RIGHT V H D S R L	LEG LF RT V H V H	HAND LEFT V - H D / Z T C	HAND RIGHT V - H D / Z T C	ARM LF RG V D V D	SHLDR LF RG V D V D	TRNK S R L	HEAD S R L D	SPEECH
5	3 4 5 1 3 1	3 6 5 1 1 3	2 3 2 3	0 8 6 6 4 3 3 2	0 8 6 7 2 3 2 3	4 0 4 4	2 1 2 1	3 3 1	1 3 4 1	
10									3 5 2	XX
15									2 3	
20				1	7 1				1 5	
25				3	8 2				3	
30				6					5 1	XXX XX
35				4					3	XX XX
40							5		1 3 2	XX
45							4			XXXXXX
50									1	XXXXXX
55									5	
60									7	XXX XX
65										XXXXXX
70									3 3	X
75									1	XXXXXX
80								3		XXXX
85					3				1 3	XXXXXX
90					7 5 9 5 5	5	1	3	3	XXXXXX
95					8 6 2 3 2	4	2	1	1 1	XXXXXX
100				1					3 5 2	XXXXXX
105				2					1 3	XXXXXX
110				5 7 5 1 4	5 9 5 5				1	XXXXXX
115				4						XXXXXX
120				6 6 6 3 2 3	7 6 1 4	5		3	5 1	XXXXXX
125					8 6 2 3 2 2	4		1	3 2	XXXXXX
130									4	XXXXXX
135					4					XX
140										
145		7 5	1		1 2	5			1 1 1	XXX XX
150		3							3 3 3	XX XX
155		5							1	XX XX
160		3	3			4			2	XXXXXX
165									3	XXXXXX
170				9	9				1	XXXXXX
175				8	8		1 3		5 2	XXXXXX
180			1	1	2		2 2			XXXXXX
185			2	4 3	4 3				3 1	XXXXXX
190								3	5 5	XXXXXX
195		7		3				1	7 1	XXXXXX
200				5 2	2			2	5 3	XXXXXX
205					1 4 1	5			1 3	XXXXXX
210									1 1	XXXX
215										
220						6		5		XXXXXX
225				5 3	2 2	4		3	3 3	XXXXXX
230				7	6 7 3 4					XXXXXX
235				6 6 6 3	1 4	7 6	1		3 3	XXXXXX
240				6 7 4 4	5 9 5 5 3	6 3 5	2		5 1	XXXXXX
245				7 6 1 3	7 6 1 3	4 4	1		1 3 2	XXXXXX
250				9 4 1 2	8 6 2 2 2	4 0	2		1	XXXXXX
255										
260				5 6 3	1 3			2		
265									1 5	XXXXXX
270				9 4 1	2		1		3	XXXXXX
275					1		2		5	XXX
280					3			2		XXXXXX
285				8 5 9 5	7 1				1	XXXXXX
290				6 7 7 3 4 4	7 3 5					XXXXXX
295				7 5 9 5 5 2	6 7 4 2 3				3	XXXXXX
300				9 6 4 1 1 4	8 6 2	4 0				XXXXXX

Figure 14.5. Sample Data Matrix resulting from Time-Series Notation of two persons for one minute. (From *Nonverbal Behavior and Communication*, 2nd Ed. by Aron W. Siegman & Stanley Feldstein. © 1987 Lawrence Erlbaum Associates. Reprinted with permission of the publisher.)

Person B

TIME	SPEECH	HEAD (S R L D)	TRNK (S R L)	SHLDR (RG V D · LF V D)	ARM (RG V D · LF V D)	HAND RIGHT (V - H D / Z T C)	HAND LEFT (V - H D / Z T C)	LEG (RG V H · LF V H)	FOOT RIGHT (V H D S R L)	FOOT LEFT (V H D S R L)
5	XXXXX	5 3 5 1	3 1 1	2 1 2 1	4 4 5 4	0 8 6 6 2 3 2 2	0 8 6 6 6 3 1 3	1 4 1 5	3 2 4 1 2 1	3 6 4 1 3 1
10	XXXXXX	5				7 5 1 1 3				
15	XXXXXX				6 3	6 7 9 5 4				
20	XXXXXX				4 2	8 6 6 2 3 3				
25	XXXXXX	3 3								
30	XXXXX	1								
35	XXXXXX									
40										
45										
50		1 7		2 2	6 4 5	6 8 5 1 2 4	2 7 5 7 2 5			
55		3			3 6 2 6		3 4			
60		5					3 3			
65					5					
70							4 6 2			
75										
80		1								
85		3								
90										
95										
100										
105										
110	XX									
115										
120										
125										
130	XXXXXX	2 5								
135	XXXXXX	1								
140	XXXXXX	3								
145	XX									
150										
155										
160										
165										
170										
175										
180	XXX	1 1								
185		3								
190		1 3								
195										
200										
205							3 6 1			
210		2 5 3					2 5 5 2			
215		4					7			
220		2 3					3 5			
225		1					1			
230										
235										
240										
245										
250							4 6 7 3 3			
255	XXXXXX		1 2	1	4 5 7 4	2	8 5 7 8 2 2	3 3	2	2
260	XX				6 3	3		1 1	1	1
265					3	2				
270					4	3				
275						2				
280	XXX	2				3				
285		1		3 3	1 1					
290			5							
295		2								
300		1								

Figure 14.5. Cont.

						Person A				
	FOOT	FOOT	LEG	HAND	HAND	ARM	SHLDR	TRNK	HEAD	
TIME	LEFT	RIGHT	LF RT	LEFT	RIGHT	LF RG	LF RG			SPEECH
305				6 2 3	9 6 2				5	XXX
310									3	XXXXXX
315				5 7 3 3	8 5 7 9 5				1	XXXXXX
320				5				3		
325				7 9 5 1	7 6 1 3 5 3				1 3 2	XXXXXX
330				6 3 2						XXXXXX
335				8 4 5	8 2		3 3		7	XXXXXX
340				9 6 1	5 3		2 2		5	XXX
345				8 4 7 3	4 9 5				1	XXXXXX
350				9 6 6 1 1	9 6 6 2 3 2					
355										
360									2	
365				1					3 1	XXXXXX
370				2					3	XXXXXX
375				8 6 3 1	4	8 0 8 6	3 2 3 2		2 1 2	XXXXXX
380				6 3 7 9 5 5	6 4 7 3 5	6 0 6			4	XXXXXX
385				9 6 6 1 1 4	8 6 6 2 2	4 0 5 5	2 1 2 1		1 3 1	XXXXXX
390					1		1 1		2 5 2	XXXXXX
395				3	4		2 1		1 3 1	XX XX
400				1					5	XXXXXX
405									2	
410										
415										
420										
425					2				1 3	
430				6 3 2			1		2	XXXXXX
435					1		2		1	XXXXXX
440										
445				8 5 7 9 5	1 3					
450				4 1	5					
455				3 2	2 3					
460				9 6 6 4 1 4 3						
465									2	
470									1	
475									2	
480										
485										
490										
495									1 1	XXXXXX
500										X
505										
510										
515										
520										XX XX
525									2	XXX XX
530										
535					1					XXXXXX
540										XXXXXX
545					2					XX
550				2						
555				4	1					
560										
565				2	2					
570				4						
575									1	
580					1					
585										
590										
595					2			3	5	
600										

Figure 14.5. Cont.

Person B

TIME	SPEECH	HEAD	TRNK	SHLDR RG	SHLDR LF	ARM RG	ARM LF	HAND RIGHT	HAND LEFT	LEG RG	LEG LF	FOOT RIGHT	FOOT LEFT
305		2											
310		1											
315													
320													
325													
330													
335					1	4	5 4	7 7 6 1 2	9 6 6 1 4 3	3	3		2
340			2	2	2	5	4 5	1 0 6 4 4 3	1 0 6 4	1 6	1 7		1
345			4	2	4	3 4	3 4	7 2	6			3	
350		3	2	1	2							1	
355	XXXX	1	3	1	1	4	5 4	0 8 6 3 1	0 8 3 3				
360		3	5	3		4	5	5 4	5 1	4	5		
365		1							2	6	7		
370		3											
375													
380										3			
385		1								1			
390		3											
395	XX	1											
400			1										
405	XXXXXX	3	1					5 4 7 3 5 3	6 1				
410	XXXXXX	1	3					8 6 6 2 3 2 2	5 3				
415	XXXXXX	3						3	1				
420			5					4					
425								3					
430													
435		4	3					1	3				
440	XX	6											
445													
450													
455													
460		2	5					2	2				
465	XXXXXX	1	3					5 6 7 1 5	3				
470	XXXXXX	1						4 8 6 2 1					
475		3											
480	XXXXXX							2	2				
485	XXXXXX												
490													
495	XXX	4											
500		3		1									
505		1		3									
510			5	1									
515		1		3					7 7 8				
520			7			5	4 7	6 7 5 1 1 1 2	2 5 7 1 4				
525			2			4							
530		1				3 5	6	5 8 3 2 2 3	6 8 6 2				
535		3	5			4	5	6 1 4 4	8 2	2	3		
540		1											
545										4	5		
550										4		3 2 2	
555													
560													
565		3								1 4	2		
570	XXX	2	7	3							2		4
575	XXXXXX					7 4	6 4	5 6 6	5 4 6 7 3				
580	XXXXXX	3	1			6	3	4 4 3	5 5 1				
585	XX	3	2		2		5 3	5 5 7 1	7 7 8				
590	XX XX							8 2	8 6 6 6 3 4				
595	XXXXXX	1	2		1			7 4 9 5 1 4	7 4 7 9 5 3				
600	XXXXXX	3	1					5	3				

Figure 14.5. Cont.

intervals) appears down the center with the speech for each subject indicated on either side of the time code (in this example, Xs are used to indicate speech). The position codes for person A are found in the nine large columns on the far left, and the position codes for person B are found in the nine large columns on the far right. Each of these columns indicates movement in all dimensions for one body part (see labels in Figure 14.5). The blank spaces signify that the last coded position has not changed.

The data matrix is the empirical basis for assessing the dependent nonverbal variable(s) in a study. It can be examined visually and/or with the aid of specially prepared computer programs. Visual inspection ("eye-balling the data") alone can provide researchers with considerable information and provide insights into what should be analyzed in depth. By comparing the clear areas to those blackened by entries, for example, one immediately observes how nonverbal activity occurs in clusters and how these clusters coordinate with the speech and movement of both participants. The temporal structure of movement increases and decreases is seen in the vertical succession of entries and blanks. Without even reading the words or examining the type of movement that is occurring, the transactional nature of verbal and nonverbal behavior of both interactors becomes obvious. Interactors seldom move, for example, when the other person is talking.

As one visually examines the data matrix more closely by looking at the number of entries in various rows or movement clusters, the volume and complexity of body movement by each participant becomes apparent. The suddenness of movement starts and stops can be judged by observing the number of simultaneous dimensions being activated or deactivated within one or two seconds. Differences in the suddenness of movement, for example, often occur between reactions to prolonged speech versus short feedback utterances.

Visual data inspection can get even more specific by comparing individual body parts of a single person or the same body part for both interactors. At this level the way in which each dimension contributes to total movement activity can be assessed. Even something as specific as lateral dominance can be judged by comparing left hand, arm, shoulder, leg, and foot movement to that on the right side of the body. These are only a few examples of the vast amount of information that can be gained by merely looking at a data matrix (Frey, 1983, pp. 17–18).

Visual inspection of a data matrix, however, taps only the surface of the available information. To really understand the significance of the data and discover underlying patterns, computer analysis is necessary. Frey and his colleagues have developed a comprehensive software library consisting of over eighty programs which offer many options for both graphic representation and quantitative analysis of data matrix information (Frey & Hirsbrunner, 1983a, 1983b; Hirsbrunner, 1979; Hirsbrunner et al., 1983). The following comment by Dr. Frey gives you an idea of the extent to which TSN data is being analyzed by researchers around the world. You will notice that variables parallel in many respects what is examined with less precision visually.

> Thus, depending upon the questions being asked in a particular study, the investigator might want to measure a set of parameters as global as, for instance, the amount of verbal and nonverbal activity an entire dyad displays during a given observation period, the complexity of the interlocutors' hand movement, the lateral dominance of right hand activity over left hand activity, the symmetry in the interlocutors' positional alignment, the disparity between verbal and nonverbal activity, the immediacy of the interactive response, the degree of simultaneous activity or inactivity, the degree to which speech or movement activity predominates or underscores the partner's activity, the rapidity with which an initial predominance disappears or further increases as time passes, etc. Besides such complex parameters, very specific behavioral aspects might be of interest, e.g. the size of a vertical hand movement, the closure of the arms at a given moment, the degree to which an interlocutor turns his head away from the partner, the frequency of trunk movements, the percentage of time an interlocutor holds his head higher than his partner, etc. Or the investigator might want to monitor the occurrence of a wide variety of very specific events whose definition can assume any complexity, from a simple head nod, or shoulder shrug, to a more complicated hand movement consisting, for example, of a simultaneous lifting, opening and upward turning of both hands, or to highly complex verbal/nonverbal patterns, involving a specific sequence of changes in all coding dimensions. (Hirsbrunner et al., 1983, p. 20)

Sample Research Studies Using TSN

The first real research test of TSN examined the interaction between doctors and patients in a psychiatric interview (Frey, Jorns, & Daw, 1980; Fisch, Frey, & Hirsbrunner, 1983). Thirteen severely depressed patient interviews (9 female and 4 male) within the first four days of admission and three days before discharge were videotaped. Three minutes of each interview were coded using TSN. The investigators examined both global and specific patterns of patient and doctor movement during the admission and discharge interviews. The global measures were (1) **mobility**, the number of time periods when movement occurred in at least one body part, (2) **complexity**, the average number of dimensions moving during the same time period, and (3) **dynamic activation**, the swiftness of movement increase and decrease. The results showed that, "upon recovery, patients spent more time in motion, displayed a more complex pattern of movement, and initiated and terminated movement activity more rapidly than when they were depressed" (Fisch, 1983, p. 316).

When specific movement activity was examined, several other differences appeared. For both doctors and patients, there was a clear rank order of movement activity in the various body parts. There was a tendency for average movement activity to cluster into four distinct geometrically progressive levels, each of which showed increasing movement activity by a factor of about three. The lowest level consisted of right and left upper leg and shoulder movement (mobility = 1 percent of observation time). At the next level trunk and right/left foot mobility reached a level of about three percent of observation time. The third level consisted of hand movement (mobility = 9 percent of observation time), and the most movement occurred in the head (mobility = 26 percent of observation time). This finding suggests that body part participation in total movement is more highly structured than previously thought.

Several other findings which relate to dyadic interaction in general were found in this study. For example, the participants seldom displayed movement while the other person was moving. In those rare instances when both did move at the same time, it was the doctor who tended to cut off movement activity first. This could indicate control of the interaction by the patient. Also, it was found that 22 head positions (out of a possible 110) accounted for four-fifths of the total observation time. It was the rare positions, however, which seemed to be most sensitive to the independent variables. This would suggest that unusual nonverbal behavior has the most communicative value.

One of the most amazing findings regarding depression was found in analyzing head movement. It is a common belief by psychiatric professionals that depressive patients will hold their head down with their chin almost touching the chest. In this study, the doctors tended to assume this downward sagittal position *more* often than the patients. Also, while the patients preferred an "upright" head position in both interviews, the doctors only raised their head in the second or discharge interview. In other words, the doctors acted more depressed in the initial interview than the patients. Several possible explanations come to mind, the most obvious being that in attempting to nonverbally empathize with the patient, the doctor was unwittingly reinforcing "sick" or depressive behaviors. Several other interesting findings were reported in this study, but space prevents our discussion of all of the results. This study demonstrates, however, the power TSN offers for nonverbal communication measurement.

A second area of investigation where TSN has been utilized is the nonverbal behavior of stutterers. This research was begun by Rainer Krause (1980, 1981) and is continuing in our laboratory (Donaghy & Kohler, 1984). Krause recorded interactions of 26 stutterers interacting with nonstuttering partners and 11 fluent speakers talking with fluent partners (control group) under conditions of "getting acquainted" and "solving political and social problems." Sixteen of the subjects stuttered audibly with different intensities and ten "either used hiding techniques or really did not stutter in this social situation" (Krause, 1980, p. 263).

The dependent variables which were examined included facial expression and paralinguistic data as well as TSN. The TSN results showed the total number of head movements, range and angle of head position, turning of the head toward partner, head downward position, and head nods were all significantly reduced for the stutterers. Fluent partners of manifest stutterers reacted with increased head movement. Even though their head was turned away from the speaking partner, the stutterers' trunk was usually turned toward the partner. Stutterers also showed less frequent movement of the hands away from the trunk (openness), fewer symmetrical leg positions, and less complex and varied movement (Krause, 1981, p. 39). Krause attributes this "behavioural rigidity" on the part of stutterers to an affect display rule of "inhibiting spontaneous affective and expressive behaviour in the speaking partner as well as their own behaviour" (1980, p. 265), therefore causing the dyad to be inhibited. He points out that many of these inhibited behaviors, such as head nods and turning of the head toward the partner, are primarily listener behaviors. "They [stutterers] seem to be pretty bad listeners" (1980, p. 265). Finally, Krause reports that "fluent speakers adapt their behavior to the stutterer and never the other way round" (1980, p. 265).

After studying Krause's results and finding some methodological difficulties, we decided to replicate and extend this research (Donaghy & Kohler, 1984). We have thus far examined eight stutterers and eight fluent speakers interacting in stutterer/stutterer, fluent/fluent, and stutterer/fluent dyads. "Get acquainted" and "problem solving" conditions were designed similar to those used by Krause. The data were analyzed using the measures of mobility, complexity, and dynamic activation (developed by Fisch, 1983, p. 316—see description above) for all subjects in both speaking and listening roles. We found significant differences for both mobility and complexity, with reduced levels of both for stutterers as compared with fluent speakers in the *speaking* role, but increased stutterer mobility and complexity when compared to nonstutterers in the *listener* role. Contrary to the findings reported by Krause, differences due to interaction partner were nonsignificant. These findings raised several questions which cannot be explained by or contradict most contemporary stuttering theories. The question that is most interesting is why stutterers move less than normal while speaking and more than usual while listening. We are in the process of adding more data to the overall TSN matrix and examining it in greater depth to determine what specific movement differences differentiate stutterers from nonstutterers as speakers and listeners.

In summary, the potential contribution of TSN to the future development of body movement measurement should be obvious. Its major advantages are (1) the simplicity of training and coding, (2) the overall code resolution, and (3) the ability to apply sophisticated analysis procedures to the data. The main disadvantages of TSN are the lack of availability of a coding manual in English and the amount of time it takes to code nonverbal behavior. If you think about how we communicate nonverbally, however, you will quickly realize that body movement is only one part of the whole complex picture. Another very important way individuals exchange information nonverbally is through facial expression. The following section will examine another fairly recent multi-user measurement system designed to study this aspect of nonverbal communication.

FACIAL ACTION CODING SYSTEM

The Facial Action Coding System (FACS) is probably the most widely used nonverbal measurement strategy. It was developed by Paul Ekman and Wallace Friesen in their San Francisco (University of California) based Human Interaction Laboratory. It is the successor to several other nonverbal measurement techniques developed by these leaders in the area of facial expression research (Ekman, 1957, 1982; Ekman & Friesen, 1969a, 1975, 1976; Ekman, Friesen, & Ellsworth, 1972) including the Visual Information Display and Retrieval—VID-R (Ekman, Friesen, & Taussig, 1969) and the Facial Affect Scoring Technique—FAST (Ekman, Friesen, & Tomkins, 1971). The idea for FACS occurred around 1970. Ekman and Friesen credit Silvan Tomkins' two volumns titled *Affect, Imagery, Consciousness* (1962, 1963) with providing the initial incentive.

Theoretical Approach

FACS is different from most other facial expression coding systems in two important ways. First, it is based on the anatomical features of the face (i.e., the facial muscles, skin, etc.). Most previous investigators differentiated facial expressions based on visual appearance of the entire face; a typical study projected a slide of a face on a screen and asked raters to judge the expression in some way. Instead, Ekman and his colleagues studied anatomy texts, felt the surface of their own faces, and examined scrambled and unscrambled photographs to understand facial movement. A second way in which FACS differs from other previous facial coding strategies is that it separates **description** (how the expression is produced) from **inference** (what the expression means). Most other facial expression researchers have attempted to *infer* the communicative function of each expression; for example, they would ask subjects to label an expression as "anger," "flirtation," or "dominance" (see the discussion of the direct evaluation coding strategy above). Like TSN, FACS is a purely descriptive system. FACS researchers are continually discouraged from discussing function or meaning. The advantage of description over inference is that the guesswork is eliminated.

A further development of Ekman's system called **EMFACS** (Emotion Facial Action Coding System) does get into meaning and inference (Ekman, 1982, pp. 77–78). Its main advantages is that EMFACS takes approximately one-fifth the time to code as FACS. Like TSN, the amount of time it takes to code behavior has always been recognized as a major disadvantage with FACS.

With EMFACS each emotion is broken down according to its most common facial movements. If none of the facial movements indicating anger, fear, happiness, sadness, surprise, etc. are evident, the action is ignored. Intensity of expression and the timing of actions are also ignored. This, of course, makes EMFACS another type of restrictive coding strategy with all of the disadvantages discussed earlier. It is beyond the scope of this chapter to discuss EMFACS in detail.

Coding Procedure

From the very beginning FACS was designed to be comprehensive and cover all possible facial expressions. Researchers who want to use FACS must first master the anatomy and physiology of the face. In the Facial Action Coding System the muscles and other features that produce facial expression are called "**Action Units** or **AUs**." Table 14.2 lists the names, numbers and anatomical basis of each Action Unit. In addition to the AUs listed in Table 14.2, there are more than 44 AU combinations to learn. An **AU combination** consists of any two or three AUs which can occur together to produce a distinctive (rather than an additive) expression.

A comprehensive FACS training kit is available which includes a manual (Ekman & Friesen, 1978b), two-part investigator's guide (Ekman & Friesen, 1978c), photographs and films (including a hand-held viewer) demonstrating each Action Unit, practice photos, and a package of scoring sheets. The training manual describes the different AUs and AU combinations as falling within two major groups and several subgroups: the *upper face* ("responsible for changing the appearance of the eyebrows, forehead, eye cover fold, and the upper and lower eyelids" — Ekman & Friesen, 1978b, pp. 2 — 1) and the *lower face*.

> There are many Action Units responsible for the changes in the appearance of the lower face. These units can be divided into five major groupings. The first major group of Action Units, *Up/Downs,* moves the skin and features in the center of the face upward towards the brow or downward towards the chin. The second group of Action Units, *Horizontals,* move the skin and features sideways stretching from center line of the face out towards the ears, or conversely pulling in from the outer edges towards the center line. The third group of Action Units, *Obliques,* pull in an angular direction from the lips upwards and outwards towards the cheekbone. The fourth group of Action Units, *Orbitals,* involve muscles which run around the mouth opening, moving the lips and skin adjacent to the mouth. The fifth group involves a number of *Miscellaneous* actions. (Ekman & Friesen, 1978b, p. 4–1)

Ekman and Friesen (1978c, p. 12) prefer to call these miscellaneous action units "**Action Descriptors (AD)**" because they usually do not involve facial muscles, and they treat them somewhat differently from Action Units. Action Descriptors include Tongue Out (AD 19), Neck Tightener (AD 21), Jaw Thrust

TABLE 14.2. SINGLE ACTION UNITS (AU)

AU Number	FACS Name	Muscular Basis
1.	Inner Brow Raiser	Frontalis, Pars Medialis
2.	Outer Brow Raiser	Frontalis, Pars Lateralis
4.	Brow Lowerer	Depressor Glabellae; Depressor Supercilli; Corrugator
5.	Upper Lid Raiser	Levator Palpebrae Superioris
6.	Cheek Raiser	Orbicularis Oculi, Pars Orbitalis
7.	Lid Tightener	Orbicularis Oculi, Pars Palebralis
8.	Lids Toward Each Other	Orbicularis Oris
9.	Nose Wrinkler	Levator Labii Superioris, Alaeque Nasi
10.	Upper Lip Raiser	Levator Labii Superioris, Caput Infraorbitalis
11.	Nasolabial Furrow Deepener	Zygomatic Minor
12.	Lip Corner Puller	Zygomatic Major
13.	Cheek Puffer	Caninus
14.	Dimpler	Buccinnator
15.	Lip Corner Depressor	Triangularis
16.	Lower Lip Depressor	Depressor Labii
17.	Chin Raiser	Mentalis
18.	Lip Puckerer	Incisivii Labii Superioris; Incisivii Labii Inferioris
20.	Lip Stretcher	Risorius
22.	Lip Funneler	Orbicularis Oris
23.	Lip Tightener	Orbicularis Oris
24.	Lip Pressor	Orbicularis Oris
25.	Lips Part	Depressor Labii, or Relaxation of Mentalis or Orbicularis Oris
26.	Jaw Drop	Masetter; Temporal and Internal Pterygoid Relaxed
27.	Mouth Stretch	Pterygoids; Digastric
28.	Lip Suck	Orbicularis Oris
38.	Nostril Dilator	Nasalis, Pars Alaris
39.	Nostril Compressor	Nasalis, Pars Transversa and Depressor Septi Nasi
41.	Lid Droop	Relaxation of Levator Palpebrae Superioris
42.	Slit	Orbicularis Oculi
43.	Eyes Closed	Relaxation of Levator Palpebrae Superioris
44.	Squint	Orbicularis Oculi, Pars Palpebralis
45.	Blink	Relaxation of Levator Palpebrae and Contraction of Orbicularis Oculi, Pars Palpebralis
46.	Wink	Orbicularis Oculi

(AD 29), Jaw Sideways (AD 30), Jaw Clencher (AD 31), Lip Bite (AD 32), Cheek Blow (AD 33), Cheek Puff (AD 34), Cheek Suck (AD 35), Tongue Bulge (AD 36), Lip Wipe (AD 37), Head Turn Left (AD 51), Head Turn Right (AD 52), Head Up (AD 53), Head Down (AD 54), Tilt Left (AD 55), Tilt Right, (AD 56), Head Forward (AD 57), Head Back (AD 58), Eyes Left (AD 61), Eyes Right (AD 62), Eyes Up (AD 63), Eyes Down (AD 64), Walleye (AD 65), and Cross-Eye (AD 66).

A novice learning FACS must be able to distinguish each of the different AUs, AU combinations, and ADs. In order to help accomplish this, the FACS manual describes each AU in terms of (1) its muscular basis, (2) the changes it makes in the appearance of the face, (3) how to make the movement on one's own face, and (4) a set of rules for determining minimal facial change needed to justify scoring. Especially important AUs, such as Upper Lid Raiser (AU 5), Upper Lip Raiser (AU 10), Lip Corner Puller (AU 12), Lip Corner Depressor (AU 15), and Lip Stretcher (AU 20), are also coded according to intensity (low, medium, high). Action Units can occur on one (unilateral) or both (bilateral) sides of the face. Table 14.3 illustrates the type of information provided for each Action Unit and AU combination. Figure 14.6 provides a picture of AU 15.

FACS is designed to be self-taught. According to the FACS training materials, the system can be learned in about 100 hours and takes approximately five weeks, in which coders spend three to four hours per day reading and practicing. The FACS authors feel it is essential that coders learn to perform each of the AUs on their own face. To do this a potential FACS coder must use a mirror and practice until he or she can train each facial muscle to imitate the AU demonstration photographs such as the one found in Figure 14.6. The demonstration and practice photographs always include a picture of the model in a "neutral face" (without any AUs) because permanent facial features (such as lines, wrinkles, etc.) can sometimes cause a learner to misinterpret an expression. The investigator's guide is very thorough; it supplies norms for assessing learner progress, practice pictures, and even a final test of FACS proficiency. The training manual reports reliability of .822 when six novice coders were compared with experts and .756 when compared to one another.

The large amount of time it takes to learn FACS is due not so much to remembering each Action Unit, Action Descriptor, or AU combination, but to learning all of the guidelines that have been built into FACS to avoid disagreements and improve coder reliability. **Combination rules**, for example, prescribe how AUs should be scored when they interact with one another. There are three combination rules: **dominance rules**, which tell coders how to score facial expressions in which a strong AU overshadows a weak one, **substitution rules**, which lay out scoring procedures for facial expressions when similiar appearing AU combinations occur, and **alternative rules**, which prescribe scoring procedures for facial expressions in which "two AUs cannot both be scored because they cannot be performed simultaneously or it is hard to distinguish one from the other" (Ekman & Friesen, 1978c, p. 11).

TABLE 14.3. EXAMPLE OF INFORMATION GIVEN IN FACS FOR EACH ACTION UNIT

Action Unit 15—Lip Corner Depressor

Figure 4–1 shows that the muscle underlying AU 15 emerges from the side of the chin and runs upwards attaching to a point near the corner of the lip. In AU 15, the corners of the lips are pulled down.

A. *Appearance Changes due to 15*

   (1) Pulls the corners of the lips down.

   (2) Changes the shape of the lips so they are angled down at the corner, and usually somewhat stretched horizontally.

   (3) Produces some pouching, bagging, or wrinkling of skin below the lips corners, which may not be apparent unless the action is strong.

   (4) May flatten or cause bulges to appear on the chin boss, may produce depression medially under the lower lip.

   (5) If the nasolabial furrow* is permanently etched, it will deepen the lower portion and may appear pulled down or lengthened.

   (6) If AU 12 combines with 15, confusion can arise between 6 + 15 and 12 + 15. Later in Chapter 6 when you learn AU 12, you will also learn how to score 12 + 15 and of the difficulty in making this distinction.

The photographs 15X and w15X show weak versions of this Action Unit, while 15Z and w15Z show stronger actions. Note that appearance change (3) is most apparent in the stronger versions. Note also that in w15Z, the nasolabial furrow* is deepened as compared to wO, but this is because there is a permanently etched nasolabial furrow* on one side of the face in wO. Examine also the photographs of 6 + 15X, 6 + 15Z, w6 + 15X and w6 + 15Z. Later, in Chapter 6, when you learn to distinguish 6 + 15 from 12 + 15 these photographs will be important. For now they simply repeat for you the signs of 15 and the addition of the appearance changes due to 6. Note that photograph j1 + 4 shows a trace of AU 15, not sufficient to score. Inspect the film of AU 15.

B. *How to do 15*

Pull your lip corners downwards. Be careful not to raise your lower lip at the same time— do not use AU 17. If you are unable to do this, place your fingers above the lip corners and push downwards, noting the changes in appearance. Now, try to hold this appearance when you take your fingers away.

C. *Minimum Requirements for scoring 15*

   (1) If the lip line is straight or slightly up in neutral the lip corners moved *slightly* down.

   or (2) If lip line is slightly or barely down in neutral, then the lip corners moved slightly down more than neutral and it is not due to 17 or 20.

*A wrinkle extending from beyond the nostril wings down to beyond the lip corners. (Reprinted with permission of Consulting Psychologist Press. Further reproduction prohibited without permission of publisher.)

A second set of important guidelines are called **minimum scoring require-ments**. A sample of the minimum requirements to score AU 15 was provided in Table 14.3. Minimum scoring requirements were developed in order to identify very minor changes in facial expression which cannot be reliably coded. The developers of FACS admit that "many of the cut-offs established for Minimum Requirements are arbitrary" (Ekman & Friesen, 1978c, p. 81). Some type of

Figure 14.6. Photograph of Paul Ekman demonstrating AU 15 (Z = High Intensity). (Reprinted with permission of Consulting Psychologist Press. Further reproduction prohibited without permission of publisher.)

minimum requirements are necessary, however, for any multi-user system to maintain consistency. As the authors state, "they are internally consistent and provide a basis for standardization" (Ekman & Friesen, 1978c, p. 81). After learning the FACS scoring standards a coder is allowed to deviate to fit individual research projects as long as that information is communicated to others sharing the data. A final set of FACS guidelines are called **subtle difference tables**. These prescribe ways of comparing and contrasting AUs and AU combinations that differ only slightly. There are over *400* subtle difference tables. All of these guidelines take time to learn but are necessary as multi-user measurement systems develop.

Data Analysis

The data one obtains using FACS are primarily **nominal,** that is, the system primarily identifies and categorizes attributes, although the intensity rating (low, medium, high) of some AUs makes them ordinal as well. This means data analysis is primarily carried out using some form of descriptive or nonparametric statistics. The FACS investigator's guide provides a format for recording a facial expression (or "event" as it is called in FACS) on an IBM computer card. The guide also provides programs to help coders avoid errors and check reliability. It is recommended that when scoring an AU, the investigator look for the **onset** (beginning), the **apex** (strongest appearance) and **offset** (ending) of the facial movement. What the FACS authors do not provide are software programs for analyzing facial expression changes over time such as those developed for use with TSN. It is assumed that individual researchers will develop their own system for identifying and quantifying important information from the data.

Some Sample Studies Using FACS

The scope of possible research where FACS might apply is endless. Several very interesting studies have already employed FACS as the nonverbal measurement instrument. One area of research that has been of long-time interest (over 15 years) to Ekman and Friesen is the universality of facial expression (Ekman, 1972, 1973; Ekman & Friesen, 1971; Ekman, Sorenson, & Friesen, 1969). The purpose of this line of research is to determine which facial expressions have a common universal meaning. A recent study (Ekman & Friesen, 1986) explored the question of whether the emotion of contempt has a distinct universal meaning separate from disgust. They examined "three different expressions that have been suggested as contempt signals: tightening and slightly raising the corner of the lip unilaterally . . .; (2) the same expression bilaterally . . .; and (3) raising the entire upper lip slightly, without tightening or raising the lip corners" (Ekman & Friesen, 1986, p. 160). Pictures of these facial actions (along with pictures of several other emotional expressions) were scored with FACS to verify the AUs. These pictures were then shown to people in ten different countries. This was the first study where observers could indicate "contempt" rather than "disgust and contempt." They found that subjects could distinguish contempt from disgust with agreement as high (75%) as that found for the other emotions (i.e., happy = 90.1%, surprise = 85.8%, sad = 80.4%, fear = 73.8%, disgust = 73.8% and anger = 73.8%).

A second study by Ekman et al. (1985) also dealt with the facial expression of emotion. They attempted to determine whether the startle reaction was an emotion or a reflex. This is a major source of debate by emotion theorists (see Landis & Hunt, 1939; Averill, 1980; Lazarus, 1982; Zajonc, 1980; and Tomkins, 1962 for the arguments on both sides). In short, the design of the study was to fire a .22 caliber blank "starters" pistol behind the head of subjects in conditions where they (1) did not know when the shot was coming, (2) did know when it was coming, and (3) tried to inhibit their startle reaction. They also had subjects simulate the startle reaction with no shot actually being fired. They examined the subject's facial expressions using FACS, especially tightening of the muscles around the eyes—AUs 7 and 8; stretching the lips horizontally—AU 20; tightening neck muscles—AU 21; closing the eyes—AU 45; and moving the head and shoulders upward. Based on their findings Ekman and Friesen proposed that startle be considered a reflex, not an emotion. They came to this conclusion after finding that the startle is easy to elicit, is shown reliably as an initial response by every subject, cannot be totally inhibited, and cannot be simulated with the correct latency (Ekman, Friesen, & Simons, 1985, p. 1424).

A third area of interest to FACS researchers relates to the asymmetry of facial actions (Ekman, 1980; Ekman, Roper, & Hager, 1980; Ekman, Hager, & Friesen, 1981; Hager, 1982). Several cerebral hemispheric specialization theories exist which differ as to whether the right, the left, or both hemispheres cause facial asymmetry. Some theories even suggest that the right hemisphere is specialized for negative emotions and the left for positive emotions (see Reuter-Lorenz & Davidson, 1981 for review) or the right hemisphere for avoidance emotions and the left for approach emotions (see Davidson & Fox, 1982 for review). A recent contribution to this literature (Hager & Ekman, 1985) examined the asymmetry of many AUs individually (AUs 1, 2, 4, 6, 7, 9, 10, 12, 14, 15, 16, 20, and 45), in combination (AUs 1 + 2) and under several different eliciting conditions (spontaneous and simulated startles and smiles, deliberate actions, and simulated emotions). None of the hemispheric specialization models were substantiated. The only consistent finding was that spontaneous facial actions were more symmetrical than deliberate, simulated actions. This finding could, however, have interesting implications for our understanding of deception, which is another topic of interest to FACS researchers (Ekman, 1985; Ekman & Friesen, 1969b, 1974).

It might appear, at this point, that all of the studies using FACS are being conducted by Ekman, Friesen, and their colleagues. This is certainly not the case. The Krause stuttering study (1980, 1981) discussed above, for example, employed FACS as well as TSN. For the stutterers, he found reduced levels of movement in the forehead and eye areas, smiling, and expressions of negative emotion. Instead, he found more lip press (AU 24) behavior by stutterers while they were speaking and listening. Also a recent study by Patrick, Craig, and Prkachin (1986) examined facial reactions (AUs 6, 7, 10, 12, 25, 26, and 45) to a series of painful and nonpainful electric shocks after earlier exposure to three social influence conditions (tolerant, intolerant, and neutral models). This is the latest contribution to a whole series of studies that have examined the expression of pain under various conditions (Craig, 1978; Craig, Best, & Ward, 1975; Craig & Patrick, 1985; Craig & Prkachin, 1978, 1980, 1983; Prkachin, Currie, & Craig, 1983; Le Resche, 1982). Patrick et al. (1986) found that the pain experience and facial behavior are affected by psychological, situational and social influences and that discrepancies often occur between the nonverbal cues and the self-reported experience of pain. Space does not permit a complete review of all of the studies that have employed the FACS procedure. This brief overview, however, should give you some idea of the many ways in which it could be used.

We have now examined two comprehensive nonverbal measurement systems. These are probably the newest and most extensive multi-user systems available. Both have their strengths and weaknesses, but each is constantly undergoing revision to make it more efficient. Studying any single mode of nonverbal communication alone, however, causes one to miss the multichannel nature of the phenomena. The question that occurs to serious students of nonverbal communication is "Why can't we integrate the advances introduced by the TSN and FACS as well as other nonverbal coding systems?" As you will see in the next section, this is exactly what is happening. Nonverbal communication researchers are no longer content to simply develop multi-user measurement systems for coding various modes of nonverbal communication; they are also attempting to develop ways of combining these individual systems, which examine only one nonverbal modality into larger systems that allow for multimodal analysis of nonverbal behavior.

MULTIMODALITY NONVERBAL COMMUNICATION MEASUREMENT

> The problem of isolating particular aspects of behavior or modalities of behavior out of an integrative whole has only rarely been considered. This is unfortunate, because such isolation precludes an analysis of the relationships between different aspects of nonverbal behavior. (Ekman, 1982, p. 33)

> Thus, after a period of research governed by single-channel approaches (owing in part to the many methodological difficulties, the complexity, and the expense of studying nonverbal cues), research is now turning toward multichannel approaches combining measures from different modalities of nonverbal behavior.... It should be noted, however, that such multimodality measurement approaches can succeed only to the degree that conceptually and methodologically sound measurements are available for each individual modality. (Scherer, 1982, pp. 179 and 182)

A few attempts have already been made to develop multimodal measurement systems. In Giessen, West Germany, for example, a research group headed by Dr. Klaus R. Scherer has begun to incorporate a movement system developed in their laboratory with their sophisticated system for analyzing vocalics (Scherer, 1982, 1984b; Ekman & Friesen, 1972; Scherer, Wallbott, & Scherer, 1979; Scherer & Scherer, 1980; Donaghy, 1984). **Vocalics,** or paralanguage as it is commonly known, refers to characteristics of the voice, other than words, which have nonverbal importance. Pauses, pitch, loudness, and speech rate are examples of vocalics. The Giessen *movement* coding system, however, is nowhere near as sophisticated as TSN, recording only when a position change occurs and how long it lasts with little indication of direction or intensity.

Some mention should be made, at this point, of contemporary methods used to study vocalics since this mode of nonverbal behavior should be included in any multimodal measurement system. The analysis of vocalic aspects of nonverbal communication has taken a somewhat different measurement thrust from the body movement and facial expression approaches described above. Whereas human coders appear at this point in our scientific development to be the best instruments for examining nonverbal behavior of the body and face, they are not the best measurement technique for studying linguistic (oral) information. Efficient contemporary acoustic analysis requires the use of some very sophisticated and expensive equipment such as highly sensitive audio recorders and microphones, a sound spectrograph or sonagraph, and small laboratory or large university computers with analog-to-digital (A/D) and digital-to-analog (D/A) conversion periphery. The mechanics of all this is much too complex to go into here. The point to remember is that we can (and should) use special equipment to analyze *vocal* nonverbal communication, whereas only the human eye is currently capable of coding *visual* nonverbal communication.

The Giessen Group has been working for some time to develop valid and reliable measures of such vocalic characteristics as silent pauses, voiceless speech segments, fundamental frequency (usually perceived as pitch), and amplitude (loudness) over time (rate). Their current equipment is capable of analyzing a voice segment and producing a graphic display or printout of several voice variables, similar to the illustration in Figure 14.7.

The Giessen vocalics laboratory is one of the most prolific and sophisticated in the world (recent publications include Scherer, 1984a, 1984b, 1986; Scherer & Ekman, 1984; Scherer, Feldstein, Bond, & Rosenthal, 1985; Helfrich, Standke, & Scherer, 1984; Johnson, Emde, Scherer, & Kinnert, 1986; Ladd, Silverman, Tolkmitt, Bergmann, & Scherer, 1985; O'Sullivan, Ekman, Friesen, & Scherer, 1985; Tolkmitt & Scherer, 1986; Wallbott & Scherer, 1986). As you might imagine, an enormous amount of time is necessary to produce this type of analysis. Scherer's computers often work around the clock to analyze a small segment of speech. The Giessen Group has also experimented with digitalization devices, such as an ultrasonic pen to record movement as well as vocalic parameters directly into a computer. The problems they have discovered, however, in trying to develop equipment capable of analyzing the visual modalities only reinforce the point made earlier—that the human eye is still the best instrument for coding visual nonverbal communication. The last I heard they have given up all such attempts for the time being.

A move is currently under way to combine Ekman and Friesen's FACS system, Frey's Time-Series Notation System, and Klaus Scherer's computerized vocalics analysis system. There are still many problems to work out, but it should not be too long before this next major step in nonverbal communication measurement occurs. In order to video and audio record this much nonverbal informaton from a pair of interacting subjects, some very special laboratory procedures and equipment are necessary in addition to the voice measurement instruments described above. A minimum of four cameras and three video recorders are needed along with a time code generator, and highly sensitive microphones. Figure 14.8 will give you an oversimplified idea of how such a laboratory might be set up.

Even with all these obstacles and the time involved, multimodal nonverbal

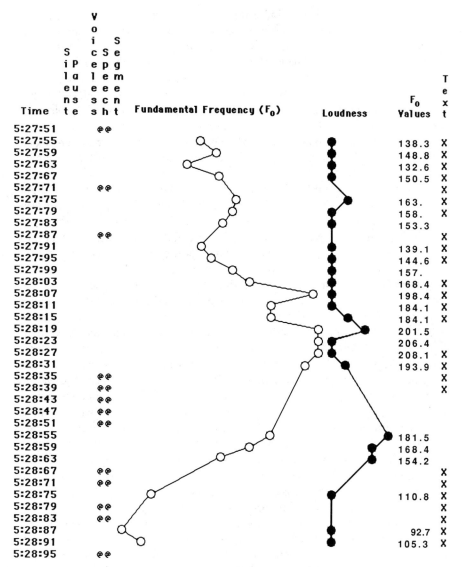

Figure 14.7. Sample Vocalics Computer Plot. (Adapted from Scherer, "Methods of research on vocal communication: Paradigms and parameters" (p. 181). Cambridge University Press, 1982).

research efforts are on the upswing. There is no doubt that these investigators feel the potential findings are worth the cost and effort. What is most encouraging is that researchers are not only aware of the importance of examining multiple channels of nonverbal communication, but they are also becoming convinced of the importance of studying the interrelationship of verbal and nonverbal communication.

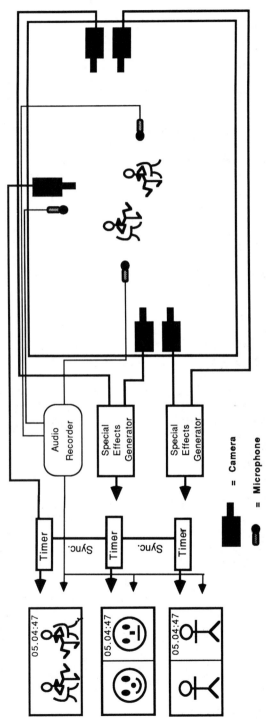

Figure 14.8. Sample Laboratory Setup for Multimodal Nonverbal Communication Measurement

= Camera

= Microphone

SUMMARY

The purpose of this chapter was to examine contemporary multi-user approaches to the measurement of nonverbal behavior. Two such systems were examined in depth: the Bernese Time-Series Notation System (TSN) and the Facial Action Coding System (FACS). The discussion of each system included an examination of its theoretical approach, how one codes data, and available data analysis procedures. Sample studies using each procedure were also presented. After examining TSN and FACS in depth, a third aspect of nonverbal communication, vocalics, was also discussed briefly, especially in light of how it might be combined with TSN and FACS to achieve a multimodality nonverbal communication measurement system. It appears that the outlook is very bright for this type of communication research. I hope that this chapter has excited your interest in the possibilities for nonverbal communication measurement in the future and encouraged you to study these measurement systems in greater depth. I think this "frontier of communication research" (Barker & Collins, 1970, p. 343) is on the brink of becoming the most exciting and fruitful of all those previously presented in this book.

NOTES

With the permission of Drs. Frey and Hirsbrunner, I developed a brief training manual in English in 1983. By the time you read this chapter, a large and more complete training manual should be available. If you would like a copy, send a self-addressed and stamped envelope to William Donaghy, Department of Communication, Box 3341, University Station, Laramie, WY 82071 or call 307–766–6277.

STUDY QUESTIONS

1. What is "nonverbal communication"?
2. How does nonverbal communication measurement differ from that used to study other forms of communication?
3. Why does the author state that "until recently little of any empirical value has been learned" from nonverbal research?
4. Why is it so important to convert visual records into digital form?
5. What are the names of the two major nonverbal measurement approaches that are discussed in this chapter?
6. How do the generic, restrictive, direct evaluation, and time-series coding strategies differ?
7. What are the three main problems with generic coding?
8. How does the "unique symbol" coding approach of Birdwhistell differ from that employed in TSN?
9. How does TSN define "body movement"?

10. What is the difference between nonverbal "movement" and "position"?
11. How does one code the sagittal, rotational, lateral, and depth position of the head?
12. How does a TSN coder record data?
13 What is a "data matrix," and how is it created?
14. What types of information can be gained from visually examining and computer analyzing a data matrix?
15. How do mobility, complexity, and dynamic activitation differ?
16. What are some studies that have used TSN?
17. Can you design a study using TSN?
18. How does FACS differ from most other facial expression coding systems?
19. What is an "Action Unit (AU)"?
20. How does one learn FACS?
21. Why does a FACS coder first have to master the anatomy of the face?
22. How do "AU Combinations" and "AU Descriptors" differ?
23. Why is it important for FACS coders to learn combination rules, minimum scoring requirements, and subtle difference tables?
24. What are the basic FACS combination rules?
25. What is the "onset," "apex," and "offset" of a nonverbal behavior?
26. What are some studies that have used FACS?
27. Can you design a study using FACS?
28. What is meant by "multimodality nonverbal behavior measurement"?
29. What is "vocalics," and why are its research methods different from those used to study movement and facial expression?
30. What type of audio and video equipment is necessary to do multimodal research?

ANNOTATED READINGS

Burgoon, J.K. (1985a). Nonverbal signals. In M. L. Knapp & G. Miller (Eds.), *Handbook of interpersonal communication* (pp. 344–389). Beverly Hills, CA: Sage.
This is an excellent, up-to-date chapter on nonverbal research methods and results. Dr. Burgoon reviews typical methods used to study self-disclosure, relational control, negotiation and persuasion strategies. She also has sections on limiting the nonverbal domain, structure of nonverbal code systems, usage norms and differences, and social functions of nonverbal communication. The emphasis in this chapter is on understanding and examining the nonverbal behaviors that form a socially shared coding system.
Ekman, P., & Friesen, W. V. (1978). *Facial action coding system: Full training materials.* Palo Alto, CA: Consulting Psychologists.
I have already included a great deal of information from and about this publication in the chapter. This work includes all of the information one needs to begin learning FACS. The information is easy to read and represents a great deal of

time and effort on the part of the authors. This material is an essential part of the library of any serious nonverbal communicaton scholar, if not to use in research, at least to demonstrate how a multi-user coding system must be documented in order to achieve validity and reliability.

Frey, S., Hirsbrunner, H. P., Florin, A., Daw, W., & Crawford, R. (1983). A unified approach to the investigation of nonverbal and verbal behavior in communication research. In W. Doise & S. Moscovici (Eds.), *Current issues in European social psychology*. Cambridge: Cambridge University Press.

Frey, S., Hirsbrunner, H. P., & Jorns, U. (1982). Time-Series-Notation: A coding principle for the unified assessment of speech and movement in communication research. In E. W. B. Hess-Luttich (Ed.), *Multimedial communication: Semiotic problems of its notation* (pp. 30–58). Tubingen: Narr.

Hirsbrunner, H. P., Frey, S., & Crawford, R. (1983). *Movement in human interaction: Description, parameter formation, and analysis*. Research Reports from the Department of Psychology. Berne, Switzerland: Univeristy of Berne.

These are the main publications currently available in English on the Bernese Time-Series Notation system. They include the basic rationale for the development of TSN, descriptions of how to use the system and sample studies in which TSN has been employed. What is left out of this material is the specific description of the coding dimensions which has thus far only been published in Frey, S., Hirsbrunner, H. P., Pool, J., & Daw, W. (1981). Das berner system zur untersuchung nonverbaler interaktion: I. Die erhebung des rohdatenprotokolls. In P. Winkler (Ed.), *Methoden der analyse von face-to-face situationen* (pp. 203–236). Stuttgart: Metzler. It is that void which my new coding manual is trying to fill.

Knapp, M. (1984). The study of nonverbal behavior vis-à-vis human communication theory. In A. Wolfgang (Ed.), *Nonverbal behavior: Perspectives, applications, intercultural insights* (pp. 15–40). New York: C. J. Hogrefe.

This recent chapter approaches nonverbal communication from a fairly unique angle. Dr. Knapp examines nonverbal communication research from the perspective of five basic assumptions regarding human communication theory. These assumptions are that human communication (1) is a process, (2) involves both purposive and expressive messages, (3) is primarily composed of multi-signal units, (4) is composed of multi-level signals, and (5) is critically dependent on context for the meanings generated. He constantly examines how well various research strategies apply to "real life" events and encourages social science researchers to develop new paradigms which do not copy those used in the physical sciences.

Scherer, K. R., & Ekman, P. (Eds.). (1982). *Handbook of methods in nonverbal behavior research* Cambridge: Cambridge University Press.

Several articles from this book are cited in the bibliography, but the text itself is not. The text is entirely devoted to examining the various ways in which nonverbal communication research is conducted. The contributors are some of the most important individuals currently conducting studies in this area. Special chapters are devoted to such topics as facial action, eye gaze, vocalics, body movement, judgment studies, and conversational analysis. An excellent introductory chapter addresses the most important methodological issues facing nonverbal communication research, and a technical appendix is devoted to audiovisual recording procedures, equipment, and troubleshooting. This reference should be on the bookshelf of any serious nonverbal communication scholar.

Glossary

Accretion measures. Measures derived from the accumulation or deposit of materials.

Act. A single unit of behavior, generally a speaking turn, in interaction analysis.

Action descriptors (ADs). Miscellaneous action units which are treated somewhat differently from Action Units because they usually do not involve facial muscles.

Action potential. A sequence of changes in the electrical charge along the membrane of a cell or muscle fiber.

Action Units (AUs). A Facial Action Coding System designation for the muscles and other features that produce facial expression.

Afferent pathway. Nerve impulses from various receptors that travel to the central nervous system to some part of the brain.

Alpha wave. Rhythmic signals from an EEG having a frequency of 8–13 Hz that indicate a state of relaxation.

Alternative rules. Combination rules which prescribe scoring procedures for facial expressions in which two Action Units cannot both be scored because they cannot be performed simultaneously or it is hard to distinguish one from the other.

Amplitude. A property of a wave form that refers to the height of a given wave, often indicating its intensity.

Apex. The strongest appearance of a nonverbal behavior.

Asymmetry. A reference to human brain function that identifies unequal responses performed by one side of the brain or the other. In EEG research, beta waves are emitted from the left side of the brain in a cognitive task, while none are emitted from the right side.

Attitude pie. Attitude measurement procedure based on the theoretical assumptions of the Social Judgment-Involvement Approach. Using circles and subject-marked "pie wedges" which represent favorable and unfavorable feelings toward an attitude object, this procedure produces ratio data.

Attitude. Hypothetical construct/term employed by behavioral scientists to represent evaluative consistencies in behaviors of people toward persons, places, things, and ideas. Frequently used as a dependent variable in behavioral science research.

Attitude scale. An instrument consisting of several items which measure people's evaluations on sentiments about given concepts. Some common types are Likert, Guttman, and Thurstone scales.

AU combination. Any two or three Action Units which can occur together to produce a distinctive (rather than an additive) expression.

Auxiliary measurement theory. A statement of the logical linkage between actual measured phenomena and the constructs they are supposed to represent.

Auxiliary memory. An electronic storage device (tape or disk) where information can be held until required for use by the computer.

Behaviorist. A person who believes the primary datum for study should be people's actual behaviors.

Belief. People's perceptions of reality in their environment.

Beta wave. EEG rhythms emitted from the brain with a frequency of 14–30 Hz. These are present during thinking or arousal conditions.

Biased sample. A sample which does not accurately reflect the population of interest to the researcher.

Binary decision tree. A common coding strategy in interaction analysis in which a sequence of yes-no questions are asked for every behavioral unit; when the answer is "no," another question is asked; when the answer is "yes," the behavioral unit is coded.

Bipolar electrode. A measure technique employing the use of two electrodes that are placed close to each other to assess the electrical charge between them.

Bit. The basic unit of information handled by a computer. In electronic terms, it is a switch that is either on or off.

Bivariate data. Measurements taken on two variables.

Body movement. The change of body part position over time.

Body position. The static location of a body part.

Byte. A basic grouping of bits which define a character, number, special symbol, or an instruction.

Categories. The classes, groups, or characteristics derived from the hypotheses or research questions which are used to analyze the content of materials. Categories are usually explicitly defined so that their boundaries (what should be included and excluded in each category) are clear to coders.

Categorizing reliability. See interpretative reliability.

Classical coding. In interaction analysis when coders utilize categories that describe manifest characteristics of the verbal interaction.

Census. The process of collecting data from every member of a group.

Central processing unit. The core memory of a computer where most of the basic work of the computer takes place. The size of the central processing unit (CPU) is one of the measures of the "brainpower" of that computer.

Chi-square test. Test which attempts to assess the difference between the expected frequency (expected on the basis of chance) in a cell of a contingency table with the observed frequency (what was actually observed or coded for a particular cell) in that cell. Designed to assess if the differences are significant enough to be unexplainable by change occurrence.

Closed-ended question. Question that asks for a response to be selected from a predetermined list provided by the researcher.

Codebook. A version of the coding instrument with detailed definitions and explanations of the categories and subcategories to be coded.

Coder drift. See reliability decay.

Coders. Also called judges or observers. The persons (sometimes may be a computer) who actually carry out the analysis of the content using the category system provided by the researcher.

Coding instrument. A form used by coders to code the material and on which the researcher puts the categories and subcategories and instructions for coding the units of analysis.

Coding strategies. Ways in which researchers convert visual records of nonverbal behavior into digital form.

Combination rules. Method of scoring Action Units when they appear together or interact with one another.

Compiler. A translator of a computer program written in a high level language into the machine language required for the computer to "understand."

Complexity. The average number of nonverbal dimensions (body parts) moving during the same time period.

Computers. An information processing system which permits the entry, transformation, and output of electronically mediated information.

Computer program. A sequencing of instructions which tell a computer how to read information, transform it, and output the information for subsequent usage by the user(s).

Computer word. The number of bits which can be moved from one place to another at a single point in time.

Computerized vocalics analysis system. A procedure developed by Klaus Scherer's group at Giessen, West Germany, to examine vocalics.

Concepts. Ideas or abstractions about a set of objects, persons, attributes, or events. Concepts more precisely clarify fuzzy ideas.

Concurrent behaviors. Behaviors occurring simultaneously in the behavioral streams analyzed in interaction analysis.

Concurrent validity. An index that compares two or more measures of the same variable or construct.

Confederates. Individuals whom the researcher instructs to behave in a specific way in order to assess the effect of that behavior on some other person.

Confidence level. An estimate of the degree to which a description of a sample matches an accurate description of a population, could the latter description be obtained.

Constructs. Scientific concepts created by scholars for purposes of research and theory.

Construct validity. Argument for the validity of a measurement procedure based on the ability of the measure to theoretically predict other variables.

Content analysis. A procedure whereby a researcher creates an operational definition of a phenomenon and then codes instances of the occurrences as operationalized.

Content categorizing system. In interaction analysis categorizing systems which code the manifest denotative or connotative semantic content of verbal interaction.

Content validity. Argument for the validity of a measurement procedure based on whether or not a procedure has completely sampled from the entire universe of possible items.

Contingency analysis. A method used to test the relationship among the units of analysis and the categories or subcategories.

Contingency table models. A method for finding the statistical probability of one category of behavior in a behavior stream being associated with other categories of behavior even when they are not contiguous.

Control. An attempt by the researcher to ensure that variables that might negatively affect the outcome of a research project are accounted for or minimized.

Convergent validity. A type of construct validity in which instruments which measure the same construct should (theoretically) correlate highly with one another.

Conversational analysis. Uses ethnomethodology to examine how conversation is constructed so that it is coherent to its participants; concerned with describing and explaining competences of ordinary speakers during conversations.

Coordinated management of meaning. An action-oriented, rules-based theory that holds that social behaviors such as communication can best be understood by examining the meanings people assign to various social situations and the ways they coordinate these meanings to achieve social objectives.

Covert behavior. Bodily events that are not observable without the use of various physiological equipment. The event can be either muscular or neural.

Criterion-related validity. Argument for the validity of a measurement procedure that is based on a correlation between the results of the measure with some external criterion. The two types are concurrent and predictive.

CRT. Cathode ray tube, i.e., the monitor by which we view informaton entered into and output from the computer. It may be monochrome (single color) or chromatic (color).

Data field. In survey research, the specific card column or columns associated with a given variable.

Dependent variable. A concept capable of taking on different values whose value is affected by, or determined by, other variables. Also termed a "consequent" or "effect."

Depolarization. A change in the electrical potential of a cell making it less negative and therefore at a level of excitation.

Depth head position. The forward or backward extension of the head and neck.

Description. How a nonverbal behavior is produced.

Direct evaluation. A coding strategy which requires coders to ascribe "meaning" or tranform observations into the psychological dimensions in which the researcher is interested.

Discourse analysis. Examines conversation using traditional linguistic theories, concepts and methodologies.

Discriminant validity. A type of construct validity in which different or opposing concepts and their operationalizations should be distinct from one another because they measure different traits even though a similar method of measurement is used.

Dominance rules. Combination rules which prescribe how to score facial expressions in which a strong Action Unit overshadows a weak one.

Dross rate. The ratio of relevant to irrelevant data; high dross rates occur when researchers must observe numerous instances of human behavior before they get examples of behaviors relevant to their inquiry.

Dynamic activitation. The swiftness of movement increase and decrease.

Efferent pathway. Nerve pathways that move away from the brain toward other effectors or organs such as heart or limbs of the body.

Electrode. Devices for sensing electrical activity of the body, usually made of silver silver-chloride or other precious metals.

Element. The smallest individual unit (e.g., person, family, group, or company) in a survey sample or population.

Emotion facial action coding system (EMFACS). A system for coding nonverbal facial behavior which is derived from FACS and infers meaning.

Empirical. Based on careful observation rather than abstract concepts.

Empirical verification. Assessment of the validity of knowledge claims by recourse to observation; e.g., if someone claims, "Women are more persuasible than men," the validity of the claim would be assessed by a series of related observations.

Empiricism. The belief or view that observations made with the senses are the primary source of knowledge.

Equivalence assumption. In interaction analysis all utterances coded into a category are regarded in the analysis as having all aspects of that category when they may have only one or a few; may introduce bias into a coding system.

Erosion measures. Measures that are created by observing the selective wear on some material.

Ethical concerns. The judgment about the rightness or wrongness of a particular research method in terms of its consequence to research subjects.

Event behavioral unit. A single occurrence of the behavior in the behavioral stream which is to be coded in interaction analysis.

Exhaustive coding system. In interaction analysis events are often chosen so that they are contiguous, so that no gaps remain in the behavioral stream where noncoded behavior occurs, so that there is some code for every behavior.

Experienced mode. Approach in interaction analysis in which the purpose of a study is to examine interaction solely from a theoretical perspective and which is not concerned with the interpretations of participants in the interaction.

Experiencer mode. Approach in interaction analysis in which the purpose of a study is to examine the idiosyncratic meaning of interaction for those participants actually involved in the interaction.

Experiencing mode. Approach in interaction analysis in which the purpose of a study is to examine the shared meanings for interaction among the members of a particular culture; this is sometimes implicit in a study resulting from the hypotheses being examined.

Experimenter effect. A potential source of bias in an experiment caused by appearance, personality, or behaviors of the experimenter/researcher.

Explanation. The aspect of theory or conceptualization which seeks to answer why and how questions. It particularly deals with causes and consequences of actions or variations.

Expressive categorizing system. In interaction analysis categorizing systems which code the extralinguistic, nonverbal characteristics of verbal interaction.

External validity. The degree to which results of a study are generalizable to "real world" situations.

Face validity. Argument for the validity of a measurement procedure based on the notion that the measurement looks as though it measures what it is supposed to measure.

Facial action coding system (FACS). A descriptive method of coding nonverbal facial behavior based on the anatomical features of the face (i.e., the facial muscles, skin, etc.).

Factor analysis. Factor analysis is a statistical method for determining the number and nature of underlying variables from a larger number of measures.

Falsification. A scientific process used to fairly test a hypothesis or theory by creating the conditions for the hypothesis or theory to fail or be disproven.

Frequency. A property of a wave that refers to the number of cycles per second which a wave passes in a given period of time. The hertz (Hz) is a reference to this property.

Galvanic skin response. Abbreviated (GSR), this is an electronic measurement of skin conductivity. Higher GSR scores are indicants of arousal, excitement or anxiety.

Generic coding. A strategy in which data is recorded into categories labeled with generic terms and covering a number of obviously different behaviors.

Ground. A critical procedure utilized in electrical measurement to allow extraneous electrical signals to be conducted to the earth (ground).

Grounded theory. A theory which has been developed as a result of extensive testing and data gathering.

Habituation. The decrease in either behavioral or neural activity that occurs with repeated or continuous stimulation.

Hardware. The physical properties of a computer system such as the computer, a disk drive, or the printer.

Hertz (Hz). The term used in electrical measurement to indicate cycles per second. 1 Hz is equal to 1 cycle per second.

Heuristic. The property of science or inquiry which leads to further questions, hypotheses, and discoveries.

Hidden hardware. Videocameras, electronic listening devices, and other technological instruments designed to record events as they occur without the participants noticing their presence.

Homeostasis. A balanced or steady-state of an organism where the right temperature, nourishment, oxygen, or fluids are at a balanced level.

Hypothesis. A declarative conjectured statement proposing a relationship between two or more variables.

Hypothetical construct.. A term used to stand for a process that is unobservable and must be inferred from observable behaviors.

Illocutionary acts. A classification of acts that denotes the role an utterance plays in the interpersonal relationship between speaker and listener.

Independent variable. A concept capable of taking on different values and whose value is unaffected by other variables in a given study. Also commonly referred to as an "antecedent" or "cause."

Inductive/grounded theory approach. In interaction analysis when the categories in the coding system, as well as the hypotheses and concepts being studied, are generated from the data or interactions being examined; the discourse and not *a priori* theory generate the coding system.

Inference. What a nonverbal behavior means.

Input. Information that is introduced to the computer to be read for analysis and/or transformation by that computer.

Interact. Two contiguous acts, generally speaking turns; the minimal unit of behavior which is analyzed in the most stringently defined of interaction analysis studies.

Interaction analysis.. Methodologies that are concerned with the systematic analysis of behavior streams, particularly with identifying sequences or repetitive patterns of behaviors.

Intercoder reliability. The degree to which coders agree in their application of the categories in analyzing the materials; usually expressed as a correlation or percentage.

Internal validity. The degree to which a research instrument measures what it purports to measure.

Interpolated measurement. The use of a measuring instrument in situations when it is not usually present, causing possible errors in measurement.

Interpretative reliability. The proportion of units of behavior which the coders classify similarly using the categories in the coding system.

Intersubjective categorizing system. In interaction analysis, categorizing systems that code the syntactically implied and other inferred relationships between the sender and receiver.

Interval scales. Level of measurement that contains all of the information of nominal and interval scales, plus the characteristic of equality of intervals. Interval scales also have an arbitrary zero point.

Intracoder reliability. The degree to which an individual coder is consistent in applying the categories to the content during coding.

Ion. An atom which has lost or gained an electron making it capable of conducting an electrical charge.

Item analysis. Procedures used to select items for the construction of a questionnaire. Usually of critical importance for developing a valid and reliable instrument.

Kilobytes. A thousand bytes of information.

Kinesics notation system. A nonverbal communication measurement system developed by Birdwhistell which creates a different symbol for each individual movement pattern.

Lag sequential analysis. A method for finding the statistical probability of one category of behavior in a behavior stream being associated with other categories of behavior even when they are not contiguous.

Latency. Refers to the period of time between stimulus presentation and response onset.

Lateral head position. The movement of the head at a 45 degree angle, sometimes referred to as "cocking" or "tilting" of the head.

Laws. Broad statements of general principles which have been empirically demonstrated and are believed to be universal.

Level of confidence. An exact probability that results of a given experiment are not caused by chance.

Level of data. Nominal, ordinal, interval, and ratio data represent four different levels of data which may be obtained from subjects.

Likert-type scales. Scales that follow the visual format of a Likert scale without using the item analysis procedures of Likert.

Logical/deductive approach. In interaction analysis, when the categories in the coding system are created using previously developed theory to create the decision rules about how particular behaviors are to be classified; generally used to test hypotheses generated *a priori* by logical deductions from theory; the type of discourse being studied is not taken into account.

Log-linear models. A method for finding the statistical probability of one category of behavior in a behavior stream being associated with other categories of behavior even when they are not contiguous.

Manifest content. Content that is explicit, overt, apparent, readily discerned, as opposed to latent.

Markov models. A method for finding the statistical probability of one category of behavior in a behavior stream being associated with other categories of behavior even when they are not contiguous.

Measurability index. The degree to which a given variable or construct lends itself to accurate measurement.

Measurement. The assignment of numbers by a specified procedure to represent phenomena such as objects, persons, events, and constructs.

MegaK. A million bytes of information.

Method of equal appearing intervals. Sometimes known as "Thurstone scales" after their developer, these were the first attempt at psychometric measurement of attitude. Most attitude measures developed since have been compared with these, either directly or indirectly, to establish validity.

Method of internal consistency. Method of estimating reliability coefficient of a test by estimating an average correlation of all possible items to halves of a test with each other.

Method of ordered alternatives. Based on the theoretical assumptions of the Social Judgment-Involvement Approach, this procedure permits subjects to indicate their latitudes of acceptance, rejection, and noncommitment on a nine-point continuum. No assumptions are made about interval width and the resulting data are nominal data.

Method of summated ratings. Often referred to as "Likert scales" after its originator, this procedure is less complex than the Thurstone procedure yet produces similar results.

The key to understanding the procedure is the item analysis method used in constructing the questionnaire. An attitude score is a single point on a continuum.

Minimum scoring requirements. A method of identifying very minor changes in facial expression which cannot be reliably coded.

MIPS. Refers to a million instructions per second, a unit for describing the speed of a computer.

Mobility. The number of time periods during which movement occurs in at least one body part.

Monopolar electrode. A reference to the use of electrodes being placed at positions on the body where there is a common electrode and no chance of conductivity between other placement of electrodes.

Multidimensional. Refers to constructs which, rather than being composed of a single dimension/component, are made up of more than one dimension/factor/component.

Multidimensional measures. Those which measure several variables with one instrument.

Multimodality nonverbal behavior measurement. The examination of several nonverbal communication modes in the same research project.

Multivariate data. Measurements taken on three or more variables.

Mutually exclusive categories.. In interaction analysis categories are created so that any given behavioral event in the behavioral stream is associated with only one code.

Natural observation. A data collection procedure whereby the researcher is a hidden spectator watching and noting events as they naturally occur.

Nominal scales. The lowest level of measurement. Numbers are used as symbols in much the same manner as categories or names.

Non-probability sample. A sample in which some members have a greater chance than others of being selected.

Nonreactive measures. A synonym for unobtrusive measurement methods.

Nonverbal communication measurement. Procedures for examining and analyzing nonverbal behavior.

Oddball methods. A synonym for unobtrusive measurement; oddball was an earlier term that was almost used instead of unobtrusive.

Offset. The ending of a nonverbal behavior.

Onset. The beginning of a nonverbal behavior.

Open-ended question. Question which asks a respondent to provide his or her own answer.

Operational definition. Concrete, specific definition which specifies methods for its measurement.

Operational parallel. A lower level construct between the construct of interest and the actual measured behaviors.

Optical scanners. A piece of hardware capable of reading a barcode, or typewritten materials for storage in computer memory.

Ordinal scales. A measurement scale that ranks data (from slight to extreme, most to least, from best to worst, for example) but there is no assumption that the differences between the various categories represent equal intervals.

Ostensive definition. To define by pointing to an example of the concept being defined; e.g., when asked, "What is a fire truck?" one might respond by directing the questioner's attention to a fire truck and saying, "There's a 'fire truck.'"

Output. Information that is produced by the computer after transformation by the computer.

Overt behavior. That behavior capable of being sensed by typical receptor organs such as sight or sound.

Own categories procedure. Based on the theoretical assumptions of the Social Judgment-Involvement Approach, this procedure is used to measure latitudes of acceptance, rejection, and noncommitment without any defined number of intervals on a continuum. The data produced is nominal data.

Parallel test reliability. Procedure for computing a reliability coefficient by correlating two forms of the same test.

Period. A property of a wave that refers to the amount of time a wave form takes to complete a cycle.

Periodicity. Associated with systematic samples; the danger of a cyclical pattern occurring in the sampling frame.

Phenomenologist. A person who believes the primary datum for study should be people's phenomenal states, i.e., the things they are thinking or the contents of their minds.

Physical traces. A kind of unobtrusive measure where a researcher collects the physical evidence that earmarks the occurrence of an activity.

Pilot study. A miniature walk-through of the entire survey, conducted before the final study begins.

Polarization. The difference in charge, either positive or negative, on the outside or inside of a cell membrane.

Population. All of the members of a group in which a survey researcher is interested.

Practice effect. A potential source of bias caused by giving subjects initial tests that serve as practice for tests administered later in the experiment.

Pragmatics. The study of the relationship between signs and language and their interpreters.

Pragmatic coding. In interaction analysis, when coders utilize categories that require them to make inferences about characteristics of the communicator, such as his or her internal state or intentions, from characteristics of the discourse.

Prediction. The aspect of theory which enables scientists to explain and anticipate future events or relationships based on their knowledge of past events or relationships.

Pre-test. Initial testing of some aspect or portion of a survey design (e.g., questionnaire, sample design, or data analysis).

Probability. Although this term is used in many ways, in chapter 2 it refers to relative frequency. So, for example, if a rat turns left in a t-maze 15 out of 30 times, then the probability of turning left would be estimated as 15/30 = .5.

Probability sample. A sample in which every member of the population has an equal and known probability of being selected.

Problem. A scientific issue, question, or statement that focuses on investigation or study.

Qualitative. A type of research, usually descriptive and nonnumeric, used to interpret and understand patterns of relationships.

Quantitative. A type of research in which numbers are assigned to phenomena for the purpose of objectively explaining and predicting relationships.

RAM. Random-access-memory, which is a place where information is stored on a CPU that can be read or written over. It is usually volatile, meaning that a loss of electrical power will erase information in RAM.

Random selection. The process by which members of a survey are sampled; ensures an equal and known chance of each member of a population being selected; associated with probability sampling primarily.

Randomization. The process of selecting subjects or assigning subjects on a probability basis—where all subjects have an equal chance to be selected without bias.

Rating coding. In interaction analysis, when coders rate each message using a set of Likert scales.

Rating scale. Scales used to measure attitudes, opinions, or behaviors.

Ratio scales. The level of measurement that includes the information of nominal, ordinal, and interval scales plus an absolute zero point. It is appropriate to analyze ratio data with parametric statistics.

Rationale. A section in a research report which provides systematic and logical reasons for conducting the investigation.

Reactive measurement. A process by which the act of measuring behaviors creates uncontrolled reactions in some subjects.

Relational analysis. A type of interactional analysis which distinguishes the "content," or what is said, from the "relationship," or how something is said; generally uses intersubjective categorizing systems to make inferences from verbal and nonverbal messages about how two or more people regard each other, their relationship, themselves within the context of that relationship.

Relational patterns. The systematic rhythms, designs, structures or episodes manifested by dyads or groups in human interactions.

Reliability. Hypothetical construct/term used to indicate the extent to which a measurement procedure produces consistent results. Also used to refer to the amount of random error in a measurement.

Reliability decay. A decrease in an individual coder's consistency from his or her original training level over time.

Replicable. Repeatable. The process of specifying the methods of a study such that other scientists can attempt to duplicate the results of a study.

Repolarization. Recovery by a cell during which the inside of a cell returns to a negative charge relative to the outside.

Representative sample. A sample which accurately reflects its overall population.

Representational validity. The requirement in the experiencing mode in interaction analysis that the particular constructs or functions categorized by the coding system should reflect the meaning of utterances for average participants in the culture.

Restrictive coding. A measurement strategy which confines coding to the assessment of a small subset of specific movements which are well defined, easily observed and difficult to mistake.

Rotational head position. The left/right turn of the head.

ROM. Read-only-memory, which is a place where information is permanently stored on a memory chip that can only be read, not written over. It is considered non-volatile, meaning that a loss of electrical power will not erase information in ROM.

Rules. Norms or conventions of human behavior followed by particular cultures, groups, or individuals.

Sagittal head position. The up or down movement of the head.

Sample. That portion of a group or population which is targeted for a survey.

Sampling. The process of collecting data from a portion of a group or population.

Sampling error. Inaccuracies which are generated throughout the measurement process in a survey.

Sampling interval. In a systematic sample, the distance between elements to be selected in a sampling frame; computed by dividing the desired sample size by the pupulation size (e.g., $K = 4$).

Sampling ratio. In a systematic sample, the proportion of elements in the population to be sampled; calculated by dividing the desired sample size by the population size (e.g., 1/4).

Scaling. A way of measurement which is composed of several items that have a relationship to each other.

Scalogram analysis/cumulative scaling. Frequently referred to as "Guttman scales" after their developer, this procedure is based on the premise that items on an attitude questionnaire can be ordered so that a response to one item enables the user to predict responses to all other items. The procedure is intended to result in completely unidimensional scales.

Science. A systematic process of discovery and problem solving based on empirical research and leading toward explanatory and predictive theory.

Semantic differential technique. Procedure developed by Osgood, Suci, and Tannenbaum for the measurement of meaning. The procedure makes use of bipolar adjectival scales which are factor analyzed, resulting in dimensions of meaning. Osgood, Suci, and Tannenbaum suggested that the scales which measure the evaluative dimension could be used as attitude scales.

Semi-Markov models. A method for finding the statistical probability of one category of behavior in a behavior stream being associated with other categories of behavior even when they are not contiguous.

Sequential behaviors. Behaviors occurring one after the other in the behavioral streams analyzed in interaction analysis.

Sieve codes. In interaction analysis, when only particular events are coded when they occur in the behavioral stream; they are not exhaustive.

Significance. The rejection of a null hypothesis through statistical tests.

Social judgment-involvement approach. Theoretically based approach to attitude measurement developed by Sherif, Sherif, and Nebergall. Focuses on the measurement of latitudes of acceptance, rejection and noncommitment rather than measuring a single point on a continuum.

Software. The operating systems and computer programs which control the work of the computer.

Sources of invalidity. Interfering factors that affect the outcome of a study but are not attributable to the research variables.

Split-half reliability. Procedure for computing a reliability coefficient by correlating one half of a test with the other half.

Standard error. A statistic which allows the researcher to estimate the sampling error generated in a survey.

Statistical archives. Repositories of statistical information; these can be privately or publicly maintained.

Statistical regression. The effect of pretesting or initial testing on subsequent test scores in an experimental study.

Stratifying variable. Associated with stratified sampling; any important variable which allows the researcher to locate important homogeneous groups within a population.

Substitution rules. Combination rules which prescribe scoring procedures for facial expressions when similar appearing Action Unit combinations occur.

Subtle difference tables. FACS guidelines for comparing and contrasting AUs and AU combinations which differ only slightly.

Summated scale. Scores on a number of attitude scales that have been added to provide a total score reflecting the person's attitude on a topic.

Test-retest reliability. Procedure for computing a reliability coefficient in which scores from a measurement instrument administered at two points in time are correlated with each other.

Theory. A highly organized set of statements about reality, logically tied together and empirically testable.

Theoretically based/discourse analytical approach. In interaction analysis, when the categories in the coding system code the relevant functions in the discourse field being studied from a theoretical perspective; both *a priori* logical deductions from theory and type of discourse are taken into account.

Time interval behavioral units. Time units in interactional analysis which are created by coding what is occurring every 10 seconds, or 2 minutes—whatever unit of time is chosen.

Time-series notation. The recording of body position, sound, etc. change over time. It is the methodological basis for literally every efficient approach to the registration and storage of audiovisual information.

Traits. Relatively enduring characteristics of people.

Triangulation. The acceptance and embracement of multiple research methods, tactics, and strategies to address the same issue.

Type I error. An error which occurs when the researcher rejects the null hypothesis when it actually is "true."

Type II error. An error which occurs when the researcher retains the null hypothesis when it actually is "false."

Unidimensional measures. Those which measure a single variable with one instrument.

Unit of analysis. The smallest component of the material which is to be analyzed according to the category system. For example, the unit of analysis can be a political ad, a newspaper story, a 20-minute public speech, or a camera shot.

Unit of enumeration. The way in which each unit of analysis is counted or quantified.

Unitizing reliability. The consistency with which coders select the same amount of verbal behavior to be classified in each category in interaction analysis.

Univariate data. Measurements taken of only one variable.

Unobtrusive methods. Research tactics that allow data collection without interference in the process being studied.

Validity. Hypothetical construct/term used to indicate the extent to which a measurement procedure measures the construct it is said to measure. Also used to refer to the amount of nonrandom error in a measurement.

Values. Relatively long-lasting judgments about the desirability of people, ideas, and objects.

Variables. Measured concepts or constructs. Attributes which can be measured quantitatively.

Visual data inspection ("eyeballing the data"). The analysis of a data matrix without the aid of specially prepared computer programs.

Vocalics (or paralanguage). Characteristics of the voice other than words, such as pauses, pitch, loudness, and speech rate.

Wave form. The shape a wave can take relative to a straight line. Waves take many forms relative to their properties of frequency and amplitude.

References

Adams, W., & Schreibman, F. (Eds.). (1978). *Television network news: Issues in content research*. Washington, D.C.: George Washington University Television and Politics Study Program.

Adamson, L. B., & Bakeman, R. (1985). Affect and attention: Infants observed with mothers and peers. *Child Development, 56*, 582–593.

Alberts, J. K. (1986). The role of couples' conversation in relational development: A content analysis of courtship talk in Harlequin romance novels. *Communication Quarterly, 34*, 127–142.

Allen, M. J., & Yen, W. M. (1979). *Introduction to measurement theory*. Monterey, CA.: Brooks/Cole.

Allport, G. W. (1935). Attitudes. In C. Murchison (Ed.), *Handbook of social psychology*. Worcester, MA: Clark University Press.

American Psychological Association. (1973). *Code of ethics of the American Psychological Association*. Washington, D.C.: Author.

Amidon, E. J., & Hough, J. B. (Eds.). (1967). *Interaction analysis: Theory, research and application*. Reading, MA: Addison-Wesley.

Andersen, J. F., Anderson, P. A., & Jenson, A.D. (1979). The measurement of nonverbal immediacy. *Journal of Applied Communication Research, 7*, 153–180.

Andersen, P. A. (1984, April). *An arousal-valence model of nonverbal immediacy exchange*. Paper presented at the Central States Speech Association Convention, Chicago.

Andersen, P. A. (1985). Nonverbal immediacy in interpersonal communication. In A. W. Seigman & S. Feldstein (Eds.), *Multichannelled integrations of nonverbal behavior* (pp. 1–29). Hillsdale, NJ: Lawrence Erlbaum.

Andersen, P. A. (1986). Consciousness, cognition, and communication. *Western Journal of Speech Communication 50*, 87–101.

Andersen, P. A. (1987). The trait debate: A critical examination of the individual differences paradigm in the communication sciences. In B. Dervin & M. Voi (Eds.), *Progress in the Communication Sciences*, (Vol. 3, pp. 47–81). Norwood, NJ: Ablex.

Andersen, P. A., Garrison, J. P., & Andersen, J. F. (1979). Implications of a neurophysiological approach for the study of nonverbal communication. *Human Communication Research, 6*, 74–88.

Andersen, P. A., Lustig, M. W., & Andersen, J. F. (1987). Regional patterns of communication in the United States: A theoretical perspective. *Communication Monographs, 54*, 128–144.

Anderson, H. H. (1937a). An experimental study of dominative and integrative behavior in children of pre-school age. *Journal of Social Psychology, 8*, 335–345.

Anderson, H. H. (1937b). Domination and integration in the social behavior of young children in an experimental play situation. *Genetic Psychology Monographs, 19*, 341–408.

Anderson, H. H. (1939a). The measurement of domination and of socially integrative behavior in teachers' contacts with children. *Child Development, 10*, 73–89.

Anderson, H. H. (1939b). Domination and social integration in the behavior of kindergarten children in an experimental play situation. *Journal of Experimental Education, 8*, 123–131.

Anderson, J. A. (1987). *Communication Research: Issues and Methods*. New York: McGraw-Hill.

Anderson, P. A. (1983). Decision making by objection and the Cuban missile crisis. *Administrative Science Quarterly, 28*, 201–222.

Andreassi, J. L. (1973). Alpha and problem solving: A demonstration. *Perception and Motor Skills, 36*, 905–906.

Andreassi, J. L. (1980). Psychophysiology: Human behavior and physiological response. New York: Oxford University Press.

Andren, G. (1981). Reliability and content analysis. In K. E. Rosengren (Ed.), *Advances in content analysis*. Beverly Hills, CA: Sage.

Argyle, M. (1975). *Bodily communication*. New York: International Universities.

Arnold, W. E. (1985). *Empathic listening and the significant other*. Paper presented to the International Listening Association, Orlando, Fla.

Arnold, W. E., & Jae Won Lee. (1974). Academic convention as the ritual of an epistemic community. *ACA Bulletin, 9*, 24–31.

Arundale, R. B. (1977). Sampling across time for communication research: A simulation. In P. M. Hirsch, P. V. Miller, & F. G. Kline (Eds.), *Strategies for communication research* (pp. 257–285). Beverly Hills, CA: Sage.

Arundale, R. B. (1980). Studying change over time: Criteria for sampling from continuous variables. *Communication Research, 7*, 227–263.

Austin, J. L. (1962). *How to do things with words*. Oxford: Clarendon Press.

Averill, J. R. (1980). A constructivist view of emotion. In R. Plutchik & H. Kellerman (Eds.), *Emotion: Theory, research and experience* (pp. 305–340). New York: Academic Press.

Ayres, J., & Miura, S. Y. (1981). Construct and predictive validity of instruments for coding relational control communication. *Western Journal of Speech Communication, 45*, 159–171.

Babbie, E. R. (1973). *Survey research methods*. Belmont, CA: Wadsworth.

Babbie, E. R. (1986). *The practice of social research* (4th ed.). Belmont, CA: Wadsworth.

Backstrom, C. H. & Hursh-Cesar, G. (1981). *Survey research* (2nd ed.). New York: John Wiley.

Bakeman, R. (1978). Untangling streams of behavior: Sequential analysis of observation data. In G. P. Sackett (Ed.), *Observing behavior* (Vol. 2). *Data collection and analysis methods* (pp. 63–78). Baltimore: University Park Press.

Bakeman, R., & Dabbs, J. M., Jr. (1976). Social interaction observed: Some approaches to the analysis of behavior streams. *Personality and Social Psychology Bulletin, 2,* 335–345.

Bakeman, R., & Gottman, J. M. (1986). *Observing interaction: A introduction to sequential analysis.* Cambridge: Cambridge University Press.

Bales, R. (1950). *Interaction process analysis: A method for the study of small groups.* Reading, MA: Addison-Wesley.

Bardo, J. W. (1976). Internal consistency and reliability in Likert-type attitude scales— some questions concerning the use of pre-built scales. *Sociology and Social Research, 60,* 403–420.

Barker, L. L., & Collins, N. B. (1970). Nonverbal and kinesic research. In P. Emmert & W. D. Brooks (Eds.), *Methods of research in communication* (pp. 343–372). Boston: Houghton-Mifflin.

Bartz, A. E. (1981). *Basic Statistical Concepts* (2nd ed.). Minneapolis: Burgess.

Bateson, G. (1951). *Information and codification: A philosophical approach.* In J. Ruesch & G. Bateson (Eds.). *Communication: The social matrix of psychiatry* (pp. 168–211). New York: W. W. Norton.

Bateson, G. (1958). *Naven.* Stanford: Stanford University Press.

Bateson, G., & Jackson, D. D. (1964). Some varieties of pathogenic organization. In D. McK. Rioch (Ed.), *Disorders of human communication, 42,* 270–283. Association for Research in Nervous and Mental Disease: Research Publications. Baltimore: Williams & Wilkins.

Beaumont, J. G., Young, A. W., & McManus, I. C. (1984). Hemisphericity: A critical review. *Cognitive Neuropsychology, 1,* 191–211.

Becker, Samuel. (1970). Rating scales. In P. Emmert and W. D. Brooks (Eds.). *Methods of research in communication.* Boston: Houghton Mifflin.

Benke, R. R. (1970). Psychophysiological technologies. In P. Emmert and W. D. Brooks (Eds.), *Methods of research in communication* (pp. 429–452). Boston: Houghton Mifflin.

Berelson, B. (1952). *Content analysis in communication research.* New York: The Free Press of Glencoe.

Bergan, J. R., & Tombari, M. L. (1975). The analysis of verbal interactions occurring during consultation. *Journal of Social Psychology, 13,* 209–226.

Berger, C. R., & Calabrese, R. J. (1975). Some exploration in initial interaction and beyond: Toward a developmental theory of interpersonal communication. *Human Communication Research, 1,* 99–112.

Berger, C. R., Gardner, R. R., Clatterbuck, G. W., & Schulman, L. S. (1976). Perceptions of information sequencing in relationship development. *Human Communication Research, 3,* 29–46.

Birdwhistell, R. (1952). *Introduction to kinesics.* Louisville: University of Louisville.

Birdwhistell, R. (1970). *Kinesics and context.* Philadelphia: University of Pennsylvania.

Blalock, H. M. (1982). *Conceptualization and measurement in the social sciences.* Beverly Hills, CA: Sage.

Blalock, H. M., & Blalock, A. B. (1968). *Methodology in social research.* New York: McGraw-Hill.

Blalock, H. M., & Blalock, A. B. (1982). *Introduction to social research* (2nd ed.). Englewood Cliffs, NJ: Prentice-Hall.

Bloom, A. J. (1986). An anxiety management approach to computerphobia. *Training & Development Journal, 39*(1), 90–92.

Boring, E. G. (1961). The beginning and growth of measurement in psychology. In H. Woolf (Ed.), *Quantification* (pp. 108–127). Indianapolis: Bobbs-Merrill.

Bostrom, R. N. (1980). Altered physiological states: The central nervous system and persuasive communication. In M. F. Roloff and G. R. Miller (Eds.), *Persuasion: New Directions in theory and research*. Beverly Hills, CA: Sage.

Bostrom, R. N. (1983). *Persuasion*. Englewood Cliffs, NJ: Prentice-Hall.

Boucher, J. D., & Ekman, p. (1975). Facial areas of emotional information. *Journal of Communication, 25*, 21–29.

Bowers, J. W. (1970). Content analysis. In P. Emmert & W. D. Brooks (Eds.), *Methods of research in communication* (pp. 291–314). Boston: Houghton Mifflin.

Bowers, J. W., & Courtright, J. A. (1984). *Communication research methods*. Dallas, TX: Scott, Foresman.

Bradley, P. H. (1978). Power, status, and upward communication in small decision-making groups. *Communication Monographs, 45*, 33–43.

Brannigan, C. R., & Humphries, D. A. (1972). Human non-verbal behavior, a means of communication. In N. Blurton Jones (Ed.), *Ethological studies of human behaviour* (pp. 37–64). Cambridge: Cambridge University.

Brockriede, W. (1982). Arguing about human understanding. *Communication Monographs, 49*, 137–147.

Brockriede, W. (1983). Lecture on criticism and quantitative research. California State University, Fullerton.

Brown, H. (1975). *Brain and behavior*. New York: Oxford University Press.

Brown, T. S., & Wallace, P. M. (1980). *Physiological psychology*. New York: Academic Press.

Brown, P., & Levinson, S. C. (1978). Universals in language usage: Politeness phenomena. In E. Goody (Ed.), *Questions and politeness: Strategies in social interaction* (pp. 56–310). Cambridge: Cambridge University Press.

Brown, W. (1910). Some experimental results in the correlation of mental abilities. *British Journal of Psychology, 3*, 296–322.

Budd, R. W., Thorp, R. K., & Donohew, L. (1967). *Content analysis of communications*. New York: Macmillan.

Bull, P. (1983). *Body movement and interpersonal communication*. New York: John Wiley.

Burggraf, C. E. (1985, November). *Relational communication: Which comes first, the relationship or the behavior?* Paper presented at the meeting of the Speech Communication Association, Denver, CO.

Burgoon, J. K. (1980). Nonverbal communication research in the 1970s: An overview. In D. Nimmo (Ed.), *Communication yearbook* (pp. 179-197). New Brunswick, NJ: Transaction. Books.

Burgoon, J. K. (1985a). Nonverbal signals. In M. L. Knapp & G. Miller (Eds.), *Handbook of interpersonal communication* (pp. 344-389). Beverly Hills, CA: Sage.

Burgoon, J. K. (1985b). The relationship of verbal and nonverbal codes. In B. Dervin & M. J. Voight (Eds.), *Progress in communication sciences* (Vol. 6). Norwood, NJ: Ablex.

Burgoon, J. K., Buller, D. B., Hale, J. L., & deTurck, M. A. (1984). Relational messages associated with nonverbal behaviors. *Human Communication Research, 10*, 351–358.

Burgoon, J. K., & Hale, J. L. (1981). *Dimensions of relational messages*. Paper presented at the Speech Communication Association Convention, Anaheim, CA.

Burgoon, J. K., & Hale, J. L. (1984). The fundamental topoi of relational communication. *Communication Monographs, 51*, 193–214.

Burgoon, J. K., & Jones, S. B. (1976). Toward a theory of personal space expectations and their violations. *Human Communication Research, 2*, 131–146.

Burgoon, J. K., & Saine, T. (1978). *The unspoken dialogue: An introduction to nonverbal communication*. Boston: Houghton-Mifflin.

Buros, O. (1985). *The ninth mental measurements yearbook*. Highland Park, NJ: Gryphon Press.

Cacioppo, J. T., Petty, R. E., & Quintinar, L. (1982). Individual differences in relative hemisphere alpha abundance and cognitive response to persuasive communications. *Journal of Psychology and Social Psychology, 43*, 623–636.

Cacioppo, J. T., & Petty, R. E. (Eds.). (1983). *Social psychophysiology: A source book*. New York: Cuilford.

Cairns, R. B., & Green, J. A. (1979). How to assess personality and social patterns: Observations or ratings? In R. B. Cairns (Ed.), *The analysis of social interactions: Methods, issues, and illustrations* (pp. 209–226). Hillsdale, NJ: Lawrence Erlbaum.

Campbell, D. T., & Stanley, J. C. (1963). *Experimental and quasi-experimental designs for research*. Chicago, IL: Rand McNally.

Cannon, W. B. (1915). *Bodily changes in pain, hunger, fear, and rage*. New York: Appleton.

Cansler, D. C., & Stiles, W. B. (1981). Relative status and interpersonal presumptuousness. *Journal of Experimental Social Psychology, 17*, 459–471.

Cappella, J. N. (1979). Talk-silence sequences in informal conversations I. *Human Communication Research, 6*, 3–17.

Cappella, J. N. (1980). Talk and silence sequences in informal conversations II. *Human Communication Research, 6*, 130–145.

Cappella, J. N., & Greene, J. O. (1982). A discrepancy-arousal explanation of mutual influence in expressive behavior for adult and infant-adult interaction. *Communication Monographs, 49*, 89–114.

Cappella, J. N., & Planalp, S. (1981). Talk and silence sequences in informal conversations III. Interspeaker Influence. *Human Communication Research, 7*, 117–132.

Carkhuff, Robert. (1969). *Helping and human relations*. Two Volumes. New York: Holt, Rinehart, and Winston.

Carmines, E. G., & Zeller, R. A. (1979). *Reliability and validity assessment*. Beverly Hills, CA: Sage.

Carr, L. J. (1929). Experimental sociology: A preliminary note on theory and method. *Social Forces, 8*, 63–75.

Carver, R. P. (1978). The case against statistical significance testing. *Harvard Educational Review, 48*, 378–399.

Catalano, R. A., Dooley, D., & Jackson, R. (1983). Selecting a time-series strategy. *Psychological Bulletin, 94*, 506–523.

Cawes, P. (1965). *The Philosophy of Science*. Princeton: Van Nostrand., Inc.

Chronbach, L. J. (1951). Coefficient alpha and the internal structure of tests. *Psychometrika, 16*, 297-334.

Clevenger, T., Jr. (1959). A synthesis of experimental research in stage fright. *Quarterly Journal of Speech, 45*, 134–145.

Clevenger, T., Jr. (1963). The influence of sex appeal upon ratings of speaking performance. *Worm Runner's Digest, 5*, 35–39.

Clevenger, T., Jr. (1964). The influence of scale complexity on the reliability of ratings of general effectiveness in public speaking. *Speech Monographs, 31*, 153–156.

Cohen, J. (1960). A coefficient of agreement for nominal scales. *Educational and Psychological Measurement, 20*,37–46.

Cohen, J. (1968). Weighted kappa: nominal scale agreement with provision for scaled disagreement or partial credit. *Psychological Bulletin, 70*, 213–220.

Cohen, J. (1977). *Statistical power analysis for the behavioral sciences*. London: Academic Press.

Coombs, C. H. (1964). *A Theory of Scaling*. Ann Arbor: University of Michigan Press.

Corballis, M. C. (1980). Laterality and myth. *American Psychologist, 35*, 284–295.

Coulthard, M., Montgomery, M., & Brazil, D. (1981). Developing a description of spoken discourse. In M. Coulthard & M. Montgomery (Eds.), *Studies in discourse analysis* (pp. 1–50). London: Routledge & Kegan Paul.

Courtright, J. A., Millar, F. E., & Rogers-Millar, L. E. (1979). Domineeringness and dominance: Replication and extension. *Communication Monographs, 49*, 179–192.

Courtright, J. A., Millar, F. E., & Rogers, L. E. (1980). Message control intensity as a predictor of transactional redundancy. In D. Nimmo (Ed.), *Communication yearbook, 4*(pp. 199–216). New Brunswick, NJ: Transaction Books.

Craig, K. D. (1978). Social modeling influences on pain. In R. A. Sternbach (Ed.), *The psychology of pain* (pp. 73–109). New York: Raven.

Craig, K. D., Best, H., & Ward, L. M. (1975). Social modeling influences on psychophysical judgments of electrical stimulation. *Journal of Abnormal Psychology, 84*, 366–373.

Craig, K. D., & Patrick, C. J. (1985). Facial expression during induced pain. *Journal of Personality and Social Psychology, 48*, 1080–1891.

Craig, K. D., & Prkachin, K. M. (1978). Social modeling influences on sensory decision theory and psychophysiological indexes of pain. *Journal of Personality and Social Psychology, 36*, 805–815.

Craig, K. D., & Prkachin, K. M. (1980). Social influences on public and private components of pain. In I. G. Sarason & C. D. Spielberger (Eds.), *Stress and anxiety* (Vol. 7, pp. 57–72). New York: Hemisphere.

Craig, K. D., & Prkachin, K. M. (1983). Nonverbal measures of pain. In R. Melzack (Ed.), *Pain measurement and assessment* (pp. 173–179). New York: Raven.

Cronen, V. E., Pearce, W. B., & Shavely, L. (1979). A theory of rule structure and types of episodes and a study of perceived enmeshments in undesired repetitive patterns (UREPS). In D. Nimmo (Ed.), *Communication yearbook 3* (pp. 225–240). New Brunswick, NJ: Transaction Books.

Cronen, V. E., Pearce, W. B., & Harris, L. M. (1982). The coordinated management of meaning: A theory of communication. In F.E.X. Dance (Ed.), *Human communication theory: Comparative essays* (pp. 61–89). New York: Harper & Row.

Cronkhite, G. (1969). *Persuasion: Speech and behavioral change*. Indianapolis: Bobbs-Merrill.

Cronkhite, G. (1976). Effects of rater-concept scale interactions and use of different factoring procedures upon evaluative factor structure. *Human Communication Research, 2,* 316–329.

Cronkhite, G., & Liska, J. R. (1980). The judgment of communicant acceptability. In M. E. Roloff and G. R. Miller (Eds.), *Persuasion: New directions in theory and research.* Beverly Hills, CA: Sage.

Crouch, W. W. (1980). The nonverbal communication literature: A book review. *Australian Soan: Journal of Human Communication, 7 & 8,* 1–11.

Cummings, H. W., & Renshaw, S. W. (1976). SLCA-II: *A computerized technique for the analysis of syntactic language behavior. Minneapolis: Burgess.*

Cummings, H. W. (1985). Microcomputing in Speech Communication: A Report of the Task Force on Use of Computers. Annandale, VA: Speech Communication Association.

Cushman, D. P. (1977). The rules perspective as a theoretical basis for the study of human communication. *Communication Quarterly, 25,* 30–45.

Cushman, D. P., & Pearce, W. B. (1977). Generality and necessity in three types of theory about human communication with special attention to rules theory. *Human Communication Research, 3,* 344–353.

Cushman, D. P., Valentinsen, B., & Dietrich, D. (1982). A rules theory of interpersonal relationships. In F.E.X. Dance (Ed.)., *Human communication theory: Comparative essays* (pp. 90–119). New York: Harper & Row.

Cushman, D. P., & Whiting, G. (1972). An approach to communication theory: Towards consensus on rules. *Journal of Communication, 22,* 217–238.

Darnell, D. K. (1966). Concept scale interaction in the semantic differential. *Journal of Communication, 16,* 104–115.

Darwin, C. (1965). *The expression of the emotions in man and animals.* Chicago: University of Chicago Press. (Original work published 1872).

Davidson, R. J., & Fox, N. A. (1982). Asymmetrical brain activity discriminates between positive and negative stimuli in human infants. *Science, 218,* 1235–1237.

Davies, P. M., & Coxon, A.P.M. (Eds.). (1982). *Key texts in multidimensional scaling.* Exeter, NH: Heinemann Educational Books.

Davis, M. (1975). *Understanding body movement: An annotated bibliography.* New York: Arno.

Davis, M. (1979). *The state of the art: Past and present trends in body movement research.* New York: Academic Press.

Dawes, R. M. (1972). *Fundamentals of attitude measurement.* New York: John Wiley.

Delbruck, M (1986) *Mind from matter.* Palo Alto, CA: Blackwell Scientific Publications.

de Vaus, D. A. (1986). Surveys in social research. London: George Allen & Unwin.

Dick, W., & Hagerty, N. (1971). *Topics in measurement: Reliability and validity.* New York: McGraw-Hill.

Dindia, K. (1982). Reciprocity of self-disclosure: A sequential analysis. In M. Burgoon (Ed.), *Communication yearbook, 6* (pp. 506–528). Beverly Hills, CA: Sage.

Donaghy, W. C. (1980). *Our silent language: An introduction to nonverbal communication.* Dubuque, IA: Gorsuch Scarisbrick.

Donaghy, W. C. (1984). Data collection and analysis approaches in nonverbal behavior research. In A. Wolfgang (Ed.), *Nonverbal behavior: Perspectives, applications, intercultural insights* (pp. 253–315). New York: C. J. Hogrefe.

Donaghy, W. C., & Kohler, R. R. (1984, November). *Analyzing nonverbal behavior of stutterers and nonstutterers*. Paper presented at the annual meeting of the American Speech-Language-Hearing Association, San Francisco, CA.

Donohue, W. A. (1981). Analyzing negotiation tactics: Development of a negotiation interact system. *Human Communication Research, 7*, 273–287.

Doob, L. W. (1947). The behavior of attitudes. *Psychological Review, 54*, 135–156.

Druckman, D., Rizelle, R. M., & Baxter, J. C. (1982). *Nonverbal communication: Surveys, theory, and research*. Beverly Hills, CA: Sage.

Dubin, R. (1969). *Theory building*. New York: Free Press.

Dubin, R. (1978). *Theory Building* (Rev. ed.). New York: Free Press.

Duffy, E. (1957). The psychological significance of the concept of "arousal" or "activation." *Psychological Review, 64*, 265–275.

Duffy, E. (1962). *Activation and Behavior*. New York: Wiley.

Eadie, W. P., & Paulson, J. W. (1984). Communicator attitudes, communicator style, and communication competence. *Western Journal of Speech Communication, 48*, 390–407.

Edwards, A. L. (1957). *Techniques of attitude scale construction*. New York: Appleton-Century-Crofts.

Edwards, A. L., & Kenney, K. C. (1946). A comparison of the Thurstone and Likert techniques of attitude scale construction. *Journal of Applied Psychology, 30*, 72–83.

Ekman, P. (1957). A methodological discussion of nonverbal behavior. *Journal of Psychology, 43*, 141–149.

Ekman, P. (1972). Universals and cultural differences in facial expressions of emotion. In J. Cole (Ed.), *Nebraska symposium on motivation* (Vol. 19, pp. 207–282). Lincoln: University of Nebraska.

Ekman, P. (1973). Cross-cultural studies of facial expression. In P. Ekman (Ed.), *Darwin and facial expression: A century of research in review*. New York: Academic Press.

Ekman, P. (1977). Biological and cultural contributions to body and facial movement. In J. Blacking (Ed.), *Anthropology of the body* (pp. 39–84). London: Academic Press.

Ekman, P. (1978). Facial expression. In A. W. Siegman & S. Feldstein (Eds.), *Nonverbal behavior and communication* (pp. 97–116). Hillsdale, NJ: Lawrence Erlbaum.

Ekman, P. (1980). Asymmetry in facial expression. *Science, 209*, 833–834.

Ekman, P. (1981). Mistakes when deceiving. *Annals of the New York Academy of Sciences, 364*, 269–278.

Ekman, P. (1982). Methods for measuring facial action. In K. R. Scherer & P. Ekman (Eds.), *Handbook of methods in nonverbal behavior research* (pp. 45–90). Cambridge: Cambridge University Press.

Ekman, P. (1984). Expression and the nature of emotion. In K. Scherer & P. Ekman (Eds.), *Approaches to emotion* (pp. 319–343). New York: Erlbaum.

Ekman, P. (1985). *Telling lies: Clues to deceit in the marketplace, politics, and marriage*. New York: Norton.

Ekman, P., & Friesen, W. V. (1969a). A tool for the analysis of motion picture film or video tape. *American Psychologist, 24*, 240–243.

Ekman, P., & Friesen, W. V. (1969b). Nonverbal leakage and clues to deception. *Psychiatry, 32*, 88–106.

Ekman, P., & Friesen, W. V. (1971). Constants across cultures in the face and emotion. *Journal of Personality and Social Psychology, 17*, 124–129.

Ekman, P., & Friesen, W. V. (1972). Hand movements. *Journal of Communication, 22,* 353–374.

Ekman, P., & Friesen, W. V. (1974). Detecting deception from the body or face. *Journal of Personality and Social Psychology, 29,* 288–298.

Ekman, P., & Friesen, W. V. (1975). *Unmasking the face.* Englewood Cliffs, NJ: Prentice-Hall.

Ekman, P., & Friesen, W. V. (1976). Measuring facial movement. *Environmental Psychology and Nonverbal Behavior, 1,* 56–75.

Ekman, P., & Friesen, W. V. (1978a). *Facial action coding system: Full training materials.* Palo Alto, CA: Consulting Psychologists.

Ekman, P., & Friesen, W. V. (1978b). *Facial action coding system: Manual.* Palo Alto, CA: Consulting Psychologists.

Ekman, P., & Friesen, W. V. (1978c). *Facial action coding system: Investigator's guide* (Parts 1 & 2). Palo Alto, CA: Consulting Psychologists.

Ekman, P., & Friesen, W. V. (1982). Felt, false and miserable smiles. *Journal of Nonverbal Behavior, 6,* 238–252.

Ekman, P., & Friesen, W. V. (1986). A new pan-cultural facial expression of emotion. *Motivation and Emotion, 10,* 159–168.

Ekman, P., Friesen, W. V., & Ancoli, S. (1980). Facial signs of emotional experience. *Journal of Personality and Social Psychology, 39,* 1125–1134.

Ekman, P., Friesen, W. V., & Ellsworth, P. (Eds.). (1972). *Emotion in the human face: Guidelines for research and an integration of findings.* New York: Pergamon. (2nd ed., P. Ekman [Ed.], Cambridge: Cambridge University Press, 1982).

Ekman, P., Friesen, W. V., O'Sullivan, M., Scherer, K. (1980). Relative importance of face, body, and speech in judgments of personality and affect. *Journal of Personality and Social Psychology, 38,* 270–277.

Ekman, P., Friesen, W. V., & Scherer, K. (1976). Body movement and voice pitch in deceptive interaction. *Semiotica, 16,* 23–27.

Ekman, P., Friesen, W. V., & Simons, R. C. (1985). Is the startle reaction an emotion? *Journal of Personality and Social Psychology, 49,* 1416–1426.

Ekman, P., Friesen, W. V., & Taussig, T. (1969). Vid-R and SCAN: Tools and methods for the automated analysis of visual records. In G. Gerbner, O. Holsti, K. Krippendorf, W. Paisley, & P. Stone (Eds.), *Content analysis.* New York: John Wiley.

Ekman, P., Friesen, W. A., & Tomkins, S. (1971). Facial affect scoring technique (FAST): A first validity study. *Semiotica, 3,* 37–38.

Ekman, P., Hager, J. C., & Friesen, W. V. (1981). Symmetry and the nature of facial action. *Psychophysiology, 18,* 101–106.

Ekman, P., Levenson, R. W., & Friesen, W. V. (1983). Autonomic nervous system activity distinguishes among emotions. *Science, 221,* 1208–1210.

Ekman, P., & Oster, H. (1979). Facial expressions of emotion. *Annual Review of Psychology, 30,* 527–554.

Ekman, P., Roper, G., & Hager, J. C. (1980). Deliberate facial movement. *Development, 51,* 267–271.

Ekman, P., Sorenson, E. R., & Friesen, W. V. (1969). Pan-cultural elements in facial displays of emotions. *Science, 164,* 86–88.

Ellgring, H. (1984). The study of nonverbal behavior and its applications: State of the art in Europe. In A. Wolfgang (Ed.), *Nonverbal behavior: Perspectives, applications, intercultural insights* (pp. 115–138). New York: C. J. Hogrefe.

Ellingson, R. J. (1956). Brain waves and problems of psychology. *Psychological Bulletin,* *53,* 1–34.

Ellis, D., & Fisher, B. A. (1975). Phases of conflict in small group development: A Markov analysis. *Human Communication Research, 1,* 195–212.

Ellis, D. G., Fisher, B. A., Drecksel, C. L., Hock, D. D., & Wertel, W. S. (1976). *A system for analyzing relational communication.* Unpublished manuscript, Department of Communication, University of Utah.

Ellyson, S. L., & Dovidio, J. F. (Eds.). (1985). *Power, dominance, and nonverbal behavior.* New York: Springer-Verlag.

Emery, D. (1982). Marital interaction: Perceptions and behavioral implications of control. In M. Burgoon (Ed.), *Communication yearbook, 6* (pp. 489–505). Beverly Hills, CA: Sage.

Emmert, P. (1970). Attitude scales. In P. Emmert and W. D. Brooks (Eds.), *Methods of research in communication.* Boston: Houghton Mifflin.

Emmert, P. (1986). Credibility: Perception or process? Paper presented at Speech Communication Association Conference, Chicago.

Emmert, P., & Brooks, W. D. (Eds.). (1970). *Methods of reseach in communication,* Boston: Houghton Mifflin.

Emmert, P., & McDermott, P. J. (1976). Evaluative response behaviors: A message-centered suggestion for communication theory. Paper presented at the Western Speech Communication Association Conference, San Francisco.

Erickson, P. M., & Rogers, L. E. (1973). New procedures for analyzing relational communication. *Family Process, 12,* 245–267.

Feldman, R. S, (Ed.). (1982). *Development of nonverbal behavior in children.* New York: Springer-Verlag.

Ferguson, G. A. (1981). *Statistical analysis in psychology and education* (5th ed.). New York: McGraw-Hill.

Ferguson, L. W. (1939). The requirements of an adequate attitude scale. *Psychological Bulletin, 36,* 665–673.

Festinger, L., & Maccoby, N. (1964). On resistance to persuasive communication. *Journal of Abnormal and Social Psychology, 68,* 359–366.

Fisch, H. U., Frey, S., & Hirsbrunner, H. P. (1983). Analyzing nonverbal behavior in depression. *Journal of Abnormal Psychology, 92,* 307–318.

Fisher, B. A. (1970). Decision emergence: Phases in group decision making. *Speech Monographs, 37,* 53–66.

Fisher, B. A. (1983). Differential effects of sexual composition and interaction context on interaction patterns in dyads. *Human Communication Research, 9,* 225–238.

Fisher, B. A., & Hawes, L. C. (1971). An interact system model. Generating a grounded theory of small groups. *Quarterly Journal of Speech, 57,* 444–453.

Flamer, S. (1983). Assessment of the multitrait-multimethod matrix validity of Likert scales via confirmatory factor analysis. *Multivariate Behavioral Research, 18,* 275–308.

Flanders, N. A. (1960). *Interaction analysis in the classroom: A manual for observers.* Ann Arbor: University of Michigan Press.

Fleiss, J. L. (1971). Measuring nominal scale agreement among many raters. *Psychological Bulletin, 76,* 378–382.

Fleiss, J. L. (1981). *Statistical methods for rates and proportions.* New York: John Wiley.

Folger, J. P., Hewes, D., & Poole, M. S. (1984). Coding social interaction. In B. Dervin & M. Voight (Eds.), *Progress in the communication sciences* (pp. 115–161). New York: Ablex.

Folger, J. P., & Poole, M. S. (1982). Relational coding schemes: The question of validity. In M. Burgoon (Ed.), *Communication yearbook, 5* (pp. 235–247). New Brunswick, NJ: Transaction Books.

Folger, J. P., & Puck, S. (1976). *Coding relational communication: A question approach.* Paper presented at the International Communication Association Convention, Portland, Oregon.

Folger, J. P., & Sillars, A. (1980). Relational coding and perceptions of dominance. In B. Morse & L. Phelps (Eds.), *Interpersonal communication: A relational perspective* (pp. 322–333). Minneapolis: Burgess.

Fowler, F. J., Jr. (1984). *Survey research methods.* Beverly Hills, CA: Sage.

Frankel, R. M., & Beckman, H. B. (1982). Impact: An interaction-based method for preserving and analyzing clinical interactions. In L. S. Pettegrew, P. Arnston, D. Bush, & K. Zoppi (Eds.), *Explorations in provider and patient interaction* (pp. 71–86). Nashville: Humana.

Frye, J. K. (1980). *FIND: Frye's index to nonverbal data.* Duluth, MN: University of Minnesota Computer Center.

Frey, S. (1973). A method for the assessment of body movement variability. In M. von Cranach & J. Vine. (Eds.), *Social communication and movement* (pp. 389–418). London: Academic Press.

Frey, S. (1976). The assessment of similarity. In M. von Cranach (Ed.), *Methods of inference from animal to human behavior.* The Hague: Mouton.

Frey, S. (1983). Unexplored dimensions of human communication. In 1983 Annual Report Standard Elektrik Lorenz AG. *He want to overcome distances* (pp. 63–66). Stuttgart: Standard Elektrik Lorenz.

Frey, S. (1984). *Die nonverbale kommunikation.* Stuttgart: Standard Elektrik Lorenz.

Frey, S., & Hirsbrunner, H. P. (1983a). *Software manual for the analysis of nonverbal and verbal behavior in communication research.* Research Reports from the Department of Psychology. Berne, Switzerland: University of Berne.

Frey, S., & Hirsbrunner, H. P. (1983b). *Software manual for the analysis of nonverbal and verbal behavior in communication research* (Rev. ed.). Research Reports from the Department of Psychology. Berne, Switzerland: University of Berne.

Frey, S., Hirsbrunner, H. P., & Bieri-Florin, A. (1979). Vom bildschirm zum datenprotokoll: Das problem der rohdatengewinnung bei der untersuchung nichtverbaler interaktion. *Zeitschrift fur Semiotik, 1,* 193–209.

Frey, S., Hirsbrunner, H. P., Florin, A., Daw, W., & Crawford, R. (1983). A unified approach to the investigation of nonverbal and verbal behavior in communication research. In W. Doise & S. Moscovici (Eds.), *Current issues in European social psychology.* Cambridge: Cambridge University Press.

Frey, S., Hirsbrunner, H. P., & Jorns, U. (1982). Time-Series-Notation: A coding principle for the unified assessment of speech and movement in communication research. In E. W. B. Hess-Luttich (Ed.), *Multimedial communication: Semiotic problems of its notation* (pp. 30–58). Tubingen: Narr.

Frey, S., Hirsbrunner, H. P., Pool, J., & Daw, W. (1981). Das berner system zur untersuchung nonverbaler interaktion: I. Die erhebung des rohdatenprotokolls. In P. Winkler (Ed.), *Methoden der analyse von face-to-face situationen* (pp. 203–236). Stuttgart: Metzler.

Frey, S., Jorns, U., & Daw, W. A. (1980). A systematic description and analysis of nonverbal interaction between doctors and patients in a psychiatric interview. In S. A.

Corson (Ed.), *Ethology and nonverbal communication in mental health* (pp. 231–258). New York: Pergamon.

Frey, S., & Pool, J. (1976). *A new approach to the analysis of visible behavior.* Research Reports from the Department of Psychology. Berne, Switzerland: University of Berne.

Galin, D., & Ornstein, R. (1972). Lateral specialization of cognitive mode: An EEG study. *Psychophysiology, 9,* 412–418.

Gardner, E. (1975). *Fundamentals of neurology.* Philadelphia: Saunders.

Geddes, L. A. (1972). *Electrodes and the measurement of bio electric events.* New York: Wiley-Interscience.

Gerbner, G., Gross, L., Morgan, M., & Signorielli, N. (1980, Summer). The "mainstreaming" of America: Violence profile no. 11. *Journal of Communication, 30,* 10–29.

Gerbner, G., Holsti, O. R., Krippendorff, K., Paisley, W. J., & Stone, P. J. (Eds.). (1969). *The analysis of communication content: Developments in scientific theories and computer techniques.* New York: John Wiley.

Gevins, A. S., Zeitlan, E. M., Yingling, C. D., Doyle, J. C., Dedon, M. F., & Schaffer, R. E. (1979). EEG-patterns during cognitive tasks I. Methodology and analysis of complex behaviors. *Electro Encephalography and Clinical Neuropsychology, 47,* 693–703.

Giannitripanni, D. (1966). Electroencephalographic differences between resting and mental multiplication. *Perceptual and Motor Skills, 22,* 399–405.

Glaser, B. G., & Strauss, A. L. (1967). *The discovery of grounded theory: Strategies for qualitative research.* Chicago: Aldine.

Gorden, Raymond. (1977). *Unidimensional scaling of social variables.* New York: Free Press.

Goss, B. (1982). *Processing communication.* Belmont, CA: Wadsworth.

Gottman, J. M. (1979a). Marital interaction: Experimental investigations. New York: Academic Press.

Gottman, J. M. (1979b). Time-series analysis of continuous data in dyads. In M. E. Lamb, S. J. Sumoi, & G. G. Stephenson (Eds.), *Social interaction analysis: Methodological issues* (pp. 207–229). Madison: University of Wisconsin Press.

Gottman, J. M. (1980). Analyzing for sequential connection and assessing interobserver reliability for the sequential analysis of observational data. Behavioral Assessment, *2,* 361–368.

Gottman, J. M. (1981). *Time-series analysis: A comprehensive introduction for social scientists.* New York: Cambridge University Press.

Gottman, J. M., & Bakeman, R. (1979). The sequential analysis of observational data. In M. E. Lamb, S. J. Suomi, & G. R. Stephenson (Eds.), *Social interaction analysis: Methodological issues* (pp. 185–206). Madison: University of Wisconsin Press.

Gottman, J. M., Markman, H., & Notarius, C. (1977). The topography of marital conflict: A sequential analysis of verbal and nonverbal behavior. *Journal of Marriage and the Family, 39.* 461–477.

Gottman, J. M., Rose, F., & Mettetal, G. (1982). Time-series analysis of social interaction data. In T. Field & A. Fogel (Eds.), *Emotion and interactions* (pp. 262–289). Hillsdale, NJ: Lawrence Erlbaum.

Gouran, D., & Whitehead, J. (1971). An investigation of ratings and discussion statements by participants and observers. *Central States Speech Journal, 21,* 263–268.

Graber, D. A. (1985). Approaches to content analysis of television news programs. *Communications: The European Journal of Communication, 11 (2),* 25–36.

Greenfield, N. S., Sternbach, R. A. (1972). *Handbook of psychophysiology.* New York: Holt, Rinehart and Winston.

Greenwald, A. G. (1968). Cognitive learning, cognitive response to persuasion and attitude change. In A. G. Greenwald, T. C. Brock, & T. M. Ostrom (Eds.), *Psychological Foundations of Attitudes.* New York: Academic Press.

Grings, W. W., & Dawson, M. E. (1978). *Emotions and bodily responses. A psychophysiological approach.* New York: Academic Press.

Guetzkow, H. (1950). Unitizing and categorizing problems in coding qualitative data. *Journal of Clinical Psychology, 6,* 47–58.

Guilford, J. P. (1954). *Psychometric methods* (2nd ed.). New York: McGraw-Hill.

Guttman, L. L. (1944). A basis for scaling qualitative data. *American Sociological Review, 9,* 139–150.

Guttman, L. (1954). A basis for analyzing test reliability. *Psychometrika, 10,* 255–282.

Hager, J. C. (1982). Asymmetries in facial expression. In P. Ekman (Ed.), *Emotion in the human face* (2nd ed., pp. 318–352). Cambridge: Cambridge University Press.

Hager, J. C., & Ekman, P. (1985). The asymmetry of facial actions is inconsistent with models of hemisphere specialization. *Psychophysiology, 22,* 307–318.

Haley, J. (1963). Marriage therapy. *Archives of General Psychiatry, 8,* 213–224.

Hall, J. A. (1984). *Nonverbal sex differences: Communication accuracy and expressive style.* Baltimore: Johns Hopkins University Press.

Handel, W. (1979). Normative expectations and the emergence of meaning as solutions to problems: Convergence of structural and interactionist views. *American Journal of Sociology, 84,* 855–881.

Harper, R. G., Wiens, A. N., & Matarozzo, J. D. (1978). *Nonverbal communication: The state of the art.* New York: John Wiley.

Harré, R. (1983). *An introduction to the logic of the sciences.* London: Macmillan.

Harré, R., & Secord, P. F. (1973). *The explanation of social behavior.* Totowa, NJ: Littlefield, Adams.

Harris, R. J. (1975). *A primer of multivariate statistics.* New York: Academic Press.

Harrison, R. P. (1973). Nonverbal communication. In I. de Sola Pool, F. W. Frey, W. Schramm, N. Maccoby, & E. B. Parker (Eds.), *Handbook of communication.* Chicago: Rand McNally.

Harrison, R. P. (1974). *Beyond words.* Englewood Cliffs, NJ: Prentice-Hall.

Hart, R. P. (1984). *Verbal style and the presidency.* Orlando FL.: Academic Press.

Hart, R. P. (1985). Systematic analysis of political discourse: The development of diction. In K. S. Sanders, L. L. Kaid, & D. Nimmo (Eds.), *Political communication yearbook 1984* (pp. 97–134). Carbondale, IL: Southern Illinois University Press.

Hartmann, D. P. (1977). Considerations in the choice of interobserver reliability estimates. *Journal of Applied Behavior Analysis, 10,* 103–106.

Hartmann, D. P. (1982). Assessing the dependability of observational data. In D. P. Hartmann (Ed.), *Using observers to study behavior: New directions for methodology of social and behavioral science* (No. 14, pp. 51–65). San Francisco: Jossey-Bass.

Hartup, W. W. (1979). Levels of analysis in the study of social interaction: An historical perspective. In M. E. Lamb, S. J. Suomi, & G. R. Stephenson (Eds.), *Social interaction analysis: Methodological issues* (pp. 11–32). Madison: University of Wisconsin Press.

Hatfield, J. D., & Weider-Hatfield, D. (1978). The comparative utility of three types of behavioral units for interaction analysis. *Communication Monograhs, 45,* 44–50.

Hawes, L. C. (1972). Development and application of an interview coding system. *Central States Speech Journal, 23,* 92–99.

Hawes, L. C. (1975). *Pragmatics of analoguing: Theory and model construction in communication.* Reading, MA: Addison-Wesley.

Hawes, L. C., & Foley, J. (1973). A Markov analysis of interview communication. *Communication Monographs, 40,* 208–219.

Helfrich, H., Standke, R., & Scherer, K. R. (1984). Vocal indicators of psychoactive drug abuse. *Speech Communication, 3,* 245–252.

Helmstadter, G. C. (1964). *Principles of psychological measurement.* New York: Appleton-Century-Crofts.

Henley, N. M. (1977). *Body politics: Power, sex and nonverbal communication.* Englewood Cliffs, NJ: Prentice-Hall.

Heritage, J., & Atkinson, J. M. (1984). Introduction. In J. M. Atkinson & J. Heritage (Eds.). *Structures of social action: Studies in conversational analysis* (pp. 1–15). Cambridge: Cambridge University Press.

Herkimer, B. J. (1985). *Computer anxiety as state anxiety and time-on-task and their relationship to sex, age, previous experience, and typing ability.* Unpublished doctoral dissertation, University of Southern California.

Hertel, R. K. (1968). *The Markov modeling of experimentally induced marital conflict.* Unpublished doctoral dissertation, University of Michigan, Ann Arbor.

Heslin, R., & Patterson, M. L. (1982). *Nonverbal behavior and social psychology.* New York: Plenum.

Hewes, D. E. (1975). Finite stochastic modelling of communication processes. *Human Communication Research, 1,* 217–283.

Hewes, D. E. (1979). The sequential analysis of social interaction. *Quarterly Journal of Speech, 65,* 56–73.

Hewes, D. E., & Haight, L. R. (1979). The cross-situational consistency of communication behaviors: A preliminary investigation. *Communication Research, 6,* 243–270.

Heyman, R., & Shaw, M. (1978). Constructs of relationships. *Journal for the Theory of Social Behavior, 8,* 231–262.

Heyns, R. W., & Zander, A. F. (1953). Observation of group behavior. In L. Festinger & D. Katz (Eds.), *Research methods in the behavioral sciences* (pp. 381–417). New York: Dryden Press.

Hirsbrunner, H. P. (1979). *Sequel-analysis. Ein Zeitgenaues verfahren zur visiellen verlaufsanalyse des sprachsignals.* Berne, Switzerland: University of Berne.

Hirsbrunner, H. P., Florin, A., & Frey, S. (1981). Das berner system zur untersuchung nonverbaler interaktion: II. Die auswertung von zeitreihen visuell-auditiver information. In P. Winkler (Ed.), *Methoden der analyse von face-to-face situationen* (pp. 237–268). Stuttgart: Metzler.

Hirsbrunner, H. P., Frey, S., & Crawford, R. (1983). *Movement in human interaction: Description, parameter formation, and analysis.* Research Reports from the Department of Psychology. Berne, Switzerland: University of Berne.

Hirsbrunner, H. P., Frey, S., & Crawford, R. (in press). Movement in human interaction: Description, parameter formation, and analysis. In A. W. Siegman & S. Feldstein (Eds.), *Nonverbal behavior and communication* (2nd. ed.). Hillsdale, NJ: Lawrence Erlbaum.

Hoffman, R. J. (1976). A computerized approach for determining equal appearing interval attitude scales. *Behavior Research Methods and Instrumentation, 8,* 462.

Hollander, M. & Proschan, F. (1984). *The statistical exorcist: Dispelling statistics anxiety.* New York: Dekher.

Holbrook, M. B. (1977, December). More on content analysis in consumer research. *Journal of Consumer Research, 4,* 176, 177.

Hollenbeck, A. R. (1978). Problems of reliability in observational research. In G. P. Sackett (Ed.), *Observing behavior* (Vol. 2). *Data collection and analysis methods* (pp. 79–98). Baltimore: University Park Press.

Holsti, O. R. (1968). Content analysis. In G. Lindzey & E. Aronson (Eds.), *The handbook of social psychology.* (Vol. 3, pp. 596–692). Reading, MA: Addison-Wesley.

Holsti, O. R. (1969). *Content analysis for the social sciences and the humanities.* Reading, MA: Addison-Wesley.

Holt, R. W. (1981). *Theory, evidence, inference: A handbook on the scientific method.* Washington D.C.: University Press of America.

Homans, G. C. (1961). *Social behavior: Its elementary forms.* New York: Harcourt, Brace & World.

Hovland, C. I., Janis, I. L., & Kelley, H. H. (1953). *Communication and Persuasion.* New Haven, CT: Yale University Press.

Hovland, C. I., & Sherif, M. (1952). Judgmental phenomena and scales of attitude measurement: Item displacement in Thurstone scales. *Journal of Abnormal and Social Psychology, 47,* 822–832.

Hovland, C. I., & Sherif, M. (1961). *Social judgment.* New Haven, CT.: Yale University Press.

Howard, G. S. (1984). *Computer anxiety and other determinants of managers' attitudes toward the usefulness of microcomputers in management.* Unpublished doctoral dissertation, Kent State University.

Izard, C. E. (1977). *Human emotions.* New York: Plenum.

Izard, C. E., & Dougherty, L. M. (1981). Two complementary systems for measuring facial expressions in infants and children. In C. E. Izard (Ed.), *Measuring emotions in infants and children.* Cambridge: Cambridge University Press.

Izard, C. E., Kagan, J., & Zajonc, R. E. (Eds.). (1984). *Emotions, cognitions, and behavior.* New York: Cambridge University Press.

Jackson, D. D. (1959). Family interaction, family homeostasis, and some implications for conjoint family psychotherapy. In J. H. Masserman (Ed.), *Individual and family dynamics* (pp. 122–141). New York: Grune and Stratton.

Jackson, D. D. (1965). The study of family. *Family Process, 4,* 1–20.

Jackson-Beeck, M., & Kraus, S. (1980). Political communication theory and research: An overview 1978–1979. In D. Nimmo (Ed.), *Communication yearbook, 4* (449–465). New Brunswick, NJ: Transaction Books.

Janis, I. L., & Feshbach, S. (1953). Effects of fear-arousing communications. *Journal of Abnormal and Social Psychology, 48,* 78–92.

Jasper, H. H. (1958). Report of the committee on methods of clinical examination in electro encephalography. *Electro Encephalography and Clinical Neurophysiology. 10,* 370–375.

Johnson, S. M., & Bolstad, O. D. (1973). Methodological issues in naturalistic observation: Some problems and solutions for field research. In L. A. Hamerlynch, L. C. Handy, & E. J. Mash (Eds.). *Behavior change: Methodology, concepts, and practice* (pp. 7–67). Champaign, IL: Research Press.

Johnson, W. F., Emde, R. N., Scherer, K. R., & Klinnert, M.D. (1986). Recognition of emotion from verbal cues. *Archives of General Psychology, 43,* 280–283.

Jones, E. E., & Davis, K. E. (1965). From acts to dispositions. In L. Berkowitz (Ed.),

Advances in experimental social psychology (Vol. 2, pp. 219–256). New York: Academic Press.

Jones, E. E., Kanouse, D. E., Kelley, H. H., Nisbett, R. E., Valins, S., & Weiner, B. (Eds.). (1972). *Attribution: Perceiving the causes of behavior*. Morristown, NJ: General Learning Press.

Joslyn, R. A. (1980). The content of political spot ads. *Journalism Quarterly, 57*, 92–98.

Kachigan, S. K. (1986). *Statistical analysis*. New York: Radius Press.

Kaid, L. L., & Foote, J. (1985). How network television coverage of the President and Congress compare. *Journalism Quarterly, 62*, 59–65.

Kaplan, A. (1964). *The conduct of inquiry*. San Francisco: Chandler.

Kassarjian, H. H. (1977). Content analysis in consumer research. *Journal of Consumer Research, 4*, 8–18.

Katz, J. M. (1981). *Why don't you listen to what I'm saying?* Garden City, NY: Anchor.

Kelley, H. H. (1967). Attribution theory in social psychology. In D. Levine (Ed.), *Nebraska symposium on motivation* (Vol. 15, pp. 192–237). Lincoln: University of Nebraska Press.

Kemper, T. D. (1978). *A social interactional theory of emotions*. New York: John Wiley.

Kendon, A. (1981). Introduction: Current issues in the study of "nonverbal communication." In A. Kendon (Ed.), *Nonverbal communication, interaction, and gesture*. The Hague: Mouton.

Kendon, A. (1983). Gesture and speech: How they interact. In J. M. Wiemann & R. P. Harrison (Eds.), *Nonverbal interaction* (pp. 13–45). Beverly Hills, CA: Sage.

Kerlinger, F. N. (1964). *Foundations of behavioral research: Educational and psychological inquiry*. New York: Holt, Rinehart and Winston.

Kerlinger, F. N. (1973). *Foundations of behavioral research* (2nd ed.). New York: Holt, Rinehart and Winston.

Kerlinger, F. N. (1979). *Behavioral research: A conceptual approach*. New York: Holt, Rinehart and Winston.

Kerlinger, F. N. (1986). *Foundations of behavioral research* (3rd ed.). New York: Holt, Rinehart & Winston.

Key, M.R. (1977). *Nonverbal communication: A research guide and bibliography*. Metuchen, NJ: Scarecrow.

Key, M. R. (Ed.). (1980). *The relationship of verbal and nonverbal communication*. New York: Mouton.

Kibler, R. J. (1970). Basic communication research considerations. In P. Emmert & W. D. Brooks (Eds.), *Methods of research in communication* (pp. 9–49). Boston: Houghton Mifflin.

Kidder, L. H. (1981). Selltiz, Wrightsman and Cook's *Research methods in social relations*. New York: Holt, Rinehart and Winston.

Kirk, J., & Miller, M. L. (1986). *Reliability and validity in qualitative research*. Beverly Hills, CA: Sage.

Kirk, R. E. (1984). *Elementary statistics* (2nd ed.). Belmont, CA: Brooks/Cole.

Knapp, M. L. (1978a). *Nonverbal communication in human interaction*. New York: Holt, Rinehart & Winston.

Knapp, M. L. (1984). The study of nonverbal behavior vis-a-vis human communication theory. In A. Wolfgang (Ed.), *Nonverbal behavior: Perspectives, applications, intercultural insights* (pp. 15–40). New York: C. J. Hogrefe.

Knapp, M. L., Wiemann, J. M., & Daly, J. A. (1978). Nonverbal communication: Issues and appraisal. *Human Communication Research, 4*, 271–280.

Kohen, J. A. S. (1975). The development of reciprocal self-disclosure in opposite-sex interaction. *Journal of Counseling Psychology, 22,* 404–410.

Koocher, G. P. (1977). Bathroom behavior and human dignity. *Psychological Bulletin, 29,* 725–739.

Krass, R. M., Apple, W., Morency, N., Wenzel, C., & Winton, W. (1981). Verbal, vocal, and visible factors in judgments of another's affect. *Journal of Personality and Social Psychology, 40,* 312–320.

Krause, R. (1980). Stuttering and nonverbal communication: Investigations about affect inhibition and stuttering. In H. Giles, P. Robinson, & P. Smith (Eds.), *Language: Social psychological perspectives* (pp. 261–266). New York: Pergamon.

Krause, R. (1981). A social psychological approach to the study of stuttering. In A. Fraser & K. R. Scherer (Eds.), *A social psychological approach to the study of stuttering.* Cambridge: Cambridge University Press.

Krippendorff, K. (1980). *Content Analysis: An introduction to its methodology.* Beverly Hills, CA: Sage.

Krueger, D. L. (1985). Communication patterns and egalitarian decision making in dual-career couples. *Western Journal of Speech Communication, 49,* 126–145.

Kruskal, J., & Wish, M. (1980). *Multidimensional scaling.* Beverly Hills, CA: Sage.

Kuhn, T. S. (1970). *The structure of scientific revolutions.* Chicago: University of Chicago Press.

Labov, W., & Fanshel, D. (1977). *Therapeutic discourse: Psychotherapy as conversation.* New York: Academic Press.

Lacey, J. I. (1967). Somatic response patterning and stress: Some revisions of activation theory. In M. H. Appleby and R. Trunbull (Eds.), *Psychological stress.* New York: Appleton-Century-Crofts.

Ladd, D. R., Silverman, K., Tolkmitt, F., Bergmann, G., & Scherer, K. R. (1985). Evidence for the independent function of intonation contour type, voice quality, and F_0 range in signalling speaker affect. *Journal of the Acoustical Society of America, 78,* 435–444.

LaFrance, M., & Mayo, C. (1978). *Moving bodies.* Monterey, CA: Brooks/Cole.

Landis, C., & Hunt, W. A. (1939). *The startle pattern.* New York: Farrar, Straus & Giroux.

Langs, R. J.(1983). *Unconscious communication in everyday life.* New York: Aronson.

Laswell, H. D., & Associates. (1942). The politically significant content of the press: Coding procedures. *Journalism Quarterly, 19,* 12–23.

Laswell, H. D., Leites, N., & Associates. (1949). *Language of politics.* New York: George W. Stewart.

Laver, J. (1980). *The phonetic description of voice quality.* Cambridge: Cambridge University Press.

Lazarsfeld, P. T. (1961). Notes on the history of quantification in sociology-trends, sources and problems. In H. Woolf (Ed.), *Quantification* (pp. 147–203). Indianapolis: Bobbs-Merrill.

Lazarsfeld, P., & Barton, A. (1969). Qualitative measurement: A codification of techniques for the social sciences. In L. Krimmerman (Ed.), *The nature and scope of the social sciences* (pp. 514–539). Englewood Cliffs, NJ: Prentice-Hall.

Lazarus, R. S. (1982). Thoughts on the relations between emotion and cognition. *American Psychologist, 37,* 1019–1024.

Leathers, D. G. (1976). *Nonverbal communication systems.* Boston: Allyn & Bacon.

Leedy, P. D. (1980). *Practical research: Planning and design* (2nd ed.). New York: Macmillan.

Leik, R. K., & Meeker, B. F. (1975). *Mathematical sociology*. Englewood Cliffs, NJ: Prentice-Hall.

Lemon, N. (1973). *Attitudes and their measurement*. New York: Halsted Press.

LeResche, L. (1982). Facial behavior in pain: A study of candid photographs. *Journal of Nonverbal Behavior, 7*, 46–56.

Levinson, S. C. (1983). *Pragmatics*. Cambridge: Cambridge University Press.

Lichty, L. W., & Bailey, G. A. (1978). Reading the wind: Reflections on content analysis of broadcast news. In W. Adams & F. Schreibman (Eds.), *Television network news: Issues in content research* (pp. 111–137). Washington, D.C.: Television and Politics Study Program, George Washington University.

Likert, R. (1932). A technique for the measurement of attitudes. *Archives of Psychology, 140*, 1–55.

Littlejohn, S. W., & Jabusch, D. M. (1987). *Persuasive transactions*. Glenview, IL: Scott, Foresman.

Lindsey, D. B. (1951). Emotion. In S. S. Stevens (Ed.), *Handbook of experimental psychology*. New York: John Wiley.

Lodge, M. (1981). *Magnitude scaling: Quantitative measurement of opinions*. Beverly Hills, CA: Sage.

Lull, J., & Cappella, J. (1981). Slicing the attitude pie: A new approach to attitude measurement. *Communication Quarterly, 29*, 67–80.

Luria, A. R. (1973). *The working brain: An introduction to neuropsychology*. New York: Basic Books.

Lustig, M. W. (1986). Theorizing about human communicaton. *Communication Quarterly, 34*, 451–459.

Mabry, E. A. (1975). An instrument for assessing content themes in group interaction. *Speech Monographs, 42*, 292–297.

Malendro, L. A., & Barker, L. (1983). *Nonverbal communication*. Reading, MA: Addison-Wesley.

Manderscheid, R. W., Rae, D. S., McCarrick, A. K., & Silbergeld, S. (1982). A stochastic model of relational control in dyadic interaction. *American Sociological Review, 47*, 62–75.

Maranell, G. M. (Ed.). (1974). *Scaling: A sourcebook for behavioral scientists*. Chicago: Aldine.

Mark, R. (1971). Coding communication at the relational level. *Journal of Communication, 21*, 221–232.

Martin, I., & Venables, P. H. (Eds.). (1980). *Techniques in psycholophysiology*. New York: Wiley.

Martindale, C. (1984). Newspaper and wire service leads in coverage of the 1980 campaign. *Journalism Quarterly, 61*, 339–345.

Maslach, C. (1979a). Cover response patterns during the processing of language stimuli. *Interamerican Journal of Psychology, 3*, 289–299.

Maslach, C. (1979b). Emotional consequences of arousal without reason. In C. E. Izard (Ed.), *Emotions in personality and psychopathology*. New York: Plenum.

Mayo, C., & Henley, N. M. (Eds.). (1981). *Gender and nonverbal behavior*. New York: Springer-Verlag.

McCarrick, A. K., Manderscheild, R. W., & Silbergeld, S. (1981). Gender differences in competition and dominance during married-couples group therapy. *Social Psychology Quarterly, 44,* 164–167.

McCombs, M. E., & Shaw, D. L. (1972). The agenda-setting function of the mass media. *Public Opinion Quarterly, 36,* 176–187.

McCroskey, J. C. (1966). Scales for the measurement of ethos. *Speech Monographs, 33,* 65–72.

McCroskey, J. C., (1978). Validity of the PRCA as an index of oral communication apprehension. *Communication Monographs, 45,* 192–203.

McCroskey, J. C. (1982). Oral communication apprehension: A reconceptualization. In M. Burgoon (Ed.), *Communication yearbook, 6* (pp. 136–170). Beverly Hills, CA: Sage.

McCroskey, J. C. (1984). The communication apprehension perspective. In J. A. Daly & J. C. McCroskey (Eds.), *Avoiding communication* (pp. 13–38). Beverly Hills, CA: Sage.

McCroskey, J. C., & McCain, T. A. (1974). The measurement of interpersonal attraction. *Speech Monographs, 41,* 261–266.

McCroskey, J. C., Prichard, S., & Arnold, W. E. (1967). Attitude intensity and the neutral point on semantic differential scales. *Public Opinion Quarterly, 31,* 642–645.

McGuigan, F. J. (1979). *Psychophysiological measurement of covert behavior: A guide for the laboratory.* Hillsdale, NJ: Lawrence Erlbaum.

McGuigan, F. J., & Baily, S. C. (1969). Covert response patterns during the processing of language stimuli. *Interamerican Journal of Psychology, 3,* 289–299.

McGuigan, F. J., Keller, B., & Stanton, E. (1964). Covert language responses during silent reading. *Journal of Education Psychology, 55,* 339–343.

McGuigan, F. J., & Rodger, W. I. (1968). Effects of auditory stimulation on covert oral behavior during silent reading. *Journal of Experimental Psychology, 76,* 649–655.

McIver, J. P., and Carmines, E. G. (1981). *Unidimensional scaling.* Beverly Hills, CA: Sage.

McLaughlin, M., & Cody, M. (1982). Awkward silences: Behavioral antecedents and consequences of the conversational lapse. *Human Communication Research, 8,* 299–316.

McPhee, R. D., & Poole, M. S. (1982). Mathematical modeling in communication research: An overview. In M. Burgoon (Ed.), *Communication yearbook, 5* (pp. 159–161). New Brunswick, NJ: Transaction Books.

Mehrabian, A. (1972). *Nonverbal communication.* Chicago: Aldine-Atherton.

Meister, D. (1985). *Behavioral analysis and measurement methods.* New York: John Wiley.

Merton, R. K. (1946). *Mass persuasion: The social psychology of a war bond drive.* New York: Harper.

Mesulam, M., & Perry, J. (1972). The diagnosis of love-sickness: Experimental psychophysiology without the polygraph. *Psychophysiology, 9,* 546–551.

Meyer, D., Hecht, M., & Arnold, W. (1987). *Empathic listening, comforting behavior, and other orientation.* Paper presented at the International Listening Association meeting in New Orleans.

Middlemist, R. D., Knowles, E. S., & Matter, C. F. (1977). Personal space invasion in the laboratory: Suggestive evidence for arousal. *Journal of Personality and Social Psychology, 35,* 122–124.

Millar, F. E., & Rogers, L. E. (1975). A relational approach to interpersonal communication. In G. R. Miller (Ed.), *Explorations in interpersonal communication* (pp. 3–11). Beverly Hills, CA: Sage.

Miller, G. A. (1956). The magic number seven, plus or minus two: Some limits on our capacity for processing information. *Psychological Review, 53,* 81–97.

Miller, G. A. (1967). The magic number seven, plus or minus two: Some limits on our capacity for processing information. In G. A. Miller, *The psychology of communication* (pp. 14–44). Baltimore: Penguin Books.

Miller, G. R. (1983). Taking stock of a discipline. *Journal of Communication, 33,* 31–41.

Miller, G. R., & Berger, C. R. (1978). On keeping the faith in matters scientific. *Western Journal of Speech Communication, 42,* 44–57.

Miller, G. R., & Nicholson, H. E. (1976). *Communication inquiry: A perspective on a process.* Reading, MA: Addison-Wesley.

Mitchell, R. E. (1967). The use of content analysis for explanatory studies. *Public Opinion Quarterly, 21,* 230–241.

Monge, P. R. (1973). Theory construction in the study of communication: The system paradigm. *The Journal of Communication, 23,* 5–16.

Monge, P. R., Farace, R. V., Eisenberg, E. M., Miller, K. I., & White, L. L. (1984). The process of studying process in organizational communication. *Journal of Communication, 34,* 22–43.

Morris, D. (1977). *Manwatching: A field guide to human behavior.* New York: Henry N. Abrams.

Morris, D., Collett, P., Marsh, P., & O'Shaughnessy, M. (1979). *Gestures.* New York: Stein & Day.

Morris, C. W. (1938). Foundations of the theory of signs. In O. Neurath, R. Carnap, & C. W. Morris (Eds.), *International encyclopedia of unified science* (Vol. 1, no. 2, pp. 77–137). Chicago: University of Chicago Press.

Neale, J. M., & Liebert, R. M. (1980). *Science and behavior: An introduction to methods of research* (2nd ed.). Englewood Cliffs, NJ: Prentice-Hall.

Noller, P. (1984). *Nonverbal communication and marital interaction.* Oxford: Pergamon.

Nunnally, J. C., Jr. (1967). *Psychometric theory.* New York: McGraw-Hill.

Nunnally, J. C., Jr. (1978). *Psychometric theory* (2nd ed.). New York: McGraw-Hill.

Ochs, E. (1979). Transcription as theory. In E. Ochs & B. Schieffelin (Eds.), *Developmental pragmatics* (pp. 43–72). New York: Academic Press.

O'Donnell-Trujillo, N. (1981). Relational communication: A comparison of coding schemes. *Communication Monographs, 48,* 91–105.

Ornstein, R., Thompson, R. F., & McCauley, D. (1984). *The amazing brain.* Boston: Houghton Mifflin.

Osgood, C. E., Suci, G. J., and Tannenbaum, P. H. (1957). *The measurement of meaning.* Urbana: University of Illinois Press.

O'Sullivan, M., Ekman, P., Friesen, W. V., & Scherer, K. (1985). What you say and how you say it: The contribution of speech content and voice quality to judgments of others. *Journal of Personality and Social Psychology, 48,* 54–62.

Parks, M. R. (1977). Relational communication. *Human Communication Research, 3,* 372–381.

Patrick, C. J., Craig, K. D., & Prkachin, K. M. (1986). Observer judgments of acute pain: Facial action determinants. *Journal of Personality and Social Psychology, 50,* 1291–1298.

Patterson, G. R., & Moore, D. (1979). Interactive patterns as units of behavior. In M. E. Lamb, S. J. Suomi, & G. R. Stephenson (Eds.), *Social interaction analyis: Methodological issues* (pp. 77–96). Madison: University of Wisconsin Press.

Patterson, M. L. (1983). *Nonverbal behavior: A functional perspective.* New York: Springer-Verlag.

Patterson, M. L. (Ed.). (1984). *Nonverbal intimacy and exchange.* New York: Human Sciences.

Pearce, W. B., & Cronen, V. E. (1980). *Communication, action and meaning: The creation of social realities.* New York: Praeger.

Pedhazur, E. J. (1982). *Multiple regression in behavioral research: Explanation and prediction* (2nd ed). New York: Holt, Rinehart and Winston.

Penfield, W., & Roberts, L. (1959). *Speech and brain mechanisms.* Princeton: Princeton University Press.

Petty, R. E., & Brock, T.C. (1979). Effects of Barnum personality assessments on cognitive behavior. *Journal of Consulting and Clinical Psychology, 47,* 201–203.

Phillips, D. P. (1982). The impact of fictional television stories on U.S. adult fatalities: New evidence on the effects of the mass media on violence. *American Journal of Sociology, 87,* 1340–1359.

Planalp, S. (1983). *A test of the impact of three levels of relational knowledge on memory for relational implications of messages.* Paper presented at the meeting of the International Communication Association, Dallas, TX.

Pliner, P., Krames, L., & Alloway, T. (Eds.). (1975). *Advances in the study of communication and affect* (Vol. 2). New York: Plenum.

Polanyi, M. (1958). *Personal knowledge.* New York: Harper Torchbooks.

Poole, M. S., & Folger, J. P. (1981a). A method for establishing the representational validity of interaction coding systems: Do we see what they see? *Human Communication Research, 8,* 26–42.

Poole, M. S., & Folger, J. P. (1981b). Overture to interaction research: Modes of observation and the validity of interaction coding systems. *Small Group Research, 17,* 477–494.

Poole, M. S., McPhee, R. D., & Seibold, D. R. (1982). A comparison of normative and interactional explanations of group decision making: Social decision schemes versus valence distributions. *Communication Monographs, 49,* 1–19.

Poole, M.S., & McPhee, R. D. (1985). Methodology in interpersonal communication research. In M. L. Knapp & J. R. Miller (Eds.), *Handbook of Interpersonal Communication* (pp. 100–170). Beverly Hills, CA: Sage.

Popper, K. R. (1959). *The logic of scientific discovery.* New York: Harper and Row.

Pribram, K. H. (1971). *Language of the brain: Experimental paradoxes and principles in neuropsychology.* Englewood Cliffs, NJ: Prentice-Hall.

Pribram, K. H. (1986). The cognitive revolution and mind/brain issues. *American Psychological, 41,* 507–520.

Price, W. L. (1986). *The effects of in-service workshops on computer anxiety in elementary teachers.* Unpublished doctoral dissertation, Virginia Polytechnic Institute and State University.

Prkachin, K. M., Currie, A. N., & Craig, K. D. (1983). Judging nonverbal expressions of pain. *Canadian Journal of Behavioural Science, 15,* 409–421.

Putnam, L. (1982). Procedural messages and small group work climates: A lag sequential analysis. In M. Burgoon (Ed.), *Communication yearbook, 5* (pp. 331–350). New Brunswick, NJ: Transaction Books.

Raub, A. C. (1982). *Correlates of computer anxiety in college students.* Unpublished doctoral dissertation, University of Pennsylvania.

Rausch, H. L., Barry, W. A., Hertel, R. K., & Swain, M. A. (1974). *Communication and conflict in marriage.* San Francisco: Jossey-Bass.

Ravetz, J. R. (1973). *Scientific knowledge and its social problems.* New York: Oxford University Press.

Ray, W. J., & Cole, H. W. (1985). EEG alpha activity reflects attentional demands, and beta activity reflects emotional and cognitive processes. *Science, 228,* 750–752.

Redding, W. C. (1970). Research settings: Field studies. In P. Emmert & W. D. Brooks (Eds.), *Methods of research in communication* (pp. 105–159). Boston: Houghton-Mifflin.

Restak, R. M. (1979). *The brain: The last frontier.* New York: Warner Books.

Reuter-Lorenz, P., & Davidson, R. J. (1981). Differential contributions of the two cerebral hemispheres to the perception of happy and sad faces. *Neuropsychologia, 19,* 609–613.

Riccillo, S. C., & Watterson, T. (1984). The suppression of crying in the human neonate: Response to human vocal track stimuli. *Brain and Language, 23,* 34–42.

Robinson, J. P., & Shaver, P. R. (1969). *Measures of social psychological attitudes.* Ann Arbor: Michigan Institute for Social Research.

Robinson, M. J., & Appel, K. R. (1979). Network news coverage of Congress. *Political Science Quarterly, 94,* 407–418.

Rogers, E. M. (1982). The empirical and critical schools of communication research. In M. Burgoon (Ed.), *Communication yearbook, 5* (pp. 125–144). New Brunswick, NJ: Transaction Books.

Rogers, E. M., & Chaffee, S. H. (1983). Communication as an academic discipline. *Journal of Communication, 33,* 18–30.

Rogers, L. E., & Farace, R. (1975). Analysis of relational communications in dyads: New measurement procedures. *Human Communication Research, 1,* 222–239.

Rogers, L. E. (1973). Dyadic systems and transactional communication in a family context (Doctoral dissertation, Michigan State University, 1972). *Dissertation Abstracts International, 33,* 6450A.

Rogers, L. E. (1979). *Relational communication control coding manual.* Paper presented at the International Communication Association Convention, Philadelphia.

Rogers, L. E., Courtright, J. A., & Millar, F. E. (1980). Message control intensity: Rationale and preliminary findings. *Communication Monographs, 47,* 201–219.

Rogers, L. E., & Millar, F. E. (1982). The question of validity: A pragmatic response. In M. Burgoon (Ed.), *Communication yearbook, 5* (pp. 249–257). New Brunswick, NJ: Transaction Books.

Rogers, L. E., Millar, F. E., & Bavelas, J. B. (1985). Methods for analyzing marital conflict discourse: Implications for a systems approach. *Family Process, 24,* 175–187.

Rogers-Millar, L. E., & Millar, F. E. (1979). Domineeringness and dominance: A transactional view. *Human Communication Research, 5,* 238–246.

Rokeach, M. (1968). *Beliefs, attitudes and values.* San Francisco: Jossey-Bass.

Romanczyk, R. G., Kent, R. N., Diament, C., & O'Leary, K. D. (1975). Measuring the reliability of observational data: A reactive process. *Journal of Applied Behavior Analysis, 6,* 175–184.

Rosenbleuth, A. (1969). *Mind and brain: A philosophy of science.* Cambridge: M.I.T. Press.

Rosenblum, L. (1978). The creation of a behavioral taxonomy. In G. P. Sackett (Ed.), *Observing behavior* (Vol. 2). *Data collection and analysis methods* (pp. 15–24). Baltimore: University Park Press.

Rosenfeld, H. M. (1982). Measurement of body motion and orientation. In K. R. Scherer & P. Ekman (Eds.), *Handbook of methods in nonverbal behavior research* (pp. 199–286). Cambridge: Cambridge University Press.

Rosenthal, R. (Ed.). (1979). *Skill in nonverbal communication: Individual differences.* Cambridge, MA: Oelgeschager, Gunn & Hain.

Rosenthal, R., Hall, J. A., MiMatteo, M. R., Rogers, P. L., & Archer, D. (1979). *Sensitivity to nonverbal communication: The FONS test.* Baltimore: Johns Hopkins University Press.

Rubin, R. B., Rubin, A. M., & Piele, L. J. (1986). *Communication research: Strategies and sources.* Belmont, CA: Wadsworth.

Rudner, R. S. (1966). *Philosophy of social science.* Englewood Cliffs, NJ: Prentice-Hall.

Ruesch, J., & Bateson, G. (1951). *Communication: The social matrix of psychiatry.* New York: W. W. Norton.

Ruesch, J., & Bateson, G. (1968). *Communication: The social matrix of psychiatry* (rev. ed.). New York: W. W. Norton.

Russell, R. L., & Stiles, W. B. (1979). Categories for classifying language in psychotherapy. *Psychological Bulletin, 86,* 404–419.

Ryan, M. (1980). The Likert scale's midpoint in communications research. *Journalism Quarterly, 57,* 305–313.

Sackett, G. P. (1974). *A nonparametric lag sequential analysis for studying dependency among responses in observational scoring systems.* Unpublished manuscript.

Sackett, G. P. (1978). Measurement in observational research. In G. P. Sackett (Ed.), *Observing behavior* (Vol. 2). *Data collection and analysis methods* (pp. 25–43). Baltimore: University Park Press.

Sackett, G. P. (Ed.). (1978). *Observing behavior* (Vols. 1–2). Baltimore: University Park Press.

Sackett, G. P. (1979). The lag sequential analysis of contingency and cyclicity in behavioral interaction research. In J. Osfsky (Ed.), *Handbook of infant development* (pp. 623–649). New York: John Wiley.

Sackett, G. P. (1980). Lag sequential analysis as a data reduction technique in social interaction research. In D. B. Sawin, R. C. Hawkins, L. O. Walker, & J. H. Penticuff (Eds.), *Exceptional infant* (Vol. 4). *Psychosocial risks in infant-environment transactions.* New York: Brunner/Mazel.

Sackett, G. P., Holm, R., Crowley, C., & Henkins, A. A. (1979). A FORTRAN program for lag sequential analysis of contingency and cyclicity in behavioral interaction data. *Behavior Research Methods and Instrumentation, 11,* 366–378.

Sackett, G. P., Ruppenthal, G. C., & Gluck, J. (1978). Introduction: An overview of methodological and statistical problems in observational research. In G. P. Sackett (Ed.), *Observing Behavior* (Vol. 2, pp. 1–14). Baltimore: University Park Press.

Sackiem, H. A., Weiman, A. L., & Grega, D. M. (1984). Effects of predictors of hemispheric specialization on individual differences in hemispheric activation. *Neuropsychologia, 22,* 55–64.

Sacks, H., Schegloff, E. A., & Jefferson, G. (1974). A simplest systematics for the organization of turn-taking in conversation. *Language, 50*, 696–735.

Sacks, H., Schegloff, E. A., & Jefferson, G. (1978). A simplest systematics for the organization of turn-taking in conversation. In J. N. Schenkein (Ed.), *Studies in the organization of conversational interaction* (pp. 7–55). New York: Academic Press.

SAS User's Guide: Basics. (1982). Carey, NC: SAS Institute.

Schacter, S., & Singer, J. E. (1962). Cognitive, social and physiological determinants of emotional state. *Psychological Review, 69*, 379–399.

Schacter, S., & Singer, J. E. (1979). Comment on Maslach and Marshall-Zembardo experiments. *Journal of Personality and Social Psychology, 37*, 989–995.

Scheflen, A. E. (1974). *How behavior means.* Garden City, NY: Anchor Books.

Scherer, K. R. (1982). Methods of research on vocal communication: Paradigms and parameters. In K. R. Scherer & P. Ekman (Eds.), *Handbook of methods in nonverbal behavior research* (pp. 136–198). Cambridge: Cambridge University Press.

Scherer, K. R. (1984a). State of the art in vocal communication: A partial view. In A. Wolfgang (Ed.), *Nonverbal behavior: Perspectives, applications, intercultural insights* (pp. 41–73). New York: C. J. Hogrefe.

Scherer, K. R. (1984b). Emotion as a multicomponent process: A model and some cross-cultural data. In P. Shaver (Ed.), *Review of personality and social psychology* (Vol. 5, pp. 37–63). Beverly Hills, CA: Sage.

Scherer, K. R. (1986). Vocal affect expression: A review and a model for future research. *Psychological Bulletin, 99*, 143–165.

Scherer, K. R., Abeles, R. P., & Fischer, C. (1975). *Human aggression and conflict: Interdisciplinary perspectives.* Englewood Cliffs, NJ: Prentice-Hall.

Scherer, K. R., & Ekman, P. (1982). Methodological issues in studying nonverbal behavior. In K. R. Scherer & P. Ekman (Eds.), *Handbook of methods in nonverbal behavior research* (pp. 1–44). Cambridge: Cambridge University Press.

Scherer, K. R., & Ekman, P. (Eds.). (1984). *Approaches to emotion.* Hillsdale, NJ: Lawrence Erlbaum.

Scherer, K. R., Feldstein, S., Bond, R. N., & Rosenthal, R. (1985). Vocal cues to deception: A comparative channels approach. *Journal of Psycholinguistic Research, 14*, 409–425.

Scherer, K. R., Scherer, U., Hall, J. A., & Rosenthal, R. (1977). Differential attribution of personality based on multichannel presentation of verbal and nonverbal cues. *Psychological Research, 39*, 221–247.

Scherer, K. R., Summerfield, A. B., & Wallbott, H. G. (1983). Cross-national research of antecedents and components of emotion: A progress report. *Social Science Information, 22*, 355–385.

Scherer, K. R., Wallbott, H. G., & Scherer, U. (1979). Methoden zur klassifikation von bewegungsverhalten: Ein funktionaler ansatz. *Zeitschrift fur Semiotik, 1*, 187–202.

Scherer, U., & Scherer, K. R. (1980). Psychological factors in bureaucratic encounters: Determinants and effects of interaction between officials and clients. In W. T. Singleton, P. Spurgeon, & R. B. Stammers (Eds.), *The analysis of social skill.* New York: Plenum.

Schneider, B. (1970). Relationships between various criteria of leadership in small groups. *Journal of Social Psychology, 82*, 253–261.

Schutz, W. C. (1952). Reliability, ambiguity and content analysis. *Psychological Review, 59*, 119–129.

Scott, W. A. (1955). Reliability of content analysis: The case for nominal scale coding. *Public Opinion Quarterly, 19*, 321–325.

Searle, J. R. (1968). Austin on locutionary and illocutionary acts. *Philosophical Review, 77*, 405–424.

Searle, J. R. (1976). A classification of illocutionary acts. *Language in Society, 5*, 1–23.

Sechrest, L. (1975). Another look at unobtrusive measures: An alternative to what. In W Sinaiko and L. Broeding (Eds.), *Perspectives on attitude assessment: Surveys and their alternatives.* Washington, D.C.: Smithsonian Institution.

Sechrest, L., & Phillips, M. (1979). Unobtrusive measures: An overview. In L. Sechrest (Ed.), *New directions for methodology of behavioral science: Unobtrusive measurement today.* San Francisco, CA: Jossey-Bass.

Selltiz, C., Johada, M., Deutsch, M., & Cook, S. W. (1959). *Research methods in social relations.* New York: Holt, Rinehart and Winston.

Selltiz, C., Wrightsman, L. S., & Cook, S. W. (1976). *Research methods in social relations.* New York: Holt, Rinehart and Winston.

Sepstrup, P. (1981). Methodological development in content analysis. In K. E. Rosengren (Ed.), *Advances in content analysis* (pp. 133–158). Beverly Hills, CA: Sage.

Shannon, C. E., & Weaver, W. (1949). *The mathematical theory of communication.* Urbana: The University of Illinois Press.

Shaw, M. E., & Wright, J. M. (1967). *Scales for the measurement of attitudes.* New York: McGraw-Hill.

Sherif, C., & Sherif, M. (Eds.). (1967a). *Attitude, ego-involvement and change.* New York: John Wiley.

Sherif, M., & Sherif, C. (1967b). Attitude as the individual's own categories: The social judgment-involvement approach to attitude change. In C. Sherif and M. Sherif (Eds.), *Attitude, ego-involvement and change* (pp. 105–139). New York: John Wiley.

Sherif, C., Sherif, M., & Nebergall, R. (1965). *Attitude and attitude change.* Philadelphia: W. B. Saunders.

Shimanoff, S. B. (1985). Expressing emotions in words: Verbal patterns of interaction. *Journal of Communication, 35*, 16–31.

Shyles, L. C. (1983). Defining the issues of a presidential election from televised political spot advertisements. *Journal of Broadcasting, 27*, 333–343.

Siegman, W., & Feldstein, S. (Eds.). (1979). *Of speech and time: Temporal patterns in interpersonal contexts.* Hillsdale, NJ: Lawrence Erlbaum.

Simons, H. (1976). *Persuasion: Understanding, practice, and analysis.* Reading, MA: Addison-Wesley.

Skinner, B. F. (1953). *Science and human behavior.* New York: Macmillan.

Skinner, B. F. (1957). *Verbal behavior.* New York: Appleton-Century-Crofts.

Sluzki, C. E., & Beavin, J. (1977). Symmetry and complementarity: An operational definition and a typology of dyads. In P. Watzlawick & J. H. Weakland (Eds. and Trans.), *The interactional view* (pp. 71–87). New York: Norton.

Smythe, D. W., & Dinh, T. V. (1983). On critical and administrative research: A critical analysis. *Journal of Communication, 33*, 117–127.

Soskin, W. F., & John, V. P. (1963). The study of spontaneous talk. In R. G. Barker (Ed.), *The stream of behavior: Explorations of its structure and content* (pp. 228–287). New York: Appleton-Century-Crofts.

Spearman, C. (1910). Correlation calculated from faulty data. *British Journal of Psychology, 3,* 271–295.

Speer, D. C. (Ed.). (1972). *Nonverbal communication.* Beverly Hills, CA: Sage.

Spence, K. W. (1944). The nature of theory construction in contemporary psychology. *Psychological Review, 51,* 47–68.

Spiegal, J. P., & Machotka, P. (1974). *Messages of the body.* New York: Free Press.

SPSS^x User's Guide. (1983). Chicago: McGraw-Hill.

Stacks, D. W. (1986). Statistical packages for the personal computers. *Communication Education, 35, 4,* 419–429.

Stacks, D. W., & Sellers, D. E. (1986). Toward a wholistic approach to communication: The effect of "pure" hemispheric reception on message acceptance. *Communication Quarterly, 34,* 266–285.

Stempel, G. H., III. (1952). Sample size for classifying subject matter in dailies. *Journalism Quarterly, 29,* 333–334.

Stempel, G. H., III. (1955). Increasing reliability in content analysis. *Journalism Quarterly, 32,* 449–455.

Stempel, G. H., III. (1981). Content analysis. In G. H. Stempel III & B. H. Westley (Eds.), *Research methods in mass communication.* Englewood Cliffs, NJ: Prentice-Hall.

Stern, R. M., Gaub, L., & Leonard, W. C. (1970). A comparison of GSR and subjective adaptation to stressful stimuli. *Psychophysiology, 7,* 3–9.

Stern, R. M., Ray, W. G., & Davis, C. M. (1980). *Psychophysiological recording.* New York: Oxford University Press.

Stevens, S. S. (1946). On the theory of scales of measurement. *Science, 103,* 677–680.

Stevens, S. S. (1951). Mathematics, measurement, and psychophysics. In S. S. Stevens (Ed.), *Handbook of experimental psychology,* New York: John Wiley.

Stiles, W. B. (1978). Verbal response modes and dimensions of interpersonal roles: A method of discourse analysis. *Journal of Personality and Social Psychology, 36,* 693–703.

Stiles, W. B. (1979). Verbal response modes and psychotherapeutic techniques. *Psychiatry, 42,* 49–62.

Stiles, W. B. (1980). Comparison of dimensions derived from rating versus coding of dialogue. *Journal of Personality and Social Psychology, 38,* 359–374.

Stiles, W. B. (1981). Classification of intersubjective illocutionary acts. *Language in Society, 10,* 227–249.

Stone, P. J., Bales, R. F., Namenwirth, J. Z., & Ogilvie, D. M. (1962). The General Inquirer: A computer system for content analysis and retrieval based on the sentence as a unit of information. *Behavioral Science, 7,* 484–494.

Stone, P. J., Dunphy, D. C., Smith, M. S., & Ogilvie, D. M. (1966). The General Inquirer: A computer system for content analysis in the behavioral sciences. Cambridge: M.I.T. Press.

Streeck, J. (1980). Speech acts in interaction: A critique of Searle. *Discourse Processes, 3,* 133–154.

Stubbs, M. (1981). Motivating analyses of exchange structure. In M. Coulthard & M. Montgomery (Eds.), *Studies in discourse analysis* (pp. 107–119). London: Routledge & Kegan Paul.

Suomi, S. J. (1979). Levels of analysis for interactive data collected on monkeys living in complex social groups. In M. E. Lamb, S. J. Suomi, & G. R. Stephenson (Eds.), *Social interaction analysis: Methodological issues* (pp. 119–135). Madison: University of Wisconsin Press.

Taplin, P. S., & Reid, J. B. (1973). Effects of instructional set and experimenter influence on observer reliability. *Child Development, 44*, 547–554.

Tedeschi, J. (Ed.). (1982). *Impression management theory and social psychological research*. New York: Academic Press.

Thayer, L. (1983). On "doing" research and "explaining" things. *Journal of Communication, 33*, 80–91.

Thibaut, J. W., & Kelley, H. H. (1959). *The social psychology of groups*. New York: John Wiley.

Thomas, C. W., & Petersen, D. M. (1982). Methodological issues in attitude scale construction. *Journal of Social Psychology, 116*, 245–253.

Thomas, D., Loomis, A., & Arrington, R. (1933). *Observational studies of social behavior* (Vol. 1). Yale University: Institute of Human Relations.

Thompson, E. G., Hatchett, P., & Phillips, J. L. (1981). Sex differences in the judgment of interpersonal verbs. *Psychology of Women Quarterly, 5*, 523–531.

Thurstone, L. L. (1928). Attitudes can be measured. *American Journal of Sociology, 33*, 529–554.

Thurstone, L. L. (1931). The measurement of social attitudes. *Journal of Abnormal and Social Psychology, 26*, 249–269.

Thurstone, L. L., & Chave, E. J. (1929). *The measurement of attitude*. Chicago: University of Chicago Press.

Tiemens, R. K. (1978). Television's portrayal of the 1976 presidential debates: An analysis of visual content. *Communication Monographs, 45*, 362–370.

Ting-Toomey, S. (1983). An analysis of verbal communication patterns in high and low marital adjustment groups. *Human Communication Research, 9*, 306–319.

Toffler, A. (1970). *Future shock*. New York: Bantam Books.

Tolkmitt, F. J., & Scherer, K. R. (1986). Effects of experimentally induced stress on vocal parameters. *Journal of Experimental Psychology: Human Perception and Performance, 12*, 302–313.

Tompkins, P., & Cheney, G. (1985). Communication and unobtrusive control in contemporary organizations. In R. D. McPhee and P. K. Tompkins (Eds.), *Organizational Communication: Traditional Themes and New Directions*. Beverly Hills, CA: Sage.

Tomkins, S. S. (1962). *Affect, imagery, consciousnes: (Vol. 1). The positive affects*. New York: Springer.

Tomkins, S. S. (1963). *Affect, imagery, consciousness: (Vol. 2). The negative affects*. New York: Springer.

Tucker, R. K., Weaver, R. L., & Berryman-Fink, C. (1981). *Research in speech communication*, Englewood Cliffs, NJ: Prentice-Hall.

Uebersax, J. S. (1982). A generalized kappa coefficient. *Educational and Psychological Measurement, 42*, 181–183.

Van Bezooijen, R. (1984). *The characteristics and recognizability of vocal expressions of emotion*. Dordrecht, The Netherlands: Foris.

Van der Ven, A.H.G.S. (1980). *Introduction to scaling*. New York: John Wiley.

Van Toller, C. (1979). *The nervous body*. Chricester: John Wiley.

vonRaffler-Engel, W. (Ed.). (1980). *Aspects of nonverbal communication*. Lisse: Swets and Zeitlinger.

Wadsworth, A. J. (1986). *Incumbent and challenger strategies in presidential communica-

tion: A content analysis of television campaign ads from 1952 to 1984. Unpublished doctoral dissertation, University of Oklahoma, Norman.

Waid, W. M. (Ed.). (1984). *Sociophysiology.* New York: Springer-Verlag.

Wallbott, H. G. (1985). Hand movement quality: A neglected aspect of nonverbal behavior in clinical judgment and person perception. *Journal of Clinical Psychology, 41,* 345–359.

Wallbott, H. G., & Scherer, K. R. (1986). Cues and channels in emotion recognition. *Journal of Personality and Social Psychology, 51,* 690–699.

Warland, R. H., & Sample, J. (1973). Response certainty as a moderator variable in attitude measurement. *Rural Sociology, 38,* 174–186.

Watterson, T., & Riccillo, S. C. (1983). Vocal suppression as a neonatal response to auditory stimuli. *The Journal of Auditory Research, 23,* 205–214.

Watzlawick, P., Beavin, J. H., & Jackson, D. D. (1967). *Pragmatics of human communication: A study of interactional patterns, pathologies, and paradoxes.* New York: W. W. Norton.

Watzlawick, P., & Weakland, J. H. (Eds.) (1977). *The interactional view: Studies at the mental research institute. Palo Alto, 1965–1974.* New York: W. W. Norton.

Weaver, D. H., Graber, D. A., McCombs, M. E., & Eyal, C. H. (1981). *Media agenda-setting in a presidential election: Issues, images, and interest.* New York: Praeger.

Webb, B. W. (1984). *The impact of computer training on computer anxiety in the organizational setting.* Unpublished doctoral dissertation, University of Maine.

Webb, E. J., Campbell, D. T., Schwartz, R. D., & Sechrest, L. (1966) *Unobtrusive measures: Nonreactive research in the social sciences.* Chicago, IL: Rand McNally.

Weick, K. E. (1969). *The social psychology of organizing.* Reading, MA.: Addison-Wesley.

Weitz, S. (Ed.). (1979). *Nonverbal communication: Readings with commentary* (2nd ed.). New York: Oxford University Press.

Wenger, M. A., & Cullen, T. D. (1972). Studies of autonomic balance in children and adults. In N. S. Greenfield & R. A. Sternbach (Eds.), *Handbook of psychophysiology.* New York: Holt.

Werts, C. E., Linn, R. L., & Joreskog, K. G. (1974). Quantifying unmeasured variables. In Hubert M. Blalock, Jr. (Ed.), *Measurement in the social sciences* (pp. 270–292). Chicago: Aldine.

Widmer, C., & Parker, I. (1984). Computerphobia: causes and cures. *Action in Teacher Education, 5* (4), 23–25.

Wilder, C. (1979). The Palo Alto Group: Difficulties and directions of the interactional view for human communication research. *Human Communication Research, 5,* 171–186.

Wilder, J. (1958). Modern psychophysiology and the law of initial value. *American Journal of Psychotherapy, 12,* 199–221.

Wilder, J. (1967). *Stimulus and response: The law of initial value.* Bristol, England: Wright.

Williamson, J. (1983). Computerphobia: How to conquer it before it conquers you. *Case Currents, 9* (3) 6–8.

Zajonc, R. B. (1980). Feeling and thinking: Preferences need no inferences. *American Psychologist, 33,* 151–175.

Zeller, R. A., & Carmines, E. G. (1980). *Measurement in the social sciences: The link between theory and data.* New York: Cambridge University Press.

Ziman, J. (1968). *Public knowledge.* Cambridge: Cambridge University Press.

Index

Page numbers in *italics* indicate illustrations. Page numbers followed by *t* indicate tables.